CLASSROOM MOTIVATION

SECOND EDITION

Eric M. Anderman
The Ohio State University

Lynley H. Anderman
The Ohio State University

PEARSON

Boston Columbus Indianapolis New York San Francisco Upper Saddle River
Amsterdam Cape Town Dubai London Madrid Milan Munich Paris Montreal Toronto
Delhi Mexico City São Paulo Sydney Hong Kong Seoul Singapore Taipei Tokyo

Vice President and Editorial Director: Jeffery
  W. Johnston
Vice President and Publisher: Kevin Davis
Editorial Assistant: Lauren Carlson
Vice President, Director of Marketing: Margaret Waples
Senior Marketing Manager: Joanna Sabella
Senior Managing Editor: Pamela D. Bennett
Project Manager: Kerry Rubadue
Production Manager: Laura Messerly

Senior Art Director: Jayne Conte
Cover Designer: Bruce Kenselaar
Cover Photo: © Andrey Shadrin/Shutterstock
Full-Service Project Management: Mansi Negi/
  Aptara®, Inc.
Composition: Aptara®, Inc.
Printer/Binder: Courier/Westford
Cover Printer: Courier/Westford
Text Font: Palatino LT Std

Credits and acknowledgments for material borrowed from other sources and reproduced, with permission, in this textbook appear on the appropriate page within the text.

Every effort has been made to provide accurate and current Internet information in this book. However, the Internet and information posted on it are constantly changing, so it is inevitable that some of the Internet addresses listed in this textbook will change.

Photo Credits: Ramona Heim/Fotolia, p. 3; jirasak pakdeeto/Fotolia, p. 9; Scott Cunningham/Merrill, pp. 14, 18, 83, 105, 134, 166; Anthony Magnacca/Merrill, pp. 15, 19, 50, 66, 69, 95, 104, 123, 128, 177, 201, 207, 217, 224; Larry Hamill/Merrill, pp. 26, 75; Yael Weiss/Fotolia, p. 28; mostafa fawzy/Fotolia, p. 37; Katelyn Metzger/Merrill, pp. 42, 57; Laura Bolesta/Merrill, p. 44; Patrick White/Merrill, pp. 64, 149; Maria B. Vonada/Merrill, p. 67; Ken Karp/Prentice Hall College, p. 85; Robert Kneschke/Fotolia, p. 97; Auremar/Fotolia, p. 119; Gennadiy Poznyakov/Fotolia, p. 148; Tim Cairns/Merrill, p. 158; Robert Vega/Merrill, p. 167; Andres Rodriguez/Fotolia, p. 168; KS Studios/Merrill, p. 183; Julie Peters/Merrill, p. 215; Todd Yarrington/Merrill, p. 221; Kathy Kirtland/Merrill, p. 227; Jasmin Merdan/Fotolia, p. 232.

Library of Congress Cataloging-in-Publication Data
Anderman, Eric M.
  Classroom motivation / Eric M. Anderman, The Ohio State University, Lynley Hicks Anderman, The Ohio State University. Second edition.
    pages cm
  ISBN-13: 978-0-13-301788-5
  ISBN-10: 0-13-301788-5
  1. Motivation in education. I. Anderman, Lynley Hicks. II. Title.
  LB1065.A56 2014
  370.15′4—dc23

      2012046095

10 9 8 7 6 5 4 3 2 1

ISBN 10:   0-13-301788-5
ISBN 13: 978-0-13-301788-5

TO SARAH AND JACOB

Preface

Few educators or parents would argue with the need for students to be motivated to learn and succeed, yet motivation for academic and school-related activities often is not well understood. Student motivation is complex and arises from a number of sources, including characteristics of the individual students and the classrooms, teachers, and schools. Whereas teachers need to be aware of the potential influence of students' individual and group differences, it is also particularly important for them to understand how aspects of the learning context and instructional practices can motivate students to engage optimally in learning activities.

Despite ongoing development of motivational theories and continued progress in empirical studies within the research literature, many important implications of this scholarly work do not get translated into the everyday practice of education. This problem lies, to at least some degree, with the very richness of the field. As multiple theories compete to explain similar behaviors and research designs increase in complexity, it becomes increasingly difficult for educators to distill a manageable set of principles to inform their daily instructional practice. This is unfortunate because the body of research now available does provide quite consistent support for a number of recommendations for teachers and administrators. Furthermore, although researchers operate within a range of theoretical frameworks and recognize fine distinctions among motivational concepts, the implications of many theories are actually quite similar. These common principles provide a core set of recommendations for practice that cut across theoretical lines.

This second edition of this text focuses first on dimensions of practice rather than starting with theory. As former classroom teachers as well as motivation researchers, we wanted to design a text that would be particularly accessible and useful for preservice teachers, practicing teachers, administrators, and anyone who cares about fostering the academic motivation of students. We started by thinking about the kinds of tasks and decisions teachers engage in every day: What kinds of tasks should I assign my students? How will I group them for instruction and help them to feel confident that they can be successful? We then integrated explanations of relevant theories around those questions. We clearly define psychological terms as they arise throughout the text and support them with many examples of motivational principles in context. This focus makes the text especially useful for practicing teachers as well as for those preparing for a teaching career. It is also appropriate for educational administrators, parents, and others interested in creating schools and classrooms that foster motivation.

NEW TO THIS EDITION

There are several changes to the new edition. These include:

- An increased focus on how the use of technology affects student motivation
- Updated reviews of motivation research from diverse theoretical perspectives
- The addition of new learning activities at the end of the chapters
- Case studies of teachers who provide exceptional examples of putting motivation theory and research into practice
- A discussion of the effects of high-stakes assessments on academic motivation
- A more in-depth examination of the relations between motivation and academic cheating
- Additional tables that provide clear definitions and examples

ORGANIZATION OF THIS TEXT

The text contains 11 chapters. Following an introductory chapter, Part II (Chapters 2 through 6) focuses on specific instructional practices, including choosing academic tasks, evaluating and rewarding student work, grouping students for instruction, and working with parents. In Part III (Chapters 7 through 10) we discuss broader aspects of creating a classroom climate that promotes and sustains students' motivation. Topics addressed include promotion of autonomy in the classroom, holding high expectations for learning, and dealing with motivational problems. Part IV (Chapter 11) completes the text, with an examination of how to put together all the pieces in the preceding chapters to create positive learning environments that support academic motivation.

ACKNOWLEDGMENTS

We want to thank many people for their assistance during the production of this text and for their roles in shaping our thinking about motivational processes in both research and practice. First, we want to thank our editor, Kevin Davis, for his belief in this project, for his extremely helpful and constructive feedback along the way, and for his consistent encouragement.

Over several years, we have benefited from many stimulating conversations and research interactions with numerous mentors, colleagues, and students, including Phyllis Blumenfeld, Lyn Corno, Pamela Cupp, Fred Danner, Heather Dawson, Jacque Eccles, DeLeon Gray, Avi Kaplan, Kristy Leigh, Martin Maehr, George McCormick, Katherine McCormick, Mike Middleton, Mike Townsend, Tim Urdan, Chris Wolters, Anita Woolfolk Hoy, Michael Yough, Allison Young, and, especially, the late Carol Midgley and the late Paul Pintrich. In addition, Lynley is especially indebted for the combined personal and professional benefits she has enjoyed from her "AERA dinner group": Liz DeGroot, Deb Meyer, Tamera Murdock, Helen Patrick, Allison Ryan, Julianne Turner, and Shirley Yu.

We would like to thank the reviewers of our manuscript for their comments and helpful insights: Darren Akerman, University of New England; Nancy Harding, Pepperdine University; William Lan, Texas Tech University; Jeffrey Liew, Texas A&M University; and Sarah Peterson, Duquesne University.

Finally, we thank our children, Jacob and Sarah, for reminding us every day that the work that we do, and the information in this text, really does have an impact on children and adolescents.

Eric M. Anderman
Lynley H. Anderman
The Ohio State University

Brief Contents

Contents

What Is Motivation?

Few educators or parents would argue the need for students to be motivated. Nevertheless, many individuals do not fully understand the complexity of academic motivation. Although many educators know much about human motivation, more can always be learned.

As you will learn, motivation is an interesting and multifaceted topic, and it can be thought of in many different ways. Consider the following examples:

Seth is a fourth-grader who hates reading. His teacher and parents say that Seth is "not motivated" when it comes to reading.

Molly is a ninth-grader who takes advanced science courses and spends much time working on science assignments. Molly spends too much time working on science because her parents give her $100 every time she brings home an A for science on her report card.

Claire is a 12th- grader who has just about given up on school. She feels that she simply doesn't have the ability to succeed in her classes. She feels like she is "dumb," and she just doesn't want to continue to struggle with academic work that she feels she can't handle and that she doesn't think is important.

Ryan is a second-grader who loves school. He enjoys every academic task that is presented to him, and he approaches each activity with a positive attitude.

Kyle is a first-year college student who wonders why he is getting low grades in his first-year writing course. He used to get great grades when he was in high school, but now he wonders if that was all an act, and if he really doesn't have the ability to be successful in college.

Dave is an extremely competitive 10th grader. He likes to show everyone how smart he is; in addition, he is very concerned about not appearing "stupid" by making mistakes in front of other students.

These examples all describe different types of academic motivation. The preceding examples all deal with different types of motivated behaviors. Seth and Claire are students who have motivational problems: Seth appears to dislike reading, whereas Claire doesn't believe in her own abilities and is ready to forego her formal education. In contrast, Molly and Ryan appear to be highly motivated: Molly is motivated to work on science assignments, albeit to receive rewards provided by her parents; Ryan seems to be motivated to do anything and everything. Academic success used to be a normal part of Kyle's school experience, but since he has transitioned into college, he has begun to question his abilities. The case of Dave is intriguing: He seems to be motivated by competition, but he is also afraid of failing in front of others.

These examples represent different types of academic motivation that will be examined in this text. We could provide several examples of other motivational issues that confront students, teachers, and parents daily. Nevertheless, these six brief cases illustrate the complexity of motivation. This text is about the multifaceted topic of academic motivation. However, the goal of this text is to make the broader topic of *motivation* as uncomplicated as possible. When you have completed reading and studying this text, you will understand the complexity of academic motivation, but also have some clear strategies available so that you can help to maintain and facilitate optimal motivation in your students. Also, you will probably gain some important insights into yourself and better understand what motivates you as a learner!

THE CLASSROOM TEACHER AND MOTIVATION

Mrs. Taylor is a middle school principal. She is fond of stating that middle school students are "hormones with legs" and that, because of puberty and the physiological changes associated with adolescence, it is impossible to motivate teenagers. She believes that middle school is a place where students really can't be motivated to learn (because of their physiological development), so she sees middle school as a place where students should be strictly disciplined until they get to high school, at which time they'll be better able to control their impulses and learn.

Is there any hope for the students in Mrs. Taylor's school? Will her negative attitudes toward adolescent motivation be mirrored in her teachers? Will her evaluations of her teachers' performance reflect these attitudes? The answer to every one of these questions is "yes." Negative attitudes and misperceptions about student motivation can have deleterious effects on students. However, hope exists. One of the goals of this text is to highlight and correct some misconceptions about student motivation so that teachers' instructional practices can reflect current research findings.

The Bottom Line

In this text, we explore the various motivation-related issues that teachers confront daily. Although most books don't start out with the ending, we want to mention our most important conclusion up front: *Teachers can and do have an impact on student motivation!* If you remember nothing else after reading this text, please remember that. You, as a teacher, will have dramatic and important effects on your students' academic motivation.

Teachers influence student motivation in many ways: Through daily interactions with students, they influence students' beliefs about their own abilities, their attitudes toward certain subject areas, their immediate and long-term goals, their beliefs about the causes of their successes and failures, and their reasons for ultimately choosing to do their academic work. As you will see, the types of instructional practices that you choose to use

Most teachers want to have highly motivated students in their classes.

with your students can affect their current motivation, as well as their future motivation to take additional coursework and even to enter into certain careers. A student who has very unpleasant experiences during math classes or math lessons may develop such a displeasure with math that she may rule out math-related careers altogether; in contrast, a student who becomes deeply engaged and interested in French may decide to major in French, to study abroad in France, and even to live in a French-speaking country during adulthood. Thus the ways that teachers motivate (or don't motivate) their students can have profound effects on the choices that students make later in life.

SHORT-TERM AND LONG-TERM EFFECTS   Teachers' interactions with their students affect both short- and long-term outcomes for students. Consider the following example:

> *Mrs. Weiss is a fourth-grade teacher. She displays the math work of her highest achieving students on the bulletin boards in her classroom. She believes that this will serve as an incentive and will help to motivate some of her lower achieving students. David is a student in Mrs. Weiss's class. He does not do well in math, and he actually resents the fact that his work is never displayed. David does not exert more effort in math as a result of the bulletin board; he just gets angry when he looks up at it.*

Mrs. Weiss's strategy is certainly well intentioned, but it does not have the desired positive influence on David's motivation. Let's consider both the possible short-term and long-term effects on David. In the short-term, David may resent his teacher and may feel that he is not good at math, compared to other students in his class. Now imagine the effects on David if he has had similar experiences with other teachers, or if he continues to have experiences of this nature in the future. Although David may initially enjoy math activities, we can expect that he will gradually lose confidence in his math abilities and come to dislike math more and more each year. David would probably be unlikely to consider a career involving math because his school experiences may have led him to believe that he is unable to do well in it. This is a sad example, but it's quite realistic for students like David who might be able to improve their confidence and competence in mathematics if they were to experience a motivationally supportive environment. However, if instructional practices lead David and students like him to believe that they are "bad" at mathematics, they may never realize that under other circumstances they might be able to learn mathematics quite effectively.

It also is important to note that some instructional practices may have different effects on individual students. For example, whereas hanging up the work of the best students did not motivate David, it may have the opposite effect on other students. Some students might be positively motivated by this type of practice and might try harder in mathematics so that they could get their own work displayed.

If the same practices can benefit some students and hurt others, what should a teacher do? We explore those questions in this text. We present strategies for motivating all students, and we explore how teachers can make decisions that will affect the motivation of all their students in a positive way.

INTRODUCTION TO THE THEORIES

Much of the research on academic motivation is guided by well-developed, research-based theories. Whereas many textbooks on motivation are organized around theoretical perspectives, this text is organized around *instructional practices*. Rather than introducing the theories in their own chapters, the theories are integrated throughout the text.

In this chapter, we briefly introduce these theories. The brief comments about each theory are intended to simply introduce you to these perspectives. There are large literatures that examine the intricacies of these theories, and researchers continue to debate many of the ideas espoused in these theories (see E. Anderman & Dawson, 2011, for a review). In later chapters, we present research supporting each theory, as well as implications for various instructional practices.

Basic Definitions

Certain terms are used consistently in motivation research. Two of the most common are *intrinsic motivation* and *extrinsic motivation*. A student is *intrinsically motivated* to engage in an academic task when the student truly wants to learn about something and engages in a task for its own sake. Students who are intrinsically motivated engage in tasks voluntarily and are learning simply for the sake of learning. For example, a child who is fascinated by cats might choose to read many books about breeds of cats, simply to learn more about the topic.

In contrast, students who are *extrinsically motivated* engage in academic tasks to earn some type of reward or to avoid an externally imposed punishment. For example, another child might read books about cats because she has to write a report for school about cats and wants to get a good grade on the report. The child might have no genuine interest in cats, but still would read many books to earn the good grade.

Stop and Think

How are intrinsic and extrinsic motivation related? In your own experience, are you both intrinsically and extrinsically motivated in some activities?

Self-Determination Theory

One quite prominent theoretical perspective in the current research literature is *self-determination theory* (SDT; Deci, 1980). Self-determination theorists study an array of motivated human behaviors. In general, they are interested in issues related to intrinsic and extrinsic motivation. In addition, these researchers also note that some individuals, whom they refer to as *amotivated*, have low beliefs in their own abilities and often do not value academic tasks; these individuals are motivated neither intrinsically nor extrinsically (Ryan & Deci, 2009).

Self-determination theorists also argue that humans have three basic needs: the need for *autonomy* (i.e., to feel a sense of self-directedness), the need for *competence* (i.e., to feel capable of performing certain tasks), and the need for *relatedness* (i.e., to feel connected to and accepted within a larger social network; Deci & Ryan, 1985; Ryan & Deci, 2000). Individuals are motivated to engage in activities that will help them meet these needs.

Attribution Theory

Attribution theory provides us with a model of how individuals explain to themselves the reasons for certain occurrences in their lives (Graham & Weiner, 1996). Whenever something happens in our lives, especially when an outcome was unexpected, we want to know why the event occurred. The answer to the question "Why?" is the basis of attribution theory; indeed, our answers to this question direct our motivation toward further engagement with or disengagement from similar activities (Weiner, 1986, 1992).

Stop and Think

Imagine that you are surprised to find out you received a failing grade on an essay you had recently written for one of your classes. Upon receiving the bad grade, what would you be asking yourself?

The basic process of attribution is as follows: Something happens. The individual then tries to determine "why" the event happened. The individual attributes the occurrence to one of several possibilities and then experiences certain feelings as a result. In turn, those feelings are predictive of one's decision regarding whether or not to engage in a similar task in the future (Weiner, 1985).

For example, suppose a student fails a chemistry test. The student will then attribute the failure to a cause, perhaps to a lack of ability in chemistry. At that point, the student might experience negative feelings or emotions, such as a sense of shame. This negative affect might lead the student to choose not to continue to study chemistry in the future. In contrast, the student might attribute the failure to insufficient studying. This attribution may lead to feelings of guilt and increased efforts in future chemistry tests.

Attribution theorists note that attributions can be described by three dimensions: *stability, locus,* and *control. Stability* has to do with whether the perceived cause of an event is constant across time and situations; *locus* refers to whether the cause of an event is believed to be internal or external to the individual; *control* refers to an individual's beliefs about whether or not he or she can personally control the causes of certain events. As you will read in later chapters, the process of attribution is extremely important in terms of academic motivation.

Expectancy–Value Theory

Expectancy–value theories represent a broad class of theories of achievement motivation. Briefly summarized, those who study academic motivation from an expectancy–value perspective are interested both in students' beliefs about their abilities to succeed with tasks (expectancies) and in individuals' valuing of various tasks (Atkinson, 1957, 1964; Eccles et al., 1983 ; Wigfield & Eccles, 2000).

Although this theory appears in various formulations, the basic tenet underlying all of them is that motivation to engage with a task is determined by both one's expectancies for success at a task *and* one's perceived valuing of the task. Values consist of students' beliefs about the importance of a task, how interesting a task is, how useful a task is, and whether or not it is worth spending the time to engage with the task ("cost"). As will be illustrated in later chapters, teachers' instructional practices can dramatically influence students' expectancy beliefs and values. This is important because these beliefs are related to students' subsequent motivation to persist with and engage in certain tasks, courses, and even careers (Wigfield & Eccles, 1992, 2000).

Social Cognitive Theory

Social cognitive theory is another term that actually encompasses a number of different theoretical frameworks. Much of the original work in this area is attributed to Albert Bandura, who introduced a number of important concepts within this broad framework. Briefly summarized, Bandura argued that human behavior involves *triadic reciprocality* among an individual's personal attributes, environmental characteristics, and behaviors (Bandura, 1986)—that is, each of those three variables influence and are influenced by each of the others.

Bandura also introduced two other concepts that are important when studying academic motivation. First, he demonstrated that individuals often learn and subsequently engage in new behaviors that are observed in others (Bandura, 1969). In other words, students can be motivated to engage in behaviors they see modeled by others, especially if the individual being observed is perceived as being similar to the observer. For example, a child who is learning how to play tennis may be motivated to replicate a technique he or she observes in a more experienced player.

Bandura also introduced the concept of *self-efficacy*, which refers to an individual's belief that he or she has the ability to perform a specific task (Bandura, 1986, 1997; Pajares, 1996; Schunk, 1991; Schunk & Pajares, 2009). Consider the following mathematics problem:

$$3x + 7 = 99$$

When some students see an algebraic expression such as this, they believe that they can easily solve the problem; however, other students see the same math expression and feel a sense of incompetence. The student who believes that she can solve the problem has high self-efficacy toward the problem, whereas a student who feels that she can't solve the problem has low self-efficacy. Self-efficacy researchers note that efficacy beliefs often are highly task specific (Bandura, 1997; Pajares, 1996); thus, a student might be low in self-efficacy for one math problem but have much higher efficacy beliefs for another type of problem. Self-efficacy beliefs are strongly related to student learning and achievement, and teachers have the potential to greatly influence these beliefs.

Goal Orientation Theory

Goal orientation theorists are interested in students' reasons for engaging in academic tasks. Although the literature is filled with various terms, goal orientations fall primarily into two categories: *mastery goals* and *performance goals* (Ames, 1992; Ames & Archer, 1988; Dweck & Leggett, 1988; Elliot, 1995; Maehr, 2001; Nicholls, 1989; Pintrich, 2000). For a given academic task, a student who endorses *mastery goals* is involved with the task to truly master the material that is being learned. When students are mastery oriented, they exert much effort at academic tasks, and they compare their current performance with their own past performances at the same task. In contrast, a student who endorses *performance goals* engages in a task to demonstrate his or her ability at the task. When students are performance oriented, they are interested in how their performance compares with the performance of other students or how they are being judged and evaluated by others.

Goal theorists also distinguish between *approach* and *avoid* dimensions of goals (Elliot, 1999; Middleton & Midgley, 1997). Approach dimensions represent positive types of motivation, whereas avoidance dimensions represent more negative types of motivation. Both mastery and performance goals have been classified according to the approach/avoid dimensions. In terms of mastery goals, a *mastery-approach* goal involves a focus on mastering the task at hand and truly learning and understanding the material; in contrast, a *mastery-avoid* goal involves a focus on avoiding misunderstanding of the task. For performance goals, a *performance-approach* goal involves a focus on demonstrating one's ability relative to others; in contrast, a *performance-avoid* goal involves a focus on avoiding being perceived as "dumb" or incompetent.

Teachers' instructional practices influence the goals that students adopt. The choices that teachers make about issues—such as grading student work, grouping of students, and how students are recognized for their successes—all influence the types of goals that students adopt; in turn, these goals affect a number of important motivational outcomes.

Table 1-1 provides an overview of theories of academic motivation.

TABLE 1-1   Overview of Theories of Academic Motivation

Theory	General Description	Important Concepts in Theory
Self-Determination Theory	Focuses on intrinsic and extrinsic motivation. Humans engage in activities to meet basic needs (need for competence, relatedness, and autonomy).	Intrinsic Motivation Extrinsic Motivation Need for Competence Need for Relatedness Need for Autonomy
Attribution Theory	Focuses on how we explain events that have happened in our lives.	Stability Locus Control
Expectancy–Value Theory	Focuses on (a) our beliefs about our expectancies for success at various academic tasks, and (b) the value that we plan on those tasks.	Expectancy Value – Importance – Interest – Utility – Cost
Social Cognitive Theory	Focuses on how individuals learn behaviors by observing others, and our beliefs about our abilities to perform certain tasks.	Triadic Reciprocity Self-efficacy
Goal Orientation Theory	Focuses on the reasons why individuals work on specific academic tasks. Two main goals are the goal of mastering a task and the goal of demonstrating one's ability at a task.	Mastery approach goals Mastery avoid goals Performance approach goals Performance avoid goals

MOTIVATION: WHAT DO YOU KNOW?

Before we examine these theories and their applications in classroom contexts more specifically, stop for a moment and think about your current beliefs and preconceptions about student motivation. Consider the following questions, then write down your answer to each:

1. Does motivation come solely from the student, or do other variables influence academic motivation?
2. How much impact can any individual teacher have on student motivation?
3. Do older students tend to be motivated differently than younger students?
4. Are gender and ethnic differences present in student motivation?
5. How do the policies set forth by schools and districts affect student motivation?
6. How do classroom-based and standardized assessments affect student motivation?
7. How can teachers work effectively with parents to enhance student motivation?
8. Can we motivate students to want to learn about topics they find boring?
9. Is motivation the same across all subject areas?
10. How has the increased use of technology in education affected student motivation?

An understanding of how to apply theories of motivation to classroom instruction will allow you to help students avoid feeling bored and frustrated.

Save your answers to these questions. You will find it interesting to compare your current responses with those you give after having read this text.

Summary

In this chapter, we introduced the scope of this text, which focuses on practical applications of motivation theory that occur daily in classrooms and emphasizes the decision-making processes that teachers must consider every day. We introduced some key motivation theories so that basic terminology will be familiar. However, these theories will be presented in greater detail and more thoroughly examined throughout the following chapters.

References

Ames, C. (1992). Achievement goals and the classroom motivational climate. In D. H. Schunk & J. L. Meece (Eds.), *Student perceptions in the classroom* (pp. 327–348). Hillsdale, NJ: Erlbaum.

Ames, C., & Archer, J. (1988). Achievement goals in the classroom: Students' learning strategies and motivation processes. *Journal of Educational Psychology, 80*(3), 260–267.

Anderman, E. M., & Dawson, H. (2011). Learning with motivation. In R. E. Mayer & P. A. Alexander (Eds.), *Handbook of research on learning and instruction* (pp. 219–241). New York, NY: Routledge.

Atkinson, J. W. (1957). Motivational determinants of risk taking behavior. *Psychological Review, 64*, 359–372.

Atkinson, J. W. (1964). *An introduction to motivation.* Princeton, NJ: Van Nostrand.

Bandura, A. (1969). *Principles of behavior modification.* New York, NY: Holt, Rinehart, & Winston.

Bandura, A. (1986). *Social foundations of thought and action: A social cognitive theory.* Englewood Cliffs, NJ: Prentice Hall.

Bandura, A. (1997). *Self-efficacy: The exercise of control.* New York, NY: Freeman.

Deci, E. (1980). *The psychology of self-determination.* Lexington, MA: Heath.

Deci, E., & Ryan, R. M. (1985). *Intrinsic motivation and self-determination in human behavior.* New York, NY: Plenum.

Dweck, C. S., & Leggett, E. L. (1988). A social-cognitive approach to motivation and personality. *Psychological Review, 95*(2), 256–273.

Eccles, J. S., Adler, T. F., Futterman, R., Goff, S. B., Kaczala, C. M., Meece, J. L., & Midgley, C. (1983). Expectancies, values and academic behaviors. In J. T. Spence (Ed.), *Achievement and achievement motivation* (pp. 75–146). San Francisco, CA: Freeman.

Elliot, A. J. (1995). Approach and avoidance achievement goals: An intrinsic motivation analysis. *Dissertation Abstracts International: Section B: The Sciences and Engineering, 55*(7-B), 3061.

Elliot, A. J. (1999). Approach and avoidance motivation and achievement goals. *Educational Psychologist, 34*(3), 169–189.

Graham, S., & Weiner, B. (1996). Theories and principles of motivation. In D. C. Berliner & R. C. Calfee (Eds.), *Handbook of Educational Psychology* (pp. 63–84). New York, NY: Macmillan Library Reference USA.

Maehr, M. L. (2001). Goal theory is not dead—Not yet, anyway: A reflection on the special issue. *Educational Psychology Review, 13*(2), 177–185.

Middleton, M. J., & Midgley, C. (1997). Avoiding the demonstration of lack of ability: An underexplored aspect of goal theory. *Journal of Educational Psychology, 89*(4), 710–718.

Nicholls, J. G. (1989). *The competitive ethos and democratic education.* Cambridge, MA: Harvard University Press.

Pajares, F. (1996). Self-efficacy beliefs in academic settings. *Review of Educational Research, 66*(4), 543–578.

Pintrich, P. R. (2000). Multiple goals, multiple pathways: The role of goal orientation in learning and achievement. *Journal of Educational Psychology, 92*(3), 544–555.

Ryan, R. M., & Deci, E. L. (2000). Intrinsic and extrinsic motivations: Classic definitions and new directions. *Contemporary Educational Psychology, 25,* 54–67.

Ryan, R. M., & Deci, E. L. (2009). Promoting self-determined school engagement. In K. R. Wentzel & A. Wigfield (Eds.), *Handbook of motivation at school* (pp. 171–195). New York, NY: Routledge.

Schunk, D. H. (1991). Self-efficacy and academic motivation. *Educational Psychologist, 26,* 207–231.

Schunk, D. H., & Pajares, F. (2009). Self-efficacy theory. In K. R. Wentzel & A. Wigfield (Eds.), *Handbook of motivation at school* (pp. 35–53). New York, NY: Routledge.

Weiner, B. (1985). An attribution theory of achievement motivation and emotion. *Psychological Review, 92,* 548–573.

Weiner, B. (1986). *An attributional theory of motivation and emotion.* New York, NY: Springer-Verlag.

Weiner, B. (1992). *Human motivation: Metaphors, theories, and research.* Newbury Park, CA: Sage.

Wigfield, A., & Eccles, J. S. (1992). The development of achievement task values: A theoretical analysis. *Developmental Review, 12*(3), 265–310.

Wigfield, A., & Eccles, J. S. (2000). Expectancy-value theory of achievement motivation. *Contemporary Educational Psychology, 25*(1), 68–81.

CHAPTER 2

Choosing Academic Tasks for Your Students

One of the most important and frequent decisions that a teacher makes concerns the nature of the tasks that will be assigned to students. Such decisions are significant because the tasks that students perform at school and at home are important and strong determinants of the quality of your students' motivation to learn. Every decision about classroom activities that you make as a teacher will have an effect on your students' motivation. As a teacher, you will be challenged daily to make academic tasks more appealing and educationally relevant for your students.

Consider the following examples. Both of these fourth-grade classrooms are in the same school, but the teachers are different. Both teachers are introducing a unit on fractions:

Example #1: Mrs. Rodriguez decides to provide her students with a task that will allow them explore the nature of fractions. After an initial lesson on halves and quarters, she divides her students into groups of three and provides each group with two Twinkies and a plastic knife. She then tells each group to cut one Twinkie into two equal-size pieces and the other Twinkie into four equal-size pieces. She then tells each group that they are to use the Twinkie pieces to demonstrate whether one half (1/2) or three fourths (3/4) is the bigger fraction. Mrs. Byrnes then visits each group, and the members must explain their work to her. When they are correct, they get to eat the Twinkies.

Example #2: Mr. Jackson gives the same initial lesson on halves and quarters. He then provides each student with a worksheet with a few simple questions that are designed to help the students to learn about fractions. For these questions, the students are to imagine that they have several pieces of paper and that they cut the paper with scissors into various quantities (e.g., they cut one paper into four equal-size pieces, they cut another paper into two equal-size pieces). The students are then asked to demonstrate whether one half (1/2) or three fourths (3/4) is the bigger fraction. They then have to write down their answer, along with a brief explanation.

Given these two examples, which task appears to you to be more motivating? Most individuals (although not all) would assume that the first task is more motivational, and for most people it probably is. The first task contains several different qualities that researchers have found to be motivating:

1. It involves an authentic (real-world) task that students are likely to encounter in their own lives (cutting food).
2. It involves social interaction and cooperation among students.
3. It encourages students to apply principles of mathematics to a real-world situation.
4. A clear reward is given when the students demonstrate competence at a specific task (eating the Twinkies).

Later in this chapter, we will return to some of the reasons these task qualities are motivational. It is also important, however, to realize that some students may be put off by some of the supposed "motivational" qualities of the task. For example, an extremely shy student might not enjoy participating in group activities. In addition, a diabetic student who cannot eat Twinkies might resent the task because she could not share in the reward. Finally, a student who has recently moved to your school from overseas may not be familiar with "Twinkies" and may be reluctant to touch or eat this new food. As we will discuss throughout this text, other strategies can be used to plan around some of these issues to motivate individual students.

THE PURPOSE OF TASKS

The types of tasks that we choose for our students lead to important consequences for learning and motivation. When teachers make decisions about the kinds of tasks that they will present to their students, they can focus on a number of different dimensions of the task. Some teachers may deeply ponder the effects of various tasks on their students' learning, development, and motivation, whereas others may think about assigning tasks that will simply keep their students quiet and help to maintain an orderly classroom environment (without much regard to the effects of the task on student learning). As we will see in this chapter, many important dimensions can be used to describe academic tasks; each of these dimensions in turn is related in important ways to students' motivation. Whereas the choice of appropriate tasks can spark remarkable interest in a topic area for some students, the choice of inappropriate or ineffective tasks can turn a student off to a field of study for a lifetime.

The task that you choose directly affects students' cognitive engagement with the material—that is, it affects the ways that students think about and engage with their work (Doyle, 1983). When academic tasks do not match the students' needs and the teacher's goals, then poor learning outcomes may result (Miller & Blumenfeld, 1993). Moreover, the choice of academic task directly influences the quality and quantity of thinking of our students. All too often, teachers simply choose tasks that are convenient, without considering the cognitive and motivational ramifications of those tasks. The selection of cognitively simple tasks will encourage students to use certain types of learning strategies, whereas the choice of more cognitively demanding tasks will elicit different, more sophisticated types of cognitive processing.

For example, after a lesson on categorizing rocks, a teacher could assign several different types of tasks. One teacher might assign a worksheet reviewing basic principles covered in this lesson; this type of assignment might encourage rote memorization of facts about rocks. Another teacher might ask students to write a story about the "life cycle" of a particular type of rock that was studied; this type of assignment would not only require memory of the principles involved but also might encourage creativity and the application of principles to an example. Still another teacher might ask students to work in groups to prepare PowerPoint presentations about the similarities and differences between the different categories; this type of assignment would allow students to apply their newly acquired knowledge and to practice communicating that knowledge effectively to audiences.

Consider the following true case:

Krystyna Boyer taught high-school Spanish for 32 years. During much of her career, she taught Spanish in a fairly traditional way, using the district-mandated textbook. Krystyna noticed over many years that the students often seemed bored during class and that the students seldom actually wanted to speak Spanish during class. Several years ago, she decided it was time for a radical change. Instead of teaching her first- and second-year Spanish classes using the traditional textbook, Krystyna abandoned the textbook and began teaching Spanish using storytelling. She adapted a well-known program, called TPR Storytelling (Ray & Seely, 2008). Specifically, Krystyna taught vocabulary by engaging students in conversation about their personal lives and personal interests. Students would then act out the stories in Spanish. Afterward the class would write stories together (in Spanish), incorporating the students' own experiences and interests into the stories. Other times, the students would be given the current vocabulary and would write their own original story. Students learned vocabulary and grammar as new words and grammatical constructions naturally occurred, rather than as stand-alone topics. Assessments were based on the stories that the students created. At the end of each school year, students took the district speaking assessment, which was very vocabulary-specific to the textbook the district used. Krystyna noticed remarkable changes in her students' motivation. After dropping the textbook and incorporating the story method, students were no longer bored during Spanish class. In particular, Krystyna noted that many of the quieter students suddenly began to participate more in class. Perhaps most telling is the fact that students started to spontaneously use Spanish during class time (that had rarely if ever occurred when the textbooks were used).

In this example, the teacher realized that many of the academic tasks that she had been using with her students (i.e., tasks that went along with using the textbook) were not motivating her students. She reinvented her classes by incorporating entirely new tasks. The students continued to learn, and their motivation was enhanced by thinking about and changing the types of tasks that were used in the classroom. This is an example of how the choices that you, as the teacher, make about what academic tasks to use in the classroom can have important effects on your students' motivation.

Types of Tasks

Doyle (1983) identified four types of tasks, each of which elicits different types of cognitive processes. Although there are some more recent developments in the classifications of

Academic tasks can differ in terms of both content and the location in which they are completed.

academic tasks that we will review later, it is useful to recognize the different types of academic tasks that were described by Doyle because many of the materials that are available for teachers to use with their students (and that teachers create for their students) can be classified across these four dimensions:

1. *Memory Tasks:* In this type of task, students are required to either directly recognize material that they have learned previously or to actually reproduce specific information. Examples of memory tasks include reciting the times tables, taking a spelling test, or memorizing the locations of nations or states on maps.

2. *Procedural/Routine Tasks:* In this type of task, students are required to apply a specific algorithm to solve a problem. This type of task is particularly common in mathematics, although it certainly is also typical in other academic domains. Examples of procedural tasks include solving a series of division problems or applying rules of conjugation to a series of verbs in a foreign language.

3. *Comprehension/Understanding Tasks:* In these tasks, students are required to recognize information that they already have encountered (e.g., recognize a descriptive paragraph as the story of Harry Potter's battle against Voldemort). Comprehension tasks can include complex math problems in which students must decide on a particular strategy or algorithm before applying it. Rather than simply applying a formula or algorithm, the student must know *why* the formula or algorithm is appropriate. Comprehension/understanding tasks also might involve making future decisions based on previously learned material (e.g., after a lesson on nutrition, asking the students to make and report decisions about what they will eat over the next week). Students should have a well-developed schema for a particular topic before they attempt comprehension tasks.

Some tasks, such as reading a novel, can help encourage students to form their own opinions.

Anthony Magnacca/Merrill

4. *Opinion Tasks:* In these tasks, students state their own thoughts about particular situations, readings, or issues. Examples of opinion tasks include writing a journal response to a prompt, reflecting on how a literary work relates to one's life (Faircloth, 2009), or engaging in a class debate. For example, students might be asked to write and justify their opinions about U.S. military involvement in Afghanistan. This type of task would require students to describe their opinions about the issue and to justify their thinking.

As noted by Doyle (1983), engagement with one type of task (e.g., procedural tasks) does not necessarily facilitate future engagement with another type of task (e.g., comprehension tasks). Indeed, one might apply the formula to calculate the standard deviation of a series of numbers many times but still be unable to understand when one would actually want to use that formula in the real world (i.e., under what conditions would computing a standard deviation be useful?). Thus, one decision that teachers have to make in choosing tasks for their students relates to the type of learning that they want to take place and whether they want students to be able to understand and apply information or simply to be able to recall a body of information.

Another decision that teachers have to make when choosing tasks has to do with how academic tasks are structured. As we will see later, the structure of academic tasks is related to student motivation in important ways. Some educators distinguish between *independent* and *cooperative task structures.* When teachers use independent task structures, students generally are expected to work on tasks by themselves; in contrast, when teachers use cooperative task structures, students work together in groups to help each other (Bossert, 1977; Slavin, 1992). Given recent developments in technology, cooperative tasks can now be accomplished by groups of students interactively via the Internet and other online learning environments, as well as in person (Lynch, 2010; Naismith, Lee, & Pilkington, 2011). Academic tasks that are pursued independently are likely to elicit different types of motivation in students than are tasks that are pursued in groups. These issues are discussed in detail in Chapter 5.

BLOOM'S TAXONOMY   Teachers can think about and organize academic tasks in a number of ways. One of the most influential frameworks for examining academic tasks is Bloom's taxonomy (Bloom, Engelhart, Furst, Hill, & Krathwohl, 1956). The taxonomy includes possible learning objectives in the cognitive, psychomotor, and affective domains. This method of classifying tasks has been very influential in the development of P–12 and college curricula. Bloom's original taxonomy for the cognitive domain includes the following six components, which represent distinct objectives that are the goals of engagement with specific academic tasks:

1. Knowledge
2. Comprehension
3. Application
4. Analysis
5. Synthesis
6. Evaluation

Teachers have used the taxonomy to foster task engagement in several ways. One of the most important exercises for a classroom teacher is to consider whether or not a specific academic task fosters one or more of the components of the taxonomy.

Bloom's original taxonomy was revised in 2001 to better reflect cognitive processes (Anderson et al., 2001). The original six categories were reorganized into six dimensions. The revised taxonomy emphasizes the specific thought processes that students must apply to accomplish academic tasks:

1. Remember (Can the student recall information?)
2. Understand (Can the student explain what has been learned?)
3. Apply (Can the student use the information in a new situation?)
4. Analyze (Can the student use the information to explain other similar phenomena?)
5. Evaluate (Can the student assess the quality of something?)
6. Create (Can the student use information to produce new exemplars of some phenomenon?)

Stop and Think

Think about the last assignment that you completed for one of your courses. How many of the six components of Bloom's revised taxonomy were evident in that assignment? Were you asked to analyze, synthesize, or evaluate material, or just to understand and remember it? Could other components have been included, and would that have enhanced what you learned?

When teachers consider the types of academic tasks that will be motivational for their students, the revised taxonomy may be particularly useful because it emphasizes the specific skills and processes that students will need to use to complete a task. For example, in the development of a history lesson, the original taxonomy suggested that tasks used in the lesson should emphasize knowledge; with the new taxonomy, the emphasis is the same, but the focus is on the cognitive process used to maintain knowledge (remembering) rather than simply on knowledge. Thus teachers can use the taxonomy to consider the types of skills that they would like their students to use and to practice while engaging with classroom tasks.

A MOTIVATIONAL PERSPECTIVE ON TASKS

One of the most influential motivational theories is referred to as *expectancy–value theory*. This perspective assumes that motivation is a combination of students' expectations for being successful at a given task and their valuing of the task. In this chapter, we are particularly interested in the *value* component of the theory.

Expectancy–value researchers have conducted many studies on this topic. The research, conducted with children, adolescents, and adults, includes four components of value; these components are basically different reasons individuals give for valuing academic tasks (Eccles, 1983; Wigfield & Eccles, 1992, 2000; Wigfield, Tonks, & Lutz Klauda, 2009). In thinking about this section, keep in mind that these terms do not refer to more global life values, such as honesty or integrity, but refer specifically to reasons for valuing a particular task or activity. The following reviews each of the four components:

1. *Attainment Value:* Attainment value refers to the importance to students of doing well on a task. The attainment value of a task helps students to confirm or disconfirm various aspects of their self-concept (Wigfield & Eccles, 1992). For example, a student who sees herself as logical and analytic may have high attainment value for academic tasks involving abstract problem solving; a student who sees himself as altruistic may hold high attainment value for tasks involving social action, such as fund-raising for a local charity; a student who sees herself as a talented athlete may have high attainment value for physical education activities.
2. *Intrinsic Value:* Intrinsic value refers to how inherently interesting, enjoyable, or likeable a task is to students. In this instance, the tasks are valued simply for the pleasure of engaging in them, regardless of other considerations. When students are interested in a task, they are likely to persevere with the task. For example, students may intrinsically value reading novels about vampires because popular culture in recent years has glamorized vampires through books and movies such as the *Twilight* series. More discussion of the role of students' interests follows in a later section.
3. *Utility Value:* Utility value refers to students' perceptions of the usefulness of a particular task. The perceived utility value of a task often is related to students' future goals, including future educational or career goals (Pintrich & Schunk, 2002). For example, a student may be motivated to persist with a task that she does not particularly enjoy if a good grade is required to gain entry to the college of her choice; a student may perceive a course on marketing as having high utility value if the student plans to apply for jobs in the marketing industry after graduation.
4. *Cost:* In this theory, cost refers to negative aspects of engaging in a task. Students want to know that it will be worth their time and effort to engage in a task. For many students, a type of cost-benefit analysis is associated with any task: Is the "cost" of doing the task worth the potential benefits that will be derived from being involved with the task? Some tasks, even those that are viewed as important or useful, might not be "cost effective" for students if engagement in the task will lead to anxiety, requires too much effort, or precludes the student from engaging in other preferred activities.

Some tasks are inherently enjoyable and help promote students' motivation.

Why Are Task Values Important?

It seems obvious that most teachers, and parents, would want children and adolescents to value academic subjects. Indeed, we often hear phrases such as "creating lifelong learners," which assume that students value at least some aspects of academic learning. Indeed, today, many colleges and universities advertise adult education courses that are aimed at the "lifelong learner." However, there are other reasons to encourage the development of positive task values. Research suggests that students who value certain academic subjects are likely to choose to engage in similar activities in the future. In particular, work by Eccles and her colleagues suggests that students who value mathematics are likely to actually enroll in future math courses when courses become optional (Simpkins, Davis-Kean, & Eccles, 2006; Wigfield & Eccles, 1992). Thus teachers increase students' long-term engagement and persistence with academic subjects when they promote positive task values in their classrooms by choosing and implementing tasks that are perceived as being important, interesting, useful, and worthy of a time commitment. Positive values regarding academic subjects that are developed early in life may lead to enhanced career possibilities, academic choices, and opportunities in the future (Durik, Vida, & Eccles, 2006). In contrast, a student is less likely to choose a profession that involves the use of a subject such as mathematics if the student does not hold positive achievement values for mathematics. In addition, longitudinal research indicates that students' valuing of academic subjects declines over time. For example, a recent longitudinal study of children's and adolescents' valuing of literacy indicated that subjective task values decrease between the 1st and the 12th grades (Archambault, Eccles, & Vida, 2010). Thus it is particularly important for teachers to acknowledge that students' valuing of academics tends to decline and consequently to pay particular attention to the types of tasks that are assigned to their students.

Questions to Ponder

Think about one of the courses you are taking currently. Which of the four achievement value components match your beliefs about the course?
How does that affect your personal motivation toward the work in that course?

Student Interest and the Academic Task

We have already noted that one of the components of the Eccles et al. expectancy–value model of motivation is *intrinsic value,* a term that refers to students' perceptions that a task is interesting and enjoyable in its own right (remember the definition of intrinsic motivation from Chapter 1). It is important to note, however, that no one task is going to be uniformly interesting for all students. It also is important to recognize that some tasks that you (as the classroom teacher) may not find interesting might be very enjoyable for some of your students. Be careful not to communicate your own lack of interest in a topic to your students! Teachers' enthusiasm for what they teach is an important influence on students' engagement (Patrick, L. H. Anderman, Ryan, Edelin, & Midgley, 2001).

Some researchers have examined student interest in depth (e.g., Hidi, Renninger, & Krapp, 2004). An examination of some of this research provides additional information that can help teachers to make academic tasks more interesting and motivational for their students. Specifically, there is a distinction between personal interest and situational interest. *Personal interest* is an individual characteristic that people may have over a long period of time and across situations; this type of interest resembles a personality trait of the individual learner (Krapp, Hidi, & Renninger, 1992; Renninger, 1992; Schiefele, Krapp, & Winteler, 1992). Thus some students come into music classes "interested" in music,

Student interest in academic tasks is determined both by the students' personal interest and situational factors that teachers can influence.

whereas others come into the same classroom totally disinterested in music. Personal interest represents the interest that students "bring with them" to a given situation.

In contrast, *situational interest* refers to interest that is elicited by environmental variables, such as characteristics of a particular task or subject matter (Hidi, 1990; Hidi & Harackiewicz, 2000; Schraw & Lehman, 2001). Regardless of their personal interest, therefore, students are more likely to become interested in particular tasks or activities because of particular qualities of the classroom or task. Much of the research on situational interest arose from studies of aspects of texts that elicit interest in students.

Both personal and situational interest offer important implications for the development of motivational academic tasks. In terms of personal interest, teachers must realize that their students enter their classrooms with varying levels of personal interest in a particular topic. Thus in a fourth-grade unit on astronomy, some students may come into the situation greatly intrigued by the study of astronomy (i.e., a student who has been fascinated with science fiction); another student may come into the situation completely uninterested in the subject. Inevitably, all students are going to have to engage with some tasks that are not personally interesting to them. Being aware of students' interests, however, can provide opportunities to use those interests to enliven potentially routine content. For example, students who are interested in sports could practice basic math operations by calculating batting averages; similarly, students interested in drama might be able to present their book report as a performance, rather than as a written product. John Guthrie and his colleagues performed experiments in which they manipulated situational interest to enhance personal interest in reading. They demonstrated that by providing children with stimulating reading tasks, both motivation and reading comprehension could be enhanced. Specifically, these researchers asked teachers to link interesting science experiments to both fiction and nonfiction reading tasks in third-grade classrooms. Their research demonstrated that the use of a greater quantity of stimulating tasks was related to increased motivation and to improved reading comprehension. The tasks included observations of interesting fish and insects (Guthrie et al., 2006).

How can teachers get to know about their students' personal interests? Here are a few suggestions:

1. Discuss future academic units that you will be covering in class with your students. From the conversation, you should be able to identify different students' interest in various topics.
2. Ask students and parents about extracurricular activities, hobbies, or areas of expertise.
3. Present older students who can read well with a brief survey assessing their interests.
4. Ask students to write a brief paragraph about their interest in a particular topic.
5. Conduct small discussion groups with students, examining their interests in various topics.
6. Ask students to engage in an online discussion in which they have the opportunity to describe and share some of their interests.

In terms of *situational interest*, teachers have a variety of options. Schraw, Flowerday, and Lehman (2001) have suggested the following six strategies to increase student interest in academic tasks:

1. *Offer meaningful choices to students.* These can include choices about what texts to read, which problems to work on for homework, or the topics for a project. As we will learn in later chapters, providing students with choices enhances intrinsic motivation.

2. *Use well-organized texts.* Students in your classrooms will certainly be at different reading levels. When students can follow and understand the material that they are reading, they are likely to maintain a higher level of interest in the assignment.

3. *Select texts that are vivid.* Schraw and Lehman (2001) noted that vivid imagery in texts can help to maintain and promote student interest in the text, as long as the imagery is related to the topic.

4. *Use texts that students know about.* When students have prior knowledge about a topic, they are likely to be interested in learning more about it (Tobias, 1994). Thus, the student who already has at least some background knowledge of astronomy would probably be more interested in reading a chapter about the solar system than would a student who knows nothing about astronomy; the student's familiarity with some astronomical concepts and terminology will help her to better process and maintain interest in the newer text. Similarly, a student who already has read some of the *Harry Potter* book series will be likely to want to read further novels in the series.

5. *Encourage students to be active learners.* Encourage your students to think deeply about the material that they are learning about. Ask them to discuss the material, to make predictions about what is coming next in a text, or to think creatively of alternative endings to stories. As students do more than merely sit in their chairs and read or listen, they are likely to become more interested in the task.

6. *Provide relevant cues for students.* Teachers need to assist some students in focusing on the important aspects of the task. One good way to accomplish this is through the use of *advance organizers,* which are outlines or summaries of tasks that are presented to students at the beginning of a class or unit to help them understand the overall purpose of the task (i.e., the goals for the day).

Goal Orientations and Academic Tasks

Goal orientations represent the reasons that students report for engaging in academic tasks. These are very important motivational perceptions because they represent students' beliefs about the reasons for engaging in academic work. Although goal orientations are relatively stable (Tuominen-Soini, Salmela-Aro, & Niemivirta, 2011), as a teacher, you will be able to shape students' goals related to their academic tasks.

Let's look at an example. When a student is reading a book, he or she generally has an achievement-related "goal" for the particular task. One type of goal that has been found to be particularly adaptive is referred to as a *mastery goal* (also referred to as a *task-involved goal* or a *learning goal* in the research literature). When oriented toward a mastery goal for a particular academic task, the student is interested in truly engaging with and "mastering" the task. Students who are mastery oriented are concerned with self-improvement and developing their competence. In contrast, when oriented toward a *performance goal* (also referred to as an *ego-involved goal* or an *ability goal*), the student is concerned with *looking* competent or comparing his or her own performance to that of others (Ames, 1992; Ames & Archer, 1988; E. M. Anderman, Austin, & Johnson, 2002; E. M. Anderman & Wolters, 2006; Elliot & Harackiewicz, 1996; Harackiewicz & Elliot, 1993; Maehr & E. M. Anderman, 1993; Meece, Blumenfeld, & Hoyle, 1988; Midgley, 1993; Pintrich, 2000). It is important to note that these goals are specific to particular subject areas or classes and are not stable for individuals. That is, it is not the case that certain students will always be oriented toward mastery or performance, although there may be a personal tendency toward one orientation or the other.

Research indicates that it is beneficial to encourage students to hold mastery goals for academic tasks. The adoption of mastery goals is related to many positive outcomes (E. M. Anderman & Maehr, 1994; Dweck & Leggett, 1988; Huang, 2011). For example, research has shown that mastery goals are associated with increased effort and persistence (Miller, Greene, Montalvo, Ravindran, & Nichols, 1996), increased engagement in tasks (Archer, 1994; Fredricks, Blumenfeld, & Paris, 2004; Wolters, 2004), improved academic achievement (Linnenbrink-Garcia, Tyson, & Patall, 2008), and less use of ineffective cognitive and self-regulatory strategies (Midgley & Urdan, 2001). Fortunately, students' orientation toward mastery can be influenced by the ways their teachers design and implement instruction. Students are more likely to focus on mastery goals when they see their teachers as emphasizing mastery, effort, and improvement (Midgley, Anderman, & Hicks, 1995).

An observational study conducted by Patrick and her colleagues (Patrick et al., 2001) examined the relations between students' goal orientations and academic tasks. These researchers identified four fifth-grade classrooms that students viewed as high in either mastery or performance goals. Some important differences in the use of academic tasks were noted in the mastery and performance-focused classrooms (see L. H. Anderman, Patrick, & Ryan, 2004, for a fuller description of the high mastery-focused classrooms).

In the high mastery-focused classrooms, all students were encouraged to verbally participate in discussions about academic tasks. One teacher in the study accomplished this by assigning a number to all students and then randomly drawing numbers to determine who would answer questions when discussing academic work. High mastery-focused teachers also exhibited high levels of enthusiasm for tasks they were introducing and communicated a strong sense of enjoyment in different lessons. In addition, these teachers emphasized the importance of thinking creatively and understanding content, rather than focusing on superficial or procedural aspects of tasks.

Research on the relations between performance goals and academic tasks is less consistent; however, research suggests that the adoption of performance-approach goals (i.e., the goal of appearing more competent than others at a task) does not negatively affect students' attention to academic tasks, whereas the adoption of performance-avoid goals (i.e., the goal of avoiding appearing incompetent when performing a task) does distract students from focusing on the task at hand (Senko, Hulleman, & Harackiewicz, 2011).

Culturally Based Academic Tasks

One extremely important aspect of developing motivational tasks is the consideration of the cultural backgrounds of students. Students from different ethnic, socioeconomic, linguistic, and religious backgrounds may have very different task preferences. What "counts" as valid learning in one culture may sharply contrast with what "counts" in another culture (Greenfield et al., 2006). Thus teachers need to be sensitive to cultural differences when designing motivational tasks (Gay, 2000; Hurley, Allen, & Boykin, 2009; Tyler, Haines, & E. M. Anderman, 2006). Indeed, some research indicates that when there is a mismatch between students' cultural backgrounds and institutional practices, students may suffer; for example, colleges and universities that primarily serve white students often are less successful than are historically black colleges and universities at retaining and graduating African American students (Rodgers & Summers, 2008). Students' cultural backgrounds not only will shape their personal interests in and prior knowledge related to various subject areas and topics, but also will be reflected in their preferences for different types of social interactions in school.

Boykin and his colleagues have studied the types of tasks and learning environments that are most favorable to the learning and motivation of minority students. Research indicates that in classrooms that serve low-income African American children, mainstream behaviors and interactions are more common than are Afrocultural interactions (Boykin, Tyler, & Miller, 2005). Indeed, academic tasks that may be particularly motivational to African American children may include characteristics such as movement, communalism, and cultural themes; however, these characteristics are often lacking in contemporary classrooms (Boykin & Ellison, 1995; Boykin, Lilja, & Tyler, 2004). However, research suggests that when African American children are asked about the types of tasks in which they would like to engage, there often is a discrepancy between students' preferences for tasks and the students' perceptions of their teachers' preferences (Tyler, Boykin, Miller, & Hurley, 2006). Whereas they may report a preference for communal academic tasks, the same students often believe that their teachers would prefer for them to engage in individualistic or competitive tasks.

TASKS AND STUDENTS' SELF-CONCEPTS OF ABILITY

The types of tasks that a teacher chooses for his or her students can affect a number of different outcomes. In particular, they can communicate teachers' expectations about students' academic and intellectual abilities in ways that will influence students' beliefs about themselves.

What Kinds of Messages Do Tasks Send to Students?

During childhood and adolescence, students develop beliefs about their own abilities (Dweck & Leggett, 1988). Whereas young children tend to overestimate their academic abilities, older children and adolescents tend to appraise their abilities more realistically (Nicholls, 1990; Nicholls & Miller, 1983). Whereas many students in a first-grade classroom might consider themselves to be the best reader in the class, eighth graders tend to have more realistic perceptions of their academic standing as readers in comparison to their classmates. As a teacher, it is important to help all your students maintain confidence in their ability to learn and be successful in your class. Without such confidence, some students may form negative views of their own academic and intellectual abilities and stop trying to learn. (Remember Claire in Chapter 1?)

The types of tasks that teachers provide for students can have an effect on their developing beliefs about their abilities. Rosenholtz and Simpson (1984) distinguished between unidimensional and multidimensional classrooms. In *unidimensional classrooms,* legitimate academic ability and activity tend to be quite narrowly and rigidly defined. In this type of environment, students are likely to work on a small number of similar academic tasks, often with everyone expected to complete the same work in the same amount of time. This can be problematic in terms of students' developing beliefs about their own ability because the class organization makes it much more likely that students will compare their own work to that of other students (Pepitone, 1972). This emphasis on comparing students on a limited range of intellectual tasks will inevitably lead to a small number of students feeling confident in their abilities and many others feeling embarrassed and inadequate.

In contrast, in *multidimensional classrooms* a wide range of different types of tasks and activities, tapping different types of intellectual abilities, is provided. Thus, students have the opportunity to demonstrate their talents and learning in a variety of ways. In addition, because students may be working on different types of tasks and with different timelines, they may be less likely to directly compare their performance to that of other students (Rosenholtz & Simpson, 1984). With this class organization, a greater number of students will be able to experience success in their academic work and to develop confidence in their abilities.

The sequencing and relative difficulty of tasks can sometimes lead to ability comparisons among students. When students focus on ability differences, they may be more likely to adopt performance goals, which can have a negative impact on their motivation (E. M. Anderman & Dawson, 2011; E. M. Anderman, Gray, & Chang, 2012). For example, if students work on different tasks at different times, while all are ultimately required to complete the same tasks by the end of a given time period, then students still may compare their progress to the progress of their peers. In particular, students might focus on differences in time to task completion for various individuals and interpret this as an indicator of ability. In addition, students who appear to be engaging in more, or more difficult, tasks may be perceived as being more "able" than are other students (Marshall & Weinstein, 1984).

Simply assigning different tasks to different students, however, will not necessarily send a desired message. Care must be taken to ensure that all students can maintain a focus on engagement and improvement and can avoid becoming self-conscious and focusing on their performance relative to others. If students are assigned different types of tasks in a way that reflects your assumptions about different students' abilities, the differentiated tasks might actually *reinforce* students' perceptions of ability differences. Consider a classroom in which students are learning about plants. A teacher could create and assign academic tasks in several ways. First, in a purely unidimensional classroom, the teacher might assign the same task to all students (e.g., the students might be required to measure and graph the growth of a plant over several days). In contrast, in a multidimensional classroom, the teacher might provide several related tasks. For example, one task might be growing a plant from seeds, experimenting with different growing conditions to decide which are optimal; another might be to write a research paper about different plant habitats; another might be to do some research about the types of plants that tend to thrive in certain geographic regions; and another might be to search the Internet for pictures of plants that survive in unusual conditions and use them to create a collage. It is sometimes inevitable that students will have to work on similar or identical tasks. In these instances, teachers can limit ability comparisons by focusing on different processes and products. This is referred to as *divergent production* (Guilford, 1959). For example, a third-grade teacher might have all her students complete a book report and require inclusion of the same key concepts (summarize the plot, describe your favorite character), but allow a range of presentation formats (an oral presentation, wall poster, formal written report, etc.).

In the multidimensional classroom the teacher has two options: allow students to choose their own tasks or assign specific tasks to different students. If the teacher assigns the tasks on the basis of perceived student ability, assuming that certain students should always receive the "challenging" or "more academic" assignments and others should always receive the less demanding tasks, the assignments can reinforce the students' beliefs about their own and their peers' abilities (or lack thereof). In our example, if the teacher assigns the "easy" task (e.g., making a collage) to the lower-ability students and the more difficult tasks (e.g., a research paper) to the higher-ability students, then involvement with specific tasks may serve to reinforce the students' beliefs about which students have greater or lesser amounts of ability. In contrast, when the teacher allows all students to choose from a limited range of tasks, the teacher's beliefs about students' abilities are not communicated to students. Research indicates that students' interest in a particular task is a more important predictor of the likelihood of choosing a challenging task than is their perceived ability (Inoue, 2007). Thus some students that the teacher views as having lower ability may choose to engage in more complex tasks, particularly if they are in an environment that encourages them to take on challenges without being penalized if they do not do well. This flexibility helps protect students' perceptions of themselves as capable, and it also allows students who have been judged as having low ability to experience challenging and interesting tasks. Given the opportunity to excel, some of your students might surprise you.

The ways that academic tasks are structured by the teacher also can affect student motivation. In one study, a researcher worked with a high-school English teacher to create classroom experiences that allowed adolescents to explore their developing and changing identities within the context of literature. Students were asked to reflect on how various pieces of literature related to their lives. For example, when the students read *To Kill a Mockingbird*, the students were asked to reflect on Atticus Finch's resistance to racism and then to relate that to their own personal commitments to reducing racism. Results of this study indicated that the provision of these opportunities fostered a greater sense of belonging among these students (Faircloth, 2009).

HOMEWORK

Homework is a specific type of academic task. The types of assignments provided to students can send powerful messages to children and adolescents. Homework tasks certainly should espouse the four achievement values identified by Eccles, Wigfield, and their colleagues (i.e., homework assignments should be perceived as interesting, important, useful, and worth the time invested). For younger children in particular, homework assignments should be enjoyable and should foster the idea that learning is fun, important, and useful (Begley, 1998).

Research suggests that homework provides few benefits for young children; as students progress through middle school and high school, homework assignments begin to accrue academic benefits (Cooper & Valentine, 2001). More specifically, in early elementary school, teacher-assigned homework is related inversely to students' attitudes—students who receive less homework have better attitudes toward school. During middle school and high school, however, homework is related positively to achievement (Cooper, Lindsay, Nye, & Greathouse, 1998). Recent research suggests that although homework is related to gains in achievement for students, the actual amount of time spent on homework is not as important as are other aspects of the assigned homework tasks (e.g., frequency of assignments and quality of effort invested in the assignments by the students; Trautwein, 2007). In particular, students who perceive their homework assignments as being of high value (i.e., useful) and students who have positive beliefs in their abilities to complete their homework are likely to exert greater effort (Trautwein & Ludtke, 2007). In addition, experiencing negative emotions while completing homework assignments actually can lead to declines in achievement (Dettmers et al., 2011). Thus teachers would be well served to focus less on the amount of time that students should spend at home working on a particular assignment and to focus more on creating assignments that (a) will be perceived as useful to their students and (b) will be perceived as manageable by their students.

To make homework meaningful to students, it is important for educators to understand that their beliefs about homework may sharply contrast with the perceptions of their students (Hong, Wan, & Peng, 2011). Although teachers may see homework as an important means of allowing students to practice important skills that were learned in class, students may see homework as an annoyance that prevents them from engaging in other preferred activities (e.g., playing outside, watching television, or spending time with peers). Teachers need to keep the discrepancies between their beliefs and their students' beliefs about homework in mind when developing homework tasks. Homework clearly has its place, but the assignment of too much seemingly boring homework may result in a dislike among students for a particular subject area.

STUDENT ENGAGEMENT AND BEHAVIOR

Students who work on meaningful academic tasks are more likely to report being engaged with their work. A student who is engaged is cognitively, motivationally, and emotionally involved with the specific task at hand. Researchers recently have argued that providing engaging tasks may improve the performance of students in school (Fredricks et al., 2004). For example, as previously discussed, when students are oriented toward mastering an academic task, they are more cognitively engaged with the task; that is, they use more effective cognitive strategies and, thus, are more likely to use their time effectively and to experience success (Elliot & McGregor, 2001; Nolen, 1988).

Larry Hamill/Merrill

Students often will be better behaved when they are engaged in interesting academic tasks.

It seems logical that students will be better behaved when they are deeply engaged with academic tasks. Consider the following scenario:

Jacob and Zach are first graders. During math instruction, Jacob's teacher provides the students with an interesting hands-on activity, in which students use items available in grocery stores (e.g., boxes of cereal, fruits, vegetables) as manipulatives to complete simple addition problems. In contrast, Zach's teacher completes the same lesson but uses worksheets that present addition problems without any meaningful context, such as this:

$$4 + 1 = \underline{\quad} ?$$

In which classroom would students be more likely to lose interest with the task and misbehave? Although students certainly might misbehave in the classroom where the manipulatives are used, misbehavior is more likely to occur with the less interesting task. If the classroom teacher consistently uses tasks such as the one with items from the grocery store, then students can learn to behave well while engaging with such tasks; when teachers focus their efforts on guiding student learning, rather than on always controlling and managing student behavior, students are likely to experience more positive learning environments (Brophy, 1996). The students are more likely to become distracted and veer off task when the assignment is simply not engaging.

Another method for promoting good student behavior through tasks is to personalize the classroom environment through the use of student-created projects. When students complete various academic tasks, those tasks or projects can be displayed throughout the classroom. Students often appreciate this more than classrooms that are sterile or decorated with impersonal posters. Making the classroom environment more comfortable for students may also lead to fewer behavioral problems (Weinstein & Mignano, 1997).

As noted in our discussion of situational and personal interest, teachers can incorporate students' interests into classroom tasks to promote engagement. For example, if a teacher knows that several students are interested in soccer, the teacher might select for a reading program age-appropriate nonfiction books and stories about soccer. This would be a way to incorporate students' personal interests into the task while still addressing curricular objectives. In addition, teachers should create classroom environments that promote interest (i.e., situational interest) in their students. For example, a teacher might decorate the classroom in a new way for a new academic unit.

Mrs. Smith is a third-grade teacher who takes pride in using academic tasks that are interesting and motivational for her students. In her district, the students begin studying U.S. history during third grade. To make history interesting and enjoyable for her students, Mrs. Smith creates a "wax museum" every year. The students in her class each choose a famous American who had an impact on history (from any time period). Then the students do research on the famous person and create a "booth" that provides information about the person. The students also make recordings that describe the historical contributions of each famous individual. Then, on a special day, each child dresses up as his or her historical figure, and the child is then stationed in the appropriate "booth," pretending to be a wax figure representing that person, while the recording plays. The teachers and students from the entire school, and the students' parents, are invited to attend this event, which is a favorite of her students.

© Yael Weiss/Fotolia

If students are not engaged with academic tasks, they are likely to find other things to do during class time.

Summary

This chapter examined academic tasks. The types of tasks that teachers use during instruction have important effects on motivation and learning. Whereas some tasks are motivational to individual students, other tasks may be necessary for different groups. Here are some suggestions for choosing tasks:

1. *Choose tasks that are developmentally appropriate for students.* It is important to choose tasks that are neither too complex nor too simple. Just because a task is included in a workbook or in the curriculum doesn't necessarily mean that it is developmentally appropriate. Use your own judgment, read about the task, try out the task, and talk to your colleagues.

2. *Build on students' personal interests.* Find out what interests students, and incorporate those interests into lesson plans. Different students will have different interests, and students from different cultural backgrounds will have varied interests as well. Instruction that is differentiated and geared toward the individual learner and his or her interests can become burden-some for teachers, but also can lead to wonderful motivational outcomes for learners (Tomlinson et al., 2003).

3. *Choose tasks that will allow students to feel successful.* To motivate students toward future tasks, choose tasks that will ensure students some success. If students cannot complete tasks, they are likely to become frustrated and give up. Don't make the tasks too easy, but strive to allow all students to experience feelings of competence.

4. *Encourage mastery.* When your students are completing academic tasks, encourage mastery of the task. Try to avoid comparing one student's progress on a task to the progress of another student.

5. *Choose tasks that convey achievement values.* Think about the four components of achievement values: intrinsic value, importance, utility value, and cost. For every task that you provide to your students, think about whether or not the task conveys any of these values. If it does not, consider reorganizing the task so that at least one achievement value is evident.

Questions to Consider When Selecting Academic Tasks for Instruction

1. What is my teaching objective for this activity? Should I choose a *memory task,* a *procedural/routine task,* a *comprehension/understanding task,* or an *opinion task*?
2. How can I increase the *situational interest* of this task? Can I organize the information, build on prior knowledge, and help students identify the key points?
3. How can I communicate the *utility value* of this task to my students? How is this knowledge or skill useful for students? What makes this task worth students' investment of time and effort?
4. How can I encourage a focus on *personal mastery* and improvement and de-emphasize ability comparisons among my students?
5. How can I individualize tasks while still accomplishing my teaching objectives?
6. What aspects of individual students' *cultural backgrounds* or *personal interests* should I take into account when designing tasks?
7. Can I provide some controlled *choices* for students?

Teachers should not simply accept tasks that are presented in texts and curricula as motivational for all students; rather, they must consider the type of learning that is required by the task (e.g., rote memorization, giving opinions), students' perceptions of the value of the task (e.g., Is it useful? Is it important?), and the individual characteristics, backgrounds, and preferences of the students. Choosing the appropriate task can have profound and important positive influences on students' learning, motivation, and future choices.

LEARNING ACTIVITY 2.1   Tasks: A Student Perspective

Some students are extremely motivated to engage in the study of a given subject domain, whereas others are not. Much of this motivation stems from the tasks in which students engage. For this assignment, interview another college student. Using the following chart, ask each student to recall his or her high-school years and to describe typical academic tasks that were assigned in each subject area. Then, ask the student to dream a little: If the student could go back in time and make suggestions to teachers for an interesting educational task, what would the student recommend?

Subject	Typical Task	Motivational Task
English/Language Arts		
Mathematics		
Science		
Social Studies		
Foreign Language		
Art		
Music		
Physical Education		
Health		
Other		

LEARNING ACTIVITY 2.2   Using Expectancy–Value Theory to Enhance the Motivational Quality of Academic Tasks

As you recall, the expectancy–value model of motivation offered by Eccles et al. contains four components: attainment value, intrinsic value, utility value, and cost. Choose an authentic academic task that is currently being used in classrooms (by examining curricular materials in your library, interviewing a practicing teacher, etc.). Then evaluate the task using Eccles's four components of value. First, describe the task, using each of the four components of expectancy–value theory. Then, describe enhancements you could make to the task to improve each of the four components.

	General Description of This Aspect of the Task	How could you enhance this aspect of the task?
Attainment Value		
Intrinsic Value		
Utility Value		
Cost		

LEARNING ACTIVITY 2.3   Enhancing Situational Interest

In this chapter, we reviewed two types of interest: *personal interest* (i.e., the interest that a student brings into the classroom) and *situational interest* (i.e., interest that is created by the teacher through instructional practices). For this activity, think about a lesson that you once had to endure that was truly boring (from any level of schooling). First, provide a brief description of that lesson, Second, using what you have learned in this chapter, redesign that lesson, and incorporate at least three of the strategies suggested by Schraw, Flowerday, and Lehman (2001) to enhance the situational interest of your students. Describe the specific changes that you would make and how you think those changes would enhance your students' motivation toward the task.

References

Ames, C. (1992). Achievement goals and the classroom motivational climate. In D. H. Schunk & J. L. Meece (Eds.), *Student perceptions in the classroom* (pp. 327–348). Hillsdale, NJ: Erlbaum.

Ames, C., & Archer, J. (1988). Achievement goals in the classroom: Students' learning strategies and motivation processes. *Journal of Educational Psychology, 80*(3), 260–267.

Anderman, E. M., Austin, C. C., & Johnson, D. M. (2002). The development of goal orientation. In A. Wigfield & J. S. Eccles (Eds.), *Development of achievement motivation: A volume in the educational psychology series* (pp. 197–220). San Diego, CA: Academic Press.

Anderman, E. M., & Dawson, H. (2011). Learning and motivation. In P. Alexander & R. Mayer (Eds.), *Handbook of learning and instruction* (pp. 219–241). New York: Routledge.

Anderman, E. M., Gray, D., & Chang, Y. (2012). Motivation and classroom learning. In W. Reynolds & G. Miller (Eds.), *Handbook of psychology: Vol. 7. Educational psychology.* Hoboken, NJ: Wiley.

Anderman, E. M., & Maehr, M. L. (1994). Motivation and schooling in the middle grades. *Review of Educational Research, 64*(2), 287–309.

Anderman, E. M., & Wolters, C. (2006). Goals, values, and affect: Influences on student motivation. In P. Alexander & P. Winne (Eds.), *Handbook of educational psychology* (2nd ed., pp. 369–389). Mahwah, NJ: Erlbaum.

Anderman, L. H., Patrick, H., & Ryan, A. M. (2004). Promoting adaptive motivational beliefs in middle school classrooms. *Middle School Journal, 35*, 33–39.

Anderson, L. W., Krathwohl, D. R., Airasian, P. W., Cruikshank, K. A., Mayer, R. E., Pintrich, P. R., et al. (2001). *A taxonomy for learning, teaching, and assessing.* New York: Longman.

Archambault, I., Eccles, J. S., & Vida, M. N. (2010). Ability self-concepts and subjective value in literacy: Joint trajectories from grades 1 through 12. *Journal of Educational Psychology, 102*, 804–816.

Archer, J. (1994). Achievement goals as a measure of motivation in university students. *Contemporary Educational Psychology, 19*(4), 430–446.

Begley, S. (1998, March 30). Homework doesn't help. *Newsweek*, 30–31.

Bloom, B. S., Engelhart, M. D., Furst, E. J., Hill, W. H., & Krathwohl, D. R. (Eds.). (1956). *Taxonomy of educational objectives: Handbook I, Cognitive domain.* New York, NY: David McKay.

Bossert, S. (1977). Tasks, group management, and teacher control behavior: A study of classroom organization and teacher style. *School Review, 85*, 552–565.

Boykin, A. W., & Ellison, C. M. (1995). The multiple ecologies of Black youth socialization: An Afrographic analysis. In R. T. Taylor (Ed.), *African-American youth: Their social and economic status in the United States* (pp. 93–128). Westport, CT: Greenwood.

Boykin, A. W., Lilja, A. J., & Tyler, K. M. (2004). The influence of communal versus individual learning context on the academic performance of African American elementary school students. *Learning Environments Journal, 7*, 227–244.

Boykin, A. W., Tyler, K. M., & Miller, O. (2005). In search of cultural themes and their expressions in the dynamics of classroom life. *Urban Education, 45*, 521–549.

Brophy, J. (1996). *Teaching problem students.* New York: Guilford.

Cooper, H., Lindsay, J. J., Nye, B., & Greathouse, S. (1998). Relationships among attitudes about homework, amount of homework assigned and completed, and student achievement. *Journal of Educational Psychology, 90*, 70–83.

Cooper, H., & Valentine, J. C. (2001). Using research to answer practical questions about homework. *Educational Psychologist, 36*(3), 143–153.

Dettmers, S., Trautwein, U., Ludtke, O., Goetz, T., Frenzel, A. C., & Pekrun, R. (2011). Students' emotions during homework in mathematics: Testing a theoretical model of antecedents and achievement outcomes. *Contemporary Educational Psychology, 36*, 25–35.

Doyle, W. (1983). Academic work. *Review of Educational Research, 53*, 159–199.

Durik, A. M., Vida, M., & Eccles, J. S. (2006). Task values and ability beliefs as predictors of high school literacy choices: A developmental analysis. *Journal of Educational Psychology, 98*(2), 382–393.

Dweck, C. S., & Leggett, E. L. (1988). A social-cognitive approach to motivation and personality. *Psychological Review, 95*(2), 256–273.

Eccles, J. S. (1983). Expectancies, values and academic behaviors. In J. T. Spence (Ed.), *Achievement and achievement motivation* (pp. 75–146). San Francisco, CA: Freeman.

Elliot, A. J., & Harackiewicz, J. M. (1996). Approach and avoidance achievement goals and intrinsic motivation: A mediational analysis. *Journal of Personality and Social Psychology, 70*(3), 461–475.

Elliot, A. J., & McGregor, H. A. (2001). A 2 × 2 achievement goal framework. *Journal of Personality and Social Psychology, 80*(3), 501–519.

Faircloth, B. S. (2009). Making the most of adolescence: Harnessing the search for identity to understand classroom belonging. *Journal of Adolescent Research, 24*, 321–348.

Fredricks, J. A., Blumenfeld, P. C., & Paris, A. H. (2004). School engagement: Potential of the concept, state of the evidence. *Review of Educational Research, 74*(1), 59–109.

Gay, G. (2000). *Culturally responsive teaching: Theory, research, and practice.* New York, NY: Teachers College Press.

Greenfield, P. M., Trumbull, E., Keller, H., Rothstein-Fisch, C., Suzuki, L. K., & Quiroz, B. (2006). Cultural conceptions of learning and development. In P. A. Alexander & P. H. Winne (Eds.), *Handbook of educational psychology* (2nd ed., pp. 675–692). Mahwah, NJ: Erlbaum.

Guilford, J. P. (1959). Three faces of intellect. *American Psychologist, 14,* 469–479.

Guthrie, J. T., Wigfield, A., Humenick, N. M., Perencivich, K. C., Taboada, A., & Barbosa, P. (2006). Influences of stimulating tasks on reading motivation and comprehension. *Journal of Educational Research, 99*(4), 232–245.

Harackiewicz, J. M., & Elliot, A. J. (1993). Achievement goals and intrinsic motivation. *Journal of Personality and Social Psychology, 65*(5), 904–915.

Hidi, S. (1990). Interest and its contribution as a mental resource for learning. *Review of Educational Research, 60,* 549–571.

Hidi, S., & Harackiewicz, J. M. (2000). Motivating the academically unmotivated: A critical issue for the 21st century. *Review of Educational Research, 70,* 151–179.

Hidi, S., Renninger, K. A., & Krapp, A. (2004). Interest, a motivational variable that combines affective and cognitive functioning. In D. Y. Dai & R. J. Sternberg (Eds.), *Motivation, emotion, and cognition: Integrative perspectives on intellectual functioning and development* (pp. 89–115). Mahwah, NJ: Erlbaum.

Hong, E., Wan, M., & Peng, Y. (2011). Discrepancies between students' and teachers' perceptions of homework. *Journal of Advanced Academics, 22,* 280–308.

Huang, C. (2011). Achievement goals and achievement emotions: A meta-analysis. *Educational Psychology Review, 23,* 359–388.

Hurley, E. A., Allen, B. A., & Boykin, A. W. (2009). Culture and the interaction of student ethnicity with reward structure in group learning. *Cognition and Instruction, 27,* 121–146.

Inoue, N. (2007). Why face the challenge? The reason behind intrinsically motivated students' spontaneous choice of challenging tasks. *Learning and Individual Differences, 17,* 251–259.

Krapp, A., Hidi, S., & Renninger, K. A. (1992). Interest, learning, and development. In K. A. Renninger, S. Hidi, & A. Krapp (Eds.), *The role of interest in learning and development* (pp. 3–25). Hillsdale, NJ: Erlbaum.

Linnenbrink-Garcia, L., Tyson, D. F., & Patall, E. A. (2008). When are achievement goal orientations beneficial for academic achievement? A closer look at main effects and moderating factors. *International Review of Social Psychology, 21,* 19–58.

Lynch, D. J. (2010). Application of online discussion and cooperative learning strategies to online and blended college courses. *College Student Journal, 44,* 777–784.

Maehr, M. L., & Anderman, E. M. (1993). Reinventing schools for early adolescents: Emphasizing task goals. *Elementary School Journal, 93*(5), 593–610.

Marshall, H. H., & Weinstein, R. S. (1984). Classroom factors affecting students' self-evaluations: An interactional model. *Review of Educational Research, 54*(3), 301–325.

Meece, J. L., Blumenfeld, P. C., & Hoyle, R. H. (1988). Students' goal orientations and cognitive engagement in classroom activities. *Journal of Educational Psychology, 80*(4), 514–523.

Midgley, C. (1993). Motivation and middle level schools. In M. L. Maehr & P. R. Pintrich (Eds.), *Advances in motivation and achievement: Vol. 8. Motivation in the adolescent years* (pp. 219–276). Greenwich, CT: JAI.

Midgley, C., Anderman, E. M., & Hicks, L. (1995). Differences between elementary and middle school teachers and students: A goal theory approach. *Journal of Early Adolescence, 15*(1), 90–113.

Midgley, C., & Urdan, T. (2001). Academic self-handicapping and achievement goals: A further examination. *Contemporary Educational Psychology, 26*(1), 61–75.

Miller, R. B., Greene, B. A., Montalvo, G. P., Ravindran, B., & Nichols, J. D. (1996). Engagement in academic work: The role of learning goals, future consequences, pleasing others, and perceived ability. *Contemporary Educational Psychology, 21*(4), 388–422.

Miller, S. D., & Blumenfeld, P. (1993). Characteristics of tasks used for skill instruction in two basal reader series. *Elementary School Journal, 94*(1), 33–47.

Naismith, L., Lee, B.-H., & Pilkington, R. M. (2011). Collaborative learning with a wiki: Differences in perceived usefulness in two contexts of use. *Journal of Computer Assisted Learning, 27,* 228–242.

Nicholls, J. G. (1990). What is ability and why are we mindful of it? A developmental perspective. In R. Sternberg & J. Kolligian (Eds.), *Competence considered* (pp. 11–40). New Haven, CT: Yale University Press.

Nicholls, J. G., & Miller, A. (1983). The differentiation of the concepts of difficulty and ability. *Child Development, 54,* 951–959.

Nolen, S. B. (1988). Reasons for studying: Motivational orientations and study strategies. *Cognition and Instruction, 5,* 269–287.

Patrick, H., Anderman, L. H., Ryan, A. M., Edelin, K. C., & Midgley, C. (2001). Teachers' communication of goal orientations in four fifth-grade classrooms. *Elementary School Journal, 102*(1), 35–58.

Pepitone, E. A. (1972). Comparison behavior in elementary school children. *American Educational Research Journal, 9,* 45–63.

Pintrich, P. R. (2000). Multiple goals, multiple pathways: The role of goal orientation in learning and achievement. *Journal of Educational Psychology, 92*(3), 544–555.

Pintrich, P. R., & Schunk, D. H. (2002). *Motivation in education: Theory, research, and applications* (2nd ed.). Upper Saddle River, NJ: Merrill Prentice Hall.

Ray, B., & Seely, C. (2008). *Fluency through TPR storytelling: Achieving real language acquisition in school* (5th ed.). Berkeley, CA: Command Performance Language Institute.

Renninger, K. A. (1992). Individual interest and development: Implications for theory and practice. In K. A. Renninger, S. Hidi, & A. Krapp (Eds.), *The role of interest in learning and development* (pp. 361–395). Hillsdale, NJ: Erlbaum.

Rodgers, K. A., & Summers, J. J. (2008). African American students at predominantly white institutions: A motivational and self-systems approach to understanding retention. *Educational Psychology Review, 20,* 171–190.

Rosenholtz, S. J., & Simpson, C. (1984). The formation of ability conceptions: Developmental trend or social construction? *Review of Educational Research, 54,* 31–63.

Schiefele, U., Krapp, A., & Winteler, A. (1992). Interest as a predictor of academic achievement: A meta-analysis of research. In K. A. Renninger, S. Hidi, & A. Krapp (Eds.), *The role of interest in learning and development* (pp. 183–212). Hillsdale, NJ: Erlbaum.

Schraw, G., Flowerday, T., & Lehman, S. (2001). Increasing situational interest in the classroom. *Educational Psychology Review, 13,* 211–224.

Schraw, G., & Lehman, S. (2001). Situational interest: A review of the literature and directions for future research. *Educational Psychology Review, 13*(1), 23–52.

Senko, C., Hulleman, C. S., & Harackiewicz, J. M. (2011). Achievement goal theory at the crossroads: Old controversies, current challenges, and new directions. *Educational Psychologist, 46,* 26–47.

Simpkins, S. D., Davis-Kean, P. E., & Eccles, J. S. (2006). Math and science motivation: A longitudinal examination of the links between choices and beliefs. *Developmental Psychology, 42,* 70–83.

Slavin, R. E. (1992). When and why does cooperative learning increase achievement? Theoretical and empirical perspectives. In R. Hertz-Lazarowitz & N. Miller (Eds.), *Interaction in cooperative groups: The theoretical anatomy of group learning* (pp. 145–173). Cambridge, England: Cambridge University Press.

Tobias, S. (1994). Interest, prior knowledge, and learning. *Review of Educational Research, 64*(1), 37–54.

Tomlinson, C. A., Brighton, C., Hertberg, H., Callahan, C. M., Moon, T. R., Brimijoin, K., Conover, L. A., et al. (2003). Differentiating instruction in response to student readiness, interest, and learning profile in academically diverse classrooms: A review of the literature. *Journal of the Gifted, 27,* 119–145.

Trautwein, U. (2007). The homework-achievement relation reconsidered: Differentiating homework time, homework frequency, and homework effort. *Learning and Instruction, 17,* 372–388.

Trautwein, U., & Ludtke, O. (2007). Students' self-reported effort and time on homework in six school subjects: Between-students differences and within-student variation. *Journal of Educational Psychology, 99,* 432–444.

Tuominen-Soini, H., Salmela-Aro, K., & Niemivirta, M. (2011). Stability and change in achievement goal orientations: A person-centered approach. *Contemporary Educational Psychology, 36,* 82–100.

Tyler, K. M., Boykin, A. W., Miller, O., & Hurley, E. (2006). Cultural values in the home and school experiences of low-income African American students. *Social Psychology of Education, 9,* 363–380.

Tyler, K., Haines, R. T., & Anderman, E. M. (2006). Identifying the connection between culturally relevant motivation and academic performance among ethnic minority youth. In D. M. McInerney, M. Dowson, & S. V. Etten (Eds.), *Research on sociocultural influences on motivation and learning: Vol. 6. Effective schools.* Greenwich, CT: Information Age Press.

Weinstein, C. S., & Mignano, A. J., Jr. (1997). *Elementary classroom management.* New York, NY: McGraw-Hill.

Wigfield, A., & Eccles, J. S. (1992). The development of achievement task values: A theoretical analysis. *Developmental Review, 12*(3), 265–310.

Wigfield, A., & Eccles, J. S. (2000). Expectancy-value theory of achievement motivation. *Contemporary Educational Psychology, 25*(1), 68–81.

Wigfield, A., Tonks, S., & Lutz Klauda, S. (2009). Expectancy-value theory. In K. R. Wentzel & A. Wigfield (Eds.), *Handbook of motivation at school* (pp. 55–75). New York, NY: Routledge.

Wolters, C. A. (2004). Advancing achievement goal theory: Using goal structures and goal orientations to predict students' motivation, cognition, and achievement. *Journal of Educational Psychology, 96,* 236–250.

CHAPTER 3

Using Rewards Effectively

If you think back to your elementary-, middle-, and high-school years, undoubtedly you will remember examples of rewards that teachers or parents offered to you, either for doing well on an examination, for memorizing your multiplication tables, or perhaps for completing chores around the house. Did receiving the reward affect your motivation to engage in the activity? If the reward were not available, would you choose to engage in that activity in the future?

Today, the use of rewards in educational settings is quite profound. One area in which rewards (and punishments) are particularly important is the use of various incentives to reward students, teachers, and schools for their performance on high-stakes tests. Whereas improved scores on such exams can lead to financial bonuses and other incentives for schools, poor performance can lead to the loss of privileges and various sanctions. Thus, when we think about how to effectively use rewards, we need to be concerned with how rewards are used in diverse ways in today's schools.

In this chapter, we will examine the nature of rewards in education. Many educators firmly believe in the use of rewards; however, others vehemently oppose it. The goal of this chapter is to demonstrate that rewards can be used both effectively and ineffectively with students. The haphazard use of rewards can be problematic; however, if used carefully, rewards can maintain and even enhance students' motivation to learn.

REWARDS IN THE CLASSROOM

The following is based on a true story. Mr. Cohen was a high-school Spanish teacher. He decided that he would allow his class to play games every Friday to review the material that had been covered in class during the preceding week. The class particularly enjoyed emulating television game shows, such as *Jeopardy*. Each week Mr. Cohen divided his classes into two teams. The team that won the competition would receive two bonus points on the next examination.

The students in Mr. Cohen's classes enjoyed their Friday game days. After doing this for several weeks, however, Mr. Cohen realized that some of his students' grades were becoming inflated due to all the extra points they were earning. Consequently, the next Friday he told both classes that they would still be playing games that day but that it was just for fun; the reward of two extra points would no longer be available. How do you think the students reacted?

Stop and Think

How do you imagine the students in Mr. Cohen's class reacted to the change in procedure?

Interestingly, the students in each class reacted the same way—they became very angry with Mr. Cohen. The students were upset and said that they didn't want to play. Mr. Cohen was amazed at the consistent responses that he heard from both classes. Finally he said, "Okay, then, if you don't want to play, we will just do our regular work." The students finally acceded—but reluctantly. They offered various comments, such as, "Okay, we'll play your stupid games, but it won't be fun."

After that school year, Mr. Cohen reflected on this situation. He didn't want to eliminate games from his classes because he truly believed they were helpful and that his students learned from them. Consequently, he decided that during the next school year he would still make Friday game day but would not offer any rewards.

At the beginning of the next school year, Mr. Cohen explained to his classes that Friday was game day: a day to reflect on their learning and have fun. Mr. Cohen never mentioned the possibility of earning extra points for winning the games. The students enjoyed their Friday sessions that year. Nobody ever complained about not earning extra points. Although Mr. Cohen did occasionally reward his students with extra points for a treat, that only occurred as a special surprise event and only a few times during the year.

Questions to Ponder

Why do you think Mr. Cohen heard such different reactions to his Friday games during the two consecutive years? Why did the removal of the extra points as a reward elicit such strong reactions in students? Why was the occasional introduction of points as a surprise reward during the second year not a problem?

THEORY AND RESEARCH

The study of the use of rewards in educational settings is rooted in behaviorist theories of learning (Skinner, 1953; Watson, 1924). Behavioral theorists assume that by using rewards, teachers can get students into the habit of engaging in a particular academic task (e.g., reading, playing the piano), and that the rewards can be faded out once the behavior

© mostafa fawzy/Fotolia

Some students are highly motivated by extrinsic rewards.

is well established. This approach can work for some students and particular behaviors for which the students have no existing motivation (e.g., the introduction of rewards might get nonreaders to read a bit more, even if it is just to obtain a reward). Nevertheless, the assumption that the rewards can eventually be removed and that the behavior will continue may or may not prove to be true. In addition, the quality of students' learning from these types of behaviors is open to question. As we will see, research clearly indicates that rewards can affect learning and motivation both positively and negatively.

One way of thinking about motivation is in terms of *intrinsic* and *extrinsic* motivation. A task is intrinsically motivating when the student finds the task to be interesting and relevant. The "reward" for engaging with the task lies in the pleasure and sense of satisfaction that are inherent in engagement itself. In contrast, a task is extrinsically motivating when the student engages with it to receive some type of reward that is external to the task itself. Consider the following two examples:

Brook and Maggie are seventh graders. They are good friends. This year, they are in the same school but have different science teachers. At the beginning of the school year, both were very enthusiastic about science. Following are descriptions of their experiences in science class this year:

> *Brook likes to work on science experiments. She is particularly fascinated with physics because her class has been working on an interesting unit about physics. She finds the lessons covered in class to be appealing, and she enjoys analyzing and examining the effects of gravity on various phenomena. She looks forward to science class at school, particularly lab experiments. Her teacher gives tests once per month, but the tests only count for 10 percent of the grade; the majority of the grade comes from student involvement and participation in laboratory activities. Brook loves science class and is seriously considering a career in a science-related field. She even asked her parents to buy her a science kit for her birthday so that she could do experiments at home. When asked about her motivation to learn about*

science, Brook states, "It is because my teacher makes it so interesting. She sets up the class so that the lessons are enjoyable, and so that we are always curious about things."

Maggie also works on science experiments in her classes. Maggie does well in her science class and participates in laboratory exercises. However, she does not maintain the passion for physics experiments that Brook has. She does the required work but nothing more. Maggie's teacher doesn't do anything to make the science lessons particularly interesting. She follows the textbook closely. She gives her class a quiz every Friday on the work that has been covered during the previous week. The quizzes count for 80 percent of the students' grades. In addition, Maggie's teacher promises her students that those who earn an A grade will be honored in a special awards assembly at the end of the school year. When asked about her motivation to learn science, Maggie states, "I am motivated to get good grades on the quiz on Friday; my grades are important to me, so that is why I do my science work."

Although you do not have a lot of information about Brook and Maggie, you can see that their science teachers structure their classes very differently and that the different activities pursued in each class lead to different outcomes for these two early adolescents. Brook has a science teacher who works to make science class interesting. She does not emphasize exams, and the majority of the students' grades come from their work on engaging laboratory assignments. Thus, students in Brook's class probably perceive the class as very activity oriented. In contrast, Maggie's science teacher follows the textbook closely and stresses the importance of examinations. Students in Maggie's class probably perceive the class as very exam oriented.

Returning to our distinction between intrinsic and extrinsic motivation, we can say that Brook is probably intrinsically motivated in her science class, whereas Maggie is probably extrinsically motivated. Their individual motivations toward science are strongly affected by the ways that their teachers structure their classes. In particular, the reward structures in the classes are quite different. In Brook's class, the teacher does not really stress rewards. There are only a few exams, and although the exams do count toward the calculation of the students' grades, they are not weighed heavily. The emphasis in the class from day to day is on the actual activities and on making interesting discoveries about science.

In Maggie's class, the emphasis is on rewards, particularly in the form of grades and tests. Students are tested every week, and the results are important determinants of the students' final grades in the class. Because tests are an important part of the class, students probably spend much time thinking about them; in contrast, in Brook's class, students probably spend less time thinking about tests and more time thinking about the actual activities. Although you may think that these two examples are extreme, almost everybody can identify classes that they have had that were similar in nature to one of these.

Stop and Think

Do you remember classes in which the teacher stressed extrinsic outcomes such as tests? Do you remember classes in which teachers focused on making the class intrinsically motivating? How much did you like each of these classes? How much factual information do you now remember from those classes? Do you think that the instructional practices of the teachers affected what you remember now (years later)?

TABLE 3-1　Comparison of Intrinsic and Extrinsic Motivation

		Intrinsic Motivation	
		Low	**High**
Extrinsic Motivation	**Low**	Student is disinterested in the task, and extrinsic incentives do not improve motivation.	Student is highly interested in the task and does not care about extrinsic motivators.
	High	Student is only willing to participate in the task if a reward is offered.	Student is truly interested in the task but also cares about receiving rewards, such as grades.

Intrinsic and Extrinsic Motivation: Distinctions and Correlations

Although we review several different perspectives on intrinsic and extrinsic motivation in this chapter, it is fair to say that most researchers believe that intrinsic motivation and extrinsic motivation are distinct entities. Although extrinsic incentives can affect intrinsic motivation, the two types of motivation can exist in students simultaneously for the same task, and some studies suggest that they are at least moderately correlated (Lepper, Corpus, & Iyengar, 2005). (See Table 3-1.)

A student can be either high or low in intrinsic motivation for a task and either high or low in extrinsic motivation for the same task. This explains why many students can be truly interested in their academic work and, nevertheless, are also motivated by extrinsic incentives such as grades; such students may be high in both intrinsic and extrinsic motivation. This type of motivation is realistic, given the fact that most teachers do give exams and grades, particularly at the middle-school and high-school levels.

Perhaps the worst-case scenario is the student who is low on both intrinsic and extrinsic motivation. Such students present difficult challenges for teachers, as they are not interested in their academic work and are not motivated to work for rewards. This is probably representative of the low motivation of many adolescents who eventually drop out of school. It is a great challenge to instruct a student who is both uninterested in the material and uncaring about grades; indeed, this can be a very difficult challenge for even the most experienced teachers. Fortunately, as we will see, teachers can use certain strategies to help motivate such students.

Stop and Think

Look at Table 3-1. In which cell do you fall? Do you fall into the same cell for all your academic subject areas? Do you fall into different cells now, compared to when you were in high school?

DIFFERENT WAYS OF THINKING ABOUT REWARDS

Rewards can be conceptualized in many different ways, and research has defined many different classifications for them.

Rewards and Reinforcement

First, it is important to distinguish between a *reward* and a *reinforcer*. *Reward* is a popular term with many educators. In educational settings, a *reward* is a tangible or intangible incentive that is given to or earned by students for engagement in or completion of an activity. In contrast, the term *reinforcement* emanates from operant conditioning theory (Skinner, 1953, 1954). A *reinforcer* is an outcome that increases the occurrence of a behavior that precedes it. Reinforcement can be either positive or negative. When a *positive reinforcer* is presented to a student, it will increase the occurrence of a particular behavior; thus, if a child receives a piece of candy every time he cleans his bedroom, the cleaning behavior is likely to increase. In contrast, when a *negative reinforcer* is used, something undesirable is taken away from a student. This, too, will increase the occurrence of a behavior. For example, if a teacher decides to eliminate a (presumably undesirable) unit test for her mathematics class because students demonstrated their understanding of the topic during a class discussion, students' participation in class discussions would be reinforced (increase).

Reinforcers are always presented (or removed) *after* the desired behavior has occurred. Another example of positive reinforcement would be giving students 5 extra minutes of recess time after they behave well during art class; this would increase on-task behavior in future art classes. Another example of negative reinforcement would be excusing a child from doing her chores because she did a good job completing her homework. By taking away the unpleasant task of doing chores, the student's future effort at doing a good job with homework assignments should increase.

When rewards are valued by students, rewards may serve as positive reinforcers. That is, they usually increase the likelihood of behavior occurring again. However, as you will see from some of the other topics that are discussed in this chapter, rewards do not necessarily increase behaviors; in fact, at times they may actually lead to decreases in certain behaviors. Thus, a reward that teachers intend to be reinforcing may not be. In this way, a reward is somewhat different than a reinforcer. For the most part, positive reinforcers are rewards, but rewards are not necessarily positive reinforcers. The distinction lies in whether the targeted behavior actually increases as intended.

Stop and Think

Can you remember a time when someone offered you a reward that you were not interested in? If the reward was unappealing, did it have any influence on your future behavior?

TYPES OF REWARDS AND REINFORCERS

Educators use many different types of rewards for students. A reward can be as small as a gold star or as large as a new car. Some rewards have real material value (e.g., a new toy), whereas other rewards are symbolic in nature (e.g., a certificate of recognition).

Behaviorist theory differentiates between two types of reinforcers: primary and secondary. A *primary reinforcer* satisfies a basic need (e.g., hunger, thirst, safety). Examples of primary reinforcers in the classroom would be giving students candy, juice, or ice cream after they complete a particular task. In contrast, a *secondary reinforcer* does not satisfy a specific biological need; rather, some reinforcers increase the frequency of behaviors because of what the student has learned about the value of the specific reinforcer. Thus, secondary reinforcers often will be more effective with older students who have learned to value certain types of rewards that might not be valued by younger children. Examples of secondary reinforcers in the classroom would be teacher praise, gold stars, an A grade, or being placed on the honor roll. Whereas the meaning of being on the honor roll might be elusive to a young child, by the time an adolescent reaches high school, she has learned the meaning and value of being on the honor roll, and therefore, such a reward may become more highly valued. Another school-based example might include the receipt of a token that could be exchanged for privileges or goods at a later time; for example, students in many classrooms earn tokens that they can redeem at later times in lieu of turning in a homework assignment. At home, an example of a secondary reinforcer might be the payment of $5 to a student for every A grade earned. Although money does not satisfy an immediate primary need, most children learn to value it at a young age. The use of secondary reinforcers is probably more common in classrooms than is the use of primary reinforcers, particularly as students progress into higher grades.

Rewards Used in Classrooms

In terms of types of rewards typically used in classrooms, we can identify three categories: concrete, social, and activity rewards. *Concrete rewards* include actual physical items that can be given to a student, such as stickers, candy, and certificates. *Social rewards* include interpersonal signs of approval, including verbal rewards (praise, positive feedback) and gestures (smiling, nodding, a thumbs-up). *Activity rewards* include using a well-liked activity as a reward for another behavior, such as having free independent reading time or extra recess.

EXAMPLES OF REWARDS Several examples of rewards are presented in Table 3-2, along with grade levels in which the reward might be developmentally appropriate.

Grade levels are included in Table 3-2 to illustrate that a reward valued by young children might not be valued by adolescents. Likewise, rewards that are meaningful to adolescents might be useless with younger children. Piaget (1929, 1952, 1972) and various other developmental theorists (e.g., Vygotsky, 1978) have demonstrated that cognitive

TABLE 3-2 Examples of Rewards Used in Schools

Grade Level	Type of Reward
Kindergarten, 1st grade	Gold stars and stickers
2nd or 3rd grade	Lollipops, small plastic toys
4th or 5th grade	15 minutes of extra recess, certificates
6th or 7th grade	Permission to attend a pizza party on Friday
8th or 9th grade	Permission to go on an extra field trip
10th or 11th grade	Permission to attend "beach day"
12th grade	Permission to skip final exams at the end of the year

Katelyn Metzger/Merrill

Rewards such as stickers may be effective with younger children, but probably will not have positive effects with adolescents.

abilities change and develop over time. Thus, a 6-year-old child understands and inter-prets the world differently than would a 15-year-old adolescent; a 6-year-old child would be highly interested in rewards that are simple and concrete (e.g., a piece of candy or a gold star), whereas an adolescent would be more interested in and able to understand the value of a more complex reward (e.g., a ticket that could later be redeemed for a free meal at McDonald's). Research indicates that the understanding of rewards is developmental and changes throughout infancy (Diamond, Churchland, Cruess, & Kirkham, 1999) and during adolescence (Galvan, 2010). The receipt of a gold star might mean a great deal to a first grader, but probably wouldn't mean much to an early adolescent. In contrast, permis-sion to skip final exams might be very meaningful to high-school seniors, but probably wouldn't even be comprehensible to second graders.

Even at a particular age, rewards might carry different meanings for different stu-dents. For example, although receiving 15 minutes of extra recess might be a great reward for most fourth graders, it might actually be a punishment to a child who tends to be bul-lied on the playground; the reward of a pizza party might be attractive to most students, but not to the diabetic whose diet is highly specialized. In addition, grades may serve as rewards for some students but not for others; for example, giving a student an A grade might be motivational for high-achieving students but not for some low-achieving stu-dents who may not care as much about extrinsic rewards (Stipek, 1996). Consequently, teachers have to make many careful decisions and consider many important outcomes before employing a system of rewards. Teachers should not simply assume that rewards will be beneficial to all students in the same ways.

CHARACTERISTICS OF REWARDS   In addition to the different categories of rewards already described, other important characteristics can affect reward effectiveness. First, sometimes rewards are used to enhance learning, whereas at other times they are used to control and manage behavior. In considering the use of rewards, teachers need to ask themselves whether their goal is to help students to learn and engage in academic tasks or to increase certain socially desirable behaviors and compliance. In some cases, rewards may serve both purposes. For example, Downing, Keating, and Bennett (2005) noted that in physical education classes, rewards (reinforcers) can be used to improve behavior management in class; improved behavior generally will allow for more time for instruction and on-task activity during actual class time.

Rewards that are presented to students can be perceived as either *informational* or *controlling*. In fact, depending on how it is presented to students, the same specific reward can be either informational or controlling. A reward is perceived as *informational* if it provides specific information or feedback to the student about his or her mastery of or improvement in a particular area. In contrast, a reward is perceived as *controlling* when receipt of the reward is related to either the simple completion of a task or being able to perform the task in a particular way (Deci, 1975; Deci & Ryan, 1987). This distinction between informational and controlling rewards can apply even to routine feedback that teachers give to students. For example, when an art teacher praises a student for the subtle use of color in one specific part of a pastel drawing, that feedback is likely to be perceived as informational (the comment provides the student with information about what she has done well). In contrast, when a math teacher praises a student for following specific, predetermined steps for solving long-division problems, regardless of the student's understanding of the processes underlying division, that feedback is likely to be perceived as controlling (the comment is based on solving the problems in a particular way and does not provide information about what the student has learned).

Many teachers probably do not think about the informational or controlling nature of rewards. Nevertheless, this is an important issue for educators. Research clearly indicates that students' perceptions of rewards as either informational or controlling are strongly related to their motivation. *Informational rewards* are likely to increase the development of positive motivational beliefs in students. For example, Mrs. Stone gives her first graders Dora the Explorer stickers when they successfully demonstrate that they can write the capital letters of the alphabet. The reward (stickers) is contingent on the students being able to demonstrate that they have mastered a specific skill. Thus, when the first graders in Mrs. Stone's class receive the stickers, they know that they have truly learned how to write the letters. Therefore, their belief in their own ability to write (or their *self-efficacy* for writing) and their interest in writing are likely to increase. Research indicates that rewards that are contingent on accomplishing specific tasks and making clear progress on a task are likely to increase a student's self-efficacy (Schunk, 1983).

In contrast, rewards are likely to be perceived as controlling when the rewards are either contingent on completion of a task or on being able to perform at a specific level on a task. For example, the first graders in Mrs. Martin's class receive stickers after they are able to write the entire alphabet in 2 minutes. The reward in this classroom is contingent on the students completing a task within a predetermined (and somewhat arbitrary) time limit. The students do not gain any information about their ability to write as a result of participating in the activity. Thus, a reward of this nature will be perceived by students as controlling their behavior. This can lead to problematic motivational outcomes, such as students sacrificing accuracy for speed in their writing or losing interest in writing activities over time. Examples of controlling and informational rewards are presented in Table 3-3.

TABLE 3-3   Examples of Controlling and Informational Rewards

Reward	Presented as Informational	Presented as Controlling
Gold stars	Joe receives a gold star from his Spanish teacher for demonstrating that he can conjugate the verbs *ser* and *estar* in Spanish.	Joe receives a gold star for completing a series of workbook exercises on conjugating the verbs *ser* and *estar* in Spanish.
$100	Marie's parents promise her $100 if she demonstrates that she has mastered new skills in all her courses during this grading period. Her parents plan to call each of her teachers to get feedback on her progress in each of their classes.	Marie's parents promise her $100 if she gets A grades in all her subjects during the current grading period.
Ice cream party	Mrs. Price surprises her class with a party on Friday after they have demonstrated to her that they understand how to add two fractions with different denominators.	Mrs. Price promises her class a party on Friday if they complete all the week's work on adding fractions on time.

Stop and Think

Think about a time when you were in school when rewards were used by one of your teachers. Why was the reward used? In retrospect, would you characterize the reward as being informational or controlling? Do you think your teacher was aware of this distinction? Would knowledge of this distinction have affected the teacher's selection and use of this particular type of reward?

When rewards are given, they should provide students with specific information about what has been learned.

USING PRAISE   Teachers often praise students, and many teachers probably assume that such praise serves as an effective reward. In fact, the verbal praise that teachers offer to students can have profoundly positive effects on student learning and motivation. However, although praise is often well intentioned, sometimes its use can actually have deleterious effects as well (Henderlong & Lepper, 2002). In a now-classic article, Jere Brophy (1981) noted that teacher praise directed toward students can, but does not necessarily, serve as a positive reinforcer. Whereas praise may be reinforcing to some students, it may not be to others. Brophy argued that praise is most effective when it is "infrequent but contingent, specific, and credible" as opposed to "frequent but trivial or inappropriate" (p. 27).

> *Consider the following example: Jennifer has completed her book report, and the teacher is now having individual conferences with students about their reports. The following are two possible ways that teachers can praise Jennifer during the conference:*

TEACHER A: Good job. Your report is much better than most of the rest. You clearly listened to what I told you to do, and the fact that you followed my rules paid off for you.

TEACHER B: This is a good book report because you really proved to me that you thought about the characters in the story and how they relate to each other. This is a great improvement over your previous book report. I am really proud of the progress that you have made; you clearly worked very hard on this report, and your hard work has paid off.

What is the difference between the types of praise offered by each teacher? If you haven't already figured it out, Teacher A's praise is less effective than is the praise offered by Teacher B. Teacher B's praise is particularly effective because it provides the student with specific information about why her report was good, it compares her current performance with her previous work (as opposed to comparing it to other students' work), it shows that the teacher really cares about the student ("I am really proud of the progress that you have made"), and the teacher praises the student's effort. In contrast, the praise offered by Teacher A is ineffective because it is very general ("Good job"), it compares the student's performance to the work of other students, and it focuses attention on the teacher's control over student behavior rather than on the student's achievement or effort.

Effective and Ineffective Uses of Praise

Brophy (1981, 2004) clearly outlined effective and ineffective uses of praise. Some characteristics of effective praise include (a) specifying particular student accomplishments, (b) credibility of the praise, (c) praise in recognition of effort, (d) praise that is contingent on a specific behavior, (e) praise that emphasizes students' effort and ability, and (f) praise that compares a student's present accomplishments with his or her earlier accomplishments. In contrast, some characteristics of ineffective praise include (a) providing random or unsystematic praise, (b) praise without specific information about students' accomplishments or performance, (c) praise that compares students to one another, (d) praise that suggests that students' achievements were not due to their own efforts (e.g., "I guess it was an easier test than I'd realized" or "You got lucky!"), and (e) praise that focuses attention on the teacher as an authority figure.

> Research indicates that the specificity of praise may be particularly important. Generic praise that is provided to a child with a generic statement such as, "You are a good drawer," is less effective than is a nongeneric statement such as, "Good job drawing" (Zentall & Morris, 2010, p. 155). Generic praise focuses students on their abilities (or lack of abilities), whereas nongeneric praise focuses the students on factors that may be within their control (e.g., effort). Research with kindergartners indicates that nongeneric praise is related to enhanced motivation, whereas the use of generic praise was related to lower levels of persistence at tasks (Zentall & Morris, 2010).

EFFECTS OF REWARDS ON MOTIVATION

By now, you probably realize that the use of rewards is related to students' motivation and achievement. Whereas some types of reward structures may lead to long-term learning, other types may lead to short-term gains without deep understanding and long-term benefits. Thus, decisions about the types of rewards that teachers and parents use are very important and can have a powerful effect on learning. For the most part, research indicates that intrinsic incentives are preferred to extrinsic incentives; however, it is not realistic to think that all students will be intrinsically motivated for every task in every situation. In the next section, we review some of the research about the effects of rewards on student outcomes.

Effects of Rewards on Academic Behaviors

Research indicates that, depending on whether they are intrinsically or extrinsically motivated, students are likely to approach academic work differently. If students are working on a task that they truly enjoy and find interesting, they are likely to use different types of learning strategies than students who are working on a similar task for extrinsic reasons.

REWARDS AND COGNITIVE STRATEGIES   Much of the research on the effects on the relations between motivation and cognition has focused on personal and situational interest (Hidi, 1990; Hidi & Ainley, 2008; Hidi & Renninger, 2006; Krapp, Hidi, & Renninger, 1992; Renninger, 2009; Schiefele, Krapp, & Winteler, 1992; Schraw & Lehman, 2001). In general, research indicates that intrinsic interest in a task is related positively to a host of important educational outcomes, including memory, comprehension, achievement, and cognitive processing. When students report that tasks are intrinsically motivating, they are likely to use more effective cognitive processes, which promote deeper understanding and the ability to remember and use ideas in the future. These results hold true for both personal and situational interest.

When extrinsic rewards are used in the classroom, they may have negative effects on students' use of some cognitive processes. As mentioned previously, this outcome often is related to how the reward is presented to the students. If rewards are presented for simply completing a task and do not provide useful information to students about what they have actually learned, students may choose to do as little as possible to complete the task. After all, why should students spend a lot of time thinking deeply about and trying to understand new material if they can receive a reward simply for completing the task? In our experience, such *noncontingent* rewards are used quite often in regular classrooms. For example, students could be asked to complete a reading log by documenting the number of pages and minutes they read every day. Every student who turns in the reading log each week would receive a sticker and a positive comment such as "Well done" or "Good effort," regardless of the degree of effort or improvement shown. Although this approach may be encouraging for some students with reading difficulties or some of those who do not like to read, it actually may lead to *less* investment in recreational reading for some of the most capable students in the class. In addition, the focus in many classrooms on performance on high-stakes tests may lead some educators to use rewards to get students to answer questions quickly and efficiently (i.e., within a specific time frame), without allowing students ample time to develop their interests or to develop creative solutions to complex problems (Nichols & Berliner, 2007).

Research also shows that extrinsic incentives may lead to academic shortcuts and less cognitive engagement with tasks. For example, a study of academic cheating indicated that middle-school students who perceived their science classes as being extrinsically oriented were more likely to report that they saw cheating as an acceptable behavior (E. M. Anderman, Griesinger, & Westerfield, 1998). Other related research from a goal-orientation perspective (see Chapter 2) indicates that when students are focused on personal mastery and improvement (a *mastery goal*), they are likely to use deep-processing strategies, such as critical and strategic thinking, or paraphrasing what they read. In contrast, when students are focused on demonstrating their ability and external indicators of performance (a *performance goal*) they are likely to use surface-level cognitive strategies, such as rote learning (E. M. Anderman & Young, 1994; Nolen, 1988; Pintrich & de Groot, 1990). Students who are focused on either receiving rewards or avoiding punishment (an *extrinsic goal*) are also more likely to engage in academic self-handicapping strategies (e.g., staying out late the night before an examination; Midgley & Urdan, 1995). Research also indicates that the content of students' goals can be framed in terms of intrinsic goals (e.g., learning something will help the student to contribute to society or to the local community) or to extrinsic goals (e.g., learning something will allow the student to make more money; Vansteenkiste, Lens, & Deci, 2006). Research indicates that learning outcomes such as cognitive processing, persistence, and achievement are improved when intrinsic goal content is emphasized (Vansteenkiste, Simons, Lens, Sheldon, & Deci, 2004). In summary, when extrinsic incentives are emphasized in classrooms, students are likely to adopt different, less adaptive cognitive approaches toward learning. If this is continued over a long period, we should expect that the actual quality of their understanding of academic subjects and ability to use what they have learned will be affected.

The grades that teachers assign in classrooms certainly can be considered to be extrinsic motivators. Consequently, some teachers and parents may assume that grades will serve to motivate students to achieve. However, it is important to remember that not all students value grades and achievement in the same ways. Research indicates that when students expect to receive a grade evaluating their performance on a task, students are more likely to adopt performance-avoidance goals (i.e., the goal of avoiding looking incompetent or "dumb"; Pulfrey, Buchs, & Butera, 2011). This is troubling, because research clearly indicates that the adoption of performance-avoidance goals is related to poorer learning outcomes (see E. M. Anderman & Wolters, 2006, or Schunk, Pintrich, & Meece, 2008, for reviews). In addition, because the use of extrinsic incentives can affect the use of cognitive strategies, the use of less effective strategies can affect learning. For example, a teacher who rewards students who get 100% on spelling tests with an ice cream party might find that students are quickly memorizing the spellings of words for tests;

however, a week after the spelling test, the students may not recall how to correctly spell the words (Stipek, 1998).

This does not mean that students should be unconcerned about grades or other extrinsic signs of achievement. Optimally, we want students to care about their grades as indicators of their learning and progress but not to focus on them *too much*. A study of college students showed that those who were highly intrinsically motivated and in the mid-range on a measure of extrinsic motivation learned the most in their classes. That is, they learned more than did students who were either very low or high on a measure of extrinsic motivation (Lin, McKeachie, & Kim, 2001). Thus, when students do not care enough about grades or when they care excessively, their learning may be affected.

REWARDS AND CREATIVITY   Some studies suggest that students will be less creative when they are extrinsically motivated. Amabile (1985) asked college students to write poems under several different experimental conditions. Although there were no differences in the first poems that students wrote (prior to any experimental manipulations), the students who were provided with extrinsic incentives to write a second poem demonstrated less creativity than did students in other conditions.

Why might students be less creative when presented with extrinsic incentives? First, they may be focused on simply completing the task and may spend less time thinking about and working on the actual task. Second, creativity may be seen as "risky" by some students. If an assignment is being graded, students may be less willing to take the risk of being creative in case their grade might suffer (Clifford, 1991). Third, if the grading criteria do not involve creativity, then students probably will only feel compelled to meet the criteria that will ensure them the highest grade. Research indicates that when rewards (e.g., grades) are contingent on a certain level of performance (e.g., "You must get 90% correct to receive a certificate"), creativity is diminished (Selart, Nordström, Kuvaas, & Takemura, 2008). In contrast, if there are no extrinsic rewards involved, students may be more willing to take a creative approach to the task. If the student has nothing to lose (i.e., no risk of getting a low grade), why not be creative?

REWARDS AND CONTINUING MOTIVATION   There is much rhetoric today about creating "lifelong learners," but are schools really effective at developing a joy of and commitment to learning in students?

Stop and Think

Think about the subjects that you learned about in elementary, middle, and high school. How many of those subjects did you pursue outside the classroom? How many of those activities are interesting to you now?

Students who are intrinsically motivated to engage in activities in school are likely to continue to be motivated for the same or similar activities at home. This is what Maehr (1976) referred to as "continuing motivation." Students, such as Brook, who find physics to be fun and exciting at school are likely to want to participate in similar activities beyond school (e.g., buying a home science set, joining a science club, or selecting books about famous scientists from the library). Research supports the notion that students will choose to continue to engage in tasks that they find intrinsically motivating (E. M. Anderman & Weber, 2009). For example, E. M. Anderman and Johnston (1998) found that students who were intrinsically interested in learning about current events in the news during school were likely to engage in news-seeking behaviors outside school (e.g., reading the newspaper, watching the news on television). In other research, Wigfield, Eccles, and their colleagues found that students who valued certain school subjects were more likely to choose to enroll in similar classes in the future (Wigfield & Eccles, 1992). Clearly, such long-term engagement in academic areas, whether in future classes or outside school, is a very desirable outcome for our students.

Short-Term Benefits, Long-Term Costs

Given the potential problems associated with extrinsic motivation and the use of rewards, it is important to consider why teachers and schools continue to use them so often. Indeed, it is a rare classroom that does not provide some kind of extrinsic rewards for students. A primary reason is that rewards often bring about a desired change in students' overt behaviors in the short term. That is, they can induce students to complete an assignment, to remain seated, or stop misbehaving. In addition, many educators offer rewards to students as a more positive alternative to issuing threats, punishments, or criticisms. Thus, the use of rewards in classrooms often seems appealing to both parents and teachers. It is important to realize, however, that the learning and engagement that may occur as a result of the use of rewards may be short lived. Indeed, the presentation of rewards affects students' perceptions of the purposes of learning. Is the purpose of a biology experiment to truly learn something about biology or to earn a reward? Is the purpose of writing a critical essay to improve one's writing skills or to earn a privilege?

Because students may use less effective cognitive strategies when extrinsic rewards are present, information may not be processed effectively and, thus, may not be remembered in the future. The activity presented in Learning Activity 3.1 will allow you to explore this in your own life. It is likely that you have had to memorize many "facts" for tests and quizzes in school. You may still remember some of this information today; however, you probably also have forgotten a great deal of what you had to memorize. In contrast, you are much more likely to remember facts that proved to be useful to you beyond one specific class. Why does this happen? Refer back to the information about cognitive strategies and the use of rewards. When students learn what is intrinsically interesting or important to them, they approach tasks more effectively. If a student has to memorize a list of words for a quiz but has no other reason to remember those words, why should the student utilize cognitive resources to recall this information? It simply is not efficient or necessary to do so.

Effects of Extrinsic Rewards on Intrinsic Motivation

One of the most hotly debated issues in educational psychology is the potential negative effects of extrinsic rewards on intrinsic motivation. Does the use of rewards actually undermine intrinsic motivation? Some researchers argue that extrinsic incentives do undermine intrinsic motivation (e.g., Deci, Koestner, & Ryan, 1999a, 1999b, 2001), whereas others argue that extrinsic rewards are not detrimental to intrinsic motivation (Cameron &

When students are offered excessive extrinsic incentives, they may become less intrinsically motivated.

Pierce, 1994, 1996; Eisenberger, Pierce, & Cameron, 1999). Recent motivation research from a neuropsychological perspective even suggests that neuropsychological reactions (in the brain) account for the undermining effects of some types of rewards (e.g., monetary rewards) on intrinsic motivation (Murayama, Matsumoto, Izuma, & Matsumoto, 2010). Consider the following example:

> *Matthew's parents promise him that he can have pizza for dinner after every book that he reads that is more than 30 pages in length. Matthew eagerly agrees to this arrangement and reads 15 books in six months, after which his parents are very pleased with him. Because he is doing a lot of reading, they decide to "cut him off" from his rewards. They tell him that he is doing great and that the rewards are no longer necessary. Do you think that Matthew will continue to read books at the same rate? Why or why not?*

It is difficult to answer this question without knowing more about Matthew and his academic record, reading ability, previous reading behavior, and family. If he had no previous interest in reading, you might find that the reward system has helped him develop a habit of reading at a particular time of day and that he continues to read, even without rewards. Matthew may even have developed a greater interest in reading for its own sake. Alternatively, you may find that Matthew abruptly stops reading when no rewards are available and actually reads even less than he did before. Will Matthew still care about reading? Will he actually read less than he did before the rewards were put into place?

Next, consider this example:

> *Hannah is in third grade. She loves to read; she enjoyed pretending to read when she was very young and reads a lot at home. When she was in first grade, her teacher identified her as an accelerated reader and recommended her for advanced reading instruction.*

This year, Hannah's teacher introduced a system in which advanced students are required to read books from a specified list. The students earn "points" linked to taking brief computer-based tests after reading the books. The children are required to earn at least five points per week. Hannah talks about the points a lot at home with her mother and becomes very concerned about being able to earn the required points. Hannah's mother tries to reassure her, as Hannah is a great reader and always earns the required points. One night, Hannah looked bored and her mother asked her if she wanted to do some reading. Hannah responded, "No, because I don't have any books from my list at home tonight."

Sadly, Hannah's story is true. This child who previously loved to read became more motivated to earn points than to read. Whereas she used to read anything and everything that she could, the teacher's well-intentioned system (which was obviously designed to enhance student motivation) actually backfired, causing Hannah to only read "required" books. The reading that Hannah was doing to accumulate points was no longer motivating for her. In this instance, it is clear that the reward system led to a decrease in Hannah's intrinsic love of reading. We will return to Hannah's story in the sections that follow, as we examine two theoretical explanations for the potential negative effects of rewards on intrinsic motivation.

OVERJUSTIFICATION   Supporters of the *overjustification hypothesis* argue that working at an intrinsically interesting activity to receive a reward can lead to a decrease in subsequent intrinsic motivation for the same activity (Lepper, Greene, & Nisbett, 1973). When an individual is offered a reward in exchange for working on a task or activity, the offer of the reward overjustifies his or her reasons for participating in the activity (because he or she already liked the activity). When the reward is no longer available, little justification exists for continuing to engage with the task; consequently, intrinsic motivation for the task declines.

For example, Mr. Bishop is a fifth-grade teacher. His students love social studies because he makes his lessons very interesting and understandable. The students perform plays, dress up in costume, and use innovative software to explore social studies topics. Thus, the students in Mr. Bishop's class generally are intrinsically motivated in social studies. In February, Mr. Bishop decides that he will provide rewards for his students. Consequently, every Friday he gives his students donuts as a reward for their having worked on social studies during the week. The students do not have to perform at any particular level—they merely have to do their regular social studies work (which they already have been doing quite well), and they receive the donuts.

According to the overjustification hypothesis, Mr. Bishop's students probably will become less intrinsically motivated to learn about social studies. More specifically, the use of donuts as rewards will *overjustify* the students' reasons for learning about social studies; the students already like social studies, so the donuts will provide additional (over) justification. The overjustification hypothesis would predict that the students would actually be less intrinsically motivated to learn social studies; they might even choose to participate less in social studies.

An important assumption of this explanation is that the individual finds the activity intrinsically interesting at the start. Thus, in Hannah's case, the introduction of points for reading might not have been problematic for a student who did not like reading, but it was detrimental for Hannah.

SELF-DETERMINATION THEORY Self-determination theory offers another explanation for the potential negative effects of extrinsic rewards on intrinsic motivation. Deci, Ryan, and their colleagues argue that true intrinsic motivation can only exist when an individual feels unpressured and not dependent on any rewards (Deci & Ryan, 1985). More specifically, they argue that individuals are intrinsically motivated when they feel that their actions are self-determined. *Self-determined* behaviors are autonomously produced by individuals, and they are free from perceived external controls. When individuals are self-determined, they perceive that they have choices and options available to them and that their actions are consistent with their self-concepts. Deci and Ryan argue that self-determination is a basic human need.

As noted previously, rewards can be perceived as either *controlling* or *informational* (Deci, 1975; Deci & Ryan, 1987). Deci and his colleagues argue that when rewards are perceived as controlling behavior, individuals perceive their involvement with the task as being due to the presence of the reward. That is, their behavior is determined by external factors (i.e., the reward) and not by self-determination. Intrinsic motivation is diminished, and therefore, once the reward is no longer available, no motivation remains to engage in the task (Deci, 1975). An important point is that rewards can only be considered controlling if they are *expected*—that is, if the promise of a reward is made before a task is completed. In contrast, if a student receives recognition for achievement or hard work *after* a task is completed, without having an expectation of reward, the reward cannot be perceived as controlling. So the teacher who, in recognition of students' hard work, arranges a surprise end-of-year party for her class or spontaneously allows extra recess time is not going to undermine anyone's intrinsic motivation. The teacher who uses a reward system as an incentive to participate in learning tasks, however, might do so.

Stop and Think

If students are told that they will receive free movie passes to a local theater if they score above a certain level on the state standardized mathematics test, would the reward of the passes be perceived as informational or controlling?

According to self-determination theory, extrinsic motivation actually falls along a continuum. At one end of the continuum is *amotivation*, which represents a situation in which an individual is quite simply not motivated (i.e., she feels that she just can't or doesn't want to do anything); at the other end is *intrinsic motivation*, which represents a situation in which the individual is engaging with a task because of pure interest and enjoyment. Deci and Ryan describe the different types of extrinsic motivation that lie between amotivation and intrinsic motivation in terms of the behaviors that they are related to. *External regulation* refers to the situation in which an individual performs a behavior purely to receive some kind of reward; this type of motivation is perceived by the learner as highly controlling. *Introjected regulation* describes a situation in which an individual is motivated to avoid feeling badly (e.g., guilty or nervous), to appear competent (similar to a performance-approach goal), or to avoid appearing incompetent (similar to a performance-avoid goal). *Identified regulation* refers to behaviors in which the

TABLE 3-4   Forms of Extrinsic Motivation

Type of Motivation	Example
External	Sarah reads for 3 hours per night because she gets ice cream if she completes the reading.
Introjected	Jeff plays soccer so that his friends perceive him as a great athlete.
Identified	Jodie takes a GRE test preparation course because she wants to be admitted to graduate school.
Integrated	Noah plays the bassoon because he sees himself as a "bassoonist." He truly enjoys playing the bassoon, and he sees this as part of what defines who he is.

individual is motivated for external (extrinsic) reasons, but the outcome of the behavior is something that is meaningful or important to the person. Finally, *integrated regulation* describes a situation in which individuals engage in various behaviors because those behaviors are representative of how an individual defines or sees herself (Ryan & Deci, 2000). Examples of these behaviors are provided in Table 3-4.

These descriptions of extrinsic motivation represent a continuum, from external regulation (in which behaviors are undertaken strictly because of external, controlling factors), to integrated regulation (in which behaviors are undertaken because they are representative of one's self-concept). Research indicates that extrinsic motivation that falls at the higher end of the continuum (e.g., integrated regulation) is related to greater academic achievement and engagement than is extrinsic motivation at the lower end of the continuum (e.g., external regulation; Assor, Vansteenkiste, & Kaplan, 2009; Grolnick & Ryan, 1987; Ryan & Deci, 2000).

Research results support the tenets of self-determination theory. For example, research indicates that teachers who are dedicated to enhancing self-determination in their students positively influence a number of important educational outcomes, including students' intrinsic motivation and perceptions of competence (Deci, Schwartz, Sheinman, & Ryan, 1981; Ryan & Grolnick, 1986). In addition, Deci and his colleagues found that teachers who use "controlling" teaching styles (compared to teachers who were autonomy supportive) are critical of students, give more commands to students, and provide fewer opportunities for choice (Deci, Spiegel, Ryan, Koestner, & Kauffman, 1982). These teaching styles may lead to declines in intrinsic motivation in students. In this view, it seems likely that Hannah perceived her teacher's policy of issuing reading points only for specific books as controlling her behavior, rather than as providing feedback on her performance as a reader. Thus, her intrinsic interest in reading was diminished through the introduction of the rewards.

CONSIDERING PUNISHMENT

Thus far, we have focused on the delivery of favorable rewards to students. However, we would be remiss not to address the use of punishment. There are two types of punishment. *Presentation punishment* is the presentation of something unpleasant following a response. Examples of this type of punishment used in schools might include verbally "scolding" students, having students write "I will not speak in class" 100 times, sending students to after-school detention, or even delivering corporal punishment. *Removal punishment* involves the removal of something the student values. Examples include keeping students inside during recess, taking away points or tokens previously earned, or denying permission to participate in a class field trip.

The basic assumption of either type of punishment is that if a student learns that a specific behavior will result in punishment, the student will become less motivated to engage in the behavior (rather than the assumption that punishment will act as a deterrent to others; Carlsmith, Darley, & Robinson, 2002). Punishment also can be implemented by teachers if a certain task is not completed or is completed unsuccessfully. Again, the notion is that students will be more motivated to complete the task if they know that a potential punishment will be delivered if they fail to complete the task.

Note

Many people confuse the terms *punishment* and *negative reinforcement*. However, they are not the same. Any form of reinforcement leads to an increase in the preceding behavior, whereas punishment leads to a decrease in behavior. The word *negative* in *negative reinforcement* refers to the idea that something negative is being removed (something unpleasant is being taken away) and *not* to the experience being undesirable for the student.

Skinner (1953) noted that the use of punishment in schools can lead to undesirable side effects, such as anxiety, anger, and negative feelings toward the teacher. If a teacher consistently punishes students for engaging in inappropriate behaviors, or for not completing their work, some of the students may develop negative feelings toward the teacher. Although the punishment may be introduced as a result of a specific action, the negative feelings on the part of the student may generalize toward the teacher and subsequently surface during other activities. In general, therefore, any form of punishment should be used rarely and judiciously.

When Behavior Modification Goes Awry

Interestingly, what a teacher intends to be a punishment may, at times, actually serve as a reward to some students. Consider the following example:

> *Mr. Jackson is an eighth-grade science teacher. One of the students in his class, Debra, displays very bad classroom behavior. She talks when he is talking, throws papers across the classroom, writes notes to her friends, and laughs when Mr. Jackson speaks. The other students always laugh when Debra misbehaves. Mr. Jackson constantly reprimands Debra; however, the reprimands do not seem to affect her behavior. Mr. Jackson then gives Debra extra homework assignments as a punishment; however, although Debra does the assignments, she still continues to misbehave daily in class. Mr. Jackson is frustrated, and he finally consults with the school psychologist to try to figure out how to stop Debra's behavior.*

Stop and Think

Before considering the school psychologist's recommendations about Debra, think about the situation. Mr. Jackson appears to be doing what he should; he is aware of the student's inappropriate behaviors and is applying a punishment immediately after each occurrence. Nevertheless, the behavior is not decreasing. Why? And what, if anything, might Mr. Jackson do differently?

Mr. Jackson meets with the school psychologist and explains the situation. After speaking with Debra's parents, the school psychologist spends several days observing Mr. Jackson's class. After three classes, the school psychologist has the problem figured out. He tells Mr. Jackson that, in his opinion, the "punishments" are actually serving as rewards to Debra. Mr. Jackson is surprised; he does not understand. The psychologist goes on to explain that Debra gets so much attention from her classmates when she misbehaves that the attention (e.g., the laughter and recognition) that she gets from her peers is actually reinforcing her bad behavior. She is being perceived as "cool" by her friends for defying the teacher. The reinforcement from her peers outweighs any negative effects of Mr. Jackson's punishments. The psychologist has a simple solution to the problem: He suggests that Mr. Jackson should think of a way to eliminate the "reward" of peer approval.

The next day, as soon as Debra misbehaves, Mr. Jackson immediately sends her out of the room. In this way, by removing her from the situation, she will not be able to appreciate the attention that is being bestowed on her. Mr. Jackson repeats this approach for the next several days. Debra seems very angry and, initially, increases her bad behavior in an increased attempt to get Mr. Jackson to react. He stays with his plan, however, and the reward of peer attention is consistently removed. Within 10 days, Debra's misbehavior has all but disappeared. She no longer engages in the distracting and disrespectful behaviors.

In summary, teachers should consider carefully when and why they will deliver punishments. They also should think about the expected and unexpected effects of punishments. Although punishments can be effective and are warranted in some circumstances, frequent and haphazard use of them can backfire on teachers. In addition, just as some intended rewards are not perceived as "rewarding" to some students, some intended punishments may not be perceived as aversive to some students. Careful planning and consistency are necessary for successful behavior modification.

USING REWARDS EFFECTIVELY

Rewards can be used both effectively and ineffectively in the classroom. If a teacher hands out rewards randomly, with little consistency, then rewards are likely to have no effect or possibly even detrimental effects on student motivation and learning. In contrast, if teachers carefully and critically examine their reasons for using rewards, and they plan their use of rewards accordingly, then rewards can benefit students.

The following list of recommendations should help you to make better decisions about when, if, and how you will use rewards in your classroom (also see Table 3-3):

1. *Only offer rewards for activities that students aren't already doing.* If students are already happily engaged with a task, there usually is no need to implement rewards. The presentation of rewards for engagement with intrinsically interesting activities may lower students' intrinsic motivation for the activity (Lepper, 1983). However, rewards can be used to increase behaviors that are not occurring. For example, college-level teachers, who often find that students do not complete reading assignments, can encourage students to read by rewarding participation in class that indicates students have completed reading assignments (Lei, Bartlett, Gorney, & Herschbach, 2010).

2. *Make rewards potentially available to all students.* Sometimes rewards are only available to the "best" students: the best academic students, the most outspoken students, the best athletes, and so on. Think of ways that you can set up reward structures in your classroom so that all students feel they have a good chance of earning a reward for their academic work (i.e., not just for good behavior or other nonacademic characteristics).

3. *Reward students for effort or improvement.* Students often receive rewards based on somewhat arbitrary achievement outcomes (e.g., getting 90% of the answers correct). However, some students may not be able to achieve at that level and, thus, may feel ineligible to receive the rewards. Furthermore, some students may be able to achieve that level with little effort and commitment. Consider rewarding students for their effort or improvement instead. This way, all students can potentially qualify for a reward—both high- and low-achieving students need to exert effort, and all students should be expected to improve (even A students). For example, one program has been developed in which students receive points based on how much they improve their initial baseline test scores from one week to the next (Mac Iver, 1993; Mac Iver & Reuman, 1993/1994). Mac Iver has demonstrated that the use of this program can lead to improved grades. One of the reasons cited for the success of this program is the fact that "all students have a realistic chance of beating their individualized base scores with effort. Even small improvements do not go unrecognized" (1993, p. 209).

4. *Rewards should be informational.* When students receive rewards, they should know *why* they are being rewarded: that they have learned specific information or achieved specific goals. Thus, students should know that the receipt of a reward is contingent on specific efforts or accomplishments.

5. *Rewards should not be perceived as controlling.* Rewards are perceived as controlling when they are contingent on either merely completing a task or completing a task in a specific way (Deci, 1975; Deci & Ryan, 1987). When students perceive that rewards are controlling their behavior, intrinsic motivation is likely to decline. In addition, sometimes teachers may offer a reward not in relation to a task but simply as a means of controlling student behavior (i.e., offering a reward to the student who can sit quietly for the longest period of time). These types of rewards also will be perceived as controlling and should be avoided.

When possible, provide rewards in private.

6. *Consider whether rewards should be presented privately or publicly.* Sometimes the presentation of rewards may be embarrassing to some students. It is important for teachers to consider the social nature of handing out rewards. This may be particularly true for adolescents, who are highly self-conscious. In fact, research indicates that adolescents prefer to receive immediate rewards more so when their peers are present than when they are not in the presence of their peers (O'Brien, Albert, Chein, & Steinberg, 2011). However, whereas a reward for effort may mean a great deal to a low-achieving student who tries hard, receiving the reward in front of other students may be embarrassing to that student; it might be better to present the reward to the student privately so that the student will not feel embarrassed because of his or her low achievement. In contrast, some high-achieving students do not want their repeated successes publicized among their peers. Therefore, teachers should think carefully about whether rewards are handed out in front of other students. In general, teachers should avoid making any information about students' achievement public (Midgley, 1993).

7. *Use praise effectively.* Recall that praise from teachers or parents is considered a reward by many students. Teachers should not praise students haphazardly; rather, they should carefully evaluate and consider when, why, and where they will deliver praise (Brophy, 1981).

8. *Consider whether a reward is truly a reward.* Sometimes teachers may select rewards that students do not appreciate. It is important to consider the cognitive and social development of students; rewards should be age and grade appropriate. In addition, rewards should be socially acceptable for students. In other words, a teacher may believe that a hug is a meaningful and important reward; however, for some students, it might be embarrassing to be hugged by the teacher, and the hug might actually serve as a punishment.

Summary

In this chapter, we have examined some of the research on the effective and ineffective use of rewards in the classroom. Educators are fond of using rewards; however, it is important to realize that their effective use must be carefully planned, and the effects of rewards on learning and motivation must be critically examined.

Educators who haphazardly use rewards to motivate students may at times undermine students' intrinsic motivation to learn. The following "Questions to Consider When . . ." feature provides some specifics to consider when you are contemplating implementing a reward system in your classroom.

Questions to Consider When Thinking About Rewarding Your Students

1. Why do I want to offer a reward? Do I have evidence that my students are not *intrinsically motivated* to engage in the targeted activity without an incentive, or am I just assuming that the activity is not interesting? Do *all* the students need an incentive for engagement, or is the problem really one of managing individual students' behavior?
2. Are *social rewards* and the natural consequences of behavior (i.e., what would simply happen without any intervention by the teacher) sufficient reward, or do I need to move to introducing a more concrete reward?
3. How can I design a *reward structure* that allows students at all levels of ability a realistic chance of being rewarded?
4. How can I ensure that rewards are communicated as *informational* about students' effort,

progress, or performance, rather than seeming *controlling?* Do students need to know they could receive a reward in advance? Do rewards need to be given in public?
5. How can I be sure the student in question will actually *value* the reward I plan on using? For example, could I offer a limited choice of equivalent rewards for the same level of achievement?
6. How can I ensure that students understand the specific behaviors that are being rewarded? For example, how can I ensure that students who have truly exerted effort on a project are rewarded while those who copied others' ideas or neglected their share of a collaborative task are not rewarded?

LEARNING ACTIVITY 3.1   Memorization and Grades

1. As noted in this chapter, when students are asked to memorize information and are then tested on it, they often can't recall the information later. They may memorize the information to receive the "reward" of a good grade, but they may experience difficulty recalling the information at a later time. Try to recall an experience when you had to directly rote memorize extensive information (e.g., a map of Europe, the capital cities of all 50 states, biology vocabulary words). In addition, try to think of an experience in which you had no practical use for this information later in life (e.g.,

you had to memorize a map of Europe but have never traveled to Europe and do not plan to travel there). Now try to recall the information you had to memorize. What specifically do you remember now?
2. Now try to recall an experience when you had to memorize information that was useful to you (e.g., memorizing a map of Europe, then traveling there and actually appreciating the locations of the various European nations). How much of that information can you recall today? What specifically do you remember?

References

Amabile, T. M. (1985). Motivation and creativity: Effects of motivational orientation on creative writers. *Journal of Personality and Social Psychology, 48*(2), 393–397.

Anderman, E. M., Griesinger, T., & Westerfield, G. (1998). Motivation and cheating during early adolescence. *Journal of Educational Psychology, 90,* 84–93.

Anderman, E. M., & Johnston J. (1998). Television news in the classroom: What are adolescents learning? *Journal of Adolescent Research, 13,* 73–100.

Anderman, E. M., & Weber, J. (2009). Continuing motivation revisited. In A. Kaplan, S. Karabenick, & E. DeGroot (Eds.), *Culture, self, and motivation: Essays in honor of Martin L. Maehr* (pp. 3–19). Greenwich, CT: Information Age Press.

Anderman, E. M., & Wolters, C. A. (2006). Goals, values, and affect: Influences on student motivation. In P. Alexander & P. Winne (Eds.), *Handbook of educational psychology* (2nd ed., pp. 369–389). Mahwah, NJ: Erlbaum.

Anderman, E. M., & Young, A. J. (1994). Motivation and strategy use in science: Individual differences and classroom effects. *Journal of Research in Science Teaching, 31*(8), 811–831.

Assor, A., Vansteenkiste, M., & Kaplan, A. (2009). Identified versus introjected approach and avoidance motivations in school and sports: The limited benefits of self-worth strivings. *Journal of Educational Psychology, 101,* 482–497.

Brophy, J. (1981). Teacher praise: A functional analysis. *Review of Educational Research, 51*(1), 5–32.

Brophy, J. (2004). *Motivating students to learn* (2nd ed.). Mahwah, NJ: Erlbaum.

Cameron, J., & Pierce, W. D. (1994). Reinforcement, reward, and intrinsic motivation: A meta-analysis. *Review of Educational Research, 64*(3), 363–423.

Cameron, J., & Pierce, W. D. (1996). The debate about rewards and intrinsic motivation: Protests and accusations do not alter the results. *Review of Educational Research, 66*(1), 39–51.

Carlsmtih, K. M., Darley, J. M., & Robinson, P. H. (2002). Why do we punish? Deterrence and just deserts as motives for punishment. *Journal of Personality and Social Psychology, 83,* 284–299.

Clifford, M. (1991). Risk taking: Theoretical, empirical, and educational considerations. *Educational Psychologist, 26,* 263–297.

Deci, E. (1975). *Intrinsic motivation.* New York, NY: Plenum.

Deci, E. L., Koestner, R., & Ryan, R. M. (1999a). A meta-analytic review of experiments examining the effects of extrinsic rewards on intrinsic motivation. *Psychological Bulletin, 125*(6), 627–668.

Deci, E. L., Koestner, R., & Ryan, R. M. (1999b). The undermining effect is a reality after all— Extrinsic rewards, task interest, and self-determination: Reply to Eisenberger, Pierce, and Cameron (1999) and Lepper, Henderlong, and Gingras (1999). *Psychological Bulletin, 125*(6), 692–700.

Deci, E. L., Koestner, R., & Ryan, R. M. (2001). Extrinsic rewards and intrinsic motivation in education: Reconsidered once again. *Review of Educational Research, 71*(1), 1–27.

Deci, E., & Ryan, R. M. (1985). *Intrinsic motivation and self-determination in human behavior.* New York, NY: Plenum.

Deci, E., & Ryan, R. M. (1987). The support of autonomy and the control of behavior. *Journal of Personality and Social Psychology, 53,* 1024–1037.

Deci, E. L., Schwartz, A. J., Sheinman, L., & Ryan, R. M. (1981). An instrument to assess adults' orientations toward control versus autonomy with children: Reflections on intrinsic motivation and perceived competence. *Journal of Educational Psychology, 73,* 642–650.

Deci, E. L., Spiegel, N. H., Ryan, R. M., Koestner, R., & Kauffman, M. (1982). Effects of performance standards on teaching styles: Behavior of controlling teachers. *Journal of Educational Psychology, 74,* 852–859.

Diamond, A., Churchland, A., Cruess, L., & Kirkham, N. (1999). Early developments in the ability to understand the relation between stimulus and reward. *Developmental Psychology, 35,* 1507–1517.

Downing, J., Keating, T., & Bennett, C. (2005). Effective reinforcement techniques in elementary physical education: The key to behavior management. *Physical Educator, 62,* 114–122.

Eisenberger, R., Pierce, W. D., & Cameron, J. (1999). Effects of reward on intrinsic motivation—Negative, neutral, and positive: Comment on Deci, Koestner, and Ryan (1999). *Psychological Bulletin, 125*(6), 677–691.

Galvan, A. (2010). Adolescent development of the reward system. *Frontiers in Human Neurosciences, 4.* Doi: 10.3389/neuro.09.006.2010.

Grolnick, W. S., & Ryan, R. M. (1987). Autonomy in children's learning: An experimental and individual difference investigation. *Journal of Personality and Social Psychology, 52,* 890–898.

Henderlong, J., & Lepper, M. R. (2002). The effect of praise on children's intrinsic motivation: A review and synthesis. *Psychological Bulletin, 128*(5), 774–795.

Hidi, S. (1990). Interest and its contribution as a mental resource for learning. *Review of Educational Research, 60,* 549–571.

Hidi, S., & Ainley, M. (2008). Interest and self-regulation: Relationships between two variables that influence learning. In D. H. Schunk & B. J. Zimmerman (Eds.), *Motivation and self-regulated learning: Theory, research and applications* (pp. 77–109). Mahwah, NJ: Erlbaum.

Hidi, S., & Renninger, K. A. (2006). The four-phase model of interest development. *Educational Psychologist, 41,* 111–127.

Krapp, A., Hidi, S., & Renninger, K. A. (1992). Interest, learning, and development. In K. A. Renninger, S. Hidi, & A. Krapp (Eds.), *The role of interest in learning and development* (pp. 3–25). Hillsdale, NJ: Erlbaum.

Lei, S. A., Bartlett, K. A., Gorney, S. E., & Herschbach, T. R. (2010). Resistance to reading compliance among college students: Instructors' perspectives. *College Student Journal, 44,* 219–229.

Lepper, M. R. (1983). Extrinsic reward and intrinsic motivation: Implications for the classroom. In J. M. Levine & M. C. Wang (Eds.), *Teacher and student perceptions: Implications for learning* (pp. 281–317). Hillsdale, NJ: Erlbaum.

Lepper, M. R., Corpus, J. H., & Iyengar, S. S. (2005). Intrinsic and extrinsic motivational orientations in the classroom: Age differences and academic correlates. *Journal of Educational Psychology, 97*(2), 184–196.

Lepper, M. R., Greene, D., & Nisbett, R. E. (1973). Undermining children's intrinsic interest with extrinsic reward: A test of the "overjustification" hypothesis. *Journal of Personality and Social Psychology, 28,* 129–137.

Lin, Y. G., McKeachie, W. J., & Kim, Y. C. (2001). College student intrinsic and/or extrinsic motivation and learning. *Learning and Individual Differences, 13*(3), 251–258.

Mac Iver, D. (1993). Effects of improvement-focused student recognition on young adolescents' performance and motivation in the classroom. In M. L. Maehr & P. R. Pintrich (Eds.), *Advances in motivation and achievement: Vol. 8. Motivation and adolescent development* (pp. 191–216). Greenwich, CT: JAI.

Mac Iver, D., & Reuman, D. (1993/1994). Giving their best: Grading and recognition practices that motivate students to work hard. *American Educator, 17*(4), 24–31.

Maehr, M. L. (1976). Continuing motivation: An analysis of a seldom considered educational outcome. *Review of Educational Research, 46,* 443–462.

Midgley, C. (1993). Motivation and middle level schools. In M. L. Maehr & P. R. Pintrich (Eds.), *Advances in motivation and achievement: Vol. 8. Motivation in the adolescent years* Greenwich, CT: JAI.

Midgley, C., & Urdan, T. (1995). Predictors of middle school students' use of self-handicapping strategies. *Journal of Early Adolescence, 15*(4), 389–411.

Murayama, K., Matsumoto, M., Izuma, K., & Matsumoto, K. (2010). Neural basis of the undermining effect of monetary reward on intrinsic motivation. *PNAS Proceedings of the National Academy of Sciences in the United States of America, 107*(49), 20911–20916.

Nichols, S. L., & Berliner, D. C. (2007). *Collateral damage: How high-stakes testing corrupts America's schools.* Cambridge, MA: Harvard Education Press.

Nolen, S. B. (1988). Reasons for studying: Motivational orientations and study strategies. *Cognition and Instruction, 5,* 269–287.

O'Brien, L., Albert, D., Chein, J., & Steinberg, L. (2011). Adolescents prefer more immediate rewards when in the presence of their peers. *Journal of Research on Adolescence, 21,* 747–753.

Piaget, J. (1929). *The child's conception of the world.* London, England: Routledge & Kegan Paul.

Piaget, J. (1952). *The origin of intelligence in children.* New York, NY: International Universities Press.

Piaget, J. (1972). Intellectual evolution from adolescence to adulthood. *Human Development, 15,* 1–12.

Pintrich, P. R., & de Groot, E. V. (1990). Motivational and self-regulated learning components of classroom academic performance. *Journal of Educational Psychology, 82*(1), 33–40.

Pulfrey, C., Buchs, C., & Butera, F. (2011). Why grades engender performance-avoidance goals: The mediating role of autonomous motivation. *Journal of Educational Psychology, 103*, 683–700.

Renninger, K. A. (2009). Interest and identity development in instruction: An inductive model. *Educational Psychologist, 44*, 105–118.

Ryan, R. M., & Deci, E. L. (2000). Self-determination theory and the facilitation of intrinsic motivation, social development, and well-being. *American Psychologist, 55*, 68–78.

Ryan, R. M., & Grolnick, W. S. (1986). Origins and pawns in the classroom: Self-report and projective assessments of individual differences in children's perceptions. *Journal of Personality and Social Psychology, 50*, 550–558.

Schiefele, U., Krapp, A., & Winteler, A. (1992). Interest as a predictor of academic achievement: A meta-analysis of research. In K. A. Renninger, S. Hidi, & A. Krapp (Eds.), *The role of interest in learning and development* (pp. 183–212). Hillsdale, NJ: Erlbaum.

Schraw, G., & Lehman, S. (2001). Situational interest: A review of the literature and directions for future research. *Educational Psychology Review, 13*(1), 23–52.

Schunk, D. H. (1983). Reward contingencies and the development of children's skills and self-efficacy. *Journal of Educational Psychology, 75*, 511–518.

Schunk, D. H., Pintrich, P. R., & Meece, J. L. (2008). *Motivation in education: Theory, research, and applications*. Upper Saddle River, NJ: Pearson.

Selart, M., Norström, T., Kuvaas, B., & Takemura, K. (2008). Effects of reward on self-regulation, intrinsic motivation and creativity. *Scandinavian Journal of Educational Research, 52*, 439–458.

Skinner, B. F. (1953). *Science and human behavior*. New York, NY: Macmillan.

Skinner, B. F. (1954). The science of learning and the art of teaching. *Harvard Educational Review, 24*, 86–97.

Stipek, D. J. (1996). Motivation and instruction. In D. C. Berliner & R. C. Calfee (Eds.), *Handbook of educational psychology* (pp. 85–113). New York, NY: Macmillan Library Reference USA.

Stipek, D. J. (1998). *Motivation to learn: From theory to practice* (3rd ed.). Boston, MA: Allyn & Bacon.

Vansteenkiste, M., Lens, W., & Deci, E. L. (2006). Intrinsic versus extrinsic goal contents in self determination theory: Another look at the quality of academic motivation. *Educational Psychologist, 41*, 19–31.

Vansteenkiste, M., Simons, J., Lens, W., Sheldon, K. M., & Deci, E. L. (2004). Motivating learning, performance, and persistence: The synergistic role of intrinsic goals and autonomy-support. *Journal of Personality and Social Psychology, 87*, 246–260.

Vygotsky, L. S. (1978). *Mind in society: The development of higher psychological processes* (M. Cole, V. John-Steiner, S. Scribner, & E. Souberman, Trans.). Cambridge, MA: Harvard University Press.

Watson, J. B. (1924). *Behaviorism*. New York, NY: Norton.

Wigfield, A., & Eccles, J. S. (1992). The development of achievement task values: A theoretical analysis. *Developmental Review, 12*(3), 265–310.

Zentall, S. R., & Morris, B. J. (2010). "Good job, you're so smart": The effects of inconsistence of praise type on young children's motivation. *Journal of Experimental Child Psychology, 107*, 155–163.

CHAPTER 4

Evaluating Student Progress

The assessment of students' academic progress is a driving force in education. The increased use of academic standards and the need to demonstrate that students have achieved those standards have led to greater use of assessments in recent years (Ercikan, 2006). In the United States, the rise in the use of tests has been particularly obvious, given the well-known No Child Left Behind legislation (Bourque, 2005) and the adoption of Common Core Standards by many states (Common Core State Standards Initiative, 2012). These assessments clearly have an impact on student motivation. The increased use of educational assessments, along with the continued use of more traditional classroom-based assessments, affects learning in the classroom (Hursh, 2008; Lane, 2004). Both students and teachers spend large amounts of class time involved in assessment-related activities (Marso & Pigge, 1993). In addition, the increase in standardized testing affects student motivation in a variety of ways. For example, many educators today complain that they cannot spend as much class time allowing their students to engage in creative, in-depth projects because it may take away time that can be used to prepare for examinations. Further, teachers who were trained several years ago may not feel as efficacious working in today's assessment-driven climate. In addition, students approach tests with a variety of motivational beliefs and strategies that affect their performance on those tests and on other academic tasks (Ryan, Ryan, Arbuthnot, & Samuels, 2007).

Despite a popular assumption that assessments will motivate students and teachers to achieve at high levels, pervasive problems also ensue as a result of the focus on assessments in education. As pointed out by Cronbach, individual characteristics of learners, such as their unique motivational states, are related to students' performance on assessments (Cronbach, 1946, 1950).

In this chapter, we review some basic concepts related to educational assessment. In addition, we critically examine the relations of these concepts to student motivation. Finally, we offer suggestions for ways of working within a system that is based on assessments, while maintaining positive student motivation in the classroom. We conclude by discussing ways of developing assessment plans that are sensitive to maintaining student motivation to learn.

GENERAL ISSUES RELATED TO ASSESSMENT

Consider the following students:

Matt is a 10th grader. It is the end of the academic year, and he will be taking examinations in all his classes. His scores on these examinations will count for 40% of his final grade in each class.

Heather is a first-year college student who has just made the transition from high school into college. She is taking a difficult course on Middle Eastern history. No assessments have been administered during the course. Instead, one comprehensive final examination during exam week will cover all the information from the entire semester.

José is a third grader. He will be taking his first standardized test in April. His teacher constantly talks about the importance of the test and how all the students must try really hard and do very well on the test. He spends much of his time in class during the months of February and March doing worksheets that will help to prepare him for the test.

Jade is in eighth grade. The students in her mathematics class are given a quiz once per week. Each quiz counts very little toward the overall grade in class; the quizzes are designed primarily for the students to demonstrate that they have mastered some basic skills that were taught each week. Students who do well on the weekly quizzes generally also do well on the unit exams that are given once per month.

Stop and Think

Which of these students might be most likely to feel confident about their ability to do well in the class in question? Which are most likely to feel anxious? In which situations are students likely to become self-conscious about their performance?

All the aforementioned students will be taking various forms of tests. However, as can be seen from these examples, some of these tests are part of the regular classroom experience, whereas some are extremely important and carry a great deal of weight in determining the students' overall grades in their classes. More specifically, some of these are *low-stakes assessments* (e.g., Jade's math quizzes), whereas some of these are *high-stakes assessments* (e.g., Heather's history exam). Scores on low-stakes assessments generally do not have large effect on student outcomes, whereas scores on high-stakes assessments do affect students or their schools, either positively or negatively.

From the perspective of achievement motivation, the students described all may be motivated in different ways. In addition, the types of assessments used in each classroom affect the students' motivation. For example, Matt and Heather may be highly *extrinsically motivated* (see Chapter 3) because their scores on these exams count for much of the grade they will receive. Although Matt and Heather also may be *intrinsically motivated*, extrinsic motivation may be particularly salient, given the relative importance of these assessments in determining their overall grades. Heather, in particular, may lack confidence in her ability to perform well on her final exam and may become increasingly anxious as exams approach. In contrast, Jade may be able to maintain a healthy level of confidence in her ability, particularly if she does well on the weekly quizzes. Indeed, the positive feedback that Jade may receive from these weekly quizzes may help her develop positive feelings of *efficacy* (see Chapter 8) in mathematics. Finally, José might adopt *performance goals* (see Chapter 1) because his teacher constantly talks about the importance of the standardized test and about how students' scores on the test are very meaningful.

Thus, the use of assessments may have different motivational consequences for students. Some students may be highly intrinsically motivated and see a test as a challenge; others may be intimidated by exams and may experience debilitating test anxiety; still other students may become so focused on the test that they become very performance oriented, and their need to demonstrate their ability (or hide their inability) may overcome all other motives. In addition, the ways in which teachers prepare their students for various assessments need to be considered, as does the preparation of students with special needs for various assessments (Conderman & Pedersen, 2010). Thus, the use of assessments can have both positive and negative effects for students.

Assessment and Educational Policy

Educational Policy and Assessment

Many state and national educational policies revolve around assessment. Assessments guide curricula and education, and they also play an important role in determining how resources are allotted to schools. Virtually all public schools are affected by formal assessments each year, and these assessment policies have broad impacts on student motivation. Assessment data are also often used by educators to provide useful information to guide future instruction (Monpas-Huber, 2010). One of the primary reasons for this policy emphasis on assessment is the perception that schools and teachers need to be held accountable for students' learning; in effect, this infers that student performance on standardized assessments provides evidence of how well educators are doing their jobs.

Historically, school accountability became necessary for a variety of reasons, including (a) the need to justify the expenditure of public dollars on education, (b) the need to explain declining achievement, and (c) the need to better manage expenses related to education (Phillips, 2004). The No Child Left Behind Act of 2001 (NCLB) has placed assessment and accountability at the forefront of the educational system in the United States. NCLB

Patrick White/Merrill

Assessment of student learning occurs more and more often for today's public school students.

requires schools to administer assessments, and schools are held accountable for their students' performance on these assessments. Although student motivation is clearly affected by such assessments and affects how students perform on them, motivation per se is not evaluated in most standardized tests. Nevertheless, concerns about the ways in which the presence of mandatory assessments in schools affect instruction are prominent (e.g., Longo, 2010). Indeed, many teachers' efforts to use innovative, research-based methods to engage students are thwarted by the conflict that they experience between their desires to be innovative and the pressure to maintain high test scores (Agee, 2004). As of 2012, numerous states had been granted flexibility in meeting the NCLB requirements, particularly as a result of public outcry about the emphasis on the importance of standardized test scores (Scott, 2012).

Under NCLB, each school district must issue an annual report card that indicates how well students performed on state assessments. Thus, NCLB requires the public reporting of school-level performance. Schools within each district must demonstrate adequate annual progress, as defined by each state. Schools that do not reach their goals are required to develop improvement plans and to provide special services for their students. In addition, schools and teachers can be rewarded for improving students' scores or for lowering achievement gaps between certain groups of students (U.S. Department of Education, 2003). In terms of motivation, the public reporting of schools' performances on assessments may foster the adoption of performance goals at the student, classroom, and school levels (E. M. Anderman & Maehr, 1994).

In addition to NCLB, most states also use some type of assessment of student progress. Many states have their own unique standards. In addition, all states participate in national assessments such as the National Assessment of Educational Progress (National Center for Education Statistics, 2006). More recently, states have begun to utilize value-added models of assessment, wherein individual student progress is examined longitudinally and the impacts of individual schools and teachers on student achievement can be identified (Finn, Ryan, & Partin, 2008; Meyer, 1997).

TYPES OF ASSESSMENTS

Educational assessments are categorized in a variety of ways. These categorizations are important in that different types of assessments may invoke different cognitive and motivational processes in students and are useful for different types of educational decisions. In addition, different types of assessments may lead to a variety of differing short- and long-term student outcomes.

Formal and Informal Assessments

A distinction is often made between formal and informal assessments. A *formal assessment* is one that has been planned and scheduled in advance. Such assessments include unit examinations and standardized examinations. Formal assessments generally are utilized for specific purposes; for example, a teacher might use a formal assessment at the end of a particular unit to examine what students have learned.

In contrast, *informal assessments* occur throughout the academic year as part of students' daily classroom experiences. Teachers informally assess student progress all the time, via conversations, classwork, and group activities. Informal assessments are

Informal assessments can occur during instruction, using regular classroom materials.

particularly important and useful for teachers as they make on-the-spot decisions about their interactions with students.

From a motivation perspective, formal assessments are more likely to have an influence on motivation than are informal assessments. Students generally do not think much about informal assessments unless their teacher creates a highly performance-oriented classroom and draws attention to the fact that students are constantly being assessed (Midgley, 2002). Formal assessments are more likely to focus students on extrinsic goals and incentives because the weight of the assessment toward a student's grade is often more salient.

It is important to consider grade-level differences when considering formal and informal assessments. Although formal assessments occur both at the elementary and secondary levels, many elementary-age students probably do not experience formal assessments as sources of anxiety because the high-stakes nature of such assessments is either not emphasized to the students or is beyond the students' understanding. In contrast, at the high-school level, students often are aware of the importance of formal assessments and the fact that formal assessments are related to valued outcomes. Furthermore, some high-school students are aware of the importance of high-stakes formal assessments for their teachers' and school's ratings under school accountability policies (L. H. Anderman, Kowalski, & Dawson, 2012).

In terms of informal assessments, it is much easier for elementary teachers to conduct informal assessments than it is for secondary teachers. Most elementary teachers spend the day with a group of approximately 20 to 30 students, whereas secondary teachers may teach up to 150 or more students per day. Thus, it is certainly easier for elementary teachers to make more reliable and valid informal assessments of progress than it is for the high-school teacher, who often spends only one hour with each group of 30 students.

Formative evaluation can occur either before or during regular classroom instruction.

Formative and Summative Evaluations

Another important distinction in types of assessment is between formative and summative assessments. *Formative evaluation* occurs before and during classroom instruction, whereas *summative evaluation* occurs after instruction has occurred. Thus, when students take a pretest on spelling new vocabulary words, the spelling assessment is formative; in contrast, when students take a large spelling test at the end of a unit, the spelling test is summative. Formative assessments help teachers judge their students' prior knowledge and current skills levels related to a particular topic, whereas summative assessments demonstrate how much has been learned and how much progress has been made.

Summative evaluations often are formal assessments, whereas formative evaluations can be either formal or informal. For example, a teacher might start a new unit of study by having a class discussion about the upcoming topic to gain some insight into students' prior knowledge and misconceptions in the area. This would be a form of formative evaluation. At the end of the unit, however, the same teacher is more likely to use a formal assessment to provide a summative evaluation of students' mastery of the content. Students may be more extrinsically motivated for summative than for formative evaluations because summative evaluations are often emphasized more in class and are more high stakes in nature.

Standardized Examinations

The term *standardized* refers to the idea that the examination or other assessment is administered to different students, using the same procedures for everyone. For example, all test takers are examined on the same or similar questions, within the same time constraints, and given the same directions. Scoring of the examination results also follows careful guidelines. Finally, those results are reported in a standardized form that allows comparison of an individual student's result to a specific performance criterion or to some group *norm score.*

Although the tendency is to think of standardized tests in terms of traditional, paper-and-pencil examinations, other types of tests can also be standardized (such as a driving test). Standardized tests generally are developed over a long period of time and undergo considerable revision before being made available to teachers. Thus, standardized scores can often provide useful information for teachers about students' performance and readiness for learning. Nevertheless, they are only one source of such information, and many other types of assessment also can provide important indicators of achievement.

Teacher-Prepared Assessments

A teacher-prepared assessment is created by the classroom teacher. Although teacher-prepared assessments can be useful and practical, they often lack the psychometric (mental measurement) properties that are expected in standardized tests. Whereas most teachers are not trained to consider such factors, it is important to realize that the assessment instruments used by most teachers in daily classroom activities were developed by the teachers—not by psychometricians (test developers)—and therefore, those assessments may not always be as accurate as one might expect. As with standardized assessments, therefore, the results of teacher-prepared assessments should be considered as only one type of information about students' achievement. However, a clear advantage of teacher-prepared tests is that instructors can tailor assessments to their own classes' individual learning objectives and to their students' interests and abilities.

Distinctions can also be drawn in terms of what students are actually asked to do during an assessment. That is, whereas we might typically think of assessment as involving students working independently and silently on pencil-and-paper tests, several other forms of assessment can be useful. These include authentic assessments, observational assessments, portfolio assessments, and performance assessments.

Authentic Assessments

An *authentic assessment* is implemented in a true-to-life context. That is, it is designed to evaluate students' ability to use particular knowledge or skills in a way that mirrors their use in applied settings. Traditional paper-and-pencil tests often are not *authentic* because they assess students' skills in a decontextualized way, divorced from the ways in which those skills might be used in regular life.

The types of assessments that teachers use often are not highly authentic in nature, partially due to the ways in which teachers are trained (Campbell, 1993). For example, a student could be tested on chemistry knowledge by solving some problems on a traditional written examination; alternatively, the student could be assessed in a more authentic manner, perhaps by having the student perform an actual experiment in a laboratory setting.

Authentic assessment is particularly prominent in the field of medicine, where medical students and interns must demonstrate their knowledge in real clinical settings, with actual patients. This type of assessment provides excellent on-the-job training for aspiring doctors and provides a particularly valid indication of their ability to use knowledge in the ways they will need to in the future. Whereas authentic assessments may not always be practical or cost efficient, they may be more motivational than more traditional approaches because this type of assessment requires students to

When a teacher uses authentic assessments, students are asked to perform tasks in settings that mirror true-to-life circumstances.

truly demonstrate task mastery (Ames & Archer, 1988; Meece, Blumenfeld, & Hoyle, 1988). Emphasizing the real-life application of specific knowledge and procedures may also help to enhance students' perceptions of the utility value (see Chapter 2) of what they are learning.

Observational Assessments

An observational assessment occurs when a teacher observes students while they are engaged in particular activities and then assesses student learning based on those observations. To evaluate students appropriately via observations, observers must be well trained and experienced.

Observational assessments often overestimate achievement because they frequently occur during the learning process. Thus, although it might seem easy to evaluate students based on observations of their behaviors, it is important to realize that observations must be carefully structured and evaluated.

From a motivational perspective, observations may or may not have an impact on student motivation. If the observers are conspicuously obvious to the students, then students may become self-conscious and start to focus on how they are appearing to the observers, rather than on learning (i.e., become more performance goal oriented). In contrast, if the observers are unobtrusive, motivational effects should be minimized. In addition, if somebody other than the classroom teacher is conducting the observation, then the students certainly will notice the new individual, at least initially. After the observer is present for several days, however, the observer probably will just fade into the background for most students.

Portfolio Assessments

Portfolios are representations of students' best examples of work, within a specific domain. The individual student is involved in selecting and evaluating work samples that demonstrate his or her accomplishment and progress over time. These collections of work typically are presented in a folder, although alternative formats such as electronic or Web-based portfolios are becoming more prominent (Bennett & Wadkins, 1995; Meyer, Abrami, Wade, & Scherzer, 2011).

Portfolio assessment may enhance student motivation for several reasons. First, because students are involved in the selection of materials for the portfolio, they may feel self-determined and autonomous because they are actively involved in the decision-making process. As we have noted, when students are offered the opportunity to make important decisions and to have choices, motivation is enhanced (Deci & Ryan, 1987; Eccles, 1999; Skinner, Zimmer-Gembeck, & Connell, 1998; see Chapter 8). Teachers can emphasize in their daily discourse in classrooms that students will be making important decisions about the portfolios. For example, when students are working on assignments, teachers can encourage students to think about whether or not a particular sample of work might go into their portfolio.

Second, because portfolios emphasize students' best work, students may feel a sense of pride in their accomplishments. Rather than focusing on their failures, portfolios focus on positive outcomes. This may enhance students' self-concepts of their own abilities and their valuing of the subject area and the tasks involved in developing the products for the portfolio (Wigfield & Eccles, 2002). From a motivational perspective, if the students' perceived valuing of the subject is enhanced, it may lead to the students being more likely to engage in the subject or task in the future (Wigfield & Eccles, 1992; Wigfield, Tonks, & Lutz Klauda, 2009).

Third, because portfolios are often reviewed, students have the opportunity to revisit their previous work. Unlike many assignments and assessments in school, when students have portfolios, they are constantly encouraged to reexamine their previous work and can see how their achievement and learning have progressed. This developmental focus on improvement is in line with most social-cognitive motivational frameworks. In particular, being able to review and improve one's work is especially consistent with promoting a mastery goal orientation (see Chapter 1); by improving one's work over time, students are encouraged to focus on mastery goals and to compare their current work with their own previous work (as opposed to comparing it to other students' work).

Performance Assessments

Performance-based assessments require students to complete actual tasks rather than simply to respond to questions on a written examination. They may be particularly motivating to some students because the assessments are contextualized within actual real-life applications of the task being assessed. Performance-based assessments have been in use in many arts-related and physical education contexts but can also be adapted to other domains. One well-known hands-on curriculum that lends itself well to performance assessments is Project-Based Science, in which students examine scientific questions as scientists would approach similar questions in their daily work (Krajcik, Blumenfeld, Marx, & Soloway, 2000). In addition, when teachers are trained in teacher education programs, student teachers often are evaluated during their student teaching experiences in terms of their actual "performance" as a teacher in a classroom.

The use of performance assessments has several advantages, including that they (a) allow for the assessment of skills that cannot easily be assessed with traditional paper-and-pencil tests and (b) affect instruction and learning, in that students often learn material in ways that will help them to receive good scores on tests. If the assessment requires performance of a real task in real time, then the student is more likely to learn the material in a meaningful way that may lead to enhanced motivation, learning, and memory of the task and procedures (Oosterhof, 2001).

Performance-based assessments are supported in particular by expectancy–value theory. Recall that the four core components of achievement values are interest, importance, utility, and cost (i.e., being worth one's time). Because students are actually engaging with "real" tasks during performance assessments, they may be more likely to understand why such tasks are important. In particular, they may gain an understanding of the utility value of tasks; thus a student who must demonstrate a scientific principle, rather than report it on a written examination, may better appreciate the activities in which scientists engage daily. Such experiences may further students' interest in studying science or perhaps entering a science career (E. M. Anderman, Sinatra, & Gray, 2012).

CHARACTERISTICS OF HIGH-QUALITY ASSESSMENTS

Because assessment is such a driving force in educational policy, it is important for educators to understand the characteristics of high-quality assessments. Not all assessments are equally valuable or trustworthy, and they do not all serve the same purposes or provide an appropriate assessment of all students. In addition, the different qualities of assessments may affect student motivation in a variety of ways.

Reliability and Validity

Issues of reliability and validity are paramount to appropriate assessment. If measures are not reliable and valid, their results cannot be trusted, and their inaccurate implications may have devastating effects on motivation. Although both reliability and validity are important characteristics of effective assessments, reliability remains a prerequisite for assessing validity (Oosterhof, 2001).

RELIABILITY   Reliability refers to consistency, either across time or across different scorers or assessors. Assessment reliability is important because it shows that people's scores on the test are due to their actual performance during the assessment, and not to random fluctuations in the ways answers are scored or irrelevant differences among students. Obviously, if an assessment has poor reliability, teachers cannot have confidence in the results derived from it.

In terms of the types of assessments described previously in this chapter, standardized assessments have the advantage in terms of reliability. Details on the ways in which a test's reliability was evaluated and the results of those evaluations are usually provided in the test manual that accompanies standardized examinations. Although it is less common, it is also possible to establish a reliable approach to observational and performance assessments. Doing so, however, requires specialized training. Overall, assessments tend to be more reliable when they include more items, problems, or questions; thus a 10-item test on a particular topic should be more reliable than a 5-item test. Similarly, observations of students' work in small cooperative groups should be more reliable if they are taken on 5 separate days, rather than on 1 day.

VALIDITY   Validity concerns whether or not an assessment truly measures what it is intended to measure. An assessment is considered valid if it can be established that it does indeed measure what it is supposed to measure and that scores are not really reflecting some other characteristic. As noted previously, any assessment that has poor reliability is vulnerable to being influenced by factors other than the student's performance; thus, an unreliable assessment cannot have good validity. Teachers should be suspect of standardized assessments that do not provide adequate evidence about their validity.

One of the main ways validity is established is through statistical associations with other related measures or real-life outcomes. Well-known standardized exams, such as the Scholastic Achievement Test (SAT), continue to be used because they are considered valid predictors of future success. That is, scores on the SAT correlate quite highly with college achievement scores, such as grades (Anastasi, 1988).

To understand why test validity is important in terms of student motivation, think about the value that is placed on test results and the critical decisions, based on those scores, that can be made for both students and teachers. If test scores do not, in fact, reflect the knowledge or abilities they are assumed to represent (i.e., if the test is not valid), educators run the risk of making the wrong decisions for students' future opportunities. For example, consider the following scenario:

> *Imagine that Ms. Miranda is trying to select middle-school students for inclusion in a special program in which they will learn to create and maintain interactive Web sites. The size of the program is limited, and she wants to select students with a strong interest in computer technology and mastery of basic skills (e.g., keyboarding, navigating the Web). To help in the selection process, Ms. Miranda develops a test in which students are required to write an essay outlining their experiences with technology and their reasons for wanting to participate in the program. She will use the results of this test to determine which students can participate.*

Stop and Think

What potential problems can you see in terms of the validity of this assessment approach? How well would this test identify the types of students Ms. Miranda wants for her program? What types of students might be disadvantaged by this approach?

The assessment in this scenario has several potential problems. First, by choosing to have students write an essay, Ms. Miranda has introduced a new area of competency (essay writing) that is not part of what she really wants to assess. Students do not need to be good essay writers to perform well in the Web site development program; however, poor essay writing skills may keep potentially qualified students from being admitted.

Thus, a student who is highly motivated and has the appropriate background to participate in the program may be precluded from participating due to poor writing skills. Second, Ms. Miranda's test requires students to describe their experiences with technology, but it does not test their actual skills. Therefore, some students may be able to describe many impressive-sounding experiences but, once in the program, turn out not to have the applied skills that they need. Given Ms. Miranda's intentions, this test has the potential to misidentify students for her program, both admitting students who will struggle with the activities and denying the opportunity to some who are qualified and truly interested. Thus, Ms. Miranda's assessment has poor validity: It is not well suited to its purpose.

Stop and Think

How else might Ms. Miranda design an assessment to identify students for her program? Might other types of assessments, other than essay writing, be more valid? Provide three examples of additional assessments that Ms. Miranda could use.

Although the preceding example is fictitious, very similar concerns have been raised repeatedly over many tests used widely in regular schooling. For example, many tests of content knowledge in various subjects, such as history or biology, require considerable skill in reading and comprehension and probably underestimate some students' knowledge. Similarly, many standardized tests that have been developed and normed primarily with students from the majority culture may not provide valid assessments of the knowledge and abilities of students from diverse linguistic, cultural, or economic backgrounds (e.g., McLoyd, 1998).

Reliability, Validity, and Motivation

The reliability and validity of assessments often are not considered in terms of their potential impact on student motivation. Nevertheless, these issues are related to motivation in very important ways. Consider the following example:

> *Jeffrey is a 10th-grade student. His English teacher feels that he is not doing very well in English class, so she recommends that he work with a reading specialist. The reading specialist asks Jeffrey to read three pages from a text, and then she has him answer some questions about the reading. Jeffrey is asked to repeat this exercise weekly, using a different text each time. Unfortunately, because the reading specialist is not using instruments that have been demonstrated to be reliable, Jeffrey's performance on the reading tasks varies greatly from week to week; one week he appears to be doing very well, whereas the next week he appears to perform poorly.*

Now, consider the motivational effects of the use of unreliable reading assessments. Ideally, it would be wonderful if Jeffrey could receive feedback from the assessments each week, indicating that he is making good progress and reaching his goals. Under those circumstances, we would expect Jeffrey's confidence in his reading ability (or *self-efficacy*; see Chapter 8) to increase (Schunk & Pajares, 2009; Schunk & Zimmerman, 2006). If the assessments are unreliable, however, and do not provide consistent and well-measured information for the specialist to share with Jeffrey and his teacher, his motivation may be affected adversely. If Jeffrey receives inconsistent feedback on his performance that does not accurately reflect his effort and progress, he may lose confidence in his reading ability or even decide that success is due to events beyond his control (that is, he may start making external, uncontrollable *attributions;* see Chapter 7). Jeffrey's English teacher probably had excellent intentions by sending Jeffrey to the specialist, including a desire that he develop both his skills and sense of competence as a reader. The use of poorly designed assessments, however, may not provide Jeffrey with the appropriate feedback to help build his self-efficacy as a reader. Thus, the use of an unreliable (and thus inherently invalid) assessment can adversely affect student motivation.

CRITERIA FOR SCORING OF ASSESSMENTS

Many teachers do not consider the fact that assessments can be scored in different ways. For example, students' scores on assessments may be presented in terms of how an individual student's performance compares to the performance of other students; in contrast, students' scores may be presented in terms of students' level of mastery of a topic. These issues can have important influences on motivation and long-term learning.

Norm-Referenced Scoring

A norm-referenced test compares a student's performance to that of other students who have taken the same or similar assessments. These tests assume that different students' scores will be spread out (in a *normal distribution* or *bell curve;* E. M. Anderman, 2008), and that some students must, by definition, fall below average. In norm-referenced tests, therefore, it is impossible for all students to attain the same results.

Norm-referenced tests are particularly useful when teachers need to report to parents or make recommendations concerning students' performance relative to others. For example, norm-referenced scores are often used for screening students for special services (Salvia & Ysseldyke, 1995) and for making admission decisions for selective programs. Thus, if a teacher or school psychologist believes that it is necessary to know how a particular student is performing in comparison to others of the same age or grade level, then a norm-referenced test is appropriate.

Norm-referenced test results often are reported as *percentile scores;* that is, a student's score is reported not in terms of the number of test items he or she answered correctly but rather in terms of how his or her score compares to those achieved by similar students who took the test at a previous time (the *norm group*). For example, Sandy receives a percentile score of 96 on a reading comprehension test. This means that Sandy performed better than 96% of the norm group for the same test. This score does *not* tell us how many questions Sandy answered correctly or provide information about her specific learning accomplishments and needs.

There are several important considerations in interpreting students' percentile scores. First, the validity of norm-referenced scores relies on the similarity between your students and those who were in the test's norm group. A description of the norm group is included in the test manual of most published tests, and teachers should pay attention to

Norm versus criterion-referenced scoring rubrics send students different messages about their ability to improve.

this information. If meaningful differences are noted between your students and those originally tested—for example, in terms of age, cultural background, disabilities, or educational opportunities—the scores may not be valid for your students. That is, even though a test is considered highly valid and reliable overall, scores for particular students may not be valid indicators for those individuals.

Second, remember that norm-referenced scores tell you only how students' scores compare to those of others who took the same test. They do not provide specific information about what students know, understand, or are confused about and, thus, cannot be used to make decisions for specific instructional planning.

Criterion-Referenced Scoring

Criterion-referenced scoring is based on the idea that students are assessed on how well or poorly they demonstrate previously defined skills; students must meet specific criteria that have been established prior to the examination. For example, a first-grade student may be asked to solve a series of math problems, such as the following, to demonstrate skill in subtracting with numbers up to 20:

$$15 - 6 = ?$$

Scores are based on the individual student's number of correct items and are not compared to anyone else's performance. Thus, a criterion-referenced examination allows students to demonstrate mastery of specific tasks and skills. With criterion-referenced scoring, it is possible for all students in a classroom to achieve a perfect score on an examination, if all the students can demonstrate mastery of the task. Similarly, it would be possible for all students to perform poorly on the assessment. Criterion-referenced assessments are appropriate for teachers who want to evaluate students' mastery of particular skills or course content or who want to diagnose areas of misunderstanding to plan for future instruction. Criterion-referenced assessments are particularly useful in situations where it is important for all students to demonstrate at least a minimum level of competency. For example, the decision to issue a driving license is based on the demonstration of a required level of knowledge (of traffic laws) and skill (in controlling a vehicle), regardless of how one driver's performance compares to others who have taken the same test. Similarly, some school districts require students to demonstrate specific academic competencies to graduate from high school. Because all students may perform equally on criterion-referenced tests, however, these assessments may not be useful for understanding how your students are performing in comparison to others of their age and grade level.

APPROACHES TO SCORING AND MOTIVATION   The use of norm- or criterion-referenced scoring may be related to the types of *goal orientations* (see Chapter 1) adopted by students or to the types of *goal structures* that are fostered in a classroom or school. For the most part, criterion-referenced assessments should be expected to promote mastery goals, whereas norm-referenced assessments are more likely to promote performance goals.

Recall that a student is mastery goal oriented when his or her main goal is to master the task at hand (Dweck & Leggett, 1988). Criterion-referenced tests are scored based on whether or not a student has mastered a task or skill, relative to previously defined criteria. Improvement on previous levels can be monitored easily, and no reference is made to the performance of other students. Thus, the use of criterion-referenced assessments may foster the adoption of mastery goals. This is a desirable outcome because research clearly indicates that the adoption of mastery goals is related to a number of valued educational outcomes (E. M. Anderman & Young, 1994; L. H. Anderman & E. M. Anderman, 2008; Nolen, 1988; Pintrich, 2000; Wolters, 2004).

A performance-goal-oriented student may be focused either on demonstrating his or her ability (*performance-approach goals*), or on avoiding appearing incompetent or "dumb" in comparison to others (*performance-avoid goals*; Elliot & Harackiewicz, 1996; Middleton & Midgley, 1997). Norm-referenced testing is based on the notion that some students inevitably will perform better than others on a given test. If a teacher or school emphasizes the normative nature of an assessment to students and their parents, then students may adopt performance goals. Whereas the adoption of performance-approach goals may benefit some students, particularly when combined with mastery goals, the adoption of performance-avoid goals inevitably leads to poor outcomes for students (E. M. Anderman & Wolters, 2006; Pintrich, 2000).

When using normative assessments, the key for teachers is to not focus the students on the normative nature of the scoring. If students are constantly reminded about how their scores reflect their abilities in comparison to others, it is highly likely that students will adopt performance goals. Many well-intentioned practices that publicize differences in students' performance, such as posting examples of "best projects" or the names of high-performing students, send a strong message to students about how their accomplishments compare to their peers'. Educators should think about the types of messages that they send to students when they talk about assessments, as this may inevitably have more of an effect on student motivation than will the actual nature of the exam itself.

ASSESSMENT AND STUDENT MOTIVATION

Throughout this chapter, we have indicated ways in which characteristics of assessment may influence different aspects of students' motivation. All the various motivation theories that are currently prominent in the research literature can be associated with assessment-related issues. Thus, educators must consider assessments' potential motivational effects on students from a variety of perspectives.

As we emphasize throughout this book, motivation is a multifaceted construct; indeed, motivation can be examined in many different ways. In the following sections, we summarize some of the implications of assessment within the contexts of specific theoretical perspectives.

Goal Orientations and Assessment

Recall that goal orientations (i.e., mastery and performance goals; see Chapter 1) can be conceptualized at three levels: as students' personal goals, as classroom goal structures, and as school-level goal structures. Research suggests that the contexts of schools and classrooms influence the types of personal goals that students adopt (E. M. Anderman & Maehr, 1994; Midgley, E. M. Anderman, & Hicks, 1995; Wolters, 2004). Thus, a school or classroom that is highly performance oriented is likely to induce personal performance goals in individual students.

When teachers in specific classrooms, or schools as a whole, place emphasis on the importance of testing, students are likely to adopt performance goals (E. M. Anderman & Maehr, 1994). As previously noted, the use of performance goals is related to specific types of cognitive outcomes; when used in conjunction with mastery goals, these outcomes may be adaptive—however, when performance goals (particularly performance-avoid goals) are adopted in the absence of mastery goals, students may use less effective cognitive strategies, such as rote memorization, and demonstrate less deep cognitive processing or critical thinking (E. M. Anderman & Young, 1994; Graham & Golan, 1991; Nolen, 1988; Nolen & Haladyna, 1990; Pintrich, 2000).

This may be particularly problematic in high-stakes testing environments, where the results of assessments determine financial rewards or sanctions given to or leveled against schools. If a school might be taken over by the state or the teachers or principal might lose their jobs as a result of poor scores, school personnel may be more likely to stress the importance of tests to their students and, consequently, foster the adoption of performance goals over mastery goals.

Attributions and Assessment

Students' attributions are intimately tied to assessments. Recall that an attribution represents a student's causal explanation for why an event occurred. In terms of assessments, when students receive their scores, they will make attributions for their successes or failures.

Thus, a student who performs poorly on an assessment might make an attribution to her lack of ability and infer that she is simply unable to do well in a particular subject; in contrast, another student might receive the same score and make an attribution to lack of effort and infer that she can do better in future assessments if she studies more. These differences in attributional patterns are important because they are related to students' expectations for future success (Graham & Williams, 2009; Weiner, 1986). Because of her supposed lack of ability, the first student in our example may see little reason to expect that she will perform well on future assessments; thus, there is no point in putting forth additional effort in that subject. In contrast, the second student may continue to feel competent because she has control over the amount of effort she puts into preparing for the next assessment.

As teachers, we often think about the process of assessment but rarely consider the aftereffects of assessments. Students are likely to make attributions whenever they receive a test score, particularly when those results were unexpected. It is our responsibility as educators to realize that testing is not over when the student finishes taking the examination. Educators must remain aware of the subsequent attributional processes used by students so that we can help them form accurate and adaptive attributions that will lead to enhanced motivation in the future. Helping students interpret their grades and test results can go a long way toward sustaining their continued effort; a short discussion about how students prepared for an assessment and why they think they got the results they did—whatever that result—can be very beneficial. If students consistently perform poorly on our assessments and are not coached in terms of how to improve their performance, then motivation toward that academic subject will almost certainly wane.

Expectancy–Value Theory and Assessment

The expectancy–value model of motivation suggests that students' motivation to engage in an academic task is a function of the students' expectancies for success at the task and perceptions of the value of the task (Eccles, 1983; Eccles & Wigfield, 2002). Both expectancies and values can be affected by assessments, and they also can affect the outcomes of future assessments.

If a student expects to do well at a particular task, he or she probably will also expect to perform well on an assessment of that task. Thus, a student who expects that he can learn a new list of spelling words is likely to believe that he also will be successful on a spelling assessment. In a similar manner, a student who places high value on an academic task is likely to spend more time on that type of task (Wigfield & Eccles, 1992) and, as a result, has a greater likelihood of performing well. Indeed, there is evidence that students' ability self-perceptions are related to actual achievement. Specifically, what students believe about their unique abilities to learn specific information is related to their actual achievement in that area. For example, researchers have found that students' beliefs about their abilities are predictive of standardized math achievement test scores (House & Telese, 2008; Marsh, Trautwein, Lüdtke, Koller, & Baumert, 2005).

The *utility value* construct is of particular interest in this regard. Students who perceive that a task has high utility value also feel that the task is useful in terms of helping them achieve a future goal. For example, a student who realizes that knowledge of Pythagorean theorem will assist her in her career goals, such as becoming a successful engineer, will place high utility value on understanding and applying the theorem. Thus, students may work diligently to do well on examinations and assessments simply because the utility value of tasks is high.

Research also indicates that other aspects of achievement values are related to test performance. For example, both students' interest in and enjoyment of reading are predictors of growth in reading achievement over time on assessments (Mucherah & Yoder, 2008; Retelsdorf, Köller, & Möller, 2011). Thus when teachers foster interest and enjoyment (e.g., by allowing students to choose their own reading materials), achievement on standardized assessments may be enhanced. Research also indicates that perceptions of a test as being important and useful are related to both greater effort and exam scores (Cole, Bergin, & Whittaker, 2008).

Whereas students' valuing of particular subject areas may motivate them to do well on assessments, the reverse relationship is not necessarily true; that is, some research suggests that a strong focus on assessment in class may negatively affect students' motivation toward engagement with a task. For example, one study found that in classrooms where teachers focused on assessment and performance, students' valuing of reading and mathematics declined over the course of an academic year (E. M. Anderman et al., 2001).

Self-Efficacy and Assessment

Self-efficacy is another motivational variable that can be affected by assessments and can affect student performance on assessments. Self-efficacy (see Chapter 8) refers to an individual's belief in his or her ability to succeed at a specific task (Bandura, 1997). Self-efficacy is highly predictive of academic achievement: Students who feel efficacious toward particular tasks tend to achieve at high levels when engaged with those tasks (Pajares, 1996).

Students who report high levels of self-efficacy and who have had positive experiences with specific tasks often receive good scores on task-specific assessments. If an individual believes that she has high ability in a particular area, then she is likely to be able to execute the necessary processes to successfully complete the task and, thus, perform successfully on an assessment.

Students who are high in self-efficacy are likely to do well on academic assessments; in turn, doing well on assessments serves to reinforce students' sense of self-efficacy. The corollary of this is, of course, that a negative pattern also can result. That is, students who have a low sense of self-efficacy may perform poorly on an assessment, and that poor performance in turn may further diminish the students' self-efficacy for the task.

Intrinsic/Extrinsic Motivation and Assessment

Recall that students are intrinsically motivated when they engage in an academic task without expecting anything in return for their participation, whereas students who are extrinsically motivated engage in academic tasks to earn a reward or to avoid some type of punishment. It is possible for students to be both intrinsically and extrinsically motivated for the same task (see Chapter 3).

In terms of assessments, students may be motivated both intrinsically and extrinsically. Certainly any discussion of assessments focuses students on extrinsic incentives—assessments often are related to grades, promotion, college acceptance, or receipt of certain privileges. Perhaps most salient in education is the fact that students' grades are often directly tied to assessments.

Nevertheless, assessments can also be intrinsically motivating. As discussed previously in this chapter, authentic assessments and performance-based assessments often are grounded in real-world tasks that are meaningful to students. When students perceive assessments as meaningful and useful, they may be more intrinsically motivated to engage in such tasks.

However, it is extremely important to remember that extrinsic incentives can undermine intrinsic motivation (Deci, Koestner, & Ryan, 1999, 2001; Lepper, 1983; Lepper, Greene, & Nisbett, 1973). Thus, when teachers focus on testing and emphasize the importance of tests and other assessment outcomes to their students, students' intrinsic motivation toward the topic may suffer. Recall the story in Chapter 3 about Hannah, whose intrinsic interest in reading declined after her teacher started assigning points for reading prescribed books. This scenario is quite typical of how a student's intrinsic motivation for a topic can suffer when extrinsic outcomes are emphasized by teachers. A subject that a student truly loves may become less interesting over time as a result of an increased focus on testing. Instructors must remember that although assessment of student progress is necessary and important, it should not be the major focus of all educational activities.

Test Anxiety

Many students experience debilitating anxiety when they are assessed. This anxiety often is specific to the testing situation and does not necessarily generalize to other situations in school or at home. Although a *little bit* of anxiety about an assessment situation (a feeling of heightened awareness or "having an edge") may help some students to perform well, too much anxiety is undesirable. Such anxiety can be so problematic that it may affect students' performance on assessments to the point where the assessment is no longer a reliable indicator of the students' ability.

Although the literature on test anxiety is expansive, research generally suggests that anxiety interferes with cognitive processes. More specifically, students' abilities to focus their attention and recall known information are adversely affected, thus negatively affecting their performance on assessments (Tobias, 1985; Zeidner, 1998). Test anxiety can lead to cognitive symptoms (e.g., excessive worrying), affective symptoms (feeling uncomfortably elevated levels of arousal or fear), and even physiological symptoms (such as sweating or an upset stomach; Zeidner, 1998). Overall, research suggests that when high levels of test anxiety are present in students, performance on assessments suffers (Hembree, 1998). In addition, perceiving a particular academic task as important is related to increased anxiety; this relation is weaker, however, when students report feeling higher levels of academic self-efficacy (Nie, Lau, & Liau, 2011). Thus instructional practices that enhance students' self-efficacy (see Chapter 8) may help to alleviate some aspects of test anxiety.

HIGH-STAKES TESTING AND MOTIVATION

Much has been written in recent years about high-stakes testing and the pressures that have been placed on teachers to ensure that students perform well on those examinations (e.g., Carnoy, Elmore, & Siskin, 2003; Madaus, Russell, & Higgins, 2009; Nichols & Berliner,

2007; Price & Peterson, 2009). From a motivation perspective, these pressures can lead to the use of instructional practices that may run counter to what motivation theory and research tell us.

First, there is an increased likelihood that teachers will focus on rote memorization and speed so that students can obtain maximum scores on these exams (e.g., Hursh, 2008). Whereas problem-solving and higher-order thinking skills are important, educators may focus students on simpler test-taking strategies, with the end-goal of helping their students to attain the highest possible scores. Indeed, teachers' instructional practices have been documented as changing to prepare students for high-stakes tests (e.g., Dooley & Assaf, 2009).

Second, the fact that schools are either rewarded or punished based on their test scores has important implications from a self-determination theory perspective. Ryan and his colleagues (Ryan & Brown, 2005; Ryan & Deci, 2009) noted that because high-stakes testing is tied to rewards and sanctions, teacher autonomy and satisfaction are likely to be adversely affected by such testing policies. In an earlier study, Deci, Ryan, and their colleagues (Deci, Spiegel, Ryan, Koestner, & Kauffman, 1982) examined the effects of two different types of instructions for teachers on the instructional practices used by teachers. Participants were assigned randomly to teach another student how to work with specific puzzles; participants in the *controlling* condition were told that they had to get their student to perform up to certain standards, whereas participants in the *informational* condition were told that their job was "to facilitate the student's learning how to work with the puzzles" (p. 853). Observers blind to the experimental conditions reported that the controlling teachers acted in more demanding and controlling manners than did the teachers in the informational condition. The controlling teachers talked more and in a more controlling manner than did the informational teachers; they gave more directives to students; they stated three times as many "should" statements than teachers in the informational condition; they criticized students more often; and they provided students with fewer opportunities to make choices.

Thus when teachers feel that they must get their students to perform on certain examinations at a specific required level of excellence, the types of instructional strategies and the quality of discourse used with students are clearly affected. These practices generally do not afford students opportunities to engage in tasks using many of the motivational strategies reviewed in this text.

DESIGNING AN ASSESSMENT PLAN

Classroom teachers are responsible for the development and scoring of most assessments. Although standardized summative assessments may emanate from governmental sources or from test publishers, the daily assessments used in classrooms are usually the products of regular classroom teachers. Because teachers develop and administer most assessments, it is also possible and important for teachers to develop assessment tools that support students' ongoing motivation. Some of the issues that teachers should consider when developing their own assessment tools include criteria for scoring, reporting of grades, recognition of performance and improvement, and providing feedback. All these aspects of assessment are important and send messages to students that affect their subsequent performance and motivation.

RECONSIDERING NORM- AND CRITERION-REFERENCED SCORING

Recall that when teachers use norm-referenced scoring, students' scores are determined as they relate to other students' scores on the same assessment. In contrast, when teachers use criterion-referenced scoring, students' scores are determined by demonstrations of their acquisition of a certain set of skills. When teachers grade in a norm-referenced manner, students' scores inevitably are compared to other scores; in contrast, when teachers use criterion-referenced scores, all students' scores are based on individual levels of achievement. Thus, in a classroom where criterion-referenced scoring is used, all students potentially can get an A on a project; in a classroom where norm-referenced scoring is used, only some of the students will qualify for A grades.

As noted previously, norm-referenced scoring is likely to invoke performance goals. When students' scores are implicitly based on comparisons with the performance of other classmates, students are likely to be concerned about how their scores compare to those of other students. Although norm-referenced testing may be appropriate at times, it is important for teachers to focus on mastery of academic subjects. In addition, when norm-referenced tests are used, teachers must help students and their parents interpret the scores. Misconceptions about the meaning of standardized scores (e.g., percentile ranks) are many, and misunderstandings about students' progress and achievement may lead teachers or students to make inappropriate and debilitating attributions. It is important that teachers make sure that *they* understand and can explain the meaning of all test results that are reported to students and their families.

The use of criterion-referenced tests is more likely to foster the adoption of mastery goals than is the use of norm-referenced tests. When criterion-referenced assessments are used, students can focus on their own individual learning and progress—their peers' scores should not affect their own scores on assessments. When students know that they can get a good grade for mastering a specific content area or a specific set of skills, they may be more motivated to continue to learn about such topics in the future. Thus, when it is feasible, teachers should always consider whether a criterion-referenced approach can meet their instructional and assessment goals.

Public versus Private Reporting of Assessment Scores

One area to which researchers have given little attention, but that nevertheless is very important, is the means by which students' assessment scores are reported. Consider the following examples:

> *Example 1* Mrs. Jackson is an eighth-grade math teacher. Whenever she returns quizzes to her class, she announces the students' quiz scores to the class as she hands back the students' papers.

> *Example 2* Mr. Jones is an eighth-grade math teacher. When he returns quizzes to his class, he posts the number of A's, B's, C's, D's, and F's on the board so that students can know how their scores compare to others.

> *Example 3* Mrs. Jeffries is an eighth-grade math teacher. When she returns quizzes to her class, she places the students' quizzes facedown on each student's desk so that nobody else sees or hears the students' grades.

Carefully consider the implications of publicly displaying students' test scores and projects.

Stop and Think

Which approach would you assume eighth-grade students would prefer? Why? What would you predict about the impact of each of these approaches on students' motivation? Would the effects differ, depending on students' level of math achievement? Would the effects differ for younger or older students?

You have probably encountered teachers who have used all three of these techniques. What kinds of messages do each of these techniques send to students? It is quite likely that students perceive the classrooms of both Mrs. Jackson and Mr. Jones as performance oriented. By making students' assessment scores public, these teachers do two things that encourage a performance orientation: They emphasize the importance of students' scores, and they encourage comparison among students. Thus, low-achieving students who receive poor grades are continuously reminded of their status as low achievers; furthermore, at least in Mrs. Jackson's classroom, that status is communicated to all classmates. In contrast, in Mrs. Jeffries' classroom, no student has any idea how his or her score on an assessment compares to others. Thus, students can focus on their own progress in the course content and maintain a mastery orientation. From an attributional perspective, the students in Mrs. Jeffries' classroom who do poorly on a quiz might be less likely to make attributions to a lack of ability than would the students in the other classrooms. In contrast, students who do poorly in the other classes know that they did worse than most of the other students and, therefore, would be more likely to make ability attributions, which could lead to further motivational problems.

Although it may seem as though the negative effects of public reporting will be detrimental only to those who have performed poorly on an assessment, this approach may also prove problematic for other students. In particular, students who typically perform at high levels can become very invested in maintaining their reputation as the "smartest" in class. This concern can lead high-performing students to avoid projects or courses they consider "risky" or even to engage in dishonest behaviors (such as cheating or plagiarism) to maintain their reputation. As for the low-achieving students, this concern for their academic status may lead them to devalue success and withdraw effort, or engage in other self-handicapping activities.

Finally, feedback also can be provided electronically to students through a variety of media; this type of feedback can be effective and may be preferred by some students who are uneasy about receiving other types of feedback (e.g., face-to-face feedback; Shroff & Deneen, 2011).

Considering Improvement and Effort

Educators seldom include effort and improvement as components within student assessment systems. Nevertheless, it is possible to base students' grades at least partly on effort and improvement. For example, an English teacher could grade students' writing assignments and then allow them to rewrite their assignments, basing the final grade on the improved version or at least on a score that represents the average scores of the two written products; a math teacher could give students a set of problems to solve and then allow them to redo problems that were calculated incorrectly and to explain why their first attempts were incorrect.

Some educators would argue that allowing students' grades to reflect effort and improvement is unfair to those students who work hard and do well initially on assessments. However, it is important to examine the larger context of education: If the ultimate goal of schooling is student learning, and if some students will maintain their motivation to learn better if they know that they can truly learn and improve from their mistakes, then it may be beneficial to recognize effort and improvement within our assessment systems.

Mac Iver and his colleagues (1993) described the "Incentives for Improvement" program as a model for including the recognition of effort and improvement within a system of assessment. Specifically, in this program, students have three goals: First, they are given the goal of beating baseline test scores by a certain number of points; second, the students earn improvement "points" based on how close they come to achieving their goal; and third, students who improve their performance over time are recognized with awards. Results of an evaluation of this program suggest that it has positive effects on effort, performance, and intrinsic motivation (Mac Iver, 1993).

Providing Feedback and Opportunities for Remediation

The type and quality of feedback provided to students can have a profound impact on their motivation and learning. When feedback concerning performance on an assessment is generic in nature, it may not help students to become better learners. However, when feedback provides students with *specific* information that can help them to identify their own strengths and weaknesses, then the feedback may enhance motivation and learning (Brophy, 1987; Tunstall & Gipps, 1996).

In addition, if feedback indicates ways to improve grades, students may be more likely to be motivated to continue learning the material. Thus, the opportunity to remediate when a bad score is received on an assessment can be very motivational to students. Students may choose to persist with a difficult task if they know their grades might improve if they truly demonstrate learning of the material. One criticism of allowing students to remediate is that students simply might not work hard initially if they know that they can retake a test; however, an easy solution is to allow students to retake exams or redo assignments, knowing that their final grade will be the average of the original score and the new score.

ASSESSMENT AND CHEATING

Cheating

Cheating is a common problem in schools, and one that is often associated with assessments of student learning. Research indicates that academic cheating occurs at all levels, although it is particularly prevalent during the secondary-school and undergraduate college years (E. M. Anderman, Griesinger, & Westerfield, 1998; E. M. Anderman & Murdock, 2007; Cizek, 1999; Davis, Grover, Becker, & McGregor, 1992; McCabe & Trevino, 1997).

Educators are understandably concerned about the prevention of cheating in classrooms. The prevention of academic cheating in classrooms serving young children is much simpler than is prevention in middle-school, high-school, and college classrooms. For example, research indicates that cheating can be deterred in young children by simply telling them that an invisible person is watching them (Piazza, Bering, & Ingram, 2011); however, such simple techniques would probably be greeted by laughter and ridicule by older students.

Students who are intrinsically motivated and mastery oriented are unlikely to engage in cheating behaviors.

FIGURE 4-1   Methods of Academic Cheating

Copying answers from another student
Taking a test for another student
Turning in another student's work (e.g., an older sibling's term paper)
Downloading a paper from the Internet
Plagiarism
Using cheat sheets during exams
Obtaining information via technology (PDA, cell phone, etc.)

Students can cheat in many ways. Some cheating techniques are simple (e.g., quickly glancing at another student's test answers when the teacher is looking the other way); others are highly complex (e.g., hiring an imposter to assume one's identity and take a college entrance examination). In addition, cheating in the 21st century can clearly involve the use of technology, such as cell phones, Bluetooth devices, iPads, and iPods. Some of the various methods that students use to cheat are listed in Figure 4-1.

Recently, motivation researchers have begun to examine the relations of motivational variables to academic cheating. Part of this increased interest by researchers in this topic is because of the aforementioned increased focus on the importance of the results of standardized examinations. Research conducted over the past several years has reported consistent findings regarding predictors of academic cheating.

WHY STUDENTS CHEAT   Just about everyone knows that cheating is "wrong," yet many students continue do it. So why would a student deliberately cheat? Before examining the motivational determinants of cheating, it is important to remember what is at stake for many students when they take exams or complete assignments. Specifically, success on assignments and examinations yields good grades; good grades lead to privileges, such as being on the honor roll or admission to more prestigious colleges and graduate schools. In addition, for some students getting a good grade might earn a parent's praise. In some households, parents might reward their children for getting good grades with gifts or money. It is also important to remember that some students may be punished by their parents if they do not earn good grades.

Stop and Think

Lacey's parents tell her that they will buy her a new car if she scores above the 95th percentile on her college entrance exams. Is Lacey more likely to cheat?

In summary, students experience consequences, both good and bad, for their grades; the desire to obtain or avoid these consequences is what encourages some students to cheat.

Most of the motivation research on academic cheating is framed in goal-orientation theory. Results of several studies that have conceptualized students' goals in terms of mastery and extrinsic goals indicate that the endorsement of extrinsic goals is related to increased reports of academic cheating (E. M. Anderman et al., 1998; Huss et al., 1993; Murdock, Hale, & Weber, 2001; Weiss, Gilbert, Giordano, & Davis, 1993). In addition, some studies indicate that perceptions of a mastery goal structure in the classroom are related to lower levels of cheating (Murdock et al., 2001), whereas perceptions of school-wide or classroom extrinsic or performance goal structures are related to greater reports of cheating (E. M. Anderman et al., 1998). Other results indicate that students who are habitual cheaters are less likely to report cheating when they are in classrooms that are perceived as being mastery-oriented (E. M. Anderman, Cupp, & Lane, 2009).

In a study that followed students from the end of middle school into the first year of high school, Anderman and Midgley (2004) found that cheating in math classes increased for students who moved from middle-school classrooms with a perceived high-mastery goal structure into high-school classrooms with a low-mastery goal structure. Similarly, they found that cheating also increased for students who moved from middle-school classrooms with low-performance goal structures to high-school math classrooms that were perceived as emphasizing high-performance goal structures. Interestingly, cheating *decreased* across the high-school transition for students who were in low-mastery middle-school classrooms but moved into high-mastery high-school math classrooms. These results suggest quite clearly that students' beliefs about what is valued in their classrooms influence the likelihood of cheating.

Overall, the results of studies using a goal theory perspective indicate that increased cheating is associated with performance and extrinsic goals and goal structures, whereas decreased cheating is associated with mastery goals and mastery goal structures. Thus, when students learn in classrooms that emphasize grades, performance, and relative ability, cheating may be more likely to occur. Murdock and E. M. Anderman (2006) have presented a research-based model examining the motivational determinants of academic cheating. They propose that students answer three questions when they decide whether or not to cheat:

1. What is my purpose?
2. Can I do this?
3. What are the costs?

Students' beliefs about the answers to these three questions determine whether or not they will decide to cheat.

In terms of the first question (*What is my purpose?*), when students believe that their purpose or goal is to simply earn a good grade, they will be more likely to cheat than when their goal is to truly learn and master the material being studied. Indeed, if a student's goal is to truly master a technique or body of knowledge, then cheating is probably not going to help that student reach such a goal (E. M. Anderman et al., 1998). Teachers can influence how students answer this question via their classroom policies and via discourse. If a teacher always talks about grades and tests and emphasizes the high-stakes nature of assessments, then students will be more likely to cheat; in contrast, if teachers stress mastery of skills, effort, and learning, students will be less likely to cheat.

The second question (*Can I do this?*) is related to students' self-efficacy beliefs (Bandura, 1986, 1997; Pajares, 1996) and expectancies for success (Eccles, 1983; Wigfield & Eccles, 2000). When students believe that they have the ability to succeed at a task, they will be less likely to cheat than when they harbor doubts about their abilities. Low self-efficacy may lead to failure-related anxiety; to avoid such anxiety, students may resort to cheating.

The final question (*What are the costs?*) refers to both the costs associated with being caught while cheating and the costs associated with what must be given up to do well on an academic task. There are penalties for cheating; some of these penalties are self-inflicted (e.g., a decrease in self-esteem as a result of being caught cheating and realizing that one's competence is in doubt), whereas others are externally imposed (e.g., receiving a failing grade as a punishment for cheating on a test).

However, another way of conceptualizing cheating has to do with the costs of *not* cheating. That is, students may consider the time and effort that can be saved by cheating. Consider the following example:

> *Sam wants to go to a party with his friends on Sunday night. However, he has a big calculus test on Monday morning. Sam decides to make up a tiny cheat sheet and sneak it into the exam so that he can go to the party with his friends.*

In terms of cost, the cost of giving up a night out with his friends is too much for Sam; thus, it is worth it to him to cheat.

Summary

Assessing students' learning and progress is a critical aspect of the educational enterprise and of teachers' roles. Furthermore, providing accurate, informative feedback about students' work has the potential to maintain and even increase their motivation as they develop a sense of growing competence and learn that their effort and improving skills lead to success. All too often, however, the ways in which assessments are used discourage many students, creating anxiety and taking away their confidence in their own abilities. It is very important that teachers educate themselves in the variety of approaches to assessment that are available, as well as in the strengths and weaknesses of each. In addition, teachers need to consider very carefully the potential long-term consequences of the ways in which assessments are designed, administered, and reported. Finally, all teachers need to remember that no single assessment or test is perfect. All assessment results and test scores provide an *estimate* of what students know and can do, and they should be treated as such. We should never make important decisions about students' capabilities or needs based on the results of a single assessment alone, and we should always allow for the possibility that students may prove our test scores wrong.

Questions to Consider When Assessing Your Students' Academic Work

1. Given my specific instructional goals, what type of assessment is most appropriate (e.g., a pencil-and-paper test, an observation, a performance assessment)?

2. Is an appropriate standardized assessment available? If not, how can I increase the reliability and validity of what I design?

3. Can I collect more than one type of assessment data (e.g., by combining a written and a performance task)? How can I give students the opportunity to demonstrate what they know?

4. Is there a good reason to score students in terms of how they compare to each other? If not, how can I design a criterion-referenced assessment?

5. How can I design an assessment that acknowledges students' effort and improvement over time?
6. How can I keep students' anxiety about being evaluated to a reasonable level (e.g., by eliminating unnecessary time constraints, by enhancing their self-efficacy beliefs, and by reducing the amount of emphasis placed on assessment)?
7. How can I maintain students' privacy in reporting their results? How can I ensure that students

and their families know how to interpret the results they receive?
8. How can I give students informative feedback to help them make accurate attributions for their results and maintain their motivation? Is there a way students can remediate a poor score?
9. How can I set up my instructional activities and assessment policies so that I can minimize cheating?

LEARNING ACTIVITY 4.1   Do Competition and Publicizing Scores Motivate Students to Work Harder?

This is a true story about Emma, a fifth-grade student who attends a special program within her school district for gifted education. A talented reader and writer, Emma has always considered math her weakest subject, although her cumulative grade for math in fourth grade was a B. This year, Emma has complained repeatedly about her math homework, claiming not to understand, completing only the minimum work, and sometimes not turning in her work. As a result, although she has received grades of A or B on all her tests, Emma's midsemester grade was a high C.

Soon afterward, Emma skipped her normal after-school academic team activity and came home early. After telling her mother she didn't feel well, Emma burst into tears and sobbed uncontrollably. Emma had received a score of 60 (the lowest in her class) on her most recent math exam. In class, the teacher wrote everyone's score on the board and had the students write them down. The teacher then assigned a homework task for the class to use those

scores to compute the minimum, maximum, mean, median, and modal scores. Emma's mother found her trying to complete her homework assignment and sobbing, "I'm so stupid; I'm so stupid!" Emma had to return to school the following day knowing that everyone's scores would be made public again, when her classmates reviewed their homework. When Emma's mother complained to the classroom teacher about this activity, she was informed that the assignment was the school principal's idea; he believed this task would motivate students to do better.

Based on what you have learned about assessment and student motivation, what would you predict about Emma's future motivational beliefs for math?

Which specific motivational theories help you to understand what is happening with Emma?

If you were Emma's teacher, what might you have said to the principal when he suggested this homework assignment?

LEARNING ACTIVITY 4.2   Prevention of Cheating

Imagine that you are a high school teacher. You teach a subject area that will be covered on the end-of-year state standardized examinations; those examinations are considered "high-stakes" because they are used to evaluate the school's overall effec-

tiveness. At the beginning of the school year, what are some things that you can do in your class to minimize academic cheating during the school year? How would you deal with instances of cheating if they did occur?

References

Agee, J. (2004). Negotiating a teaching identity: An African American teacher's struggle to teach in test-driven contexts. *Teachers College Record, 106,* 747–774.

Ames, C., & Archer, J. (1988). Achievement goals in the classroom: Students' learning strategies and motivation processes. *Journal of Educational Psychology, 80*(3), 260–267.

Anastasi, A. (1988). *Psychological testing.* New York, NY: Macmillan.

Anderman, E. M. (2008). Normal distribution. In E. M. Anderman & L. H. Anderman (Eds.), *Psychology of classroom learning* (pp. 648–650). Farmington Hills, MI: Cengage.

Anderman, E. M., Cupp, P. K., & Lane, D. (2009). Impulsivity and academic cheating. *Journal of Experimental Education, 78*(1), 135–150.

Anderman, E. M., Eccles, J. S., Yoon, K. S., Roeser, R. W., Wigfield, A., & Blumenfeld, P. (2001). Learning to value math and reading: Individual differences and classroom effects. *Contemporary Educational Psychology, 26,* 76–95.

Anderman, E. M., Griessinger, T., & Westerfield, G. (1998). Motivation and cheating during early adolescence. *Journal of Educational Psychology, 90,* 84–93.

Anderman, E. M., & Maehr, M. L. (1994). Motivation and schooling in the middle grades. *Review of Educational Research, 64*(2), 287–309.

Anderman, E. M., & Midgley, C. (2004). Changes in self-reported academic cheating across the transition from middle school to high school. *Contemporary Educational Psychology, 29,* 499–517.

Anderman, E. M., & Murdock, T. B. (2007). *Psychology of academic cheating.* San Diego, CA: Elsevier.

Anderman, E. M., Sinatra, G., & Gray, D. (2012). The challenges of teaching and learning about science in the 21st century: Exploring the abilities and constraints of adolescent learners. *Studies in Science Education, 48*(1), 89–117.

Anderman, E. M., & Wolters, C. (2006). Goals, values, and affect: Influences on student motivation. In P. A. Alexander & P. H. Winne (Eds.), *Handbook of educational psychology* (2nd ed., pp. 369–389). Mahwah, NJ: Erlbaum.

Anderman, E. M., & Young, A. J. (1994). Motivation and strategy use in science: Individual differences and classroom effects. *Journal of Research in Science Teaching, 31*(8), 811–831.

Anderman, L. H., & Anderman, E. M. (2008). Oriented towards mastery: Promoting positive motivational goals for students. In R. Gilman, E. S. Heubner, & M. Furlong (Eds.), *Handbook of positive psychology in the schools.* Mahwah, NJ: Erlbaum.

Anderman, L. H., Kowalski, M., & Dawson, H. (2012, August). *Student perceptions of what teachers care about: Aggravating or assuaging the temptation to cheat.* Poster presented at the biennial International Conference on Motivation, Frankfort, Germany.

Bandura, A. (1986). *Social foundations of thought and action: A social cognitive theory.* Englewood Cliffs, NJ: Prentice Hall.

Bandura, A. (1997). *Self-efficacy: The exercise of control.* New York, NY: Freeman.

Bennett, R. E., & Wadkins, J. (1995). Interactive performance assessment in computer science: The advanced placement computer science (APCS) practice system. *Journal of Educational Computing Research, 12*(4), 363–378.

Bourque, M. L. (2005). Leave no standardized test behind. In R. P. Phelps (Ed.), *Defending standardized testing* (pp. 227–253). Mahwah, NJ: Erlbaum.

Brophy, J. (1987). Teacher influences on student achievement. *American Psychologist, 41*(10), 1069–1077.

Campbell, D. (1993). Teachers' assessment of students: Roles, responsibilities and purpose. In S. L. Wise (Ed.), *Teacher training in measurement and assessment skills* (pp. 97–127). Lincoln, NE: Buros Institute of Mental Measurements.

Carnoy, M., Elmore, R. F., & Siskin, L. S. (2003). *The new accountability: High schools and high-stakes testing.* New York, NY: Routledge Falmer.

Cizek, G. J. (1999). *Cheating on tests: How to do it, detect, it, and prevent it.* Mahwah, NJ: Erlbaum.

Cole, J. S., Bergin, D. A., & Whittaker, T. A. (2008). Predicting student achievement for low stakes tests with effort and task value. *Contemporary Educational Psychology, 33,* 609–624.

Common Core State Standards Initiative. (2012). Available at: http://www.corestandards.org/

Conderman, G., & Pedersen, T. (2010). Preparing students with mild disabilities for taking state and district tests. *Intervention in School and Clinic, 45,* 232–241.

Cronbach, L. J. (1946). Response sets and test validity. *Educational and Psychological Measurement, 6,* 475–494.

Cronbach, L. J. (1950). Further evidence on response sets and test design. *Educational and Psychological Measurement, 10,* 3–31.

Davis, S. F., Grover, C. A., Becker, A. H., & McGregor, L. N. (1992). Academic dishonesty: Prevalence, determinants, techniques, and punishments. *Teaching of Psychology, 19,* 16–20.

Deci, E. L., Koestner, R., & Ryan, R. M. (1999). A meta-analytic review of experiments examining the effects of extrinsic rewards on intrinsic motivation. *Psychological Bulletin, 125*(6), 627–668.

Deci, E. L., Koestner, R., & Ryan, R. M. (2001). Extrinsic rewards and intrinsic motivation in education: Reconsidered once again. *Review of Educational Research, 71*(1), 1–27.

Deci, E. L., & Ryan, R. M. (1987). The support of autonomy and the control of behavior. *Journal of Personality and Social Psychology, 53,* 1024–1037.

Deci, E. L., Spiegel, N. H., Ryan, R. M., Koestner, R., & Kauffman, M. (1982). Effects of performance standards on teaching styles: Behavior of controlling teachers. *Journal of Educational Psychology, 74,* 852–859.

Dooley, C. M., & Assaf, L. C. (2009). Context matters: Two teachers' language arts instruction in this high-stakes era. *Journal of Literacy Research, 41,* 354–391.

Dweck, C. S., & Leggett, E. L. (1988). A social-cognitive approach to motivation and personality. *Psychological Review, 95*(2), 256–273.

Eccles, J. S. (1983). Expectancies, values and academic behaviors. In J. T. Spence (Ed.), *Achievement and achievement motivation* (pp. 75–146). San Francisco, CA: Freeman.

Eccles, J. S. (1999). The development of children ages 6 to 14. *Future of Children, 9*(2), 30–44.

Eccles, J. S., & Wigfield, A. (2002). Motivational beliefs, values, and goals. *Annual Review of Psychology, 53*(1), 109–132.

Elliot, A. J., & Harackiewicz, J. M. (1996). Approach and avoidance achievement goals and intrinsic motivation: A mediational analysis. *Journal of Personality and Social Psychology, 70*(3), 461–475.

Ercikan, K. (2006). Development in assessment of student learning. In P. A. Alexander & P. H. Winne (Eds.), *Handbook of educational psychology* (2nd ed., pp. 929–952). Mahwah, NJ: Erlbaum.

Finn, C., Ryan, T., & Partin, E. (2008). *Ohio value-added primer: A user's guide.* The Thomas B. Fordham Institute. Retrieved October 18, 2009, from http://www.edexcellence.net/issues/index.cfm?topic=1

Graham, S., & Golan, S. (1991). Motivational influences on cognition: Task involvement, ego involvement, and depth of information processing. *Journal of Educational Psychology, 83*(2), 187–194.

Graham, S., & Williams, C. (2009). An attributional approach to motivation in school. In K. R. Wentzel & A. Wigfield (Eds.), *Handbook of motivation at school* (pp. 11–33). New York, NY: Routledge.

Hembree, R. (1998). Correlates, causes, effects, and treatment of test anxiety. *Review of Educational Research, 58,* 47–77.

House, D. J., & Telese, J. A. (2008). Relationships between student and instructional factors and algebra achievement of students in the United States and Japan: An analysis of TIMSS 2003 data. *Educational Research and Evaluation, 14,* 101–112.

Hursh, D. W. (2008). *High-stakes testing and the decline of teaching and learning: The real crisis in education.* Lanham, MD: Rowman & Littlefield.

Huss, M. T., Curnyn, J. P., Roberts, S. L., Davis, S. F., Yandell, L., & Giordano, P. (1993). Hard driven but not dishonest: Cheating and the Type A personality. *Bulletin of the Psychonomic Society, 31,* 429–430.

Krajcik, J. S., Blumenfeld, P., Marx, R. W., & Soloway, E. (2000). Instructional, curricular, and technological supports for inquiry in science classrooms. In J. Minstrell & E. H. van Zee (Eds.), *Inquiring into inquiry learning and teaching in science.* Washington, DC: American Association for the Advancement of Science.

Lane, S. (2004). Validity of high-stakes assessment: Are students engaged in complex thinking? *Educational Measurement: Issues and Practice, 23*(3), 6–14.

Lepper, M. R. (1983). Extrinsic reward and intrinsic motivation: Implications for the classroom. In J. M. Levine & M. C. Wang (Eds.), *Teacher and student perceptions: Implications for learning* (pp. 281–317). Hillsdale, NJ: Erlbaum.

Lepper, M. R., Greene, D., & Nisbett, R. E. (1973). Undermining children's intrinsic interest with extrinsic reward: A test of the "overjustification" hypothesis. *Journal of Personality and Social Psychology, 28,* 129–137.

Longo, C. (2010). Fostering creativity or teaching to the test? Implications of state testing on the delivery of science instruction. *Clearing House: A Journal of Educational Strategies, Issues, and Ideas, 83,* 54–57.

Mac Iver, D. (1993). Effects of improvement-focused student recognition on young adolescents' performance and motivation in the classroom. In M. L. Maehr & P. R. Pintrich (Eds.), *Advances in motivation and achievement: Vol. 8. Motivation and adolescent development* (pp. 191–216). Greenwich, CT: JAI Press.

Madaus, G. F., Russell, M. K., & Higgins, J. (2009). *The paradoxes of high-stakes testing: How they affect students, their parents, teachers, principals, schools, and society.* Charlotte, NC: Information Age Publishing.

Marsh, H. W., Trautwein, U., Lüdtke, O., Köller, O., & Baumert, J. (2005). Academic self-concept, interest, grades, and standardized test scores: Reciprocal effects model of causal ordering. *Child Development, 76,* 397–416.

Marso, R. N., & Pigge, F. L. (1993). Teachers' testing knowledge, skills, and practices. In S. L. Wise (Ed.), *Teacher training in measurement and assessment skills* (pp. 129–185). Lincoln, NE: Buros Institute of Mental Measurements.

McCabe, D. L., & Trevino, L. K. (1997). Individual and contextual influences on academic dishonesty: A multicampus investigation. *Research in Higher Education, 38,* 379–396.

McLoyd, V. C. (1998). Socioeconomic disadvantage and child development. *American Psychologist, 53,* 185–204.

Meece, J. L., Blumenfeld, P. C., & Hoyle, R. H. (1988). Students' goal orientations and cognitive engagement in classroom activities. *Journal of Educational Psychology, 80*(4), 514–523.

Meyer, E. J., Abrami, P. C., Wade, A., & Scherzer, R. (2011). Electronic portfolios in the classroom: Factors impacting teachers' integration of new technologies and new pedagogies. *Technology, Pedagogy, and Education, 20,* 191–207.

Meyer, R. (1997). Value-added indicators of school performance: A primer. *Economics of Education Review, 16*(3), 283–301.

Middleton, M. J., & Midgley, C. (1997). Avoiding the demonstration of lack of ability: An underexplored aspect of goal theory. *Journal of Educational Psychology, 89*(4), 710–718.

Midgley, C. (Ed.). (2002). *Goals, goal structures, and patterns of adaptive learning.* Mahwah, NJ: Erlbaum.

Midgley, C., Anderman, E. M., & Hicks, L. H. (1995). Differences between elementary and middle school teachers and students: A goal theory approach. *Journal of Early Adolescence, 15*(1), 90–113.

Monpas-Huber, J. B. (2010). Explaining teachers' instructional use of state assessment data: A multilevel study of high school teachers in Washington State. *Journal of School Leadership, 20,* 208–237.

Mucherah, W., & Yoder, A. (2008). Motivation for reading and middle school students' performance on standardized testing in reading. *Reading Psychology, 29,* 214–235.

Murdock, T., & Anderman, E. M. (2006). Motivational perspectives on student cheating: Towards an integrated model of academic dishonesty. *Educational Psychologist, 41*(3), 129–145.

Murdock, T. B., Hale, N. M., & Weber, M. J. (2001). Predictors of cheating among early adolescents: Academic and social motivations. *Contemporary Educational Psychology, 26*(1), 96–115.

National Center for Education Statistics (NCES). (2006). *State Profiles.* Retrieved July 26, 2008, from http://nces.ed.gov/nationsreportcard/states

Nichols, S. L., & Berliner, D. C. (2007). *Collateral damage: How high stakes testing corrupts America's schools.* Cambridge, MA: Harvard University Press.

Nie, Y., Lau, S., & Liau, A. K. (2011). Role of academic self-efficacy in moderating the relation between task importance and test anxiety. *Learning and Individual Differences, 21,* 736–741.

Nolen, S. B. (1988). Reasons for studying: Motivational orientations and study strategies. *Cognition and Instruction, 5,* 269–287.

Nolen, S. B., & Haladyna, T. M. (1990). Motivation and studying in high school science. *Journal of Research in Science Teaching, 27,* 115–126.

Oosterhof, A. (2001). *Classroom applications of educational measurement* (3rd ed.). Upper Saddle River, NJ: Merrill Prentice Hall.

Pajares, F. (1996). Self-efficacy beliefs in academic settings. *Review of Educational Research, 66*(4), 543–578.

Phillips, K. R. (2004). *Testing controversy: A rhetoric of educational reform.* Cresskill, NJ: Hampton Press.

Piazza, J., Bering, J. M., & Ingram, G. (2011). Princess Alice is watching you: Children's belief in an invisible person inhibits cheating. *Journal of Experimental Child Psychology, 109*(3), 311–320.

Pintrich, P. R. (2000). Multiple goals, multiple pathways: The role of goal orientation in learning and achievement. *Journal of Educational Psychology, 92*(3), 544–555.

Price, T. A., & Peterson, E. A. (2009). *The myth and reality of No Child Left Behind: Public education and high-stakes assessment: A report issued on behalf of National Louis University, 2008.* Lanham, MD: University Press of America.

Retelsdorf, J., Köller, O., & Möller, J. (2011). On the effects of motivation on reading performance growth in secondary school. *Learning and Instruction, 21,* 550–559.

Ryan, K. E., Ryan, A. M., Arbuthnot, K., & Samuels, M. (2007). Students' motivation for standardized math exams. *Educational Researcher, 36*(1), 5–13.

Ryan, R. M., & Brown, K. W. (2005). Legislating competence: The motivational impact of high stakes testing as an educational reform. In C. Dweck & A. E. Elliot (Eds.), *Handbook of competence* (pp. 354–374). New York, NY: Guilford.

Ryan, R. M., & Deci, E. L. (2009). Promoting self-determined school engagement: Motivation, learning, and well-being. In K. R. Wentzel & A. Wigfield (Eds.), *Handbook of motivation at school* (pp. 172–195). New York, NY: Routledge.

Salvia, J., & Ysseldyke, J. E. (1995). *Assessment* (6th ed.). Boston, MA: Houghton Mifflin.

Schunk, D. H., & Pajares, F. (2009). Self-efficacy theory. In K. R. Wentzel & A. Wigfield (Eds.), *Handbook of motivation at school* (pp. 35–53). New York, NY: Routledge.

Schunk, D., & Zimmerman, B. J. (2006). Competence and control beliefs: Distinguishing the means and the ends. In *Handbook of educational psychology* (2nd ed., pp. 349–367). Mahwah, NJ: Erlbaum.

Scott, M. (2012, February). *Ten states granted flexibility from No Child Left Behind, Michigan hoping for future approval.* Retrieved from http://www.mlive.com/education/index.ssf/2012/02/10_states_granted_flexibility.html

Shroff, R. H., & Deneen, C. (2011). Assessing online textual feedback to support student intrinsic motivation using a collaborative text-based dialogue system: A qualitative study. *International Journal on E-Learning, 10,* 87–104.

Skinner, E. A., Zimmer-Gembeck, M. J., & Connell, J. P. (1998). Individual differences and the development of perceived control. *Monographs of the Society for Research in Child Development, 63,* 2–3.

Tobias, S. (1985). Test anxiety: Interference, defective skills, and cognitive capacity. *Educational Psychologist, 20,* 135–142.

Tunstall, P., & Gipps, C. (1996). Teacher feedback to young children in formative assessment: A typology. *British Educational Research Journal, 22,* 389–404.

U.S. Department of Education. (2003). *Questions and Answers on No Child Left Behind.* (2003). Retrieved July 26, 2008, from http://www.ed.gov/nclb/accountability/schools/accountability.html

Weiner, B. (1986). *An attributional theory of motivation and emotion.* New York, NY: Springer-Verlag.

Weiss, J., Gilbert, K., Giordano, P., & Davis, S. F. (1993). Academic dishonesty: Type A behavior and classroom orientation. *Bulletin of the Psychonomic Society, 31,* 101–102.

Wigfield, A., & Eccles, J. S. (1992). The development of achievement task values: A theoretical analysis. *Developmental Review, 12*(3), 265–310.

Wigfield, A., & Eccles, J. S. (2000). Expectancy-value theory of achievement motivation. *Contemporary Educational Psychology, 25*(1), 68–81.

Wigfield, A., & Eccles, J. S. (2002). The development of competence beliefs, expectancies for success, and achievement values from childhood through adolescence. In A. Wigfield & J. S. Eccles (Eds.), *Development of achievement motivation: A volume in the educational psychology series* (pp. 91–120). San Diego, CA: Academic Press.

Wigfield, A., Tonks, S., & Lutz Klauda, S. (2009). Expectancy-value theory. In K. R. Wentzel & A. Wigfield (Eds.), *Handbook of motivation at school* (pp. 55–75). New York, NY: Routledge.

Wolters, C. A. (2004). Advancing achievement goal theory: Using goal structures and goal orientations to predict students' motivation, cognition, and achievement. *Journal of Educational Psychology, 96,* 236–250.

Zeidner, M. (1998). *Test anxiety: The state of the art.* New York, NY: Plenum.

CHAPTER 5

Grouping Students for Instruction

A stereotypical image of schooling involves a teacher standing in front of a class of approximately 30 students, lecturing, monitoring students' behavior, and asking questions (an instructional approach known as *recitation*). In reality, however, classes today often are not structured in this way. Rather, it is more typical to see students at all levels working in groups on various activities while their teacher moves from group to group, monitoring progress and offering suggestions, while simultaneously maintaining students' engagement and managing students' behavior. The popularity of small-group instruction has been driven by a number of theories of child development and learning, especially sociocultural theories (e.g., Greeno, Collins, & Resnick, 1996; Vygotsky, 1978), which emphasize the importance of students being able to interact with one another while learning. In addition, some have advocated the use of *cooperative learning* approaches, not only to promote students' academic achievement, but also to improve the quality of social relationships between students of different cultural backgrounds (e.g., Shachet, 1997; Slavin & Cooper, 1999) and between children with disabilities and their classmates (Jacques, Wilton, & Townsend, 1998).

Although small-group instruction has become quite commonplace, it is important to recognize that the placement of students into groups for learning activities is not simple. As we shall see, grouping practices are related to motivational variables (Linnenbrink, 2005), and some grouping practices have been critiqued on theoretical grounds (e.g., Kirschner, Sweller, & Clark, 2006). As with many other aspects of teaching, a number of important decisions must be made when forming groups, and these choices have implications for students' learning and motivation. Some examples of these choices include how to organize membership in the groups, how to assign roles within the groups, and decisions about how much autonomy to afford students in the work undertaken by groups. In addition, the inherently social nature of groups also can affect how students learn and interact within various groups (Järvela & Järvenoja, 2011). In this chapter, we explore some of the issues, questions, and research regarding the grouping of students.

Instructional groups can be structured in many different ways.

MAKING DECISIONS ABOUT GROUPING

As teachers plan lessons, the decision about whether and how to group students is a major consideration. For example, a teacher may choose to present information to students in a whole-class format, to have students work individually at their desks, to have students work interactively via technology (e.g., online discussion groups), or to divide the class into smaller groups, either randomly or based on some criteria. First, we need to recognize that no one *participation structure* is going to be appropriate for all lessons or liked equally well by all students. Thus, teachers should think about their instructional objectives for a given lesson and the needs of their students when deciding on the use of small groups. They also should consider balancing different types of participation structures, to provide variety in their instruction, and to match the preferences of different students.

The ways in which teachers arrange groups in classrooms have important effects on motivation. As will be noted throughout this chapter, students' ability levels often play an important role in determining the nature of groups. The placement of an individual student into a particular group can have profound effects on the student's goals, self-efficacy beliefs, attributions, and achievement values. Students' interactions with their peers in the groups, as well as the students' beliefs about their own abilities, can affect a variety of important motivational variables. Thus, teachers must carefully evaluate the effects of group placement on motivation for individual students. The effects of being placed in a mixed-ability group, as will be explained, may be quite different for low- and high-achieving students.

Stop and Think

If a teacher sets up small groups to work on mathematics problems, what are some of the emotions that high- and low-ability students might experience while working in the group? How might that vary if the groups include students of similar math ability, or with differing levels of ability?

Types of Grouping

Grouping can be thought of in many different ways. One important distinction is the difference between *within-class* and *between-class grouping.* This chapter refers mostly to issues of within-class grouping because those decisions are generally under the control of regular classroom teachers. Nevertheless, many of the motivational principles related to within-class grouping also may apply to between-class practices. It should also be noted that both within- and between-class groupings can be used simultaneously. For example, students may be assigned to math classrooms based on prior achievement; however, within those classrooms, teachers may then arrange their students into smaller within-class subgroups.

BETWEEN-CLASS GROUPING   Between-class grouping (sometimes referred to as *tracking*) occurs when classes are formed based on students' similarities on some characteristic, usually on their prior achievement or test results in a particular subject. Between-class grouping is particularly common in middle and high schools. For example, students may be assigned to one of several different types of science classes. Some students might be in regular science, some in honors science, some in Advanced Placement science, and some might be in remedial science. Such between-class grouping based on curricular differences (e.g., advanced science versus regular science) is particularly salient with older students and in high-school settings (Baines, Blatchford, & Kutnick, 2003; Good & Brophy, 1994). Generally, the rationale for between-class grouping is that students with differing levels of prior achievement have different instructional needs that can be more easily met by teachers when classes are as *homogeneous* (i.e., uniform) as possible.

Despite its intuitive appeal to educators and pervasive use in education, research has shown that between-class ability grouping is, for the most part, not related strongly to achievement (Fuligni, Eccles, & Barber, 1995; Gamoran, 1992; Slavin, 1990). Furthermore, when there are benefits in terms of achievement, they are usually for higher-achieving students (e.g., Fuligni et al., 1995). Schofield (2010) reviewed international studies on ability grouping in secondary schools and noted that when students are grouped by ability and different types of curricula are used with the different ability groups, achievement gaps are likely to increase.

In addition, between-class grouping can reinforce existing motivational beliefs. If a student has low self-efficacy toward mathematics and is placed in a low-ability-level math class, the student's efficacy beliefs may be reinforced by being placed with other low achievers. However, as we will see later, effective instruction aimed at the students' ability levels may help to enhance efficacy beliefs by allowing these students to experience successes that they might not experience in a more heterogeneous classroom.

WITHIN-CLASS GROUPING   Within-class grouping occurs when teachers divide students into work groups within classrooms. For example, a fourth-grade teacher might divide a class of 24 students into six groups, with four students in each group. Such groups might be short term, created for just one brief project or assignment, or the groups might be long term, formed with an expectation that students will work together for longer periods (even perhaps for the entire academic year). In addition, long-term groups can vary in terms of how *stable* they are; that is, students may be able to change groups fairly readily as their work unfolds, or they may be required to stay with the same group for many weeks or even a full semester or academic year.

Students can work in groups while using technology.

ABILITY GROUPING

Quite often, teachers arrange groups based on students' differing achievement in various subject areas, with students of similar levels placed together, a practice known as *ability grouping.* Academic tracking (placing students into specific classes based on their abilities) is a clear example of ability grouping, although ability grouping also is used within classrooms. In the lower grades, for example, teachers often form groups for reading instruction within their classrooms. Thus, during reading time, students might be placed in three smaller groups that are working on different types of reading materials. The decision about which group a student should work with usually is based on some combination of standardized and classroom assessment of the individual's achievement and instructional level (see Chapter 4). This approach is often used to help teachers focus their instruction on students' differing needs, with the intention of providing more individualized help for all students. Despite these sound intentions, however, less positive motivational effects of ability grouping may result.

Consider the following example of between-class ability grouping:

> *The fourth-grade teachers at Chestnut Elementary School decide that it will be helpful to divide their students into three distinct groups for math instruction during the coming academic year. Based on students' standardized test scores from the previous academic year, the teachers divide the students into a low-ability math group, a middle-ability math group, and a high-ability math group. The teachers use the 33rd and 66th percentiles (see Chapter 4) on the previous year's standardized test scores as cutoff points for the formation of these three groups. Students report to their regular classrooms for most of the school day, but every day at 11:00 A.M. the students move to different classrooms for math instruction.*

Stop and Think

Based on what you know about assessment, is it reasonable that a student who scored at the 32nd percentile is assigned to the "low-ability" class, whereas one who scored in the 34th percentile on the same test ends up in the "average-ability" class? What other assessment approaches or sources of information might you consider in assigning students to groups? Do you think the students would be aware of the ability differences across the three math groups? If so, how might this awareness affect their sense of self-competence, expectancy for success, and goal orientations? What policies might the teachers consider in terms of allowing students to move between groups during the year?

Several issues should come to mind as you think about this quite typical scenario. First, as stated in Chapter 4, making decisions about students' assignment to different educational experiences based on a single test is not appropriate. Because no single test is perfectly valid and reliable, apparent differences between scores (such as the 32nd and 34th percentile) may be meaningless in real terms and may not reflect true ability differences between students. Furthermore, many different unit topics are included in a subject such as math; students who are very competent with one topic (e.g., computation) may not perform well in another (e.g., geometry).

In general, research indicates that ability grouping in mathematics does not provide remarkable advantages for students. In fact, for low-ability students, there are generally no positive and some negative effects of being placed in ability groups during the middle-school years. When positive effects are found, they are usually limited to higher-ability students (Fuligni et al., 1995). Furthermore, some research suggests that when high-ability students move from mixed-ability math classes into classes designed for gifted students, academic self-concept in math may decline for those students (Preckel, Götz, & Frenzel, 2010). Some research indicates that students who are placed into more advanced courses than are indicated by their test scores often rise to the occasion and learn well in those situations (Mason, Schroeter, Combs, & Washington, 1992). A further concern is that, when groups are assigned based on ability and especially when the groups remain stable over time, teachers must assume that students are aware of the ability differences among those groups. That is, your students will be well aware that one group is considered the "best" at math, whereas another is seen as the poorest. This legitimizing of and emphasis on the differences among students may have consequences for their self-concepts of ability, particularly those students in the "low-ability" groups (Felson & Reed, 1986; Henk & Melnick, 1998). That is, students are likely to see their assigned groups as an indication of their teachers' beliefs about their abilities and expectations for them, and then they are likely to internalize those beliefs for themselves. Although these effects may be minimized when whole-school grouping is used (Trautwein, Lüdtke, Marsh, Köller, & Baumert, 2006), they may be stronger when between-class ability grouping occurs within schools. Students who think their teachers see them as lacking in the ability to do challenging work, or as less competent than their peers, are likely to see themselves in the same way (Weinstein, Marshall, Brattesani, & Middlestadt, 1982; see Chapter 8). As we will discuss later, the social interactions among group members are related in important ways to whether or not students in mathematics (and other domains) benefit or not from being grouped for instruction (Turner & Meyer, 2009).

Not only are students assigned to low-ability groups likely to lower their perceptions of their own ability, but they also are quite likely to receive less challenging, less interesting, and less individualized work to complete. In general, studies comparing the instructional practices that typify high- and low-ability classes have found that students in lower tracks tend to be given more routine activities and fewer higher-order activities, such as problem solving, than are students in higher tracks. In addition, teachers of lower-ability tracks tend to focus less on students' individual interests than do those in higher tracks, and they use more worksheets and fewer hands-on activities (Borko & Eisenhart, 1986; Oakes & Lipton, 1990).

Weinstein and her colleagues have demonstrated that elementary-school children perceive their teachers as treating high- and low-achieving students differently. For example, some of their research suggests that students believe that high achievers get to make more choices and have more freedom than do low achievers. In contrast, lower-achieving students often are perceived as being under greater teacher control and hearing more negative feedback than higher achievers (Weinstein et al., 1982).

Not only are these differences in practices likely to limit the type of learning that lower-tracked students are able to achieve, but they also have implications for long-term motivation. Recall our discussion of *task values* in Chapter 2; faced with routine practice of basic skills, little attention to individual interests, and few challenging, authentic activities, students may be expected to show a decline in their valuing of academic content over time. Similarly, experiencing little autonomy in terms of their own learning is likely to reduce students' intrinsic motivation for what they are learning (see Chapter 7).

It is important to note that the use of within-class ability grouping may be associated with demographics. A recent national study of kindergarten classrooms indicated that the use of within-class ability grouping for reading instruction is greater in schools that serve large proportions of minority students, compared with schools that primarily serve majority students. This observation is related, in part, to the diversity of reading abilities of incoming kindergartners because the use of within-class ability grouping also is higher when there is greater variation in incoming students' abilities. Results from this study also indicate that in schools with high minority student populations, achievement gains are associated with the use of increased within-class ability grouping; thus although within-class ability grouping is practiced more often in these schools, it also is related to improved achievement (Buttaro, Catsambis, Mulkey, & Steelman, 2010).

Although the use of heterogenous (mixed-ability) grouping practices may seem difficult to many teachers, this approach can be used successfully. Boaler and Staples (2008) examined mathematics instruction in three high schools. Of particular interest are the instructional practices of the math teachers at Railside High School. Railside is an urban high school with a diverse population. At Railside, the combined use of a number of motivationally relevant instructional practices led to impressive motivational and academic outcomes for students. In that school, teachers taught mathematics primarily in heterogeneous groups. Students spent 72% of their time working in mixed-ability groups, with teachers circulating the classroom to work with the groups and holding high expectations for all students. Compared to the other two schools, which used more traditional formats for mathematics instruction, the students at Railside reported enjoying mathematics more. The students also achieved at higher levels on exams that were aligned with the curriculum, and achievement gaps between students from different cultural and ethnic groups were lower than in the other schools. Boaler and Staples (2008) attribute some of these positive results to the fact that students at Railside learned to appreciate and respect their peers from different backgrounds. In addition, the teachers at Railside valued many different aspects of mathematical work (not just the execution of specific procedures). For example, they encouraged students to solve problems in creative and diverse ways (i.e., to not just apply the appropriate algorithm). Teachers also worked actively to raise the perceived competence of students, particularly low achievers, by praising their successes and sharing those with the group. Finally, teachers stressed effort over ability as necessary for success.

In summary, the decision about whether to use ability-based groups presents teachers with a dilemma. On one hand, in terms of being able to select materials and activities that closely match students' learning needs, it may be advantageous to teach students of similar achievement levels together. On the other hand, assigning students to ability groups has the potential to affect students' motivation and confidence, especially for those who are placed in the lower-level groups. In addition, if ability groups are used over long periods of time and are quite rigid in membership, they may have an unintended consequence related to students' interpersonal relationships with one another and the overall tone of acceptance in the classroom. In high schools in particular, students often develop friendships with other students who are in similar ability-grouped classes and not with those with diverse levels of achievement (Oakes, Gamoran, & Page, 1992).

Given these concerns, what should a teacher do about using ability-based groups? First, make sure that students' assignments to groups are based on a range of sources of information about their achievement, including your own observations and high-quality assessments. Second, keep group memberships fluid, allowing students to change groups in response to their performance. Third, avoid using ability-based groups for all projects or for long periods of time. For example, an elementary teacher might assign students to ability-based groups for part of her reading program but also include individual and whole-class reading activities. Similarly, a middle-school math teacher might have students work in ability-based groups for 3 days a week, but use whole-class, individualized, or cooperative groups (see the following section) on the other days. The example of Railside High School provides us with an important reminder that instruction in heterogeneous groups can be successful if care is taken to provide assistance to groups, to emphasize the importance of effort, and to work with students to appreciate each other's unique qualities and contributions.

COOPERATIVE LEARNING: A MOTIVATIONAL TECHNIQUE FOR GROUPING STUDENTS

Given the concerns that have been raised about the use of ability-based groups in classes, a number of researchers have advocated *cooperative learning groups* as a more desirable approach. At the beginning of this chapter, we noted that teachers have a number of alternatives to choose among in participation structures, including whole-group instruction, small-group instruction, and individual instruction.

Another way of thinking about instructional grouping is that it can be structured as *competitive, individualistic,* or *cooperative* (Ames, 1984). Instruction is *competitive* when students' chances of being successful are limited by the success of others. For example, in classes where only a limited number of students can receive an A grade, or where students are rewarded for receiving the highest score on an exam, only a small number of students can achieve success. Students must compete with one another to do well, and they have a better chance of being successful if their classmates fail. Instruction is *individualistic* in structure if there is no link between an individual's performance and other students' success. Students' grades and progress are based on their own work and are not affected in any way by the success of their classmates. In contrast, instruction is *cooperative* if students' success is dependent on the success of their classmates. That is, in cooperative learning settings, students have to work together and ensure that their peers experience success to be successful themselves. In many cooperative learning programs, students have to both work together as a group and demonstrate individual learning (e.g., each student has to score at a specific level on a test) to be rewarded (Slavin, 1992).

A large research base supports the effectiveness of cooperative learning approaches for maintaining students' motivation to learn, as well as their achievement and enjoyment of school (e.g., Qin, Johnson, & Johnson, 1995; Slavin, 1990, 1992). The use of cooperative groups may address many of the concerns raised about ability-based groups. Furthermore, cooperative learning techniques are particularly useful in terms of working with ethnically diverse students. As noted by Gay (2000), Latino American, Native American, African American, and Asian American students in particular may benefit from cooperative learning techniques because cooperation is an important characteristic of these groups' learning preferences. Implementing cooperative learning approaches correctly, however, can be quite complex. Sometimes teachers attempt to have students work in cooperative groups and are disappointed with the outcomes. Research indicates that simply placing students into random groups with little or no direction is not likely to lead to enhanced learning or achievement. Instead, cooperative learning can be designed in a number of specific ways to be effective. Before we examine some specific types of cooperative learning techniques, we present some general principles that educators should consider when using cooperative learning.

Designing Effective Cooperative Learning Groups

1. Teachers should have specific goals and outcomes related to the use of cooperative learning groups; cooperative learning should not be used simply for the sake of cooperative learning. A good rationale should be in place for the use of cooperative groups.
2. Teachers should examine the different types of cooperative group structures (e.g., STAD, Jigsaw) and choose the type that is most appropriate for the material that is being covered in class.
3. Teachers should carefully and thoroughly explain the procedures for how the groups will operate. Teachers may even need to practice these procedures, particularly with younger children.
4. Cooperative groups must be monitored. The teacher should not retreat to his or her desk and do paperwork while students are engaged in cooperative group activities. In fact, some recent research suggests that teacher involvement with cooperative groups leads to more effective student outcomes than groups that have minimal interaction with teachers (Law, 2011).
5. Teachers must evaluate the effectiveness of cooperative groups. Did the use of groups lead to better learning? Did all students participate appropriately in the groups? How could the groups be run more effectively next time?

In the following section, we review some of the techniques that Robert Slavin and his colleagues have identified as particularly helpful.

Student Teams–Achievement Divisions

In Student Teams–Achievement Divisions (STAD), students are divided into groups of approximately four or five students per team. The teams should be *heterogeneous* in nature, representing the diversity of gender, ethnicity, and ability in the classroom. After the teacher introduces new academic material, the team members work together as a group to study the material. The group members are told that their goal is to truly understand the material, not just to complete worksheets or memorize answers. Finally, students take individual quizzes on the material. Team scores are calculated based on individual students' improvement on the quizzes.

Slavin (1991) recommends the use of a weekly newsletter to recognize both the teams with the highest scores and the students who improved the most or who received perfect scores. After successful implementation of STAD, teachers tend to see dramatic changes in classroom climate and student cooperation.

Teams–Games–Tournament

The Teams–Games–Tournament method is similar to STAD; however, games are used in place of quizzes. Specifically, weekly tournaments are held in which students of similar ability levels (from different teams) compete against each other. The competitors change each week. Students are not told specifically that they will be competing against members of other teams who are of similar ability levels; they are merely told that the competitions are designed to be fair (Slavin, 1991).

Jigsaw

In contrast to STAD and the Teams–Games–Tournament, the Jigsaw approach does not include a competition between teams of students. In this approach, teachers divide students into six-member teams. The material to be learned (e.g., a chapter of a textbook or an article to be read) is then broken into five sections, with each team member taking responsibility for learning a section (two members usually team up and share one section, so that all six members are included). The teams are then separated, and students assemble into different groups, called "expert groups." In these groups, all students responsible for learning a particular section of the unit come together to discuss their sections in greater depth. Finally, the experts return to their original teams and teach their team members about their sections (Aronson, Blaney, Stephan, Sikes, & Snapp, 1978).

In Jigsaw II, a somewhat modified version of Jigsaw, students work in groups of four to five members. All students read an entire text; however, individual members are assigned specific topics on which they are required to become an expert. Expert groups then meet to discuss these specialized topics. The experts then return to their original groups and teach their teammates about their area of expertise (Slavin, 1991).

Cooperative Learning Techniques Designed for Specific Subject Domains

Several cooperative learning techniques are recommended for use with specific subject areas. These include Team Accelerated Instruction, which is designed for mathematics, and Cooperative Integrated Reading and Composition, which is designed for reading and writing instruction.

TEAM ACCELERATED INSTRUCTION   Team Accelerated Instruction (TAI) is a particularly useful technique for math instruction in heterogeneously grouped classrooms. It is recommended for use in elementary and middle-school classrooms. Students work together in heterogeneous groups of approximately four to five students. Students work on individually selected math lessons, rather than the entire group working on the exact same unit or lesson. Team members are responsible for checking each other's work. Unit tests also are given. The teams receive scores based on both the number of units completed each week and the accuracy of the units. Teams that receive a certain number of points receive a reward (Slavin, 1991).

COOPERATIVE INTEGRATED READING AND COMPOSITION   In Cooperative Integrated Reading and Composition (CIRC), which is designed for use in upper-elementary classrooms, teachers use traditional reading materials and reading groups. Students are then placed into teams consisting of pairs of students from different reading groups. As the classroom teacher works with one group, the other students work in their pairs on various activities (Slavin, 1991). For example, a pair of students might work together on writing a summary paragraph, describing a chapter that was just read.

Benefits of Cooperative Learning

As noted previously, a large body of research examines why cooperative learning techniques are effective. Cooperative learning is not a mysterious black box that magically causes students to excel in school; rather, it affects many basic educational and psychological processes that are related to achievement and motivation. There is some debate among researchers about the importance of competition among groups, as in STAD and the Teams–Games–Tournament approaches. Although some educators favor a completely *cooperative* approach to instruction (i.e., with no competition involved), others have argued that cooperation *within* teams is sufficient. One thing that seems clear is that the positive effects of cooperative learning on academic achievement are related in particular to the use of group rewards (Slavin, 1983). In the following section, we describe some of the positive benefits that can result from the use of cooperative learning approaches.

Cooperation and Help

One potential explanation for some of the beneficial effects of cooperative learning has to do with the amount and type of *help* that students receive when working in cooperative groups. When students work individually, they may be reluctant to ask their teacher or peers for assistance. Indeed, research clearly indicates that students do not always seek help with their academic work when they need assistance (e.g., Newman, 1998; Newman & Schwager, 1992; Turner et al., 2002). In particular, lower-achieving students and those who are concerned about being judged are unlikely to seek help, even when they are aware that they need it (Ryan, Pintrich, & Midgley, 2001). When students work in small cooperative groups, however, they may be more likely to ask their peers or teacher for assistance. Because the group is required to work together to receive their reward, giving and receiving help becomes legitimized and "normal" and, therefore, less threatening for students.

Students may be more likely to seek help when they work in cooperative groups.

There is evidence that the quantity and quality of assistance that students receive may be enhanced when students work in cooperative groups. Webb (1982, 1992) has examined the nature of interactions among students within cooperative groups. She concludes that some of the benefits of cooperative learning may be due to the fact that students receive additional and effective help when they work together cooperatively. In particular, she found that when students received elaborated help (e.g., giving detailed explanations, rather than just telling students the correct answer) while working cooperatively, they were particularly likely to learn more and to perform better on tests. However, when the discourse between teachers and students in the classroom does not encourage active help seeking, then the quality of help that students offer to each other in cooperative groups often is rather low (Webb, Nemer, & Ing, 2006).

Webb (1992) suggested several ways that cooperative groups can be structured to enhance the quantity and quality of help offered by some students to their peers. For example, the use of cooperative reward structures (where rewards for the group are contingent on the learning of all group members) may be particularly effective in getting students to provide elaborated help to each other. If the group will only receive the reward if all students truly demonstrate that each individual member has learned the material, the entire group will benefit by members providing assistance to each other. In addition, Webb argued that the use of the Jigsaw method may also lead to more giving and receiving of high-quality help; recall that in Jigsaw students must become "experts" in a particular area and then must teach their area to the other students. If the expert sees that some of the other group members are having trouble learning about the domain the expert has mastered, the expert may then need to provide more detailed explanations and assistance to group members so that all members can effectively learn the material. Research indicates that when cooperative groups are structured so that students are prompted to ask for and provide help (e.g., with flashcards) and are reminded about how to take turns in conversations, both motivation and achievement can be enhanced (Saleh, Lazonder, & de Jong, 2007).

When students work cooperatively, they often develop more positive relationships with their peers.

Cooperation and Social Relationships in the Classroom

When students work together in cooperative groups, social barriers between them often change. Consider the following example:

> *In Mr. French's geography class, students are placed into cooperative groups for a 6-week period to learn about European geography. The students placed in the group are Tara, Rachel, Seth, and Jeff. Tara is a very attractive, popular student with many friends; Rachel is a very studious, quiet student, who has a small group of friends, but does not socialize with the "popular" crowd; Seth is the type of student who prefers nontraditional interests—he wears all black clothing, has a pierced tongue, and wears a dog collar around his neck; Jeff is a "jock"—he is on the football and baseball teams. The team has to work together to come up with a group presentation about their choice of the top-10 sites to visit in Western Europe. The group has to prepare a PowerPoint presentation for the class and is also required to come up with actual travel plans so that individuals who want to actually visit the 10 sites can easily travel from place to place.*

Research on social relationships during adolescence suggests that these four students probably would not socialize with each other or be friends either inside or outside of school (Brown, 2004; Wentzel & Asher, 1995). Research on cooperative learning, however, suggests that if those techniques are used appropriately and effectively by the classroom teacher, these four students can work together and actually may come to respect and like each other more after having engaged in the task. It is possible that these students all will acquire a better understanding of their peers' motives and behaviors. These effects have been shown, not only in terms of improving relationships and acceptance of students with differing interests and values, but also in the social acceptance of students with disabilities (Jacques et al., 1998; Madden & Slavin, 1983) and across cultural differences (e.g., Slavin & Cooper, 1999). In addition, some research suggests that when cooperative learning techniques are used in the classroom, students are more likely to feel that their classmates want them to do well academically (e.g., Madden & Slavin, 1983).

Some Cautions Regarding Cooperative Learning

Although cooperative learning approaches have been found to be very effective, some caution is warranted before assuming that it will always be effective. Too often, teachers assume that just assigning students to mixed-ability groups and telling them to work together will bring great benefits. Slavin (1992) noted that researchers and educators who use cooperative learning must carefully examine the types of outcomes that they want to affect.

Cautions for Cooperative Learning

Good and Brophy (1994) have reviewed the research on cooperative learning and recommend the use of cooperative learning, with some qualifications. They suggest that cooperative learning can be highly effective, but they offer several important cautions:

1. Cooperative learning should not completely replace traditional whole-class instruction; cooperative learning has its place, but so do traditional full-class instruction and other participation structures.
2. Cooperative learning may be more effective in some classes (e.g., middle school) than in other classes (e.g., elementary school or high school). Young children, in particular, may not have sufficiently mature social and self-regulatory skills to function in cooperative learning groups.
3. Teachers need to "teach" their students how to successfully use cooperative learning; educators should not simply assume that students will be able to successfully implement these techniques without practice. Cooperative learning involves specific techniques and roles, and students need to learn, practice, and master these techniques, just as they need to practice other techniques.
4. Cooperative learning may be effective in the long term for students who are socially oriented but may be less effective for other students (e.g., those who prefer to work alone or those who assume leadership roles within their groups). Some students like to work with others and interact well with their peers, whereas others become distracted when working with others and may prefer to work by themselves at times.
5. Cooperative learning may be more suited to some subject areas or specific unit topics than others. Teachers should consider whether specific tasks are suitable for cooperative learning and may need to alter and adjust tasks to make them more appropriate. Some tasks (e.g., the discussion of a chapter from a novel) may be easily adapted to cooperative learning, whereas others (e.g., memorizing the capitals of states or countries) may be less well suited to cooperative learning techniques.
6. Teachers who use cooperative learning should emphasize cooperation, while de-emphasizing competition. Some aspects of cooperative learning (e.g., the use of rewards) may induce unnecessary competition into group learning situations; such competition may undermine the potential benefits of cooperative learning.

ALTERNATIVE METHODS OF FORMING SMALL GROUPS

Ability groups are assigned based on students' prior achievement or estimated potential in a specific subject area. In contrast, cooperative learning groups are assigned in such a way to deliberately mix students of different ability levels and backgrounds. Additional methods are available to teachers who wish to form small groups for class activities. These alternative approaches are more likely to be used for temporary or informal groupings (e.g., for the duration of one specific project or activity) than over a long period of time. In using such groups, one of the most important concerns for the teacher is how the groups should be formed. Should the teacher specify the members of the group? Should students be permitted to work with whomever they choose? These decisions have a number of important motivational ramifications.

The following sections describe several alternative methods for the formation of groups, most of which have advantages and disadvantages. However, these suggestions may help you to think of creative ways to form small groups without emphasizing ability differences.

Allow Students to Choose Their Own Groups

Sometimes teachers might consider allowing students to choose with whom they will work in groups. Clearly there are numerous considerations, including how student choice will affect learning, motivation, and behavior. Research with college students suggests that when students are allowed to choose their own groups, intrinsic motivation and a sense of community are higher than when groups are formed by the instructor (Ciani, Summers, Easter, & Sheldon, 2008). When allowing students to form their own groups, teachers should specify in advance the minimum and maximum size of group that is acceptable. The group size should match the complexity and nature of the project in question and be reasonably uniform across groups. When students are afforded the opportunity to choose group members, they are likely to experience a sense of autonomy. This may have a positive impact on their intrinsic motivation; indeed, research indicates that the perception of choice is related to enhanced intrinsic motivation in students (see Chapter 7; Deci, Nezlek, & Sheinman, 1981). Even when students are only allowed to make seemingly minor choices, their intrinsic motivation may be enhanced (Swann & Pittman, 1977).

However, caution must be taken when allowing students to form their own groups. Students are likely to choose to work with their friends in small groups (Mitchell, Reilly, Bramwell, Solnosky, & Lilly, 2004). A few students often will be left out and not chosen to be in a group. This experience can be very embarrassing for those students and can draw attention to their social isolation within the class. Teachers must be aware of this possibility and take steps to prevent it from happening. One way to accomplish this would be to assign each student to a partner, and then to have each group of partners form a group with other partners. In addition, teachers should be aware that groups based on students' own preferences may have a greater tendency to get *off task* as students socialize with their friends. Therefore, greater teacher monitoring of group interactions and progress may be necessary with this approach.

Form Groups Based on Students' Interests

Much research indicates that students' motivation and achievement are improved when they are allowed to explore topics that are of personal interest (Hidi, 1990; Schraw, Flowerday, & Lehman, 2001) and are considered valuable (Eccles, 1983; Wigfield & Eccles, 2000). In addition, allowing students to enter groups based on their own personal interests will enhance autonomy because students will be making their own decisions about how they will learn (Deci et al., 1981).

Consider the following example:

> *Mrs. Hartley is a third-grade teacher. She wants to be able to work with small groups of students during reading instruction for the next several weeks. She decides to gather some reading materials related to transportation. She then tells her students that they will be reading about transportation for the next few weeks and that they will have the opportunity to choose the type of transportation that they would like to learn about. She announces that students should choose the type of transportation that is most interesting to them, from the following choices:*

> 1. *Cars*
> 2. *Buses*
> 3. *Trains*
> 4. *Airplanes*
> 5. *Ships*

> *After the students make their choices, Mrs. Hartley forms reading groups based on those choices. For example, the students in Group 1 spend the next few weeks reading about the use of cars for transportation. They use a variety of materials at different reading levels, and Mrs. Hartley can work with the students in this small group, more easily attending to individual needs.*

This type of grouping does not emphasize ability differences. Students are likely to be more motivated to read because they will be reading about topics in which they are truly interested. Thus, students of mixed-ability levels are likely to enter into groups together. In addition, after several weeks the teacher can ask students to switch to another topic, or the teacher can provide a new series of topics for the next unit of reading instruction.

Random Assignment to Groups

A final approach that can be effective in some situations is to assign students to groups randomly. This can be achieved quite easily in the classroom, for example, by taking students alphabetically from the class roster (the first four students form a group, the second four another, and so on). Another technique is to randomly assign numbers to students (e.g., if you want five groups, assign the numbers 1 through 5) and have them work with others who were assigned the same number (all 1s together, and so on). A third approach is to choose some superficial characteristic to form groups—for example, everyone wearing blue is in one group. In this instance, teachers need to quickly survey the class, to ensure groups are of reasonably equal size (assuming this is desirable for your activity). Random assignment has the advantage of forming groups that combine not only different ability levels but also require students to work with classmates with whom they do not usually interact. In addition, because the formation of the groups is so visibly random, students will not make any assumptions about your intentions or expectations in assigning them. Thus, the problems inherent in ability grouping in terms of affecting students' sense of competence or goal orientations are avoided.

Summary

In this chapter, we examined various characteristics of academic grouping. Clearly, small-group instruction is becoming more common at all levels of education. Indeed, many educators today acknowledge that having students work in groups during school prepares them for the workplace, where they will likely need to collaborate with others. Nevertheless, the research on academic grouping clearly indicates that some types of group arrangements are more effective than others. It is also important to realize that although grouping of students may be desirable for the teacher, some students may not enjoy group learning. For example, students with learning disabilities sometimes indicate that they do not enjoy working in groups (Elbaum, Moody, & Schumm, 1999).

Whereas the short-term benefits of grouping may be enticing to educators, we must also consider the long-term effects of our grouping practices. In particular, educators must consider the long-term effects of ability grouping on motivation. If a student is consistently placed in a low-ability group, the student may develop motivational beliefs that are not conducive to continued involvement with that subject area; thus, a student who is always in the low-ability math group may form persistent negative self-perceptions of ability as a math student (e.g., low self-efficacy for mathematics) and a sense that "Math is not for me." Such students are probably less likely to opt for advanced math classes or to consider entering careers that involve extensive use of mathematical skills.

During the elementary years in particular, students may be at different levels of cognitive development. Some students may be placed into a lower-ability group simply because they are somewhat behind their peers in terms of cognitive development. Although such students probably will catch up to their peers, their initial placement into low-ability academic groups may have pervasive long-term negative effects on their motivation. Placement into low-ability groups may create low self-perceptions of ability that persist into adolescence and even adulthood.

Grouping of students is an important and powerful educational tool. The decisions that teachers make regarding groups should not be taken lightly. The short-term and long-term effects of grouping practices on learning and motivation are significant and will continue to be salient issues as grouping practices become more accepted and expected in classrooms.

Questions to Consider When Assigning Your Students to Groups

1. What are my instructional objectives for this lesson or unit? What am I trying to achieve, and is the use of a small-group approach the most appropriate in this case?
2. Are my students developmentally ready to work in a group? Have I given them guidelines and provided practice in working together effectively?
3. Is there a good reason to assign students to groups based on their current achievement? How *reliable* and *valid* are the data on which I am basing those decisions? If I do decide to use *ability groups,* how can I minimize the potential negative effects of this approach on students' *self-perceptions?*
4. If groups are not based on ability, how will I assign students to groups? Is it important for groups to be balanced in terms of gender, age, and ethnicity? Should I consider students' *interests* or personal preferences in forming groups?
5. How can I adapt the task to make sure that all group members will be able to participate and make a meaningful contribution to the group's work? How can I encourage students to seek

help from each other and provide help to each other in appropriate ways?

6. How long are students going to stay in these groups? How easily can students move from one group to another and under what circumstances?

7. Have I provided instruction to the students about how to interact effectively in groups? Am I assisting them in understanding how to take turns and how to both ask for help and provide help to others?

References

Ames, C. (1984). Competitive, cooperative, and individualistic goal structures: A cognitive-motivational analysis. In R. Ames & C. Ames (Eds.), *Research on motivation in education* (Vol. 1, pp. 177–207). New York, NY: Academic Press.

Aronson, E., Blaney, N., Stephan, C., Sikes, J., & Snapp, M. (1978). *The Jigsaw classroom*. Beverly Hills, CA: Sage.

Baines, E., Blatchford, P., & Kutnick, P. (2003). Changes in grouping practices over primary and secondary school. *International Journal of Educational Research, 39,* 9–34.

Boaler, J., & Staples, M. (2008). Creating mathematical futures through an equitable teaching approach: The case of Railside school. *Teachers College Record, 110,* 608–645.

Borko, H., & Eisenhart, M. (1986). Students' conceptions of reading and their reading experiences in school. *The Elementary School Journal, 86,* 589–611.

Brown, B. (2004). Adolescents' relationships with peers. In R. Lerner & L. Steinberg (Eds.), *Handbook of adolescent psychology*. New York, NY: Wiley.

Buttaro, A., Catsambis, S., Mulkey, L., & Steelman, L.C. (2010). An organizational perspective on the origins of instructional segregation: School composition and use of within-class ability grouping in American kindergartens. *Teachers College Record, 112,* 1300–1377.

Ciani, K. D., Summers, J. J., Easter, M. A., & Sheldon, K. M. (2008). Collaborative learning and positive experiences: Does letting students choose their own groups matter? *Educational Psychology, 28,* 627–641.

Deci, E., Nezlek, J., & Sheinman, L. (1981). Characteristics of the rewarder and intrinsic motivation of the rewardee. *Journal of Personality and Social Psychology, 40,* 1–10.

Eccles, J. S. (1983). Expectancies, values and academic behaviors. In J. T. Spence (Ed.), *Achievement and achievement motivation* (pp. 75–146). San Francisco, CA: Freeman.

Elbaum, B., Moody, S. W., & Schumm, J. S. (1999). Mixed ability grouping for reading: What students think. *Learning Disabilities Research and Practice, 14,* 61–66.

Felson, R. B., & Reed, M. D. (1986). Reference groups and self-appraisals of academic ability and performance. *Social Psychology Quarterly, 49,* 103–109.

Fuligni, A. J., Eccles, J. S., & Barber, B. L. (1995). The long-term effects of seventh-grade ability grouping in mathematics. *Journal of Early Adolescence, 15*(1), 58–89.

Gamoran, A. (1992). Is ability grouping equitable? *Educational Leadership, 50*(2), 11–17.

Gay, G. (2000). *Culturally responsive teaching: Theory, research, and practice*. New York, NY: Teachers College Press.

Good, T., & Brophy, J. (1994). *Looking in classrooms* (6th ed.). New York, NY: Harper Collins.

Greeno, J., Collins, A., & Resnick, L. (1996). Cognition and learning. In D. Berliner & R. Calfee (Eds.), *Handbook of educational psychology* (pp. 15–46). New York, NY: Macmillan.

Henk, W., & Melnick, S. A. (1998). Upper elementary-aged children's reported perceptions about good readers: A self-efficacy influenced update in transitional literacy contexts. *Reading Research and Instruction, 38,* 57–80.

Hidi, S. (1990). Interest and its contribution as a mental resource for learning. *Review of Educational Research, 60,* 549–571.

Jacques, N., Wilton, K., & Townsend, M. (1998). Cooperative learning and social acceptance of children with mild intellectual disability. *Journal of Intellectual Disability Research, 42,* 29–36.

Järvela, S., & Järvenoja, H. (2011). Socially constructed self-regulated learning and motivation regulation in collaborative learning groups. *Teachers College Record, 113,* 350–374.

Kirschner, P. A., Sweller, J., & Clark, R. E. (2006). Why minimal guidance during instruction does not work: An analysis of the failure of constructivist, discovery, problem-based, experiential, and inquiry-based teaching. *Educational Psychologist, 41*, 75–86.

Law, Y. K. (2011). The effects of cooperative learning on enhancing Hong Kong fifth graders' achievement goals, autonomous motivation and reading proficiency. *Journal of Research in Reading, 34*, 402–425.

Linnenbrink, E. A. (2005). The dilemma of performance-approach goals: The use of multiple goal contexts to promote students' motivation and learning. *Journal of Educational Psychology, 97*, 197–213.

Madden, N. A., & Slavin, R. E. (1983). Effects of cooperative learning on the social acceptance of mainstreamed academically handicapped students. *Journal of Special Education, 17*, 171–182.

Mason, D. A., Schroeter, D. D., Combs, R. K., & Washington, K. (1992). Assigning average-achieving eighth graders to advanced mathematics classes in an urban junior high school. *Elementary School Journal, 92*, 587–599.

Mitchell, S. N., Reilly, R., Bramwell, F. G., Solnosky, A., & Lilly, F. (2004). Friendship and choosing groupmates: Preferences for teacher-selected vs. student-selected groupings in high school science classes. *Journal of Instructional Psychology, 31*, 20–32.

Newman, R. S. (1998). Students' help-seeking during problem solving: Influences of personal and contextual goals. *Journal of Educational Psychology, 90*, 644–658.

Newman, R. S., & Schwager, M. T. (1992). Student perceptions and academic help-seeking. In D. H. Schunk & J. L. Meece (Eds.), *Student perceptions in the classroom* (pp. 123–146). Hillsdale, NJ: Erlbaum.

Oakes, J., Gamoran, A., & Page, R. (1992). Curriculum differentiation: Opportunities, outcomes, and meanings. In P. Jackson (Ed.), *Handbook of research on curriculum* (pp. 570–608). New York, NY: Macmillan.

Oakes, J., & Lipton, M. (1990). Tracking and ability grouping: A structural barrier to access and achievement. In J. I. Goodlad & P. Keating (Eds.), *Access to knowledge: An agenda for our nation's schools* (pp. 187–204). New York, NY: College Entrance Examination Board.

Preckel, F., Götz, T., & Frenzel, A. (2010). Ability grouping of gifted students: Effects on academic self-concept and boredom. *British Journal of Educational Psychology, 80*, 451–472.

Qin, Z., Johnson, D. W., & Johnson, R. T. (1995). Cooperative versus competitive efforts and problem solving. *Review of Educational Research, 65*, 129–143.

Ryan, A. M., Pintrich, P. R., & Midgley, C. (2001). Avoiding seeking help in the classroom: Who and why? *Educational Psychology Review, 13*, 93–114.

Saleh, M., Lazonder, A. W., & de Jong, T. (2007). Structuring collaboration in mixed-ability groups to promote verbal interaction, learning, and motivation of average-ability students. *Contemporary Educational Psychology, 32*, 314–331.

Schofield, J. W. (2010). International evidence on ability grouping with curriculum differentiation and the achievement gap in secondary schools. *Teachers College Record, 112*, 1492–1528.

Schraw, G., Flowerday, T., & Lehman, S. (2001). Increasing situational interest in the classroom. *Educational Psychology Review, 13*(3), 211–224.

Shachet, H. (1997). Effects of cooperative learning on intergroup interaction in the heterogeneous classroom. *Megamot, 38*, 367–382.

Slavin, R. E. (Ed.). (1983). *Cooperative learning.* New York, NY: Longman.

Slavin, R. E. (1990). Ability grouping and student achievement in secondary schools. *Review of Educational Research, 60*, 417–499.

Slavin, R. E. (1991). *Student team learning: A practical guide to cooperative learning.* Washington, DC: National Education Association.

Slavin, R. E. (1992). When and why does cooperative learning increase achievement? Theoretical and empirical perspectives. In R. Hertz-Lazarowitz & N. Miller (Eds.), *Interaction in cooperative groups: The theoretical anatomy of group learning* (pp. 145–173). Cambridge, England: Cambridge University Press.

Slavin, R. E., & Cooper, R. (1999). Improving intergroup relations: Lessons learned from cooperative learning programs. *Journal of Social Issues, 55*, 647–663.

Swann, W., & Pittman, T. (1977). Initiating play activity of children: The moderating influence of verbal cues on intrinsic motivation. *Child Development, 48*, 1128–1132.

Trautwein, U., Lüdtke, O., Marsh, H. W., Köller, O., & Baumert, J. (2006). Tracking, grading, and student motivation: Using group composition and status to predict self-concept and interest in ninth-grade mathematics. *Journal of Educational Psychology, 98*(4), 788–806.

Turner, J. C., & Meyer, D. K. (2009). Understanding motivation in mathematics. In K. R. Wentzel & A. Wigfield (Eds.), *Handbook of motivation at school* (pp. 527–552). New York, NY: Routledge.

Turner, J. C., Midgley, C., Meyer, D. K., Gheen, M. H., Anderman, E. M., Kang, Y., & Patrick, H. (2002). The classroom environment and students' reports of avoidance strategies in mathematics: A multimethod study. *Journal of Educational Psychology, 94*(1), 88–106.

Vygotsky, L. S. (1978). *Mind in society: The development of higher psychological processes.* Cambridge, MA: Harvard University Press.

Webb, N. M. (1982). Student interaction and learning in small groups. *Review of Educational Research, 52,* 421–445.

Webb, N. M. (1992). Testing a theoretical model of student interaction and learning in small groups. In R. Hertz-Lazarowitz & N. Miller (Eds.), *Interaction in cooperative groups: The theoretical anatomy of group learning* (pp. 102–119). Cambridge, England: Cambridge University Press.

Webb, N. M., Nemer, K. M., & Ing, M. (2006). Small-group reflections: Parallels between teacher discourse and student behavior in peer-directed groups. *The Journal of the Learning Sciences, 15*(1), 63–119.

Weinstein, R. S., Marshall, H., Brattesani, K., & Middlestadt, S. (1982). Student perceptions of differential teacher treatment in open and traditional classrooms. *Journal of Educational Psychology, 74,* 678–692.

Wentzel, K. R., & Asher, S. R. (1995). The academic lives of neglected, rejected, popular, and controversial children. *Child Development, 66*(3), 754–763.

Wigfield, A., & Eccles, J. S. (2000). Expectancy–value theory of achievement motivation. *Contemporary Educational Psychology, 25*(1), 68–81.

CHAPTER 6

Working with Parents

Teachers interact with parents often. Whether it is a formal meeting about student progress or a brief conversation at the supermarket, teachers' interactions with parents are very important and can influence student motivation in many ways.

More specifically, parents have a profound influence on their children's motivation and achievement (e.g., Dornbusch & Ritter, 1988; Hoover-Dempsey & Sandler, 1997; Pomerantz & Moorman, 2010; Zhang, Haddad, Torres, & Cheng, 2011), and teachers' interactions with parents can both benefit and harm those influences. In this chapter, we examine the relations between parental attitudes and behaviors and student motivation. In addition, we examine some ways in which teachers can work with parents to improve the motivation and achievement of students.

Stop and Think

Think about your own educational experiences and about your own parents' or guardians' interactions with your teachers. When did your parents interact with teachers? Were these interactions positive or negative? How did you, as a student, feel about these interactions?

WHY IT IS IMPORTANT TO KNOW ABOUT WORKING WITH PARENTS

Students spend a great deal of time at school; however, they also interact with other individuals, across other contexts. These contexts include the home, the neighborhood, friends' homes, extracurricular activities, and a variety of other settings. Children and adolescents will experience extensive interactions with their parents across most of these contexts.

Research clearly indicates that student achievement is related to both academic and social variables (Wentzel & Wigfield, 1998). Obviously, children are greatly influenced by their parents. We know that parents' values, attitudes, behaviors, cultures, and religious beliefs all affect students in a variety of ways. The family as a whole represents an extremely important context for children's overall development (Pianta, 1999).

Parents' behaviors and attitudes are related to motivation in many ways, including the socialization of gender-related beliefs and behaviors (Eccles, Jacobs, & Harold, 1990). In addition, research also clearly indicates that parent involvement in their children's education is related to positive outcomes for both children and adolescents (e.g., Epstein, 1983).

How Parents Influence Children's Success in School

Parents affect children's and adolescents' performance in school in many ways. Laurence Steinberg and his colleagues describe three distinct ways in which parents influence their children's successes and failures, specifically in the realm of education (Steinberg, 1996):

1. *Parents communicate specific messages to children and adolescents about school and learning.* Parents communicate attitudes and values for education both intentionally and unintentionally, and both verbally and nonverbally. Whereas most parents probably believe that they are communicating important messages to children about the value of education, parents' actions may sometimes undermine this message. For example, a parent might state to a child that it is very important to do homework every night; however, the parent may do little to monitor whether or not homework is completed.

2. *Parents influence children's and adolescents' academic achievement via their own behaviors.* Parents clearly demonstrate their commitment to education by how they spend their own time. Parents who regularly attend school events, ask questions about school, and volunteer at school are communicating to their children that schooling is a worthwhile activity. In contrast, parents who never visit the school, do not spend time engaging in school-related activities, or do not monitor their child's progress may communicate to students that education is a requirement but not something to be valued.

3. *Parents influence the academic achievement of children and adolescents via the atmosphere in the home.* The styles of parenting used in various households are related to developmental and educational outcomes. We review these styles later in this chapter. Nevertheless, it is often clear to observers that some households are continuously conducive to enhancing students' education, whereas others are not. When parents spend time helping their children with homework assignments, a message is sent to children indicating that academics are important. In fact, recent research suggests that both students and teachers believe that parental involvement with academics in the home is more important than direct involvement in actual schools (DePlanty, Coulter-Kern, & Duchane, 2007).

In recent years, research has examined more specifically the ways in which academic motivation is affected by interactions with parents. As we will show, students' beliefs about their own abilities, their attributions for successes and failures, and their values for different subject areas and topics are all related to their parents' attitudes and behaviors.

Interacting with Parents

As a teacher, you will interact with parents in many ways. Consider the following examples:

- Formal teacher/parent conferences
- Individualized Educational Plan (IEP) meetings
- Meetings with school administrators about behavioral problems
- Joint consultations with special educators
- Extracurricular activities
- Phone calls to parents about student progress or behavior
- PTA meetings
- School social events
- Informal conversations before school or after dismissal at the end of the day
- E-mail communications
- School newsletters
- Conversations via electronic media (e.g., Skype)
- An unplanned meeting in the community (e.g., at the mall or at the supermarket)

Communicating with Parents

It is important to remember that communication with parents should be bidirectional. Whereas teachers can and should communicate important information to parents, it is also important for parents to communicate with teachers. Schools have a role in making it easier and more comfortable for parents to approach their children's teachers. As educators, we need to examine ways of enhancing communications between parents and teachers.

Whether or not you have formally planned a meeting, you *will* interact with your students' parents. Therefore, it is extremely important for teachers to understand the ways in which parents can and do have an impact on student motivation and achievement. It is also important that you be aware of any family situations that may make attendance and learning difficult for some students. As a teacher, you can communicate some very important information to parents, which might assist them as they work with their children on school-related assignments.

In addition, parents need to feel comfortable communicating with teachers. The most effective relationships between parents and teachers will be partnerships with communication emanating from both parties: teachers communicating with parents, and parents communicating with teachers.

PARENTING AND ITS EFFECTS ON STUDENTS

The effects of parents on children and adolescents depend on many different factors. The scope of parental effects could be the topic of an entire book. In this chapter, we focus on aspects of parenting that most directly relate to education and to student motivation.

The ways in which parents affect students may be considered from different perspectives. Some of the most powerful work in this area has been conducted in the field of developmental psychology. Whereas researchers often did not set out to examine the relations of parenting to academic motivation, many interesting and important findings have emerged from this body of research.

Parenting Styles

Consider the following situations. Think about what is different about each child's experiences with his or her parents:

> *Jeffrey's parents set firm and strict rules for him. Jeffery knows exactly what he is and is not allowed to do. His parents are warm and responsive, and they are always attending activities at Jeffrey's school. They allow Jeffrey to make many important decisions, but they also set clear boundaries for him.*
>
> *Cynthia's parents are very strict. They like to know about everything that she is doing, all the time. Cynthia rarely gets to make choices about how she will spend her time. Her parents are somewhat distant—they are not very warm and comforting to her.*
>
> *Joe and his parents have a close, affable relationship. For the most part, Joe's parents allow him to do whatever he wants. The household has few rules, and Joe can more or less come and go as he pleases.*
>
> *Michelle's parents do not demonstrate much warmth or caring, and they do not have many rules or regulations for her. Michelle does not really have a good relationship with either of her parents. Although they live in the same house, Michelle's parents are often not home, and when they are present, they express little interest in Michelle's academic or social life.*

The households described in these examples vary. In some cases, the parents have warm, openly affectionate relationships with their children, whereas in others the relationship is more distant; in some cases, parents are very clearly the authorities in the home, whereas other parents afford their children numerous opportunities to make important decisions. These differing experiences have important effects on the social, emotional, and academic development of children and adolescents. In particular, students' academic motivation can be greatly affected by the parenting style that is prominent in the home.

Diana Baumrind has examined patterns of parent–child relationships. She has developed a research-based typology that describes different patterns that occur in various households. As a classroom teacher, you may become aware that your students experience different types of parenting styles. This knowledge may be particularly useful to you as you interact with parents concerning student performance in your class.

The following describes the four types of parenting styles, which are reviewed in much greater detail elsewhere (Baumrind, 1967, 1971, 1973, 1991; Dornbusch, Ritter, Liederman, Roberts, & Fraleigh, 1987; Steinberg, 1996, 2005; Steinberg, Lamborn, Darling, Mounts, & Dornbusch, 1994):

1. *Authoritative:* These parents set strict limits and high expectations for their children's behavior, but also allow their children some independence and autonomy. Authoritative parents are warm and are involved with their children's lives. Children of authoritative parents often exhibit high levels of academic achievement and positive psychological outcomes. These students tend to attribute their academic successes to effort. The benefits of this parenting style are evident across a variety of cultures.

2. *Authoritarian:* These parents also set strict limits and have high expectations for their children but, in contrast to authoritative parents, they generally do not encourage independence and autonomy; instead, they tend to be controlling. Authoritarian parents display less warmth and expect their children to do as they are told and not to question parental authority or decisions. These students generally do not do quite as well in school as students from authoritative households.

3. *Permissive:* These parents are quite warm and loving with their children, but they do not set clear rules or boundaries. Discipline and expectations in these households often are inconsistent. These students are particularly prone to misbehavior during adolescence.

4. *Rejecting/Neglecting:* These parents stand in contrast to the other three categories in that rejecting/neglecting parents are quite uninvolved with their children. Rejecting/neglecting parents are not warm with their children, and they do not exert much control over their children's actions. Children raised under this parenting style often experience serious social and academic problems later in life.

Stop and Think

What kind of parenting style did your parents or guardians use with you? What effects did this have on you? Do you agree with Baumrind's contentions about parenting?

Research clearly indicates that, overall, authoritative parenting is the most adaptive for children and adolescents. Because parenting practices are influenced by culture and values, the prevalence of each style across different cultural groups varies. Steinberg (2005) noted that authoritative parenting is observed less often in African American, Asian American, and Hispanic American households than in Caucasian households; nevertheless, the positive effects of authoritative parenting on students are equivalent across ethnic and cultural groups. Research also indicates that authoritative parenting continues to have beneficial effects as students move into college as well (Turner, Chandler, & Heffer, 2009). Although the authoritarian parenting style is somewhat more common in ethnic minority households, its negative effects may be more pervasive for White children and adolescents than for minority students (Chao, 1994; Dornbusch et al., 1987; Steinberg, 2005). Authoritarian parenting may be beneficial to some adolescents who live in dangerous neighborhoods; in addition, phenomena such as strictness, autonomy, and control may carry different meanings within different ethnic and cultural groups (Steinberg, 2005).

Socioeconomic and Cultural Influences on Parenting

Parents' socioeconomic status is related to student achievement and learning (Blau & Duncan, 1967). When families live in economically disadvantaged environments, parents' abilities to positively affect their children across a variety of domains are diminished (e.g., Elder & Caspi, 1988). Although some variation has been observed in the strength of these relations, they do appear to be somewhat universal, transcending various cultures and countries (Müller, 1996; Schnabel, Alfeld, Eccles, Köller, & Baumert, 2002). When parents are employed and have reliable sources of income, their children are likely to do better in school.

Research suggests that even when families live in poverty, children's academic achievement can improve if parents find better employment and start to earn better wages (Huston et al., 2005). Research indicates that adolescents are more likely to perceive that their parents offer encouragement, praise, academic assistance, and attendance at school events when the adolescents live in traditional family structures and have highly educated parents (compared to nontraditional structures and having less educated parents; Deslandes, Potvin, & Leclerc, 1999). In addition, research indicates that academic success is related to parents' feelings of efficacy, particularly for low socioeconomic standing (SES) children (Ardelt & Eccles, 2001).

It is important to note that many low SES children and adolescents are also ethnic minority students; histories of discrimination against minority groups often further impede these students' abilities to succeed in school (Halle, Kurtz-Costes, & Mahoney, 1997; Huston, 1994). In particular, parents of minority students may be less likely to want to be involved with their children's education as a result of their own unpleasant experiences with schooling. In addition, some parents of ethnic minority students may feel intimidated by the largely ethnic majority school personnel (Koonce & Harper, 2005). Parents' English language skills and familiarity with local schooling policies and organization can add to these difficulties for immigrant parents. Research also suggests that the relations of parental involvement to academic achievement are sometimes weaker for ethnic minority and majority students (Desimone, 1999; Valdez, 2002). This may be because some parents (e.g., parents from Latino homes) may not feel prepared to help children and adolescents with academic assignments, despite highly valuing education (Ceballo, Huerta, & Epstein-Ngo, 2010). Such differences also might reflect different patterns of parental involvement across ethnic groups. For example, Graves and Wright (2011) used a nationally representative sample of children about to enter kindergarten and found that whereas European American parents were more likely to be engaged with their children at home (e.g., reading to their children), African American parents were more likely to be involved with children at school (e.g., volunteering).

Given these diverse findings, it is particularly important for teachers to encourage parents of low SES and minority students to communicate actively with teachers and to facilitate that communication. It is particularly important that teachers treat parents in a respectful, professional manner, so that parents will feel comfortable initiating communications with teachers.

PARENTS AND ACADEMIC MOTIVATION

Most educators accept that parents have a profound influence on student motivation. For example, many of us know of a child who eventually chooses to enter the same profession as one of her parents. We also know of a child who chooses to enter a completely different occupation than her parents did. Research has illustrated exactly how parents influence student motivation. As we stated at the beginning of the chapter, this is important information because, as a teacher, your communications with parents may help you to understand why a student is or is not motivated to learn in a particular way. Parents help their children to interpret reality (Eccles, 1993). Thus, when a child gets a low grade on a science test, comments made at home by parents about the low grade influence students' self-beliefs and future motivation toward science.

Perceived support from parents and conflict with parents also are related to motivational outcomes in students. Using a large sample of South Korean students, Bong (2008)

When parents become involved with their children's academic work, students experience many benefits.

found that students are more willing to cheat and less likely to seek academic help when they experience conflict with their parents. In addition, students who report feeling obligated to their parents also are likely to avoid seeking academic help.

Parents' Beliefs About Students' Abilities

We asked several students what their parents think about them as learners. Consider these typical responses:

> *"My mom thinks I'm great at math."*
> *"My dad thinks I am a really bad basketball player."*
> *"My parents think I'm a great student."*
> *"My parents think I'm a jerk."*

The types of responses that students offer to questions of this nature are actually quite important. In addition, students' perceptions of their parents' beliefs are also important determinants of student motivation.

Parents' beliefs about their children's abilities are related to the types of interactions that parents have with their children. When a parent believes that a child is truly talented in science, that parent can be expected to interact differently when assisting with science homework and to react differently to test results in science, than will a parent who believes that his child is unable to do well in science class.

Most important, research indicates that parents' beliefs about their children's abilities are related to children's actual beliefs about themselves (e.g., Alexander & Entwisle, 1988; Halle et al., 1997). For example, adolescents' motivational beliefs in mathematics and English are more closely related to their parents' beliefs about the children's abilities than to the students' actual grades (Frome & Eccles, 1998; Parsons, Adler, & Kaczala, 1982). Thus, a student whose mother believes that he simply is not talented when it comes to mathematical reasoning may hold similar beliefs about himself; in contrast, a student whose father believes that she is an excellent writer may adapt similar positive self-beliefs toward writing. These beliefs, once established, can be quite resistant to change.

When teachers interact with parents, we must consider parents' beliefs about their children's abilities. If you know that a student's mother believes that the student is a truly gifted mathematician, this will affect how you communicate with that parent about the student's performance. You might encourage specific strategies with a parent who believes that a child is gifted, compared to the types of strategies that you might suggest for a parent who believes his or her child has a problem with learning.

Effects of Parents' Behaviors and Beliefs on Students' Motivated Behaviors

Many parents believe that their children will adopt and internalize their family values and behaviors. For example, a parent who spends much time engaging in athletic activities may believe that his or her children will also want to spend participating in athletics. Bandura's studies of observational learning support these hypotheses (Bandura, 1997): When individuals observe others engaging in meaningful activities, they too are often motivated to engage in the same or similar activities.

Research indicates a relation between parents' participation in specific activities and children's participation in similar activities. Simpkins, Davis-Kean, and Eccles (2005) found that parents' own participation in computer, math, and science activities predicts their children's participation. Specifically, when parents provide materials for their children (e.g., computers, science kits), and when the parents interact with their children around these activities, students are likely to choose to participate in similar activities.

In another study, Jodl, Michael, Malanchuk, Eccles, and Sameroff (2001) examined parental influences on adolescents' occupational aspirations, using a large sample of seventh-graders who were living with undivorced parents. Results of this research indicated that parents' values are related directly to students' educational values and to students' occupational aspirations. Although both parents' beliefs and behaviors affect these relations, fathers in particular tend to socialize adolescents' attitudes and behaviors in the domain of sports.

Some research on motivation in science suggests that parents interact differently with boys and girls. Bhanot and Jovanovic (2009) examined the relations between parental involvement in science with children and early adolescents. Specifically, when girls discussed the importance of science and possible careers in science with their mothers, girls' beliefs about the usefulness of science and their beliefs about their own abilities in science were high. For boys, the promotion of interest in science by mothers was actually related to lower self-perceptions of ability in science. Their results also indicated that mothers often encourage science interest in girls when the girls are doing well in science (e.g., getting good grades in science), whereas they encourage science interest in boys when they are not doing well in science class.

Recent research also indicates that the provision of structure by parents is related to beneficial outcomes for students. Farkas and Grolnick (2010) identified six aspects of structure that parents provide for early adolescents: (a) providing clear and consistent guidelines, (b) predictable consequences, (c) opportunities to meet expectations, (d) information feedback, (e) rationales for rules and expectations, and (f) acting as authority figures in the home.

Analyses indicated that although these aspects of structure are related to important outcomes in early adolescents, their relations with outcomes vary. For example, providing clear and consistent guidelines is related to perceptions of control, engagement, grades, and perceived cognitive competence in early adolescents, whereas predictable consequences are just related to cognitive competence and grades, and opportunities to meet expectations are related to perceived competence, engagement, grades, and perceived control over success.

PARENT INVOLVEMENT   A related body of research literature focuses on parental involvement with children and schooling. Research indicates that when parents are involved with their children's education, beneficial results accrue, particularly in terms of motivation and academic achievement (e.g., Epstein, 1983). Some research even suggests that dropout rates are lower in schools where there is greater parent involvement (Rumberger & Palardy, 2002).

Most researchers do not distinguish between different *types* of parental involvement (National Research Council Institute of Medicine, 2004). Nevertheless, there may be reason to do so. Grolnick and Slowiaczek (1994) distinguished between three types of parent involvement: *behavioral, personal,* and *cognitive/intellectual*:

- *Behavioral involvement*, as the name implies, refers to parents' active engagement in behaviors related to their children's education. Examples of behavioral involvement include visiting the child's school and volunteering in the child's classroom.
- *Personal involvement* refers to parents talking about school with their children and displaying positive affect toward school-related issues. An example of personal involvement would be a parent asking a child each evening about the child's experiences that day in school. In particular, if a parent acts excited and interested in the child's experiences, this should convey to the child that the parent is genuinely interested in those experiences. Research suggests that discussing school-related issues with adolescents is related to academic achievement (Jeynes, 2005).
- *Cognitive/intellectual involvement* refers to parents interacting with their children at home around cognitively stimulating materials. An example of cognitive/intellectual involvement would be reading and discussing interesting books with children outside school. Research indicates that mothers who perceive their children as difficult are less likely to be cognitively/intellectually involved with them (Grolnick, Benjet, Kurowski, & Apostoleris, 1997).

Recent research indicates that parental involvement in students' learning (e.g., helping them with their homework) is related positively to students' reports of higher levels of parent-oriented motivation (e.g., doing well in school to gain parents' approval or to demonstrate responsibility); parent-oriented motivation, in turn, is related positively to self-regulated learning, which is predictive of higher grades in school (Cheung & Pomerantz, 2012). Thus parental involvement with academics may lead to changes in students' motivation toward schoolwork (vis-à-vis their parents), which in turn is related positively to adaptive academic behaviors and higher achievement.

Some research indicates that different individual and contextual variables are related to the type of parental involvement that occurs in families. For example, mothers who live in difficult social contexts and who do not have much support are particularly unlikely to be involved in their sons' school experiences (Grolnick et al., 1997). Parental work schedules, financial conditions, and obligations to other family members can make involvement in schooling very difficult. Overall, Grolnick and her colleagues (Grolnick & Slowiaczek,

1994) have found that when mothers are involved in their children's schooling, the children tend to feel competent and in control of their learning. These positive outcomes for students are ultimately predictive of higher achievement for them.

In addition, research indicates that the involvement of mothers in their children's homework can be particularly beneficial for children with negative beliefs about their abilities; specifically, the use of mastery-oriented practices with their children (e.g., encouraging children to figure out how to solve problems on their own; helping children understand homework assignments) is related to enhanced psychological well-being for such children (Pomerantz, Ng, & Wang, 2006).

STRATEGIES FOR WORKING WITH PARENTS

As a teacher, it is inevitable that you will come into contact with parents. Whereas teachers of young children often interact with parents more than teachers of adolescents, it is important for all teachers to maintain good relationships with parents. In addition, there is no reason why a middle-school or high-school teacher cannot or should not interact with parents.

How Teachers Can Communicate with Parents

Teachers can use many different methods to encourage parents to be involved in the education of their children and adolescents. Teachers do not need to wait for parents to make contact; they can initiate contact and encourage parents to be more involved in educational activities. However, teachers must also encourage parents to work as partners; they must ensure that the lines of communication are open, respectful, and bidirectional.

Epstein and her colleagues list 14 specific practices (see Table 6-1) that teachers can use with parents (Becker & Epstein, 1982; Epstein, 2001). These strategies can be communicated to parents in a variety of ways:

- Via formal parent–teacher conferences
- Via notes sent home with students
- Via school newsletters
- Via e-mail messages
- Via electronic conferencing (e.g., Skype)
- Via telephone messages
- Via notes at the end of homework assignments
- Via comments written on report cards

Teachers must be creative with the mechanisms they use to communicate with parents. The use of communication technologies such as e-mail and Skype are growing in popularity, given the prevalence of e-mail in many individuals' lives (Graham-Clay, 2005). Sensitivity is required, however, in assuming that all parents have access to such technologies. An alternative is to use a *traveling notebook*, which travels to and from school with the child every day; the teacher can write daily notes to the parents, and the parents can also write back to the teacher (Hallahan & Kauffman, 1997). In the end, we know that parental involvement is good for students. However, parents often do not always appreciate the importance of their own participation; some parents are reluctant to "interfere" with the work of professional educators. As teachers, we can inform and encourage parents to be involved with their children's academic lives.

Anthony Magnacca/Merrill

Teachers can communicate with parents in many different ways.

TABLE 6-1   Techniques for Involving Parents in Teaching Activities at Home

1. Ask parents to regularly read to their child or listen to their child reading aloud.
2. Loan materials to parents to keep at home, to use as extra learning materials.
3. Ask parents to take their child to the library.
4. Ask parents to get their child to talk about what he or she did that day in class.
5. Give an assignment that requires children to ask their parents questions.
6. Ask parents to watch a specific television show with their child and to discuss the show afterward.
7. Suggest ways for parents to incorporate their child into their own home-based activities that would be educationally enriching.
8. Send home suggestions for games or group activities that are related to the child's schoolwork and can be played by parent and child.
9. Suggest how parents might use the home environment (i.e., things they do in their daily lives) to stimulate the child's interest in reading, math, and so on.
10. Establish a formal agreement whereby the parent supervises and assists the child in completing homework tasks.
11. Establish a formal agreement whereby the parent provides rewards and/or penalties based on the child's school performance or behavior (see Chapter 3 for tips on how to administer rewards and penalties appropriately).
12. Invite parents to observe the classroom (not to "help") for part of the day.
13. Explain to parents certain techniques for teaching, for making learning materials, or for planning lessons.
14. Give a questionnaire to parents so they can evaluate their child's progress or provide some other feedback to you.

Source: Adapted from Becker & Epstein (1982).

Teachers must be highly sensitive to the fact that students live in a variety of different settings: two-parent households, single-parent households, grandparent-run households, sibling-run households, same-sex-parent households, mixed-race households, and numerous other settings. It also is important for teachers to realize that many students today live in nontraditional households, which are not necessarily the norm in many communities. Both parents and children in nontraditional households experience stressors that may be different from those of more traditional families (Bos, van Balen, van den Boom, & Sandfort, 2004; Maseko, 2003). Teachers can alleviate some of that stress by avoiding making assumptions about children's family situations and by monitoring the content of curriculum materials and communication materials. For example, when one of the authors taught in a school where many students were not living in traditional family structures, the teachers adopted a practice of referring to "the person who takes care of you at home," rather than "parents" when asking students to deliver newsletters, get homework signed, and so on.

In addition, it is important for teachers to be aware of the particular stressors that affect parents of children and adolescents with disabilities. Parents of children with learning disabilities, physical disabilities, emotional problems, mental retardation, and other exceptionalities may suffer additional stress in their lives (Beckman, 1991; Hassall & Rose, 2005; O'Neill, 2005; Singer & Irvin, 1989). When teachers contact the parents of exceptional children, they must be aware that such families have to contend with all the usual daily life stressors that parents must face, but they also have to assist their child in atypical ways. For example, if you as a teacher contact a parent because a child is having difficulty with math class work, you may learn that the child has a learning disability in the area of reading, which is affecting the child's ability to complete tasks in math (i.e., the child can't effectively read the math problems); when you speak with the parent, you must be sensitive to the fact that the parent may need to do more than just help the child with math—the parent may need to be working on reading with the child, across all subject areas. Usually special educators and school psychologists are available to assist and consult in these situations; as a teacher, you should not be shy about asking these professionals for advice and assistance. Many students with disabilities may already have Individualized Education Programs (IEPs), which outline strategies for helping these children to succeed in school.

Enhancing Student Motivation Through Contact with Parents

Central to this chapter is the notion that teachers can have a positive impact on their students' motivation via contact with parents. Although most parents want to motivate their children to learn, few may know how to accomplish this. Nevertheless, as a teacher, you have strategies to use in your interaction with parents. You can suggest to parents that they use specific strategies to help motivate their children, such as the following:

1. *Parents should offer encouragement to students.* When students are encouraged at home to persist with their academic work, motivation is likely to be enhanced (Bong, 2008; van Voorhis, 2003). Parents can encourage their children in a variety of ways. For example, they can encourage their children when homework assignments are difficult by sitting down with children and helping them break their assignments down into smaller tasks. Be aware that parents may find some homework assignments

challenging. Providing parents with resources (such as helpful Web sites or "cheat sheets" for parents) can be very helpful.

2. *Parents should be encouraged to provide cognitively engaging materials in the home.* Teachers can ask parents to make sure that books, educational videos, and other academically oriented materials are in the household. It is, of course, important to note that some low-income parents may not be able to provide some of the same resources that higher income parents can provide (Halle et al., 1997). Nevertheless, parents can be encouraged to use public libraries to borrow materials for their children. Where appropriate, teachers may facilitate students acquiring library cards.

3. *Parents should be encouraged to engage in activities at home with their children.* First, when parents participate in educationally relevant activities with their children, the children are likely to see that their parents value such activities. In addition, from a cognitive perspective, when children and adolescents work with their parents on academic tasks, cognitive development may also be enhanced (Simpkins et al., 2005). Specifically, when children and adults work together on meaningful tasks, the children may be lured into their zones of proximal development (ZPD). The ZPD represents the difference between an individual's ability to solve a problem alone and the same individual's potential to solve the same problem when working with a more experienced other (Vygotsky, 1978). Teachers should encourage parents to work on all types of academic tasks with their children because some parents may be more likely to work with children in some academic areas (e.g., reading) than in others (e.g., math; Epstein, 2001). Teachers also should recognize that parents from minority cultural and ethnic backgrounds may be less likely to work with students at home than parents from majority cultures (Graves & Wright, 2011).

4. *Parents of minority students, in particular, should be encouraged to work with their children.* As mentioned, parents of minority students may be less inclined to approach teachers and to advocate for their children due to prior unpleasant experiences with school personnel in their own lives. Teachers must be particularly aware of and sensitive to these issues and should reach out to the parents of minority students. In addition, those parents may want to partner with community agencies to advocate for their children and to improve their relationships with school personnel (Koonce & Harper, 2005). Such agencies often can help teachers and parents to communicate about important educational issues.

5. *Parents should help children and adolescents to attribute failures and successes to effort.* When children come home with graded assignments, their parents' reactions to those grades often affect the types of attributions that students will make. Consider a sixth-grade student (Tanya), who comes home with a grade of D on her math quiz. The following are two possible responses that she might hear from her mother:

Response #1: "Tanya, you didn't do well on your assignment. I know you were goofing off last night, watching TV and talking to your friends on the telephone. You simply didn't try hard enough. If you had spent more time preparing and less time fooling around, you would have gotten a better grade."

Response #2: "Tanya, you didn't do well on your assignment. Oh well, math is really difficult. Some of us just don't do well in certain classes."

In terms of attributions, Response 1 is likely to induce attributions to effort, whereas Response 2 is likely to induce attributions to ability. When students believe that their failures are due to lack of ability, they will be less likely to be motivated to engage in the same task in the future; in contrast, when students attribute their failures to lack of effort or poor studying strategies (i.e., to controllable variables), they are more likely to exert more effort and be more motivated toward the task in the future (Weiner, 1985, 1986).

As a teacher, you can help to educate parents about the ways in which they can help to shape their children's attributions. For example, during parent–teacher conferences, teachers can take more time to talk about how parents offer feedback and encouragement to children. Parents can be encouraged to use more supportive, motivationally appropriate language at home with their children. Teachers can provide examples and demonstrations of how to use such discourse during parent–teacher meetings or via handouts or e-mail messages shared with parents.

6. *Parents should be encouraged to hold high expectations for their children.* Whereas there is much rhetoric about holding high expectations (see Chapter 9), the research base regarding maintaining high expectations is sound. In particular, parents can be shown how to help their children to set realistic, proximal goals. Teachers can show parents how to help children set these goals, and parents should be encouraged to hold high expectations that their children meet those goals. When children do meet their goals, parents can provide positive reinforcement that is specifically tied to what the students have learned. This will likely lead to improved self-efficacy in the future (Schunk, 1991).

7. *Parents should encourage students to hold mastery goals.* Recall that when a student holds mastery goals, he or she is concerned about truly mastering an academic task; mastery-oriented students exert effort, are not threatened by challenging tasks, and are eager to truly learn the material that is being presented (in contrast to performance goals, for which students are concerned with either demonstrating their ability compared to others or avoiding the appearance of being incompetent; Ames, 1992; E. M. Anderman & Maehr, 1994; Dweck & Leggett, 1988; Meece, Blumenfeld, & Hoyle, 1988; Urdan, 1997). Research indicates that holding mastery goals is related to a number of positive outcomes, including the use of adaptive cognitive processing strategies, persistence, and effort (E. M. Anderman & Wolters, 2006). Parents communicate their beliefs about the types of achievement goals that students should espouse to their children. When parents constantly talk about grades and ability, students are likely to focus on performance goals; in contrast, when parents speak to their children about the importance of task mastery and truly learning and understanding the material, students may be more likely to adopt mastery goals. Research suggests that parents may more easily communicate information about performance goals than about mastery goals to their children (Bergin & Habusta, 2004); therefore, it is important for teachers to remind parents to try to emphasize mastery goals with their children at home. Benefits to the students are likely to accrue if parents stress the importance of mastery goals; some research even suggests that when parents themselves hold mastery goals, students may receive higher grades in school. This effect has been found particularly in African American adolescents (Gutman, 2006). Other research indicates that when students perceive that their parents hold mastery goals (i.e., they support mastery goals for

their children), those students are more likely to report holding personal mastery goals and to report engagement with their academic work (Gonida, Kiosseoglou, & Voulala, 2007).

8. *Parents should avoid using unwarranted extrinsic rewards.* Recall from Chapter 3 that there is much debate about the use of extrinsic rewards in education. Some research suggests that when students work at an intrinsically interesting task to receive a reward, intrinsic motivation toward the task may decline (Lepper, Greene, & Nisbett, 1973). In addition, when rewards are perceived as controlling, intrinsic motivation also is likely to decline (Deci, 1975). Parents often hand out rewards to students simply for earning a good grade. Consider the following examples:

Lacey receives $5 for every A that she gets on her report card.
Jack's parents promise to buy him a new car if he scores over the 90th percentile on the ACT.
Shirley's parents promise to send her on a trip to visit her cousins at the beach if she gets on the honor roll.

In these examples, students are rewarded for a specific outcome, not for effort, learning, or progress. Some research suggests that when students are focused only on the "prize," they will learn less and may even resort to cheating to receive the reward (E. M. Anderman, Griessinger, & Westerfield, 1998; Murdock & E. M. Anderman, 2006). Teachers should work with parents to ensure that when parents do use extrinsic rewards, the rewards are given when students actually demonstrate to the parents that they have truly learned the material (i.e., the rewards should be informational). In addition, the rewards should not be perceived by the students as controlling. Rather than merely awarding money or a prize to a child for completing a set of academic tasks, parents could offer such rewards if the children demonstrate to them that they truly understand the material they have learned in class. For example, the child might be asked to write a short paper for the parents explaining how the material learned in a class during the past semester relates to something in the "real world" that interests the child. Whereas both students and parents may find this to be time consuming, the long-term benefits are important. In the long term, the child is more likely to remember the information that has been learned and, perhaps, to actually value that information more in the future (E. M. Anderman et al., 2001; Deci, Koestner, & Ryan, 1999).

9. *Parents should be encouraged to work as partners with teachers in the school.* Teachers who maintain regular positive contact with parents are likely to develop relationships of trust with parents. Parents will be more likely to continue to work with teachers and to partner with them when they have close, caring, and professional relationships with them. It is particularly important that parents do not always have negative interactions with teachers. Educators should contact parents about students' successes and achievements, not just about problems.

10. *Parents should be encouraged to make sure that students complete their homework.* Parents have an important influence on whether, when, and how students complete their homework. Teachers can remind parents to set aside specific times for students to work on homework and to monitor progress on homework when possible. In addition, parents should be contacted about homework that is not completed, and

Teachers can communicate with parents in many different ways.

they should be encouraged to check in with teachers about whether or not homework is being turned in by students. Teachers also can instruct students in how to "invite" their parents to assist them with their homework. Research indicates that when adolescents in particular invite parents to assist them, parents are more likely to do so (Deslandes & Bertrand, 2005).

Summary

In this chapter, we have examined the roles that parents play in affecting student academic motivation. Whereas schools and peers clearly influence academic motivation, parents also have profound effects on how their children approach academic work. Parents' values, beliefs, and behaviors are all related to students' motivation toward academics. Parents affect their children both through their interactions with children at home and via their involvement with teachers and schools.

As teachers, we have the ability and responsibility to help parents understand the ways in which they can influence student motivation and achievement. We can suggest strategies that parents may find useful and that may positively benefit their children. In addition, at times teachers need to respectfully and tactfully indicate to parents that certain strategies being used in the home may in fact undermine motivation. As a teacher, it will take time to learn how to effectively communicate with students' parents but teachers will also see great payoffs in terms of how much their students will learn and achieve.

School communities as entire organizations may want to take on the issue of educating parents about student motivation. Parents hold many beliefs about motivation that may not necessarily be based in research. An entire school, under the direction of leadership that truly believes in the importance of research-based motivational practices, can provide programming and education for parents related to these issues.

If teachers take the time to communicate with parents about motivation, students ultimately will benefit. All too often, contact with parents focuses on negative events (e.g., poor grades, bad behavior). We encourage teachers also to initiate contact with parents for positive reasons—to inform parents that their children are doing well and to suggest strategies to improve motivation at home.

Questions to Consider When Communicating with Parents

1. How am I going to communicate with parents? What is the most appropriate form of communication with this particular family? A face-to-face meeting? A phone call? An e-mail message?
2. What is the status of the home life of this student? Do both parents live at home? Does the child live with foster parents or grandparents?
3. Will the parents' reactions align with my goals for the student's motivation? If I am trying to encourage intrinsic motivation and mastery goals, how can I gently persuade parents to support, rather than undermine, these goals?
4. Why am I communicating with parents? Do I always communicate negative information? Do I ever communicate positive information about this student?

LEARNING ACTIVITY 6.1   A Protocol for Conversation

Develop a protocol for a conversation that you could have with parents about a student who is not motivated to do well in your class. Consider the following issues:

1. How will you contact the parent(s)?
2. How will you communicate information about how to best motivate this student?
3. How will you convey both positive and negative information to the parent(s)?
4. How will you follow up later with the parent(s)?
5. How will you assess the effectiveness of this communication?

References

Alexander, K. L., & Entwisle, D. R. (1988). Achievement in the first two years of school: Patterns and processes. *Monographs of the Society for Research in Child Development, 53*(2) (serial no. 218).

Ames, C. (1992). Classrooms: Goals, structures, and student motivation. *Journal of Educational Psychology, 84*(3), 261–271.

Anderman, E. M., Eccles, J. S., Yoon, K. S., Roeser, R. W., Wigfield, A., & Blumenfeld, P. (2001). Learning to value math and reading: Individual differences and classroom effects. *Contemporary Educational Psychology, 26,* 76–95.

Anderman, E. M., Griesinger, T., & Westerfield, G. (1998). Motivation and cheating during early adolescence. *Journal of Educational Psychology, 90,* 84–93.

Anderman, E. M., & Maehr, M. L. (1994). Motivation and schooling in the middle grades. *Review of Educational Research, 64*(2), 287–309.

Anderman, E. M., & Wolters, C. (2006). Goals, values, and affect: Influences on student motivation. In P. Alexander & P. Winne (Eds.), *Handbook of educational psychology* (2nd ed., pp. 369–389). Mahwah, NJ: Erlbaum.

Ardelt, M., & Eccles, J. S. (2001). Effects of mothers' parental efficacy beliefs and promotive parenting strategies on inner-city youth. *Journal of Family Issues, 8,* 944–972.

Bandura, A. (1997). *Self-efficacy: The exercise of control.* New York, NY: Freeman.

Baumrind, D. (1967). Child care practices anteceding three patterns of preschool behavior. *Genetic Psychology Monographs, 75,* 43–88.

Baumrind, D. (1971). Current patterns of parental authority. *Developmental Psychology Monographs, 4*(1, pt. 2).

Baumrind, D. (1973). The development of instrumental competence through socialization. In A. D. Pick (Ed.), *Minnesota Symposium on Child Psychology: Vol. 7.* Minneapolis: University of Minnesota Press.

Baumrind, D. (1991). The influence of parenting style on adolescent competence and substance use. *Journal of Early Adolescence, 11,* 56–95.

Becker, H. J., & Epstein, J. L. (1982). Parent involvement: A survey of teacher practices. *Elementary School Journal, 83*(2), 85–102.

Beckman, J. P. (1991). Comparison of mothers' and fathers' perceptions of the effect of young children with and without disabilities. *American Journal on Mental Retardation, 95*(5), 585–595.

Bergin, D. A., & Habusta, S. F. (2004). Goal orientations of young male ice hockey players and their parents. *Journal of Genetic Psychology, 165*(4), 383–397.

Bhanot, R. T., & Jovanovic, J. (2009). The links between parent behaviors and boys' and girls' science achievement beliefs. *Applied Developmental Science, 13,* 42–59.

Blau, P. M., & Duncan, O. D. (1967). *The American opportunity structure.* New York, NY: Wiley.

Bong, M. (2008). Effects of parent-child relationships and classroom goal structures on motivation, help-seeking avoidance, and cheating. *Journal of Experimental Education, 76,* 191–217.

Bos, H. M. W., van Balen, F., van den Boom, D. C., & Sandfort, T. G. M. (2004). Minority stress, experience of parenthood and child adjustment in lesbian families. *Journal of Reproductive Infant Psychology, 22*(4), 291–304.

Ceballo, R., Huerta, M., & Epstein-Ngo, Q. (2010). Parental and school influences promoting academic success among Latino students. In J. L. Meece & J. S. Eccles (Eds.), *Handbook of research on schools, schooling, and human development* (pp. 293–307). New York, NY: Routledge.

Chao, R. (1994). Beyond parental control and authoritarian parenting style: Understanding Chinese parenting through the cultural notion of training. *Child Development, 65,* 1111–1119.

Cheung, C. S., & Pomerantz, E. M. (2012). Why does parents' involvement enhance children's achievement? The role of parent-oriented motivation. *Journal of Educational Psychology, 104,* 820–832.

Deci, E. (1975). *Intrinsic motivation.* New York, NY: Plenum.

Deci, E. L., Koestner, R., & Ryan, R. M. (1999). A meta-analytic review of experiments examining the effects of extrinsic rewards on intrinsic motivation. *Psychological Bulletin, 125*(6), 627–668.

DePlanty, J., Coulter-Kern, R., & Duchane, K. A. (2007). Perceptions of parent involvement in academic achievement. *The Journal of Educational Research, 100,* 361–368.

Desimone, L. (1999). Linking parent involvement with student achievement: Do race and income matter? *Journal of Educational Research, 93,* 11–31.

Deslandes, R., & Bertrand, R. (2005). Motivation of parent involvement in secondary-level schooling. *The Journal of Educational Research, 98,* 164–175.

Deslandes, R., Potvin, P., & Leclerc, D. (1999). Family characteristics predictors of school achievement: Parent involvement as a mediator. *McGill Journal of Education, 34,* 133–151.

Dornbusch, S. M., & Ritter, P. L. (1988). Parents of high school students: A neglected resource. *Educational Horizons, 66,* 75–77.

Dornbusch, S. M., Ritter, P., Liederman, P., Roberts, D., & Fraleigh, M. (1987). The relation of parenting style to adolescent school performance. *Child Development, 58,* 1244–1257.

Dweck, C. S., & Leggett, E. L. (1988). A social-cognitive approach to motivation and personality. *Psychological Review, 95*(2), 256–273.

Eccles, J. S. (1993). School and family effects on the ontogeny of children's interest, self-perceptions, and activity choices. In J. E. Jacobs (Ed.), *Developmental perspectives on motivation* (pp. 145–208). Lincoln: University of Nebraska Press.

Eccles, J. S., Jacobs, J. E., & Harold, R. D. (1990). Gender role stereotypes, expectancy effects, and parents' socialization of gender differences. *Journal of Social Issues, 46,* 183–201.

Elder, G. H., & Caspi, A. (1988). Economic stress in our lives: Developmental perspectives. *Journal of Social Issues, 44,* 25–45.

Epstein, J. L. (1983). Longitudinal effects of family-school-person interactions on student outcomes. In A. Kerckhoff (Ed.), *Research in sociology of education and socialization* (pp. 101–128). Greenwich, CT: JAI Press.

Epstein, J. L. (2001). *School, family, and community partnerships: Preparing educators and improving schools.* Boulder, CO: Westview Press.

Farkas, M. S., & Grolnick, W. S. (2010). Examining the components and concomitants of parental structure in the academic domain. *Motivation and Emotion, 34,* 266–279.

Frome, P. M., & Eccles, J. S. (1998). Parents' influence on children's achievement-related perceptions. *Journal of Personality and Social Psychology, 74*(2), 435–452.

Gonida, E. N., Kiosseoglou, G., & Voulala, K. (2007). Perceptions of parent goals and their contribution to student achievement goal orientation and engagement in the classroom: Grade-level differences across adolescence. *European Journal of Psychology of Education, 22,* 23–39.

Graham-Clay, S. (2005). Communicating with parents: Strategies for teachers. *School Community Journal, 15,* 117–129.

Graves, S. L., & Wright, L. B. (2011). Parent involvement at school entry: A national examination of group differences and achievement. *School Psychology International, 32,* 35–48.

Grolnick, W. S., Benjet, C., Kurowski, C. O., & Apostoleris, N. H. (1997). Predictors of parent involvement in children's schooling. *Journal of Educational Psychology, 89,* 538–548.

Grolnick, W. S., & Slowiaczek, M. L. (1994). Parents' involvement in children's schooling: A multidimensional conceptualization and motivational model. *Child Development, 65,* 237–252.

Gutman, L. M. (2006). How student and parent goal orientations and classroom goal structures influence the math achievement of African Americans during the high school transition. *Contemporary Educational Psychology, 31*(1), 44–63.

Hallahan, D. P., & Kauffman, J. M. (1997). *Exceptional learners: Introduction to special education* (7th ed.). Boston, MA: Allyn & Bacon.

Halle, T. G., Kurtz-Costes, B., & Mahoney, J. L. (1997). Family influences on school achievement in low-income, African American children. *Journal of Educational Psychology, 89,* 527–537.

Hassall, R., & Rose, J. (2005). Parental cognitions and adaptation to the demands of caring for a child with an intellectual disability: A review of the literature and implications for clinical interventions. *Behavioural and Cognitive Psychotherapy, 33*(1), 71–88.

Hoover-Dempsey, K. V., & Sandler, H. M. (1997). Why do parents become involved in their children's education? *Review of Educational Research, 67,* 3–42.

Huston, A. C. (1994). Children in poverty: Designing research to effect social policy. *Social Policy Report: Society for Research in Child Development, 8*(2), 1–12.

Huston, A. C., Duncan, G. J., McLoyd, V. C., Crosby, D. A., Ripke, M. N., Weisner, T. S., & Eldred, C. A. (2005). Impacts on children of a policy to promote employment and reduce poverty for low-income parents: New hope after 5 years. *Developmental Psychology, 41*(6), 902–918.

Jeynes, W. H. (2005). Effects of parental involvement and family structure on the academic achievement of adolescents. *Marriage & Family Review, 37,* 99–116.

Jodl, K. M., Michael, A., Malanchuk, O., Eccles, J. S., & Sameroff, A. J. (2001). Parents' roles in shaping early adolescents' occupational aspirations. *Child Development, 72,* 1247–1265.

Koonce, D. A., & Harper, W. (2005). Engaging African American parents in the schools: A community-based consultation model. *Journal of Educational and Psychological Consultation, 16,* 55–74.

Lepper, M. R., Greene, D., & Nisbett, R. E. (1973). Undermining children's intrinsic interest with extrinsic reward: A test of the "overjustification" hypothesis. *Journal of Personality and Social Psychology, 28,* 129–137.

Maseko, M. (2003). A young parent's anxieties in raising her infant in a non-traditional family structure. *Journal of Child and Adolescent Mental Health, 15*(2), 77–80.

Meece, J. L., Blumenfeld, P. C., & Hoyle, R. H. (1988). Students' goal orientations and cognitive engagement in classroom activities. *Journal of Educational Psychology, 80*(4), 514–523.

Müller, W. (1996). Class inequalities in educational outcomes: Sweden in a comparative perspective. In R. Erikson & J. O. Jonsson (Eds.), *Can education be equalized?* (pp. 145–182). Boulder, CO: Westview Press.

Murdock, T. B., & Anderman, E. M. (2006). Motivational perspectives on student cheating: Toward an integrated model of academic dishonesty. *Educational Psychologist, 41,* 129–145.

National Research Council Institute of Medicine. (2004). *Engaging schools: Fostering high school students' motivation to learn.* Washington, DC: The National Academies Press.

O'Neill, M. M. (2005). *Investigation of the prevalence of and predictors of posttraumatic stress symptomology in parents of children with disabilities.* Unpublished doctoral dissertation, University of Kentucky.

Parsons, J. E., Adler, T., & Kaczala, C. M. (1982). Socialization of achievement attitudes and perceptions: Parental influences. *Child Development, 53,* 310–321.

Pianta, R. C. (1999). *Enhancing relationships between children and teachers.* Washington, DC: American Psychological Association.

Pomerantz, E. M., & Moorman, E. A. (2010). Parents' involvement in children's schooling. In J. L. Meece & J. S. Eccles (Eds.), *Handbook of research on schools, schooling, and human development* (pp. 398–416). New York, NY: Routledge.

Pomerantz, E. M., Ng, F. F.-Y., & Wang, Q. (2006). Mothers' mastery-oriented involvement in children's homework: Implications for the well-being of children with negative perceptions of competence. *Journal of Educational Psychology, 98,* 99–111.

Rumberger, R. W., & Palardy, G. J. (2002). *Raising test scores and lowering dropout rates: Can schools do both?* Paper presented at the American Educational Research Association, New Orleans.

Schnabel, K. U., Alfeld, C., Eccles, J. S., Köller, O., & Baumert, J. (2002). Parental influence on students' educational choices in the United States and Germany: Different ramifications—same effect? *Journal of Vocational Behavior, 60,* 178–198.

Schunk, D. H. (1991). Self-efficacy and academic motivation. *Educational Psychologist, 26,* 207–231.

Simpkins, S. D., Davis-Kean, P. E., & Eccles, J. S. (2005). Parents' socializing behavior and children's participation in math, science, and computer out-of-school activities. *Applied Developmental Science, 9*(1), 14–30.

Singer, G. H. S., & Irvin, L. K. (1989). Family caregiving, stress, and support. In G. H. S. Singer & L. K. Irvin (Eds.), *Support for caregiving families: Enabling positive adaptation to disability* (pp. 3–25). Baltimore, MD: Paul H. Brookes.

Steinberg, L. (1996). *Beyond the classroom: Why school reform has failed and what parents need to do.* New York, NY: Simon & Schuster.

Steinberg, L. (2005). *Adolescence* (7th ed.). Boston, MA: McGraw-Hill.

Steinberg, L., Lamborn, S. D., Darling, N., Mounts, N. S., & Dornbusch, S. M. (1994). Over-time changes in adjustment and competence among adolescents from authoritative, authoritarian, indulgent, and neglectful families. *Child Development, 65,* 754–770.

Turner, E. A., Chandler, M., & Heffer, R. W. (2009). The influence of parenting styles, achievement motivation, and self-efficacy on academic performance in college students. *Journal of College Student Development, 50,* 337–346.

Urdan, T. (1997). Achievement goal theory: Past results, future directions. In M. L. Maehr & P. R. Pintrich (Eds.), *Advances in motivation and achievement* (Vol. 10, pp. 99–141). Greenwich, CT: JAI Press.

Valdez, J. R. (2002). The influence of social capital on mathematics course selection by Latino high school students. *Hispanic Journal of Behavioral Sciences, 24,* 319–339.

van Voorhis, F. L. (2003). Interactive homework in middle school: Effects on family involvement and science achievement. *Journal of Educational Research, 96,* 323–338.

Vygotsky, L. S. (1978). *Mind in society: The development of higher psychological processes* (M. Cole, V. John-Steiner, S. Scribner, & E. Souberman, Trans.). Cambridge, MA: Harvard University Press.

Weiner, B. (1985). An attribution theory of achievement motivation and emotion. *Psychological Review, 92,* 548–573.

Weiner, B. (1986). *An attributional theory of motivation and emotion.* New York, NY: Springer-Verlag.

Wentzel, K. R., & Wigfield, A. (1998). Academic and social motivational influences on students' academic performance. *Educational Psychology Review, 10*(2), 155–175.

Zhang, Y., Haddad, E., Torres, B., & Chen, C. (2011). The reciprocal relationships among parents' expectations, adolescents' expectations, and adolescents' achievement: A two-wave longitudinal analysis of the NELS data. *Journal of Youth and Adolescence, 40,* 479–489.

CHAPTER 7

Promoting Autonomy in the Classroom

Teachers have to make daily decisions about the amount of autonomy that will be afforded to students. Whereas some teachers provide students with many opportunities to make a variety of choices during the school day, others structure learning environments so that students have few occasions to experience autonomy. Decisions teachers make about the design of instruction, such as many of those discussed in this book, can provide students with much or little autonomy. Furthermore, the decisions that teachers make about autonomy can have profound influences on students' learning and motivation.

Consider the following two third-grade classrooms. In each scenario, the teacher is telling the students about the morning activities. Think about how student motivation might be affected in each setting.

Example #1: "*Good morning, class. Today we are going to be reading an exciting story about a brother and a sister and their pet horse. I think you will really like the story. First, we are going to read the story together. Then, right after we read the story, we are going to talk about it. After that, I will choose some of you to act out some scenes from the story. Finally, we will do an art project related to the story.*"

Example #2: "*Good morning, class. Today we are going to be reading an exciting story about a brother and a sister and their pet horse. I think you will really like the story. We will be doing several activities this morning, including reading the story, talking about the story, acting out some scenes from the story, and doing an art project related to the story. First, I am going to give you 20 minutes to read the story. Then, you will see that I have set up three tables at the back of the room. One table is for a group discussion of the story. Another table is for a group to put together a little play and "act out" some of the story. The third table is for a group to do an art project based on the story. After we read the story, you will get to participate in two of the activities of your choice. First, you will choose one of the activities, and you will have a half hour to work in that group. Then, you will choose a second activity, and you will have an additional half hour to work in that group.*"

In both scenarios, students are engaging with the same instructional tasks. However, in the second scenario, the students are given a number of choices after they read the story. In addition, in the first scenario, which is highly controlled by the teacher, all students participate in all activities; in the second scenario, the students get to choose two of the three activities and in which order they will complete those activities. How would student motivation be affected by these different practices? Would students learn the same amounts, and be motivated in the same ways, in both classrooms? Does the provision of choice (an important dimension of autonomy) affect the students' motivation to learn?

Stop and Think

As a classroom teacher, how much autonomy do you think students should have? Does your answer vary for students at different ages and grade levels? Does it vary for different academic subjects?

THEORETICAL BASIS FOR PROVIDING AUTONOMY

Much theory-based research conducted in recent years supports the provision of autonomy in the classroom. Findings from several programs of research suggest that when students are provided with the opportunity to make meaningful choices, student motivation is enhanced. Although these findings emanate from different theoretical perspectives, all converge on the same conclusions.

Students' academic motivation can be enhanced when they are given the opportunity to make meaningful choices in the classroom.

Scott Cunningham/Merrill

At this point, it is important to distinguish between autonomy and control. Autonomy is a broad concept. First, autonomy includes choice; when students feel autonomous, they feel that they can make meaningful and important choices. One of the hallmarks of autonomy is that choices are made for intrinsic reasons; a student can only feel autonomous if the choices are made freely. For example, a student may feel highly autonomous in a classroom situation in which the student can choose to write a book report on any book that the student wants, without feeling any obligation to choose a particular type of book to please a teacher or a parent. As we will discuss later, from a self-determination theory perspective, autonomy includes more than just "choice"; in the classroom, student autonomy can be expressed by allowing students to have input on important decisions, by fostering a sense of intellectual freedom, and by allowing and even encouraging students to hold different opinions than the teachers.

In contrast, control relates to the determination of outcomes; when students feel a sense of control, they feel that they can influence outcomes. Control and autonomy are related in important ways. Generally, if a student is given many opportunities to make choices (autonomy), the student will likely feel a greater sense of control over educational outcomes. Therefore, teachers who provide students with the opportunities to make choices may enhance their students' sense of control. For example, a student who is allowed to choose the topic for a social studies project is more likely to feel that he or she has some control over the quality of the project. Thus, autonomy involves the provision of choices, whereas control involves feeling able to influence the outcomes of those choices.

In general, research indicates that perceptions of control can be related to achievement in a variety of ways. For most students, perceived control is highly important—in other words, students' beliefs about how much autonomy or control they have are related to learning and motivation. Control perceptions and achievement are related reciprocally, in that students with high control beliefs are likely to confirm their own positive expectancies for success, whereas students with low control beliefs are likely to confirm negative expectancies (Schmitz & Skinner, 1993; Seligman, 1975; Skinner, Zimmer-Gembeck, & Connell, 1998).

This type of control should not be confused with *controlling instructional practices.* Reeve (2009) described various controlling practices (e.g., adopting a narrow perspective, pressuring students to think and behave in specific ways, and intruding into students' feelings and actions). These practices are related to overall poorer functioning of students in academic settings (Reeve, 2009; Reeve, Nix, & Hamm, 2003).

Locus of Control

The concept of locus of control has a long history in education and psychology. Although the term is not used much in current psychology, its historical roots are important in terms of understanding current work on attribution theory. Rotter (1990) examined reinforcements from the perspectives of *internal* and *external locus of control.* Rotter argued that individuals perceive reinforcements as being due either to internal or external factors. An *internal locus of control* is the belief that an individual controls his or her own outcomes or reinforcements; thus, control emanates from internal, personal behaviors and characteristics. In contrast, *external locus of control* is the belief that outcomes are determined by other persons or other circumstances; thus, control emanates from external sources. Locus of control is considered to be a trait that does not change much over time. That is, students are likely to enter into classrooms with strongly developed beliefs concerning their abilities to control various outcomes in their lives.

For example, a student with a high internal locus of control might come into a classroom believing that she has ample academic ability and that, if she chooses to apply herself, she can (internally) control her own academic performance and outcomes. In contrast, a student with a high external locus of control might come into a classroom believing that he really has no power over his performance. This student might feel that teachers are the sole determinants of students' grades in academic situations. Consequently, if the student feels that teachers do not like him or are unfair, he may feel that he has little hope of ever doing well academically in school.

Attribution Theory

Attribution theory emanates, in part, from research on locus of control. However, the "locus" construct within attribution theory is more complex than Rotter's original distinction between internal and external locus of control. *Attributions* are individuals' attempts at explaining why certain events have occurred in their lives. For example, when a teacher returns examination results to students, and a student sees that he has gotten a grade of D, the student is likely to make attributions for this grade. The student may decide that he received the bad grade because he simply is not intelligent. This is an attribution to *ability*—an attribution that is internal to the student and uncontrollable; this type of attribution may be maladaptive for students because they have little control over their innate ability. Alternatively, however, the student might make the attribution to lack of *effort*— perhaps the student knows that he goofed off and simply didn't study much for the examination. This type of attribution is still internal because it reflects something about the student himself and not in the context, but it is also *controllable*—that is, the student can control how much effort he or she put forth (Weiner, 1985, 1986, 1992, 2005, 2010). Students can also attribute their successes and failures to a variety of other variables, including characteristics of the teacher, luck, or illness.

Attributions are important because they are predictive of future motivation to engage in a task. If students attribute failures to *uncontrollable* factors, such as lack of ability or an unfair teacher, they are unlikely to expect to do well on similar tasks in the future. This may also make them unwilling to engage in a task again in the future. However, if students make attributions to *controllable* variables, such as effort or strategy use, they are less likely to want to avoid the task in the future.

Attributions are classified according to three criteria: *controllability, stability,* and *locus.* Thus, the concept of *controllability* is paramount to attribution theory. *Controllability* refers to whether or not the individual feels that she or he has control over the cause of an event. For example, if a student fails an examination and attributes the failure to the fact that he did not study for the exam, this is clearly a controllable situation. In contrast, a student who believes "This teacher is just too tough" is making an uncontrollable attribution.

Attribution theory is more complex than earlier notions of internal and external locus of control because the concepts of locus and controllability are distinguished. In attribution theory, the *locus* dimension pertains to whether or not the cause of an event is perceived as emanating from within the individual student (internal) or outside the individual student (external). Thus, the student who fails an examination and attributes it to his lack of ability is making an internal attribution because ability is "internal" to the individual. It is not the case, however, that lack of ability would always be considered a *controllable* cause. Thus, in attribution theory, the notions of *locus* and *control* are distinct, compared with Rotter's locus of control.

The other dimension, *stability*, refers to whether or not the cause of an event is perceived as stable or unchanging versus unstable, or varying across situations. If the cause of an event can change across situations and tasks (such as performing poorly when feeling ill), that cause would be perceived as unstable. In contrast, if a student fails an examination and attributes it to a perceived lack of intelligence, this is a stable attribution, particularly if the student believes that intelligence is fixed, or unchangeable (Dweck & Leggett, 1988).

When discussing attribution theory and student autonomy, it is important to note that there are age differences in how students' beliefs about ability and effort are related to the emergence of attributional beliefs. Young children tend to believe that ability and effort are related positively. That is, young children assume that "smart" students exert much effort, whereas "dumb" students do not put forth much effort. As students grow older, they develop more complex understandings of the concepts of ability and effort; specifically, they often arrive at the conclusion that "smart" students simply do not have to exert much effort (i.e., because they have greater innate abilities than do "dumb" students). In fact, some students come to see ability and effort as compensating for one another—students who have to work hard must not have a lot of innate ability (Folmer et al., 2008; Nicholls, 1978, 1979; Nicholls, Patashnick, & Mettetal, 1986). These beliefs can be counterproductive, leading students to avoid working hard or at least appearing to do so. In particular, students with a record of high achievement can start to believe that they should not have to exert effort to be successful. Thus, it is important for teachers to reinforce the importance of effort and practice for achievement, for students at all levels of ability.

Some students may attribute failure to strategy deficiencies. For example, a student who fails a mathematics test and realizes that she did not know the appropriate strategies for solving the problems on the test is making an attribution to the lack of knowledge of a specific strategy; a student who receives a poor grade on a written essay in a language arts class and acknowledges that he does not understand the processes for structuring a logical essay also is making an attribution to lack of strategic knowledge. These types of attributions can be adaptive because a student who realizes this may decide to learn the strategy to alleviate the deficiency. Alternatively, an observant teacher may recognize the lack of strategic knowledge and can help students to understand that the students are not "stupid"; rather, the teacher can work with the students to learn and practice the appropriate strategies, thus facilitating attributions to effort and ultimately enhanced self-efficacy.

On a daily basis, teachers can make decisions that will affect students' attributions and can help students to develop adaptive attributions. By providing students with opportunities to make choices and important decisions, teachers can help students to develop adaptive attributional beliefs. More specifically, teachers can enhance the controllability dimension by allowing students to make meaningful decisions. Examples of how to accomplish this are provided later in this chapter.

Self-Determination Theory

Deci, Ryan, and their colleagues' theory of self-determination is a comprehensive, empirically based theory concerning intrinsic motivation (Deci & Ryan, 1985, 1987; Deci, Vallerand, Pelletier, & Ryan, 1991; Deci, Schwartz, Sheinman, & Ryan, 1981; Ryan & Deci,

2000). The concept of *autonomy* is an important component of their theory. The provision of choice is one way of promoting a sense of autonomy in students. The theory is complex and has been adapted to a variety of domains, in addition to academic learning. In this chapter, we focus on the theory as it relates to academic learning and motivation. For more detailed descriptions of the theory, readers are referred to the sources cited.

Deci, Ryan, and their colleagues posit that individuals have three basic innate psychological needs:

- The need for competence
- The need for relatedness
- The need for autonomy

In terms of academics, the *need for competence* refers to an individual's need to feel adept at engaging in academic tasks. For example, a student who can successfully master the tasks assigned by a teacher in a classroom is likely to feel competent at performing those tasks. The *need for relatedness* refers to the need to feel a sense of belonging. As has been demonstrated by a variety of studies in recent years, when students feel a sense of belonging in their schools and classrooms, academic performance is enhanced, and engagement in risky behaviors is lessened (E. M. Anderman, 2002; L. H. Anderman & Freeman, 2004; Goodenow, 1993; Resnick et al., 1997; Skinner, 1995).

The *need for autonomy* refers to an individual's need to feel a sense of control or autonomy over the environment. As mentioned earlier, autonomy is a broad concept, involving more than just the provision of choice in the classroom. Thus autonomy includes feeling that one has control over interactions with other individuals, as well as control over the various events that occur in one's life. Research by Deci and Ryan, as well as other motivation researchers, indicates that as students' perceptions of control increase, intrinsic motivation also increases (e.g., Deci & Ryan, 1985; Zuckerman, Porac, Smith, & Deci, 1978).

Deci and Ryan describe three different major types of motivation: amotivation (i.e., a complete lack of motivation), extrinsic motivation, and intrinsic or self-determined motivation (Deci & Ryan, 1985; Ryan & Deci, 2000). They theorize that when an individual truly "self determines" his or her engagement in a particular task or activity, that individual will be intrinsically motivated. Truly self-determined intrinsic motivation is one type of motivation in self-determination theory.

THE IMPORTANCE OF AUTONOMY IN THE CLASSROOM

Research clearly indicates that student motivation is enhanced when students have opportunities to make choices during classes and when students perceive that their teachers provide such opportunities (e.g., Ciani, Summers, Easter, & Sheldon, 2008; Moller, Deci, & Ryan, 2006; Patall, Cooper, & Robinson, 2008; Ryan & Grolnick, 1986; Shen, McCaughtry, Martin, & Fahlman, 2009; Swann & Pittman, 1997). As we mentioned earlier, when students are provided with opportunities to make choices, their sense of autonomy is enhanced. More specifically, intrinsic motivation is enhanced when students are able to make choices. Consequently, it seems logical that teachers should provide all students with opportunities to make choices. Yet, in reality, we all know from our own experiences that some teachers provide more opportunities for students to make choices than do others. Interestingly, research also suggests that students' opportunities to make choices change as students progress through school. For example, as students move from elementary school to middle school, opportunities to make choices during the school day tend to decrease (see Midgley, 1993). That is, students often have more opportunities to make choices when they are in elementary school than when they are in middle school. This is somewhat ironic, given that students are developmentally more able to evaluate choices as they approach adolescence (Piaget, 1952; Piaget & Inhelder, 1973). In addition, it is generally believed that students' decision-making skills develop throughout childhood, adolescence, and even into adulthood (Grisso et al., 2003; Jacobs & Ganzel, 1993). Thus, ironically, although students are able to make decisions more critically as they mature, they often are given fewer opportunities in school to do so. Research shows that students' reports of autonomy support received from both parents and teachers actually decrease during adolescence (Gillet, Vallerand, & Lafreniere, 2012).

Research also suggests that students' and teachers' *beliefs* about autonomy are different throughout various periods of development. For example, Midgley and Feldlaufer (1987) found that, in mathematics, students desire greater opportunities to be able to make decisions after the transition to middle school than prior to the transition; however, in the same study, middle-school teachers reported believing that their students in the seventh grade should have *fewer* opportunities to make decisions than did the teachers of the same students when they were in sixth grade in elementary school (Midgley & Feldlaufer, 1987). Clearly, there is a mismatch between what the students want, and are ready for, and what many teachers are providing. In addition, research also suggests that early adolescents often believe that they have limited opportunities to make important decisions at home (Flanagan, 1986).

Much research in the field of motivation suggests that when students are provided with opportunities to exercise autonomy in the classroom, motivation will be enhanced. Research by Deci and his colleagues (Deci et al., 1981) indicates that students of teachers who support autonomy in the classroom tend to be more intrinsically motivated (see also Kenny, Walsh-Blair, Blustein, Bempechat, & Seltzer, 2010). Nevertheless, in many classrooms students do not receive many opportunities to make choices or have input on decisions. In a study of motivation in African American adolescents, students rarely reported any opportunities to make choices about the types of academic tasks they did during the school day (Freeman, Gutman, & Midgley, 2002).

The perception of *control* is also very important for students. When students believe that they have some control over outcomes, both students and teachers benefit. In contrast, when students do not feel that they have a sense of control, problems may ensue. In particular, children and adolescents low in perceived control may prefer simpler, less challenging tasks, set lower or easier goals for themselves, attribute failures to their ability, and may demonstrate impaired cognitive functioning, particularly on challenging tasks (Schmitz & Skinner, 1993; Skinner, 1995). In contrast, when students believe that they do have control over their own outcomes, they are more likely to prefer challenging tasks, set higher goals for themselves, and persist when faced with difficulty (Skinner et al., 1998). Perhaps not surprisingly, such perceptions of control are also related to academic achievement (e.g., Stupinsky et al., 2007).

The purpose of this chapter is to examine some of the theory and research-based evidence for autonomy in the classroom. In addition, we hope to encourage you to think about practical applications and uses of this information, so that you can think about when and how to provide opportunities for the expression of autonomy in your classroom.

DIFFERENT TYPES OF CHOICE

Classroom teachers can provide many types of opportunities for their students to make choices during the school day. Most formal curricula used in P–12 classrooms do not directly address issues of choice. Nevertheless, classroom teachers have the opportunity and responsibility to make decisions about how, when, and where to incorporate choice into their instructional plans. These important decisions can affect student motivation and learning (Guskey & E. M. Anderman, 2008).

The idea of providing opportunities for students to make choices in the classroom is not as simple as it may seem. Certainly, allowing too many choices for students could create a situation where student work and behavior become too difficult to monitor and could be overwhelming for both students and the teacher. Thus, it is important to find a balance by providing a carefully thought-out set of controlled choices or opportunities for student self-determination that still ensures that students complete work that is consistent with curricula standards and is appropriate to their current learning needs. Following are some examples of opportunities for teachers to allow students to make some controlled choices. For each of these examples, think about how you as a teacher could use these strategies in your own instruction to allow for greater autonomy for your students.

Choice of Academic Tasks

As a teacher, you can structure some lessons so that students can choose from a variety of potential academic tasks while still achieving your learning objectives. Teachers can think about task choice in two ways: *within-task choices* and *between-task choices.*

WITHIN-TASK CHOICES When students are working on a specific task, teachers can provide opportunities for students to make choices *within the task.* In other words, students can choose different ways to go about completing the task and demonstrating their understanding. For example, students in a sixth-grade class might be working on a social studies project about Japan. The teacher could tell the students that they can make their own choices about how to acquire information about Japan. The teacher might make several suggestions, such as going to the school library, going to the public library, using some books in the classroom, using the Internet, or speaking to an adult who has visited Japan. In high-autonomy classrooms, teachers would allow the students to make the ultimate decision about how to acquire this information, although they would still require that everyone produce a comparable final project.

BETWEEN-TASK CHOICES It is also sometimes possible to allow students to choose their own academic tasks, from a variety of options. For example, another group of sixth-graders might also be studying Japan. In this instance, however, the teacher could structure the lesson so that the students could choose among several different types of activities related to Japan. The teacher might tell the students that they are required to learn some new particular facts about Japan but that they can present their information using a method of their own choosing. Different students are likely to choose different activities, such as writing a traditional written report, giving an oral presentation, writing and performing a skit, making a video presentation, or creating a Web page.

Choices in Daily Schedules

When teachers have long blocks of time to spend with students, they have more flexibility to allow their students opportunities to complete various activities during the day. This is usually possible in elementary school classrooms, where teachers spend much of the day with the same students. However, providing these types of choices is becoming easier in secondary schools as well, with the increased use of block scheduling.

An Example of Block Scheduling

In a high-school math classroom using 90-minute block schedules, the teacher might announce that students must complete three tasks during the 90 minutes. Those tasks might include (a) reviewing the previous night's homework, using computers in the classroom that will provide explanations of the problems, (b) reading a magazine article that exemplifies a practical use of a technique that the students have learned, and (c) participating in a small-group lesson on some new material. The teacher could tell the students that they all have to complete all three tasks within the 90 minutes, but that they can do the tasks in any order.

Choices for Classroom Rules

At the beginning of the year, many teachers establish a series of rules for the classroom. This represents another opportunity to foster student autonomy. Rather than merely giving the students a list of predetermined rules that they must follow, the teacher could spend some time generating a short series of reasonable rules with the students. In this way, the students will feel that they have some ownership over the rules, and they might be more likely to follow them in the future. It is more effective to provide a few important rules and to consistently enforce them than to provide a long list of rules (some of which may be ignored). Some teachers also choose to hold periodic class meetings to review the class rules and discuss whether the class is operating smoothly and whether any revision to the rules is necessary.

Choices for Where to Do Work

Many people think of classrooms in a traditional arrangement, where the teacher stands near the front of the room and students sit at desks in rows. Given the increased use of cooperative and group-learning techniques, however, many administrators are encouraging and allowing teachers to physically restructure classrooms.

One method of fostering autonomy is allowing students to choose their own work locations. Rather than telling students that they have to sit at their desks to do all their work, teachers can allow students to choose from a variety of locations—at least for some activities. For example, students could choose to use their regular desks, to go to the school library, to sit outside in a supervised courtyard, to sit on the floor, or to sit in a more comfortable area (e.g., on a sofa or alternative seating, such as beanbags, if available). Some research supports allowing students to choose their own work locations. Zimmerman and Martinez-Pons (1986) found that high-achieving students tend to physically restructure learning environments more than do lower achievers. Thus, high-achieving students are more likely to think about where they will best be able to self-regulate and effectively complete their work. Perhaps with more encouragement, other students could learn how to think better about the best locations in a classroom for their own learning.

It is also important to think about using virtual learning environments to allow students to choose where and how to work. Given the availability of audio and video teleconferencing software, it is now plausible for students to be allowed to choose to work at a computer station, where they can collaborate with peers and experts who are located remotely. For example, if a student is reading a novel that nobody else in your school is reading, that student could potentially be matched with a student at another school from across the country (or even internationally) who is reading the same book; using technology, the two students could converse about the novel and perhaps work on a collaborative project. This and other uses of technology to enhance autonomy are now easily available in many classrooms.

Nevertheless, the provision of autonomy, if it is provided haphazardly, can lead to increased behavioral problems. As noted by Maehr and Midgley (1996), teachers need to carefully examine the potential effects of opportunities for choice on student behavior. Whereas teachers certainly do not want to create unsafe environments characterized by pandemonium, they need to carefully balance student autonomy with issues of safety and well-being. If teachers were to allow students to suddenly go from having no autonomy to having complete control over most of their daily activities, problems likely would arise. However, the teacher who carefully and strategically implements limited opportunities for choice into well-structured and effective lessons is unlikely to experience serious behavioral problems. As with any classroom routines, students may require some guidance and practice in working more autonomously.

Choices for What School to Attend

It is important to recognize that other types of choices sometimes are provided for students and parents. In many regions of the United States, parents and students can choose which schools students will attend. These choices of schools range from the choice to attend public school, private schools, religious schools, or to be home-schooled or attend electronic ("online") schools. In addition, within the arena of public schools, choices often exist between the types of schools that students can attend. For example, some schools offer specializations. Such "magnet" schools may offer a focus on a particular area of study.

There is some evidence that school choice can positively affect student outcomes. For example, in the state of Connecticut, where students may choose to attend magnet schools in other districts, academic achievement is enhanced in reading and mathematics for high school students who choose to attend such schools (Bifulco, Cobb, & Bell, 2009). Similar results have been reported for students in Los Angeles, California (Ledwith, 2010), and in Italy (Ponzo, 2011). In addition, data from Chicago indicate that when students choose to attend specific schools, on-time graduation rates may be enhanced (Lauen, 2009). These beneficial effects may be due to a host of factors, including the ability to attend schools that cater to students' specific interests, the ability to attend desegregated schools, and the ability to interact with diverse teachers who may better meet students' needs.

Choices for Traditional Versus Hybrid/Online Learning Environments

In recent years, the prevalence of online and hybrid learning environments has increased dramatically. Students in both K–12 and college settings now have numerous options regarding choices of learning environments. These choices can be monitored and controlled by parents to some extent. For example, a parent can certainly influence whether or not an adolescent attends a traditional high school or a "virtual" high school.

Nevertheless, there are many situations in which students can make choices about traditional versus virtual learning environments. This is particularly true at the college level, where students may have the option of choosing to attend certain classes in person or to take alternative versions of those courses in an online format. Although research on the effects of such choices on learning outcomes is nascent, some research indicates that students' motivational beliefs may influence their choices. For example, research suggests that college students are more likely to choose a traditional classroom option for a course when they endorse mastery goals and when they are interested in expending effort in a class, whereas feeling efficacious at learning in online environments is predictive of choosing a virtual learning environment (Clayton, Blumberg, & Auld, 2010).

FACTORS THAT AFFECT STUDENT AUTONOMY

Even the best-intentioned teacher must realize that there are impediments to providing students with opportunities for making choices in the classroom. Although some teachers might truly want to give their students multiple opportunities to make decisions during the school day, numerous factors can interfere with teachers' attempts to enhance student autonomy. For example, teachers may provide students with opportunities to make choices, but some students may not be comfortable with these opportunities because of a variety of factors. The next section presents some issues that teachers must seriously consider when working to provide students with opportunities for autonomy.

Gender in the Classroom

The gender breakdown of the classroom may have an influence on the types of decisions that students and teachers make in the classroom. We probably all can think of examples of situations in which we wanted to do something that might be considered gender atypical, and we consequently chose to engage in a less preferred but more socially acceptable activity. For example, a boy might truly be interested in learning ballet, but due to gender stereotypes, most boys probably would not choose to enroll in a ballet class.

Gender stereotypes emerge at very young ages. Boys generally know what boys "should" do, and girls know what girls "should" do by age 3 (Kuhn, Nash, & Brucken, 1978). In addition, particularly at young ages, children prefer to play with same-sex peers, rather than with opposite-sex peers (Maccoby & Jacklin, 1987). Such early gender stereotyping can influence the types of decisions that children make in the classroom. Indeed, when students are given opportunities to make choices, those choices often may be made along gender lines. When male students are in classrooms with many other male students, they may feel compelled to choose to engage in activities that would be perceived as masculine in nature; however, when male students are in classrooms with many female students, some males may feel compelled to make choices that will be perceived as masculine, whereas others may be more daring and willing to try an activity that might be perceived as more feminine in nature. Nevertheless, the gender distribution within a classroom certainly can affect the types of choices that students make. When teachers are aware of these concerns, they can better structure the environment so that students can be comfortable with their choices.

MALE AND FEMALE STUDENTS' EXPERIENCES IN THE CLASSROOM   Some research indicates that male and female students do have different experiences in classrooms. Indeed, both teachers and other students may respond differently to males and females, and teachers may make different decisions based on student gender.

For example, some research indicates that female students feel less confident in mixed-gender classrooms; these feelings in turn cause some female students to feel less comfortable participating in classroom activities (Orenstein, 1994). Such feelings of discomfort may hinder females' perceptions of autonomy.

Other research indicates that teachers often praise female and male students differently. This differential praise may also affect students' autonomy in the classroom. For example, male students often are praised for providing correct answers, whereas female students are often praised for just trying (Sadker & Sadker, 1994). In addition, praise given to male students often is more specific in nature than is the praise that is given to female students (Parsons, Kaczala, & Meece, 1982). Female students may become less likely to voice their opinions when given the opportunity to make autonomous decisions in environments in which they are not often praised.

These features of classrooms, as well as other factors, influence the types of choices that students make. It is important for teachers to be aware of the potential influence that gender can have on the choices that students are willing to make. Indeed, the types of choices made by students in classrooms may be precursors to future course and career choices. Unfortunately, research indicates that although gender differences between females and males in many academic subjects have decreased in recent years, many more males than females still are employed in science- and math-related careers (Eisenberg, Martin, & Fabes, 1996). Thus, teachers should be aware of gender-related influences so that they can create classroom environments in which all students' choices are valued and respected.

Ethnicity in the Classroom

The ethnic makeup of a classroom can also affect the types of choices that students make. Certain activities may be perceived as being more culturally appropriate for some ethnic groups than for others. Thus, a student might be truly interested in choosing to participate in a certain task but might ultimately choose not to because the activity is not perceived as culturally appropriate for him or her (Gay, 2000).

For example, students from some cultures may prefer working in groups more than students from other cultures. Therefore, if teachers present students with the choice of working on a class project either in a group or alone, some students may choose to work alone due to culturally based preferences. However, other students may not understand those preferences and thus may interpret the student's desire to work alone as a rejection of other classmates. Alternatively, students who regularly choose to work with others may be perceived as lacking independence or being overly reliant on their peers. Thus, misunderstandings of culturally based preferences may lead to problems for both teachers and students in the classroom. Consequently, teachers need to be sensitive to potential cultural influences on student autonomy.

Research indicates that achievement differences are correlated with culture (Steinberg, Dornbusch, & Brown, 1992). Students from different ethnic and cultural backgrounds have different childhood experiences, and these experiences affect students' later school experiences. The experiences of majority students may be more aligned with the expectations of schools than are the experiences of minority students. Work in multicultural education has received much support in terms of making learning environments more appropriate for all students (e.g., Banks, 1995). Nevertheless, potential mismatches between students' expectations and classroom practices still abound, and they certainly influence the types of decisions that students make in school.

Research also indicates that in some cultures, the relation between choice and motivation may depend on relationships with parents or teachers. Studies of Chinese children indicated that whether or not students could make choices only affected their motivation when they did not have close relationships with their mothers or their teachers (Bao & Lam, 2008). Specifically, when children had close relationships with their teachers or mothers, it didn't matter if the student or the teacher/mother made choices (e.g., chose in which activity to participate); however, if the child and the mother or teacher had poor interpersonal relationships, then student motivation only remained high if the students made the choice. Thus when these children have good relationships with their mothers or their teachers, student motivation is high whether or not choices are made by the children themselves or by the teacher or mother. One possible explanation for these findings, from a self-determination theory perspective, is that children who have good relationships with their parents or teachers have probably internalized many of their beliefs; consequently, the choices made by the mothers and teachers probably fulfill these children's need for relatedness.

Thus, ethnicity may influence the types of decisions that students make in a highly autonomous classroom. When students from diverse ethnic backgrounds are given the opportunity to make choices during the school day, some of these choices will be influenced by cultural variables. Teachers need to be keenly aware of this possibility. Again, what is important is to be aware—teachers may not want or need to change anything about their decision making; however, they do need to create classroom environments where students feel comfortable making various choices and where the choices that students make are respected by their classmates.

Peer Influences in the Classroom

Students are not alone in the classroom. They are keenly aware of the presence of their peers, particularly as they approach adolescence. Consequently, students often will be cognizant of how they are being seen by their peers and, thus, may not choose to engage in activities or tasks that their peers might ridicule.

Peer pressure can be a salient influence at any age. However, it may be particularly problematic during the early adolescent years. Research indicates that students are most likely to conform to peers' beliefs and expectations during middle adolescence (i.e., around the age of 14), although this varies somewhat depending on the particular area of conformity that is being considered (Berndt, 1979; Sim & Koh, 2003). Early adolescents who do not have strong emotional ties to their families may be particularly vulnerable to peer pressure (Erwin, 1993). Because of the desire to be perceived as not being different from one's peers, adolescents in particular may prefer to conform to perceived norms, rather than to take risks and to choose to engage in challenging and unconventional (but interesting) tasks (Hartup, 1983).

Stop and Think

How can teachers alleviate the potential negative effects of peers on student autonomy? One way is to allow students to make choices privately. Think about ways to structure the classroom environment and your lessons so that students' choices are private, not public. Another way is to emphasize to your students, from the first day of class, that all choices are valued and respected in your classroom. As the teacher, you might want to demonstrate this by doing something unconventional and by stressing to students that doing the unconventional is perfectly acceptable and even encouraged in your classroom.

DIFFERING TYPES OF AUTONOMY SUPPORT

Teachers can utilize a variety of instructional practices that support student autonomy. However, it is important to realize that there are different types of autonomy supportive behaviors; each of these may lead to different types of outcomes for students. Stefanou, Perencevich, DiCintio, and Turner (2004) have identified three types of autonomy-supportive behaviors in teachers: organizational, procedural, and cognitive.

Organizational autonomy support occurs when teachers give students the opportunity to make choices regarding aspects of the classroom environment. Examples of instructional strategies that provide organizational autonomy support include allowing students to choose group members, to help to create classroom rules, and to choose seating arrangements in the classroom.

Procedural autonomy support occurs when teachers encourage "student ownership of form" (Stefanou et al., 2004, p. 101). Examples of strategies that provide procedural autonomy support include giving students the opportunity to choose materials to be used in class projects, how work will be displayed, and how competence will be demonstrated.

Cognitive autonomy support occurs when students are given opportunities to feel ownership over their own learning. Examples of strategies that provide cognitive autonomy support include giving students the opportunity to discuss varied approaches to solving problems, freely debate ideas, and find differing solutions to problems.

Although all three types of autonomy support are important, research indicates that cognitive-autonomy-supportive practices are particularly important, as they are most likely to promote long-term engagement among students. The use of organizational and procedural autonomy practices may initially enhance students' interest in a lesson or a topic, but those strategies are unlikely to facilitate long-term cognitive engagement. In contrast, when students are allowed to explore unique ways to solve problems and given the opportunity to make decisions regarding the cognitive aspects of how they will approach and work through a problem or task, then engagement is more likely to be enhanced (Stefanou et al., 2004).

SUGGESTIONS FOR ENHANCING OPPORTUNITIES FOR STUDENT AUTONOMY

Some examples in the literature illustrate ways in which teachers can restructure learning environments to foster greater autonomy. For example, Maehr, Midgley, and their colleagues (E. M. Anderman, Maehr, & Midgley, 1999; Maehr & Midgley, 1996) worked with teachers and administrators at the elementary- and middle-school levels to enhance student motivation. Specifically, they worked with school personnel using a goal-orientation-theory perspective to change school policies and practices that directly affected student motivation.

Maehr and Midgley argue that, in terms of autonomy, school personnel need to examine the balance between staff control and student autonomy. Staff members need to critically examine the quality and quantity of choices that are afforded to students on a daily, weekly, monthly, and annual basis. If students are provided with opportunities to make meaningful choices, they are likely to feel more responsible. Thus, schools that provide few opportunities for student autonomy can be characterized as schools in which "Faculty makes the rules. Students obey—or else" (Maehr & Midgley, 1996, p. 114).

Maehr, Midgley, and their colleagues worked with school personnel to enhance opportunities for autonomy. Realizing that research indicates a clear link between perceived opportunities for autonomy and enhanced student motivation, the researchers collaborated with teachers to implement new practices that would afford students greater opportunities to make choices. For example, at the middle-school level, the team of researchers and school personnel discussed and implemented opportunities for students to make choices about course materials (e.g., what books to read in English classes). The school also implemented a "small house" at the seventh-grade level in which students could remain with a smaller group of peers and teachers, rather than traveling around from class to class. However, to enhance autonomy, teachers and administrators allowed students to make the important choice concerning whether or not they would be in the small house or in the traditional classroom (E. M. Anderman et al., 1999).

As noted by Reeve (2009), teachers can deliberately provide opportunities for students to experience greater autonomy. We present several suggestions for creative ways to enhance student autonomy throughout the school year. We urge you to consider the developmental appropriateness of each suggestion—whereas some are clearly applicable to young children, others may only be effective with adolescents.

Involve Students in Behavior Management

At the beginning of the school year, when teachers are setting up classroom rules and procedures, teachers should try to involve students in the process of deciding on class rules (Davis & Thomas, 1989). If students are involved in making these important decisions, they will feel a sense of ownership over the rules and will be more likely to adhere to them and follow the procedures. It is important to consider allowing students to make choices, even if the students experience behavioral issues or academic concerns (Harper, 2007); of course teachers must be cautious in these situations, but the benefits of autonomy should benefit all students, not just the compliant and high-achieving students.

In addition, Maehr and Midgley (1996) argued that autonomy and responsibility will be enhanced if students are actually allowed to participate in conflict-resolution programs.

Autonomy can be enhanced by allowing students to be involved in making decisions during the school day.

Rather than simply having school personnel decide on the outcomes of behavioral issues, consider allowing students to be involved in this process. Some students may become more emotionally and academically invested in schooling if they know that their voices and opinions will be valued in this way.

Present Students with Opportunities to Make Choices That Are Important to Them

The ways in which students think about the choices that they are going to make are affected by students' attitudes and beliefs about the choice. If the choice involves something that is personally meaningful to the student, he or she is likely to make the choice more carefully than if the choice is unimportant (Jacobs & Ganzel, 1993).

Eliminate Factors That Will Block Creativity in Making Choices

When making decisions, students may be affected by a variety of factors, including their peers, their parents, and social constraints. For example, a social studies teacher might allow students to choose any biography to read for their next book report. A male student might truly be interested in the biography of Susan B. Anthony, but the student might refrain from choosing this book because he might feel that his peers or his parents would make fun of him for reading such a book. Thus, teachers should allow students to make at least some of their decisions privately. If the teacher in this instance truly wants students to be creative and choose a truly interesting book, he or she could eliminate public presentations. The students could read their books at home and turn in their

Many social factors may affect the choices that our students make.

reports, which don't necessarily have to be shared with the other students. If the students know that their choices will remain private, they will be more likely to make innovative choices.

Consider Small Choices That Students Can Make Every Day

Opportunities for autonomy in the classroom can be provided in many ways. Choices don't always have to be major decisions, such as the choice for a semester-long project. Rather, it is quite possible to foster autonomy in small ways and on a daily basis.

Every day before class, try to come up with at least one way in which you can provide your students with opportunities to make choices. For example, you might have four tasks that you plan to cover during a particular class session. When it is possible, why not ask the students their preferences for the order of tasks? Of course, some tasks will naturally need to occur before others (e.g., a lesson on fractions might be necessary before doing an activity in which students use fractions). However, on other days, you may feel that you have more flexibility, and the inclusion of choices may be more readily applicable. Similarly, students might choose whether to work independently or with a partner, or whether they want to use "hands-on" manipulatives to work on math problems.

You may need to think "out of the box" to provide opportunities for autonomy on a daily basis. However, it is possible, and your students will appreciate these opportunities.

Assist Students in Attributing Failures to External, Controllable Events

As has been mentioned, attribution theorists (e.g., Weiner, 1985, 1986) classify attributions according to the dimensions of controllability, locus, and stability. The concept of *autonomy* that has been addressed in this chapter overlaps with both the controllability and locus dimensions.

When students do not succeed at academic tasks, they will make attributions as to the causes of their failure. Teachers play an important role in these situations. Without any feedback from the teacher, students may make maladaptive attributions, which ultimately may lead to declines in motivation and continued low performance. If a student does not succeed at a task (e.g., a student fails a test), as a teacher you can help students to gain some perspective in terms of issues related to autonomy. For example, if a student fails an examination, taking a few minutes to question the student about her study habits may help the student to attribute the failure to controllable, internal factors, rather than to factors that are perceived as being outside the student's control. Consider the following dialogue:

> TEACHER: Rose, you know you didn't do very well on the vocabulary quiz. Why do you think that happened?
>
> ROSE: Because I'm stupid. I can't remember anything. I try to memorize the words, but I just can't learn them. I'm just one of those dumb kids who can't learn well.
>
> TEACHER: Rose, tell me how you studied the words.
>
> ROSE: I read the list over and over again.
>
> TEACHER: For how long did you do this?
>
> ROSE: For a half hour.
>
> TEACHER: Were you doing anything else at the same time?
>
> ROSE: No, just watching TV.
>
> TEACHER: Do you think that watching the TV while you were studying affected your ability to learn the words?
>
> ROSE: Well . . . maybe a little bit.
>
> TEACHER: Did you have to keep the TV on while you were studying?
>
> ROSE: Well, no.
>
> TEACHER: So you really had control over this situation. You could have decided to turn off the TV and learn the words. Rose, I really think that you made a poor choice and that your bad grade is due not to being "dumb" but simply to the fact that you chose to pay more attention to the TV show than to your spelling words.
>
> ROSE: Well, maybe.
>
> TEACHER: Rose, I know that you can do this work, you have done well before. You can do this. You just need to try harder and think about how you are going to study.

Rose initially attributes her poor grade to lack of ability. She truly feels that she did try to study, but that she just was unable to really learn the work. However, through a brief conversation, the teacher helps Rose to see that she actually did have control over the situation and that her poor performance probably is not due to "being dumb." A few simple words from the teacher can make a big difference.

It often is difficult to have conversations of this nature with students, particularly when 30 other students are in the room. But if you can find the time to talk privately with students, those conversations can make a big difference. If you don't have time to talk to a student, another strategy would be to write a note to the student on his or her examination to get him or her to think about what to do differently to be more successful in the future.

Promote a Supportive, Caring Environment

When students perceive that their teachers care about them as learners, beneficial outcomes result (Juvonen, 2006; Wentzel, 1997). More specifically, research indicates that when students perceive that their teachers care, they are more likely to develop positive beliefs about perceived control. For example, Skinner and her colleagues (Skinner et al., 1998) found that children who perceived their teachers as warm and supportive developed positive beliefs about control, whereas students who experienced their teachers as uncaring and cold were more likely to develop external control beliefs, which ultimately led to lower academic achievement and negative feelings about school.

Summary

This chapter outlined some of the research indicating that it is beneficial and important to provide students with opportunities for autonomy in the classroom. When students are given occasions to make choices, they are likely to develop positive motivational beliefs that, in turn, may lead to enhanced feelings of autonomy and improved achievement. In addition, when students are given opportunities to control some aspects of the learning environment, they may develop adaptive attributions and, thus, be able to cope better with frustration and failure.

Teachers have to make important decisions concerning the amount of control that will be afforded to their students. When teachers make these decisions, they need to consider instructional issues, behavioral issues, and motivational issues. It is often difficult and challenging to provide students with autonomy. As students gain control in the classroom, teachers inevitably lose some control. However, research suggests that students' perceptions of control and opportunities for autonomy are extraordinarily beneficial, in terms of both their short-term learning and long-term development.

Questions to Consider

1. Is the provision of autonomy practical for this task?
2. How can I prevent behavioral problems from ensuing, while providing opportunities for autonomy?
3. How can the task be structured so that all students feel that they have a sense of autonomy?
4. How will autonomy affect student motivation and learning within this task?

LEARNING ACTIVITY 7.1   Developing Autonomy in the Classroom

Select one of the following lesson plans (one is for elementary-school students, one is for middle-school students, and one is for high-school students). Then, rewrite the lesson plan to include several opportunities for students to express autonomy.

Elementary-School Plan: You are a third-grade teacher preparing a lesson on writing in cursive letters. Students have completed learning how to write all letters. You now want them to engage in an activity that will allow them to practice this newly developed skill.

Middle-School Plan: You are an eighth-grade teacher preparing a social studies lesson on the American Civil War. Students have just read their textbook chapter on the Civil War and have also spent several days discussing the chapter in class. You now want them to engage in an activity that will allow them to apply what they have learned to some social problem in modern society.

High-School Plan: You are an 11th-grade English teacher preparing a lesson on the Shakespearean play *Macbeth*. Students have read the entire play over several days (as a group). They have also engaged in several group discussions about themes from the play. You now want them to engage in an activity that will allow them to further examine themes from the play.

References

Anderman, E. M. (2002). School effects on psychological outcomes during adolescence. *Journal of Educational Psychology, 94,* 795–809.

Anderman, E. M., Maehr, M. L., & Midgley, C. (1999). Declining motivation after the transition to middle school: Schools can make a difference. *Journal of Research and Development in Education, 32,* 131–147.

Anderman, L. H., & Freeman, T. M. (2004). Students' sense of belonging in school. In P. R. Pintrich & M. L. Maehr (Eds.), *Motivating students, improving schools: The legacy of Carol Midgley* (Vol. 13, pp. 27–63). Amsterdam, The Netherlands: JAI Press.

Banks, J. A. (1995). *Handbook of multicultural education.* New York, NY: Macmillan.

Bao, X., & Lam, S. (2008). Who makes the choice? Rethinking the role of autonomy and relatedness in Chinese children's motivation. *Child Development, 79,* 269–283.

Berndt, T. J. (1979). Developmental changes in conformity to peers and parents. *Developmental Psychology, 15,* 608–616.

Bifulco, R., Cobb, C. D., & Bell, C. (2009). Can interdistrict choice boost student achievement? The case of Connecticut's interdistrict magnet school program. *Educational Evaluation and Policy Analysis, 31,* 323–345.

Ciani, K. D., Summers, J. J., Easter, M. A., & Sheldon, K. M. (2008). Cooperative learning and positive experiences: Does letting students choose their groups matter? *Educational Psychology, 28,* 627–641.

Clayton, K., Blumberg, F., & Auld, D. P. (2010). The relationship between motivation, learning strategies and choice of environment whether traditional or including an online component. *British Journal of Educational Technology, 41,* 349–364.

Davis, G. A., & Thomas, M. A. (1989). *Effective schools and effective teachers.* Needham Heights, MA: Allyn & Bacon.

Deci, E. L., & Ryan, R. M. (1985). *Intrinsic motivation and self-determination in human behavior.* New York, NY: Plenum.

Deci, E. L., & Ryan, R. M. (1987). The support of autonomy and the control of behavior. *Journal of Personality and Social Psychology, 53,* 1024–1037.

Deci, E. L., Schwartz, A. J., Sheinman, L., & Ryan, R. M. (1981). An instrument to assess adults' orientations toward control versus autonomy with children: Reflections on intrinsic motivation and perceived competence. *Journal of Educational Psychology, 73,* 642–650.

Deci, E. L., Vallerand, R., Pelletier, L., & Ryan, R. (1991). Motivation and education: The self-determination perspective. *Educational Psychologist, 26,* 325–346.

Dweck, C. S., & Leggett, E. L. (1988). A social-cognitive approach to motivation and personality. *Psychological Review, 95*(2), 256–273.

Eisenberg, N., Martin, C. L., & Fabes, R. A. (1996). Gender development and gender effects. In D. C. Berliner & R. C. Calfee (Eds.), *Handbook of educational psychology* (pp. 358–396). New York, NY: Macmillan Library Reference USA.

Erwin, P. (1993). *Friendship and peer relations in children.* Chichester, England: Wiley.

Flanagan, C. (1986, March). *Early adolescent needs and family decision-making environments: A study of person-environment fit.* Paper presented at the American Educational Research Association, San Francisco.

Folmer, A. S., Cole, D. A., Sigal, A. B., Benbow, L. D., Satterwhite, L. F., Swygert, K. E., & Ciesla, J. A. (2008). Age-related changes in children's understanding of effort and ability: Implications for attribution theory and motivation. *Journal of Experimental Child Psychology, 99,* 114–134.

Freeman, K. E., Gutman, L. M., & Midgley, C. (2002). Can achievement goal theory enhance our understanding of the motivation and performance of African American young adolescents? In C. Midgley (Ed.), *Goals, goal structures, and patterns of adaptive learning* (pp. 175–204). Mahwah, NJ: Erlbaum.

Gay, G. (2000). *Culturally responsive teaching: Theory, research, and practice.* New York, NY: Teachers College Press.

Gillet, N., Vallerand, R. J., & Lafreniere, M. A. (2012). Intrinsic and extrinsic school motivation as a function of age: The mediating role of autonomy support. *Social Psychology of Education, 15,* 77–95.

Goodenow, C. (1993). Classroom belonging among early adolescent students: Relationships to motivation and achievement. *Journal of Early Adolescence, 13*(1), 21–43.

Grisso, T., Steinberg, L., Woolard, J., Cauffman, E., Scott, E., Graham, S., et al. (2003). Juveniles' competence to stand trial: A comparison of adolescents' and adults' capacities as trial defendants. *Law and Human Behavior, 27,* 333–363.

Guskey, T. R., & Anderman, E. M. (2008). Students at bat. *Educational Leadership, 66*(3), 8–14.

Harper, E. (2007). Making good choices: How autonomy support influences the behavior change and motivation of troubled and troubling youth. *Reclaiming Children and Youth: The Journal of Strength-Based Interventions, 16,* 23–28.

Hartup, W. W. (1983). Peer relations. In P. H. Mussen (Ed.), *Handbook of child psychology: Vol. IV. Socialization* (pp. 103–196). New York, NY: Wiley.

Jacobs, J. E., & Ganzel, A. K. (1993). Decision-making in adolescence: Are we asking the wrong question? In M. L. Maehr & P. R. Pintrich (Eds.), *Advances in motivation and achievement: Motivation and adolescent development* (Vol. 8, pp. 1–31). Greenwich, CT: JAI Press.

Juvonen, J. (2006). Sense of belonging, social bonds, and school functioning. In P. A. Alexander & P. H. Winne (Eds.), *Handbook of educational psychology* (2nd ed., pp. 655–674). Mahwah, NJ: Erlbaum.

Kenny, M. E., Walsh-Blair, L. Y., Blustein, D. L., Bempechat, J., & Seltzer, J. (2010). Achievement motivation among urban adolescents: Work hope, autonomy support, and achievement-related beliefs. *Journal of Vocational Behavior, 77,* 205–212.

Kuhn, D., Nash, S. C., & Brucken, L. (1978). Sex role concepts of two- and three-year-old children. *Child Development, 49,* 445–451.

Lauen, D. L. (2009). To choose or not to choose: High school choice and graduation in Chicago. *Educational Evaluation and Policy Analysis, 331,* 179–199.

Ledwith, V. (2010). The influence of open enrollment on scholastic achievement among public school students in Los Angeles. *American Journal of Education, 116,* 243–262.

Maccoby, E. E., & Jacklin, C. N. (1987). Gender segregation in childhood. In H. W. Reese (Ed.), *Advances in child development and behavior* (Vol. 20, pp. 239–288). San Diego, CA: Academic Press.

Maehr, M. L., & Midgley, C. (1996). *Transforming school cultures.* Boulder, CO: Westview Press.

Midgley, C. (1993). Motivation and middle level schools. In M. L. Maehr & P. R. Pintrich (Eds.), *Advances in motivation and achievement: Motivation in the adolescent years* (Vol. 8). Greenwich, CT: JAI Press.

Midgley, C., & Feldlaufer, H. (1987). Students' and teachers' decision-making fit before and after the transition to junior high school. *Journal of Early Adolescence, 7*(2), 225–241.

Moller, A. C., Deci, E. L., & Ryan, R. M. (2006). Choice and ego-depletion: The moderating role of autonomy. *Personality and Social Psychology Bulletin, 32*(8), 1024–1036.

Nicholls, J. G. (1978). The development of the concepts of effort and ability, perception of academic attainment, and the understanding that difficult tasks require more ability. *Child Development, 49*, 800–814.

Nicholls, J. G. (1979). Quality and equality in intellectual development: The role of motivation in education. *American Psychologist, 34*, 1071–1084.

Nicholls, J. G., Patashnick, M., & Mettetal, G. (1986). Conceptions of ability and intelligence. *Child Development, 57*, 636–645.

Orenstein, P. (1994). *Schoolgirls: Young women, self-esteem, and the confidence gap.* New York, NY: Doubleday.

Parsons, J. E., Kaczala, C. M., & Meece, J. L. (1982). Socialization of achievement attitudes and beliefs: Classroom influences. *Child Development, 53*, 322–329.

Patall, E. A., Cooper, H., & Robinson, J. C. (2008). The effects of choice on intrinsic motivation and related outcomes: A meta-analysis of research findings. *Psychological Bulletin, 134*, 270–300.

Piaget, J. (1952). *The origin of intelligence in children.* New York, NY: International Universities Press.

Piaget, J., & Inhelder, B. (1973). *Memory and intelligence.* London: Routledge & Kegan Paul.

Ponzo, M. (2011). The effects of school competition on the achievement of Italian students. *Managerial and Decision Economics, 32*, 53–61.

Reeve, J. (2009). Why teachers adopt a controlling motivating style toward students and how they can become more autonomy supportive. *Educational Psychologist, 44*, 159–175.

Reeve, J., Nix, G., & Hamm, D. (2003). Testing models of the experience of self-determination in intrinsic motivation and the conundrum of choice. *Journal of Educational Psychology, 95*, 375–392.

Resnick, M. D., Bearman, P. S., Blum, R. W., Bauman, K. E., Harris, K. M., Jones, J., et al. (1997). Protecting adolescents from harm: Findings from the National Longitudinal Study on Adolescent Health. *Journal of the American Medical Association, 278*, 823–832.

Rotter, J. (1990). Internal versus external control of reinforcement: A case history of a variable. *American Psychologist, 45*, 489–493.

Ryan, R. M., & Deci, E. L. (2000). Intrinsic and extrinsic motivations: Classic definitions and new directions. *Contemporary Educational Psychology, 25*, 54–67.

Ryan, R. M., & Grolnick, W. S. (1986). Origins and pawns in the classroom: Self-report and projective assessments of individual differences in children's perceptions. *Journal of Personality and Social Psychology, 50*, 550–558.

Sadker, M., & Sadker, D. (1994). *Failing at fairness: How our schools cheat girls.* New York, NY: Simon & Schuster.

Schmitz, B., & Skinner, E. A. (1993). Perceived control, effort, and academic performance: Interindividual, intraindividual, and multivariate time-series analyses. *Journal of Personality and Social Psychology, 64*, 1010–1028.

Seligman, M. E. P. (1975). *Helplessness: On depression, development, and death.* San Francisco, CA: Freeman.

Shen, B., McCaughtry, N., Martin, J., & Fahlman, M. (2009). Effects of teacher autonomy support on students' autonomous motivation on learning in physical education. *Research Quarterly for Exercise and Sport, 80*, 44–53.

Sim, T., & Koh, S. (2003). A domain conceptualization of adolescent susceptibility to peer pressure. *Journal of Research on Adolescence, 13*(1), 57–80.

Skinner, E. A. (1995). *Perceived control, motivation, and coping.* Thousand Oaks, CA: Sage.

Skinner, E. A., Zimmer-Gembeck, M. J., & Connell, J. P. (1998). Individual differences and the development of perceived control. *Monographs of the Society for Research in Child Development, 63*, 2–3.

Stefanou, C. R., Perencevich, K. C., DiCintio, M., & Turner, J. C. (2004). Supporting autonomy in the classroom: Ways teachers encourage student decision making and ownership. *Educational Psychologist, 39*, 97–110.

Steinberg, L., Dornbusch, S. M., & Brown, B. B. (1992). Ethnic differences in adolescent achievement: An ecological perspective. *American Psychologist, 47*, 723–729.

Stupkinsky, R. H., Renaud, R. D., Perry, R. P., Ruthig, J. C., Haynes, T. L., & Clifton, R. A. (2007). Comparing self-esteem and perceived control as predictors of first-year college students' academic achievement. *Social Psychology of Education, 10*, 303–330.

Swann, W. B., & Pittman, T. S. (1997). Initiating play activity of children: The moderating influence of verbal cues on intrinsic motivation. *Child Development, 48*, 1128–1132.

Weiner, B. (1985). An attribution theory of achievement motivation and emotion. *Psychological Review, 92*, 548–573.

Weiner, B. (1986). *An attributional theory of motivation and emotion.* New York, NY: Springer-Verlag.

Weiner, B. (1992). *Human motivation: Metaphors, theories, and research.* Newbury Park, CA: Sage.

Weiner, B. (2005). Motivation from an attributional perspective and the social psychology of perceived competence. In A. J. Elliot & C. S. Dweck (Eds.), *Handbook of competence and motivation* (pp. 73–84). New York, NY: Guilford Publications.

Weiner, B. (2010). The development of an attribution-based theory of motivation: A history of ideas. *Educational Psychologist, 45*, 28–36.

Wentzel, K. R. (1997). Student motivation in middle school: The role of perceived pedagogical caring. *Journal of Educational Psychology, 89*, 411–419.

Zimmerman, B. J., & Martinez-Pons, M. (1986). Development of a structured interview for assessing student use of self-regulated learning strategies. *American Educational Research Journal, 23*, 614–628.

Zuckerman, M., Porac, J. L., Smith, R., & Deci, E. L. (1978). On the importance of self-determination for intrinsically motivated behavior. *Personality and Social Psychology Bulletin, 4*, 443–446.

CHAPTER 8

The Self and Motivation

The way students feel about themselves as learners often isn't considered a major outcome of interest in today's classrooms. As long as students learn the material and do well on assessments, students' self-beliefs often are not regarded seriously in many classrooms. Consider the following examples:

> *Mac is a fourth-grade student. For the most part, she is an average-achieving student, but she has always experienced difficulty with mathematics. In particular, Mac finds division problems to be particularly challenging. Although Mac feels positively about her abilities in most areas, she simply does not believe that she has the academic prowess to successfully solve division problems.*
>
> *David is a 12th-grader. He is not happy with most parts of his life. He isn't satisfied with his academic performance, with his appearance, with his social life, or with his athletic abilities. Basically there just isn't anything that David "likes" about himself. He doesn't take pride in any of his abilities.*

What is the difference between Mac and David? In some ways, both students lack confidence in certain aspects of themselves. Mac holds negative beliefs about her abilities for a particular topic: division. In contrast, David isn't happy with any aspect of himself. He doesn't take pride in any of his qualities. As teachers, we know that all children and adolescents have positive qualities, but some of them do not feel good about these qualities. The rigors and demands of instruction often preclude classroom teachers from helping students to appreciate themselves. Nevertheless, psychological variables are important outcomes and can be influenced by teachers (E. M. Anderman, 2002; Woolfolk Hoy, Hoy, & Davis, 2009).

In this chapter, we examine the ways that teachers can influence students' beliefs about themselves. Although schools often emphasize learning and test scores as the most valued outcomes, we hope in this chapter to convince you that teachers have a responsibility to create learning environments that are psychologically healthy and safe for learners. While we are working on instructing students in important content areas, we also need to consider how school experiences are affecting students' beliefs about themselves. This is important in itself; however, it also is important to realize that self-beliefs are related in important ways to how students learn.

THE SELF AND THE CLASSROOM

Students' beliefs about themselves are very important. If students have experiences that lead to negative self-beliefs, these shortcomings in students' feelings about themselves and their abilities can have deleterious effects on a number of other academic variables. It is quite possible for some students that beliefs about their abilities might be based in fiction rather than fact; nevertheless, these beliefs can result in debilitating anxiety that can lead to poor academic performance. For example, consider the student that has come to believe over time that he simply "isn't a math student." This belief may be based on numerous negative experiences that the student has had in the past and may be extremely incapacitating to the student. Nevertheless, the belief may not be a true representation of the student's actual abilities in mathematics. Although most teachers are not trained or licensed to recognize and treat these psychological problems, teachers can become aware of their students' self-beliefs and can use instructional practices that are more conducive to students' mental health.

DIFFERENCES BETWEEN SELF-RELATED VARIABLES

When talking about students' beliefs about themselves, numerous variables can be discussed. This chapter focuses on several that have received much attention in both the research literature and the popular press. Two that have received particular attention are *self-esteem* and *self-efficacy*. Classroom teachers can have an impact on both of these variables, which is very important because these self-perceptions are related to a variety of outcomes, in different ways.

Stop and Think

How would you define **self-esteem**? What does that term mean to you? Do you think teachers should try to enhance students' self-esteem?

What Is Self-Esteem?

The term *self-esteem* is used quite freely in the media and the popular press. Low levels of self-esteem have been blamed for numerous societal problems. For example, numerous television talk shows and "self-help gurus" argue that enhancing one's self-esteem will lead to better relationships, less use of illicit substances, lower levels of aggressive behavior, and less likelihood of being victimized or bullied. Nevertheless, as we will see, many of these claims are unwarranted.

Generally, self-esteem is defined in terms of an individual's feelings about himself or herself; self-esteem is viewed as an affective evaluation of one's self-concept (Baumeister, Campbell, Krueger, & Vohs, 2003; Crocker, Lee, & Park, 2004; Malanchuk & Eccles, 2006; Wigfield & Karpathian, 1991; Wylie, 1979). Self-esteem is a *general* variable; it does not refer to specific attributes or qualities of an individual. Individuals' sense of self-esteem is based on how they feel about themselves overall; in other words, when children or

It is important for students to have a high sense of self-esteem; however, high self-esteem will not solve many other academic and social problems that students face.

adolescents look in the mirror, do they like whom they see? Do they like their physical appearance? Do they like their personality? There are many unclear definitions of self-esteem, although there is some commonality among the definitions (Harter, 1983; Wylie, 1974). Confusion and disagreement in the measurement and definitions of self-related constructs may be related to some of the weak or nonsignificant relations often found between self-related variables and numerous outcomes in research studies (Wylie, 1979; Bong & Clark, 1999).

What Is Self-Efficacy?

Whereas self-esteem is a very general feeling about oneself overall, self-efficacy is a task-specific construct. Self-efficacy refers to an individual's beliefs about whether or not he or she has the abilities to carry out a *particular task* (Bandura, 1986, 1997; Schunk & Pajares, 2009). An individual who feels highly efficacious at a given task believes that she has the abilities to successfully engage with and complete the task. Bandura defined self-efficacy as individuals' "judgment of their capabilities to organize and execute courses of action required to attain designated types of performances" (Bandura, 1986, p. 391). A large body of research indicates that self-efficacy is a complex construct. It influences human behavior through cognitive, motivational, affective, and selection processes (Bandura, 1993). Much research indicates the importance of self-efficacy as a predictor of important educational and social outcomes (see Bandura, 1986, 1997; Schunk, 1991, for reviews).

Bandura (1997) has commented on the differences between self-esteem and self-efficacy. Specifically, he indicated that although the terms often are used interchangeably, they represent "entirely different things" (p. 11). He suggested that people may be highly inefficacious at a particularly activity, without a lowering of their self-esteem. For example, an early adolescent may feel completely inefficacious at playing soccer (i.e., she may believe that she is an untalented soccer player), but if she does not highly value soccer, her self-esteem is unlikely to suffer.

Thus, a student like Mac may feel highly efficacious at mathematics addition problems, but may feel inefficacious at division problems. Although students have self-efficacy beliefs in academic subject areas (i.e., self-efficacy for mathematics), self-efficacy often is considered at the level of individual, specific tasks (Pajares, 1996). Furthermore, it is not the case that Mac's lack of confidence with solving division problems will necessarily have any bearing on her overall self-esteem.

Self-Esteem, Self-Efficacy, and Other Related Variables

The "self" has been an important construct in education and psychology since the early work of William James (1890). Quite often, terms such as *self-concept, self-efficacy, possible selves,* and *self-concept of ability* are used interchangeably with the term *self-esteem* (e.g., McEachron-Hirsh, 1993). Nevertheless, the terms all have distinct meanings, and these distinctions have important implications for how we educate children and adolescents and even adults; therefore, it is very important for teachers to be aware of the differences among these various terms because they represent different phenomena in the classroom. In addition, in research studies examining the relations of these variables to academic achievement, it is important to precisely measure these different but related constructs, so that relations to achievement can be correctly ascertained, particularly because many of these measures are highly interrelated (Marsh, Dowson, Pietsch, & Walker, 2004). To understand what self-esteem and self-efficacy are, it is important to understand what self-esteem and self-efficacy *are not.* Indeed, a number of commonly used terms in education refer to various aspects of the "self."

POSSIBLE SELVES   Markus and Nurius (1986) have discussed and researched the concept of *possible selves.* Possible selves are images and conceptions of both hoped-for and feared "selves" in the future (see also Cross & Markus, 1991). Possible selves are powerful motivational variables that serve to direct future behavior (Oyserman & Leah, 2009). They have been related to an array of valued outcomes, including academic achievement (E. M. Anderman, L. H. Anderman, & Griesinger, 1999; Leonardi, Gonida, & Gialamas, 2009; Oyserman, Bybee, & Terry, 2006). For example, in one study, Oyserman and Markus (1990) found that nondelinquent adolescents were likely to display a balance between their hoped-for and feared selves, whereas delinquent youth were less likely to experience such a balance. Consider the following example:

> Jessie is 17 years old. He has always wanted to be a football player when he gets to college. He thinks about himself as a player, and he thinks about all the rewards that come with being a college football player.

We can see that Jessie entertains a "possible self" as a football player. He sees this as a real goal for his future, and he can actually picture himself as a football player. This sense of his future self may increase Jessie's use of strategies that could help him to realize this dream.

Now consider this example:

> Susan is 15 years old. Her older sister dropped out of school and is now having a very difficult time getting and keeping a job. She thinks often about how she can avoid dropping out of school like her sister did.

In this example, we can see that Susan entertains a "feared self" as a school dropout. She wants to avoid becoming a dropout. This fear of becoming like her sister may increase Susan's use of strategies that will help her to avoid dropping out of school.

SELF-CONCEPT OF ABILITY   Measures of *self-concept of ability* emanate from a number of influential programs of research (e.g., Eccles, Barber, Jozefowicz, Malenchuk, & Vida, 1999; Eccles & Wigfield, 1995; Harter, 1982; Marsh, 1987). Self-concept of ability is a domain-specific (subject-specific) characteristic. This construct often refers to students' beliefs about their specific abilities in a particular subject domain. For example, Eccles and her colleagues (e.g., Eccles, Wigfield, Harold, & Blumenfeld, 1993; Wigfield, Eccles, Mac Iver, Reuman, & Midgley, 1991) have developed reliable and valid measures of self-concept of ability in a number of domains, including math, English, sports, and social activities. Self-concept of ability is related to valued educational outcomes, including interest (Denissen, Zarrett, & Eccles, 2007) and achievement (e.g., Wigfield & Eccles, 2002).

SELF-WORTH   Another closely related construct is *self-worth*. Covington (1984) has argued that self-worth is and should be an important educational outcome. According to Covington (1992, 2009), the search for self-worth is a fundamental priority in human nature. The concepts of self-worth and self-esteem are quite similar, and at times the terms are used interchangeably. However, a fundamental difference between self-worth and self-esteem is that, by definition, self-worth is largely determined by self-perceptions of ability and per-formance. Self-worth theory often includes references to *specific ability perceptions*, whereas self-esteem is usually a more general construct that represents how individuals feel about themselves in a very general way. The concept of self-worth, particularly as it has been used in educational research, tends to include self-perceptions of ability and performance.

For children and adolescents in school settings, self-worth is tied directly to academic performance (Covington, 1984). Much of Covington's influential work on the ways that individuals try to protect their sense of self-worth has been in the domain of education, whereas the concept of *general self-esteem* often is related to a multitude of social, psycho-logical, and educational phenomena. Students often engage in academic self-handicapping behaviors to protect their self-worth (e.g., putting off doing an assignment until the last minute; Covington, 1992). In this manner, when a student does not do well on an assignment, he or she can attribute the poor grade to a lack of effort rather than lack of ability, thus preserving a sense of self-worth.

Schools can do much to enhance students' sense of self-worth (Covington, 2009). Urdan, Midgley, and Anderman (1998) found that students were more likely to engage in self-handicapping behaviors when they were in classrooms where teachers stressed rela-tive ability, performance, and grades. Research indicates that self-worth is related to a number of important educational variables and that students often engage in such self-handicapping behaviors *to protect their self-worth* (Covington, 1984, 1992). Consequently, reducing the stress on grades, performance, and ability may help protect some children's and adolescents' belief in their own self-worth. Whereas research *directly* addressing this particular issue is scant, some related research does indicate that a decreased stress on performance, ability, and grades, combined with an increased stress on mastery, effort, and improvement, may lead to enhanced motivation and learning (e.g., Ames & Archer, 1988; E. M. Anderman & Maehr, 1994; Maehr & Midgley, 1996).

BELIEFS ABOUT INTELLIGENCE. Students' beliefs about intelligence also are related in important ways to academic motivation and achievement. Carol Dweck and her colleagues described two different types of implicit "theories" that individuals hold about intelligence. When students hold an *entity theory of intelligence*, they believe that intelligence is a fixed characteristic that does not change. Students who maintain entity theories believe that they are born with a certain "amount" of intelligence, and that it is a fixed entity that will not improve. One implication of this belief is that exerting too much effort to achieve a given outcome provides evidence of lower ability; that is, if you have to work hard to make a B, you must not be very smart. In contrast, students who hold an incremental theory of intelligence believe that intelligence can improve and change over time. These students believe, in particular, that enhanced effort will lead to improved learning and achievement; thus intelligence covaries positively with effort in the minds of these students (Dweck, 1999, 2006; Dweck & Master, 2009).

Incremental beliefs about intelligence are related to many beneficial outcomes for students in academic settings. Students who maintain incremental beliefs about intelligence demonstrate enhanced academic achievement (e.g., Blackwell, Trzesniewski, & Dweck, 2007) and better use of self-regulated learning strategies (e.g., Dweck & Master, 2008).

THE IMPORTANCE OF SELF-BELIEFS

Beliefs about the self are important in the field of education. In academic settings, high levels of self-efficacy in particular are related to more effective overall learning and achievement (Bandura, 1997; Pajares, 1996). For example, students will be more likely to persist at academic tasks when they feel self-efficacious (Schunk, 1989). This is probably because high self-efficacy beliefs are related to the use of effective cognitive strategies (e.g., focusing on the task, relating newly learned information to previously learned information, organizing one's notes effectively; e.g., Bandura, 1986, 1997; Schunk, 1989; Schunk & Pajares, 2009).

Although general self-esteem is an important psychological variable, there is little evidence that high self-esteem is related strongly to academic achievement (e.g., Baumeister et al., 2003; Valentine, DuBois, & Cooper, 2004). However, research suggests that having high-self esteem is related to some other important outcomes. For example, individuals high in self-esteem report greater happiness (Diener & Diener, 1995), whereas having low self-esteem may be related to depression in some individuals (Arndt & Goldenberg, 2002; Baumeister et al., 2003). Low self-esteem may be related to a number of psychological problems in children and adolescents, particularly when other risk factors are also present (Harter, 2006).

EXAMINING SELF-ESTEEM MORE CAREFULLY

In this section, we take a careful look at self-esteem. This is important because self-esteem is a hotly debated topic among educators and policy makers. Some schools spend much time focusing on the development of self-esteem in children and adolescents; as educators, we need to consider whether such policies are sound.

In the United States, the belief that having high self-esteem will remedy many of education's problems is prolific. Numerous guests on television talk shows, motivational speakers, and educators champion this belief. In addition, numerous schools pay large fees for programs, curricula, and speakers with the goal of raising students' self-esteem. Nevertheless, the actual scientific research evidence supporting these beliefs and practices is weak (Baumeister et al., 2003). Whereas self-esteem is an important outcome or dependent variable in education, little evidence supports its manipulation as a meaningful independent variable (Kohn, 1994). That is, there is little evidence that raising self-esteem will bring about other positive changes. In contrast, other motivational constructs, if manipulated correctly, might produce the desired academic and societal benefits and positive outcomes that often are inaccurately associated with self-esteem. Disagreement and confusion regarding a precise definition of self-esteem have contributed to this problem.

This topic is important to those involved with education because many individuals are conducting workshops, professional development seminars, and in-service programs and selling them to the general public, under the premise that increasing children's and adolescents' general self-esteem will cure many problems related to education and society. Indeed, a quick search of the Internet will reveal many individuals who sell their services as speakers who will raise children's and adolescents' self-esteem. At times, self-esteem programs have been implemented on a very large scale and at very high costs, such as the California esteem project (California Task Force to Promote Self-Esteem and Personal Social Responsibility, 1990; Leo, 1990). Although some researchers advocate self-esteem enhancement programs as approaches to the prevention of problems during the school years (e.g., Meggert, 1996), little empirical evidence supports such claims (Baumeister et al., 2003).

Nothing is inherently wrong with raising children's and adolescents' self-esteem; indeed, it would be wonderful if all youth had healthy levels of self-esteem. As educators, however, we need to be wary of programs that promise great results yet are based on little solid research. We must also be particularly concerned about the lack of a general understanding of the definition of the term *self-esteem*—whereas some programs to enhance students' self-esteem are founded on a firm, research-based understanding of self-esteem, others are instituted on a nebulous, general notion of self-esteem as something that incorporates a range of motivational beliefs, including self-concept, self-efficacy, and other related constructs. This problem is serious and widespread and has large policy implications.

Self-Esteem as a Panacea

It is a widely held belief that the raising of self-esteem will improve, if not altogether eliminate, many of society's problems (e.g., Meggert, 1996). Instead, self-esteem programs may be detrimental in some cases, particularly to children with disabilities. Tobin and Hwang (1997) argued that if educators encourage a false sense of self-esteem in children with disabilities, those children may become satisfied with their current levels of achievement and remain unmotivated to continue learning (Tobin & Hwang, 1997).

When one examines well-regarded sources in education and psychology, it becomes obvious that little, if any, empirical evidence supports the self-esteem craze. For example, the index of a scholarly volume examining the causes and suggested interventions for delinquency and violence during adolescence does not contain a single reference to self-esteem (Gullotta, Adams, & Montemayor, 1998). The index to the 1996 *Handbook of Educational Psychology* (Berliner & Calfee, 1996) does not contain a single reference to self-esteem in the subject index, and the updated 2006 edition contains only three references to the topic (Alexander & Winne, 2006). Neither the recent *Handbook of Research on Student Engagement* (Christenson, Reschly, & Wylie, 2012) nor the *Handbook of Research on Learning and Instruction* (Mayer & Alexander, 2011) contains a single reference to self-esteem. In one of the seminal reviews of the literature on self-concept, Wylie (1979) found little support for positive relations between self-esteem and valued educational and social outcomes.

Individual and Group Differences in Self-Esteem

Research has indicated the existence of individual differences and somewhat predictable trajectories for self-esteem during childhood and adolescence. Children and adolescents differ somewhat in their levels of self-esteem by gender and ethnicity, and self-esteem changes over time for some of them. It is particularly important for classroom teachers to be aware of these findings so that they can be more knowledgeable when offered the opportunity to present self-esteem lessons or curricula to their students.

Some developmental studies have indicated that self-esteem changes during child-hood and adolescence, although results have been contradictory at times. Results of a recent longitudinal study of over 7,000 participants in the United States indicate that self-esteem increases during both adolescence and young adulthood, although the rate of increase is slower during the adult years (Erol & Orth, 2011). Simmons, Blyth, and their colleagues (e.g., Simmons & Blyth, 1987; Simmons, Rosenberg, & Rosenberg, 1973) suggested that although self-esteem does not appear to change much for most early adolescents (e.g., Blyth, Simmons, & Carlton-Ford, 1983), self-esteem declines for *some* adolescents as a result of the transition from elementary school to middle school. Some of their research has indicated that adolescent females who experience a decline in self-esteem after the transition to middle school are likely to experience similar declines in self-esteem during later periods of adolescence (Simmons & Blyth, 1987). Wigfield et al. (1991) found that early adolescents' self-esteem declined immediately after the transition from elementary school to middle school, but it then rose to higher levels after some time in the middle-school environment.

Some gender differences are apparent in the self-esteem literature. For example, in a study using a large sample of early adolescents, Wigfield, Eccles, and their colleagues (Wigfield et al., 1991) found that males had higher self-esteem than did females. Other research (e.g., Simmons & Blyth, 1987) also indicates that females tend to report lower levels of self-esteem than do males, although more recent research suggests few differences between females and males in the development of self-esteem over time (Erol & Orth, 2011).

There is some evidence that minority students think about aspects of the self and respond to self-esteem measures differently than do majority students. Hispanic adolescents tend to report lower levels of self-esteem than do White and African American adolescents; however, by the age of 30, African Americans and Hispanics report higher levels of self-esteem than do Whites (Erol & Orth, 2011). However, it is important to note that one of the *criticisms* of existing measures of self-esteem is that they are insensitive to cultural differences (Padilla & Lindholm, 1995). For example, Martinez and Dukes (1987) found that minority students reported lower levels of self-esteem when questioned about *public* aspects of self-esteem, as opposed to *private* aspects of self-esteem, where minority students scored higher than nonminority students. Indeed, it has been suggested that individual differences in self-esteem should not be evaluated without simultaneously considering political and economic issues (McEachron-Hirsh, 1993).

Self-Esteem: Relations to Educational Outcomes

Stop and Think

Does raising students' self-esteem help them in any way? Should schools be in the business of trying to raise students' self-esteem? If yes, what outcomes should we expect?

Consider the following example:

> *The principal of Southern High School has decided to implement a new program designed to raise the self-esteem of adolescents. The principal requires all his teachers to attend two professional development sessions to learn about the program. In addition, the principal requires that all the school's English teachers spend one class period per month using the curriculum. The principal hopes that by making students feel better about themselves, they will do better academically and will be less likely to get into trouble in school for misbehavior.*

This scenario is quite common. Particularly in the era of high-stakes accountability, schools often look for innovative methods to improve student achievement. However, there is little evidence that directly enhancing children's and adolescents' self-esteem will lead to positive educational or societal outcomes. Whereas some correlational research indicates a positive relation between self-esteem and educational/social outcomes (particularly when self-esteem is measured in terms of how students feel about their academic abilities), little evidence indicates that the *manipulation* of self-esteem is causally related to changes in other valued variables (Kohn, 1994; Wylie, 1979).

Little evidence indicates that directly *enhancing* students' self-esteem leads to an increase in academic performance (Baumeister et al., 2003). Again, part of the problem with many studies is that some studies have used the term *self-esteem* interchangeably with *self-concept* and *academic self-esteem*. Studies of *academic self-concept* (i.e., students' self-perceptions as a student) indicate that academic self-concept and academic achievement have a reciprocal relation (Guay, Marsh, & Boivin, 2003; Marsh et al., 2007; Marsh, Trautwein, Ludtke, Koller, & Baumert, 2005). That is, students who have a high academic self-concept are likely to receive high grades in the future; those high grades, in turn, are predictive of a continued high self-concept.

In her review of the literature on self-esteem, Wylie (1979) concluded that the association between achievement and self-esteem (her term is *self-regard*) is quite low, even when ability scores are uncontrolled. She concluded that the correlations between various achievement indices and self-esteem offer "no support to the commonly accepted lore that achievement and self-regard are strongly associated" (p. 406). Pullman and Allik's (2008) recent study of self-esteem in a large representative sample of students in Estonia indicated that academic self-esteem is predictive of achievement, and that low (but not high) general self-esteem is related to achievement, when academic self-esteem is controlled. Another recent study examining self-esteem, perceived control, and academic achievement in college students indicated that when perceived control is included in analyses, self-esteem is unrelated to college grade point average (GPA), whereas perceived control is related positively to GPA (Stupinsky et al., 2007).

Research indicates that students who come from low socioeconomic status backgrounds often do not perform as well in school as do their more economically advantaged peers (e.g., Felner et al., 1995). Consequently, the assumption often is made that children and adolescents from lower socioeconomic status families are low in self-esteem. However, little research supports this view. In her review of studies of self-esteem prior to 1979, Wylie (1979) found no evidence of a relation between self-esteem and socioeconomic status.

THE POWER OF SELF-EFFICACY

In the educational psychology literature, *self-efficacy* has been identified as a variable that is related to perceived competence. Unlike self-esteem, research does indicate that self-efficacy is related quite strongly to academic achievement (Schunk, 1991; Vuong, Brown-Welty, & Tracz, 2010; Zimmerman & Bandura, 1994). Some research suggests that self-efficacy is related to adaptive achievement goals (e.g., mastery goals and performance-approach goals), which in turn are related to the use of cognitive strategies that are predictive of achievement (e.g., Diseth, 2011). Children and adolescents who believe that they have the cognitive capabilities to succeed at specific tasks tend to report high levels of task-specific self-efficacy, and they tend to perform better on those tasks.

Self-efficacy differs from other related constructs in that it refers to students' beliefs that they can attain "designated types of performances and achieve specific results" (Pajares, 1996, p. 546). Thus, one of the hallmarks of self-efficacy is that it is often a highly task-specific construct. For example, rather than referring to a student as being self-efficacious "at math," in the true spirit of self-efficacy, teachers should think in terms of students' efficacy beliefs toward specific tasks (e.g., a specific type of math problem, a specific mathematical skill).

The level of self-efficacy that is assessed should match the level of performance that one is considering (Bandura, 1997). Specifically, if a teacher is giving a French exam that expressly assesses students' knowledge of "animal" vocabulary, the teacher must be cognizant of the students' self-efficacy regarding animal vocabulary knowledge; if a French teacher is giving an exam on verb conjugation, then it would be helpful for the teacher to be cognizant of the students' self-efficacy toward the conjugation of verbs.

According to Bandura (1997), self-efficacy emanates from four sources: enactive mastery experiences, vicarious experiences, verbal persuasion, and physiological/affective arousal. Mastery experiences occur when an individual "masters" a particular task. For example, when a student masters the correct structure for writing paragraphs, the student's self-efficacy is likely to be enhanced as a result of this experience. In contrast, vicarious experiences occur when students observe others who are successful at tasks. Thus, a child who is trying to learn how to ride a bicycle without training wheels is likely to experience enhanced self-efficacy if she views one of her friends successfully riding a bicycle. Verbal persuasion occurs when other individuals provide realistic encouragement to learners. For example, if a child is struggling with learning how to breathe while swimming freestyle, realistic encouragement from a parent can enhance the child's self-efficacy. Finally, physiological and affective cues serve as important indicators to learners that affect their self-efficacy. For example, if an adolescent decides to become a jogger, goes out for a jog, and then feels her heart beating rapidly and feels out of shape, those physiological indicators may inhibit her sense of efficacy as a runner.

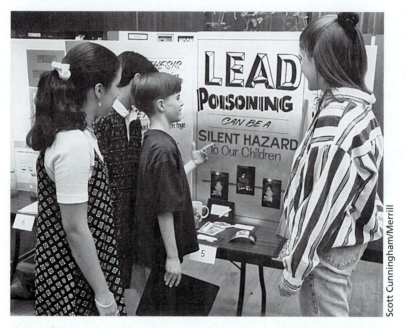

Scott Cunningham/Merrill

The use of high-quality academic tasks can enhance both self-esteem and self-efficacy.

Now consider the following two examples:

Brad is enrolled in a first-level German class. He does not enjoy the class. He has little confidence in his abilities in German, and he does not feel that he is able to pronounce the words, conjugate the verbs, or write meaningful sentences. Overall, he feels that he is incompetent when it comes to learning foreign languages.

Mia is enrolled in a first-level German class. Mia generally does well in the class, but she is very uncomfortable with pronunciation. She feels that she is unable to correctly pronounce German words. She feels good about her abilities to read and write German, but when it comes to speaking it, she feels that she does not have much ability.

What is the difference between these situations? Brad's problems with German represent a general sense of low expectancies for success in the class. His problems generalize to all areas of German. Whereas he may in fact have low self-efficacy toward specific tasks, his motivational problems in German class are quite profound and generalized. In contrast, Mia has a lack of confidence in her abilities *in one particular area:* pronunciation.

If you were a teacher and were trying to help build these students' self-efficacy, Mia would be the easier case. Her lack of efficacy matches well with the definition of self-efficacy as a highly task-specific variable. In fact, it probably would be best to assist Mia by trying to build her efficacy at specific pronunciation tasks.

Brad probably also has low self-efficacy toward many specific tasks in German class, but his low expectations are quite broad. As a teacher, where would you start? You certainly could use a self-efficacy perspective and work to build Brad's self-efficacy one task at a time, with the expectation that increased efficacy in some aspects of learning German will generalize to more positive overall expectations. However, from a self-efficacy perspective, Mia's problems are much more obvious.

ENHANCING STUDENTS' SELF-EFFICACY

Teachers can use specific research-based procedures to enhance students' self-efficacy for specific academic tasks. Contrary to the research on raising students' self-esteem, the data on self-efficacy are well supported by many years of high-quality research.

Our recommendations are largely based on the work of Schunk (1991), who described several important research-based aspects of self-efficacy. Each of these areas is described in the following sections.

Help Students to Set Realistic Goals

Students often set unrealistic goals for themselves. In addition, sometimes they don't set any goals for themselves when they engage in academic work. Researchers distinguish between *proximal goals,* which are short term and readily attainable, and *distal goals,* which are longer term and can only be reached after much time and effort.

From a self-efficacy perspective, when students set distal goals, they are unlikely to feel any immediate success. For example, if a student goes into a French I class with the goal "to learn French," then the student is unlikely to feel very efficacious at French for a long time (because the amount of material learned in a first-level French course does not equate to the amount that is necessary to approach fluency in the language). In many foreign-language classrooms, teachers try to speak the language as much as possible during class so that the students hear the language. If the student's goal is to sound as fluent as the teacher, then the student probably will not feel very successful because it takes non-native-speaking French teachers many years to learn to speak the language fluently.

In contrast, if the student knew how to set realistic proximal goals, the student might enter the course with a goal of learning how to greet a friend in French by the end of the first week. This is realistic; if the student learns the vocabulary, pronunciation, and basic

Students' self-efficacy is enhanced when they develop feelings of competence at performing specific academic tasks.

Robert Vega/Merrill

Teachers need to help students to set proximal goals so that they don't become frustrated with academic work.

syntax for greetings, and if the student gets to practice using these greetings during the week, then by the end of the week the student will feel quite good about his or her ability to greet friends in French. From a self-efficacy perspective, the student's self-efficacy at the task of using greetings in French will be enhanced. From a more long-term perspective, this increased sense of efficacy for the task is likely to motivate the student to want to continue to learn French.

WHAT CAN A TEACHER DO?   Teachers can help students to set realistic but somewhat challenging—not too simple!—proximal goals. One way to do this is to put an advance organizer on the board each week with a proximal goal for the week (e.g., "This week our goal is to learn how to greet each other in French"). Such goals are much more effective than general goals such as "Try hard" or distal goals such as "Learn to speak French." Teachers can also work with individual students to set specific short-term goals. It is, of course, important to provide students with appropriate and regular feedback so that they know they have reached these goals. When students are not achieving their goals, teachers can help students to self-evaluate and figure out whether or not goals are being attained (Schunk & Mullen, 2012).

Help Students to Believe in Their Cognitive Abilities

Many students come to academic tasks with histories of being unsuccessful in the past. From a self-efficacy perspective, students must believe that they have the cognitive abilities to successfully complete a task. When students receive feedback that indicates they are truly learning and understanding the material, self-efficacy will be enhanced. This means that the students' beliefs in their ability to cognitively process information related to the task will be strengthened, which in turn will influence their motivation toward the task.

Consider a student who is taking French for the first time, but who initially had taken German and failed. How could the French teacher help the student to believe in his abilities in the French class? One useful strategy would be for the teacher to be particularly cognizant of providing the student with positive, specific feedback about his progress. If the proximal goal for the first week is to learn how to greet one another in French, the teacher can enhance self-beliefs in this student by pointing out to the student how well he is learning and using his newly learned French greetings.

WHAT CAN A TEACHER DO? Teachers can help students to master specific learning strategies that may enhance their abilities to process newly learned information (Schunk, 1991). Examples of such strategies include monitoring one's comprehension, relating newly learned material to previously learned material, and strategies to enhance effort and persistence.

Many students do not think strategically about their learning and do not plan for their own learning. By teachers taking a step back and helping students to think about appropriate strategies to use with specific tasks, the students may experience greater success with the tasks and ultimately will experience enhanced self-efficacy.

Provide Models for Students

Bandura's work on self-efficacy originated in his more general work on social learning theory. Bandura and others have demonstrated that individuals' self-efficacy can be enhanced when students observe effective models.

Effective Models

Effective models should have the following characteristics (Pintrich & Schunk, 2002):

1. *Competence:* The model should be able to successfully carry out the task being observed.
2. *Similarity:* The model should be similar to the observer.
3. *Credibility:* Students should believe in the sincerity and credibility of the model; if students do not believe that the model truly cares about task performance and can consistently perform the task, then the model probably will not be effective.
4. *Enthusiasm:* The model should engage with the task, demonstrating a sense of enthusiasm, enjoyment, and commitment to the task.

WHAT CAN A TEACHER DO? Teachers can provide effective models for their students in several ways. First, teachers themselves can model the skills and strategies that they want their students to learn. When students observe their teacher engaging in behaviors that the students feel they actually can accomplish, students may internalize the teachers' modeled behaviors and mimic the skills necessary to effectively complete a task.

Second, teachers can use students who have mastered a task as models for other students. For example, if one student in a physical education class has mastered pitching in softball, the teacher could ask that student to slowly demonstrate the skills necessary to effectively complete the task. When the task is broken down for the students (creating proximal goals), and when the students see a peer completing the task, they can gain confidence in their own ability to complete the task.

Third, teachers can use technology to provide models for their students. The use of video technology via DVD or the Internet may be particularly useful for teachers. The availability of online videos (e.g., through publicly available sites such as YouTube) has increased the instantaneous access that teachers have to a wide range of models for many types of tasks and behaviors.

Attributional Feedback

As noted by Schunk (1991) and Bandura (1986), appropriate attributional feedback can affect students' academic self-efficacy. Recall that attributions refer to students' beliefs about why an outcome has occurred (see Chapter 7). Students make attributions to various sources, including ability, effort, task difficulty, the teacher, strategy usage, or various other factors. Research indicates that it is particularly useful for students to be provided with attributional feedback that links their successful performance on academic tasks to effort, as opposed to ability (Schunk, 1983a). Such attributions have been shown to be related to higher self-efficacy.

WHAT CAN A TEACHER DO?   Teachers can use any of several instructional practices to provide students with attributional feedback that may enhance self-efficacy. First, it is important for teachers to help their students make attributions to effort. When a student succeeds at an academic task, teachers can provide feedback that helps the student link the success to effort. For example, the teacher can make statements such as "You obviously did a good job of preparing for this test!" or "Working hard really paid off!" or "Your practice at greeting people in French really helped you to learn how to communicate well this week."

Second, teachers should give feedback as soon as possible. If a teacher is going to help students to make attributions to effort, then the teacher must act quickly. Students are likely to form attributions rapidly. For example, if a student sees that her peers all did better than she did on an assignment, she may quickly attribute her poor performance to perceived low ability; however, if the teacher acts quickly, the teacher can provide feedback that helps the student make a more adaptive attribution (i.e., to lack of effort or missing a key concept).

Third, teachers can encourage students to make attributions to strategy usage. Specifically, if a teacher can clearly communicate to a student that she is not succeeding at a task because she is not using the appropriate strategy, then the student will be more likely to try the task again and to incorporate the appropriate strategy.

Rewards

As we noted in Chapter 3, much controversy surrounds the use of rewards. However, consensus seems to be emerging that indicates rewards are effective when they are not perceived as controlling and when they provide feedback to students that indicates learning has occurred (Deci & Ryan, 1987). Schunk (1983b, 1991) noted that rewards can enhance self-efficacy when they indicate to students that they have truly made progress and learned something meaningful.

DCU Library
Express Point 2
Borrow Receipt

Customer name: MS. Carol Hughes

Title: Classroom motivation
ID: 100009751
Due: 18/03/2016 21:00

Title: Becoming a legendary teacher : to
instruct and inspire
ID: 080010490
Due: 01/04/2016 21:00

Total items: 2
11-03-2016
Checked out: 4

Thank you for using the Express Service Point.

Please keep this receipt for your due date.

WHAT CAN A TEACHER DO?   Teachers should think carefully about the types of rewards that they use. Rewards should provide students with specific and definitive information about what the students have learned. Rewards should not be given simply for engaging in a task; rather, they should indicate to students that they have learned particular information and made measurable progress. For example, a certificate that specifies "Great work mastering your multiplication facts!" is much more informative than one that states, "Great work!"

Summary

In this chapter, we have discussed a variety of beliefs about the "self." Research indicates that students' beliefs about their abilities are important predictors of subsequent motivation and achievement. Although a variety of terms are used to describe these self-related beliefs, research generally indicates that beliefs that are highly specific (e.g., "I'm not good at solving algebra equations") are much more strongly related to achievement than general beliefs about oneself ("I don't feel good about myself"). Whereas all self-beliefs are important, as teachers we can in particular influence students' beliefs about specific abilities through some of the techniques discussed in this chapter.

Schools and teachers can enhance students' beliefs about their own abilities in numerous ways (e.g., by helping them to set appropriate proximal goals and then helping them to evaluate whether or not those goals have been reached). Much research from the perspective of attribution theory (e.g., Weiner, 1986) indicates that when learners are encouraged to make success attributions to internal, stable, controllable factors, as opposed to external, unstable, uncontrollable processes, motivation and achievement are likely to be enhanced. When learners feel that they are responsible and in control of their own learning, they are likely to perceive themselves as being more competent. Schools can engage in both small- and large-scale practices to encourage perceived competence. For example, schoolwide programs recognizing *improvement*, rather than merely recognizing overall achievements (e.g.,

earning all As), may lead to an enhanced sense of perceived competence, particularly for low-achieving students.

In this chapter, we have tried to distinguish between self-efficacy, self-esteem, and other self-related beliefs. We have spent some time discussing self-esteem because much attention is paid to students' self-esteem by educators and policy makers. Some researchers (e.g., Harter, 1983) have argued that self-esteem, when considered within the broader self-system, can in fact be a useful construct. Problems arise when educators use *self-esteem* as an all-encompassing term. The problems become quite dangerous when the assumption is made that the enhancement of general self-esteem will lessen the likelihood of serious problems, such as low academic achievement, adolescent pregnancy, and school violence. Although it would be wonderful if self-esteem enhancement could eliminate those problems, evidence indicating such effects is scarce (Baumeister et al., 2003). Those of us involved with education must be particularly concerned with developing a clear understanding of the concept of self-esteem, particularly given recent publicity concerning issues such as school violence and bullying. Indeed, as the public becomes more concerned with such issues, it is important to disentangle effective from ineffective solutions. When crimes occur in society, citizens often want the police to make an arrest and to find the perpetrator of the crime as rapidly as possible; in a similar manner, when serious problems occur in schools, individuals often want administrators and teachers to quickly fix the problem. However, the danger of utilizing general self-esteem enhancement programs as panaceas may, in some cases, do more harm than good.

Self-esteem is and should be a valued outcome in education. All students should feel good about themselves, both in and out of school. Nevertheless, the belief that the enhancement of student self-esteem will lead to an increase in achievement and a decrease in social problems is not strongly supported by the research. Although many researchers are aware of the limits of the concept of self-esteem as a remedy for social and educational problems, many practitioners and popular authors appear to be unaware of the numerous methodological and conceptual problems with this concept. As public concern with issues such as academic performance, school violence, and adolescent pregnancy continues to rise, it will become increasingly important for educators, researchers, and policy makers to understand the types of programs and prescriptions that are likely to make a difference, as well as the types that may sound appealing but provide few benefits for children and adolescents.

Questions to Consider Regarding Self-Beliefs

1. Self-esteem is a popular topic, and you certainly will hear colleagues talking about the need to raise students' self-esteem. What will you say to your colleagues after reading this chapter?
2. What aspects of your instructional techniques influence your students' self-related beliefs (self-esteem, self-efficacy, etc.)?
3. Are policies in place at the school level that undermine your efforts to develop your students' sense of self-efficacy?
4. How should teachers build self-efficacy in different subject areas (e.g., English, math)? Will the same techniques work in each subject? Why or why not?

LEARNING ACTIVITY 8.1   Enhancing Students' Self-Efficacy

Reread the descriptions of Brad and Mia (page 166). Then, use the ideas presented in the section "Enhancing Students' Self-Efficacy" to come up with specific strategies that a teacher could use to help Mia improve her self-efficacy and ultimately her pronunciation skills.

References

Alexander, P. A., & Winne, P. H. (2006). *Handbook of educational psychology* (2nd ed.). Mahwah, NJ: Erlbaum.

Ames, C., & Archer, J. (1988). Achievement goals in the classroom: Students' learning strategies and motivation processes. *Journal of Educational Psychology, 80,* 260–270.

Anderman, E. M. (2002). School effects on psychological outcomes during adolescence. *Journal of Educational Psychology, 94,* 795–809.

Anderman, E. M., Anderman, L. H., & Griesinger, T. (1999). Present and possible academic selves during early adolescence. *Elementary School Journal, 100,* 2–17.

Anderman, E. M., & Maehr, M. L. (1994). Motivation and schooling in the middle grades. *Review of Educational Research, 64,* 287–309.

Arndt, J., & Goldenberg, J. L. (2002). From threat to sweat: The role of physiological arousal in the motivation to maintain self-esteem. In A. Tesser,

D. A. Stapel, & J. V. Wood (Eds.), *Self and motivation: Emerging psychological perspectives* (pp. 43–69). Washington, DC: American Psychological Association.

Bandura, A. (1986). *Social foundations of thought and action: A social cognitive theory.* Englewood Cliffs, NJ: Prentice Hall.

Bandura, A. (1993). Perceived self-efficacy in cognitive development and functioning. *Educational Psychologist, 28,* 117–148.

Bandura, A. (1997). *Self efficacy: The exercise of control.* New York, NY: Freeman.

Baumeister, R. F., Campbell, J. D., Krueger, J. L., & Vohs, K. D. (2003). Does high self-esteem cause better performance, interpersonal success, happiness, or healthier lifestyles? *Psychological Science in the Public Interest, 4,* 1–44.

Berliner, D. C., & Calfee, R. C. (1996). *Handbook of educational psychology.* New York, NY: Macmillan.

Blackwell, L. S., Trzesniewski, K. H., & Dweck, C. S. (2007). Implicit theories of intelligence predict achievement across an adolescent transition: A longitudinal study and an intervention. *Child Development, 78,* 246–263.

Blyth, D. A., Simmons, R. G., & Carlton-Ford, S. (1983). The adjustment of early adolescents to school transitions. *Journal of Early Adolescence, 3,* 105–120.

Bong, M., & Clark, E. (1999). Comparison between self-concept and self-efficacy in academic motivation research. *Educational Psychologist, 34,* 139–153.

California Task Force to Promote Self-Esteem and Personal and Social Responsibility. (1990). *Toward a state of esteem.* Sacramento: State of California.

Christenon, S. L., Reschly, A. L., & Wylie, C. (2012). *Handbook of research on student engagement.* New York, NY: Springer.

Covington, M. V. (1984). The self-worth theory of achievement motivation: Implications and findings. *Elementary School Journal, 85,* 7–20.

Covington, M. V. (1992). *Making the grade: A self-worth perspective on motivation and school reform.* New York, NY: Cambridge University Press.

Covington, M. V. (2009). Self-worth theory: Retrospection and prospects. In K. R. Wentzel & A. Wigfield (Eds.), *Handbook of motivation at school* (pp. 141–169). New York, NY: Routledge.

Crocker, J., Lee, S. J., & Park, L. E. (2004). The pursuit of self-esteem: Implications for good and evil.

In A. G. Miller (Ed.), *The social psychology of good and evil* (pp. 271–302). New York, NY: Guilford Press.

Cross, S., & Markus, H. (1991). Possible selves across the life span. *Human Development, 34,* 230–255.

Deci, E. L., & Ryan, R. M. (1987). The support of autonomy and the control of behavior. *Journal of Personality and Social Psychology, 53,* 1024–1037.

Denissen, J. J. A., Zarrett, N. R., & Eccles, J. S. (2007). I like to do it, I'm able, and I know I am: Longitudinal couplings between domain-specific achievement, self-concept, and interest. *Child Development, 78,* 430–447.

Diener, E., & Diener, M. (1995). Cross-cultural correlates of life satisfaction and self-esteem. *Journal of Personality and Social Psychology, 68,* 653–663.

Diseth, A. (2011). Self-efficacy, goal orientations and learning strategies as mediators between preceding and subsequent academic achievement. *Learning and Individual Differences, 21,* 191–195.

Dweck, C. S. (1999). *Self-theories.* New York, NY: Psychology Press.

Dweck, C. S. (2006). *Mindset: The new psychology of success.* New York, NY: Ballantine.

Dweck, C. S., & Master, A. (2008). Self-theories motivate self-regulated learning. In D. H. Schunk & B. J. Zimmerman (Eds.), *Motivation and self-regulated learning: Theory, research, and applications* (pp. 31–51). Mahwah, NJ: Erlbaum.

Dweck, C. S., & Master, A. (2009). Self-theories and motivation: Students' beliefs about intelligence. In K. R. Wentzel & A. Wigfield (Eds.), *Handbook of motivation at school* (pp. 123–140). New York, NY: Routledge.

Eccles, J. S., Barber, B., Jozefowicz, D., Malenchuk, O., & Vida, M. (1999). Self-evaluations of competence, task values, and self-esteem. In N. G. Johnson (Ed.), *Beyond appearance: A new look at adolescent girls* (pp. 53–83). Washington, DC: American Psychological Association.

Eccles, J. S., & Wigfield, A. (1995). In the mind of the actor: The structure of adolescents' achievement task values and expectancy-related beliefs. *Personality and Social Psychology Bulletin, 21*(3), 215–225.

Eccles, J. S., Wigfield, A., Harold, R. D., & Blumenfeld, P. (1993). Age and gender differences in children's self- and task perceptions during elementary school. *Child Development, 64,* 830–847.

Erol, R. Y., & Orth, U. (2011). Self-esteem development from age 14 to 30 years: A longitudinal study. *Journal of Personality and Social Psychology, 101,* 607–619.

Felner, R. D., Brand, S., DuBois, D. L., Adan, A. M., Mulhall, P. F., & Evans, E. G. (1995). Socioeconomic disadvantage, proximal environmental experiences, and socioemotional and academic adjustment in early adolescence: Investigation of a mediated effects model. *Child Development, 66,* 774–792.

Guay, F., Marsh, H. W., & Boivin, M. (2003). Academic self-concept and academic achievement: Developmental perspectives on their causal ordering. *Journal of Educational Psychology, 95*(1), 124–136.

Gullotta, T. P., Adams, G. R., & Montemayor, R. (Eds.). (1998). *Delinquent violent youth: Theory and interventions.* Thousand Oaks, CA: Sage.

Harter, S. (1982). The perceived competence scale for children. *Child Development, 53,* 87–97.

Harter, S. (1983). Developmental perspectives on the self-system. In E. M. Hetherington (Ed.) & P. H. Mussen (Series Ed.), *Handbook of child psychology: Vol. 4. Socialization, personality, and social development* (4th ed., pp. 275–386). New York, NY: Wiley.

Harter, S. (2006). The development of self-representation in childhood and adolescence. In W. Damon & R. Lerner (Eds.), *Handbook of child psychology* (6th ed.). New York, NY: Wiley.

James, W. (1890). *Principles of psychology.* New York, NY: Holt.

Kohn, A. (1994, December). The truth about self-esteem. *Phi Delta Kappan,* 272–283.

Leo, J. (1990, April). The trouble with self-esteem. *U.S. News and World Report,* p. 16.

Leonardi, A., Gonida, E. N., & Gialamas, V. (2009). "Possible" selves during middle adolescence; Relationships with school achievement and various demographic factors. *Psychology: The Journal of the Hellenic Psychological Society, 16,* 342–360.

Maehr, M. L., & Midgley, C. (1996). *Transforming school cultures.* Boulder, CO: Westview Press.

Malanchuk, O., & Eccles, J. S. (2006). Self-esteem. In J. Worell & C. D. Goodheart (Eds.), *Handbook of girls' and women's psychological health: Gender and well-being across the lifespan* (pp. 149–156). New York, NY: Oxford University Press.

Markus, H., & Nurius, P. (1986). Possible selves. *American Psychologist, 41,* 954–969.

Marsh, H. W. (1987). The big-fish-little-pond effect on academic self-concept. *Journal of Educational Psychology, 79,* 280–295.

Marsh, H. W., Dowson, M., Pietsch, J., & Walker, R. (2004). Why multicolinearity matters: A reexamination of relations between self-efficacy, self-concept, and achievement. *Journal of Educational Psychology, 96,* 518–522.

Marsh, H. W., Gerlach, E., Trautwein, U., Ludtke, O., Baer, J. S., & Brettschneider, W. (2007). Longitudinal study of preadolescent sport self-concept and performance: Reciprocal effects and causal ordering. *Child Development, 78*(6), 1640–1656.

Marsh, H. W., Trautwein, U., Ludtke, O., Koller, O., & Baumert, J. (2005). Academic self-concept, interest, grades, and standardized test scores: Reciprocal effects models of causal ordering. *Child Development, 76*(2), 397–416.

Martinez, R., & Dukes, R. L. (1987). Race, gender, and self-esteem among youth. *Hispanic Journal of Behavioral Sciences, 9,* 427–443.

Mayer, R. E., & Alexander, P. A. (2011). *Handbook of research on learning and instruction.* New York, NY: Routledge.

McEachron-Hirsh, G. (1993). Self and identity formation. In G. McEachron-Hirsh (Ed.), *Student self-esteem: Integrating the self* (pp. 1–17). Lancaster, PA: Technomic.

Meggert, S. S. (1996). Who cares what I think: Problems of low self-esteem. In D. Capuzzi & D. R. Gross (Eds.), *Youth at risk: A prevention resource for counselors, teachers, and parents* (2nd ed., pp. 81–103). Alexandria, VA: American Counseling Association.

Oyserman, D., Bybee, D., & Terry, K. (2006). Possible selves and academic outcomes: How and when possible selves impel action. *Journal of Personality and Social Psychology, 91*(1), 188–204.

Oyserman, D., & Leah, J. (2009). Possible selves: From content to process. In K. D. Markman, W. M. P. Klein, & J. A. Suhr (Eds.), *Handbook of imagination and mental stimulation* (pp. 373–394). New York, NY: Psychology Press.

Oyserman, D., & Markus, H. R. (1990). Possible selves and delinquency. *Journal of Personality and Social Psychology, 59,* 112–125.

Padilla, A. M., & Lindholm, K. J. (1995). Quantitative educational research with ethnic minorities. In J. A. Banks & C. A. M. Banks (Eds.), *Handbook of research on multicultural education* (pp. 97–114). New York, NY: Macmillan.

Pajares, F. (1996). Self-efficacy beliefs in academic settings. *Review of Educational Research, 66*(4), 543–578.

Pintrich, P. R., & Schunk, D. H. (2002). *Motivation in education* (2nd ed.). Upper Saddle River, NJ: Merrill Prentice Hall.

Pullman, H., & Allik, J. (2008). Relations of academic and general self-esteem to school achievement. *Personality and Individual Differences, 45,* 559–564.

Schunk, D. H. (1983a). Ability versus effort attributional feedback: Differential effects on self-efficacy and achievement. *Journal of Educational Psychology, 75,* 848–856.

Schunk, D. H. (1983b). Reward contingencies and the development of children's skills and self-efficacy. *Journal of Educational Psychology, 75,* 511–518.

Schunk, D. H. (1989). Self-efficacy and achievement behaviors. *Educational Psychology Review, 1,* 173–208.

Schunk, D. H. (1991). Self-efficacy and academic motivation. *Educational Psychologist, 26,* 207–231.

Schunk, D. H., & Mullen, C. A. (2012). Self-efficacy as an engaged learner. In S. L. Christenon, A. L. Reschly, & C. Wylie, (Eds.) *Handbook of research on student engagement* (pp. 219–235). New York, NY: Springer.

Schunk, D. H., & Pajares, F. (2009). Self-efficacy theory. In K. R. Wentzel & A. Wigfield (Eds.)., *Handbook of motivation at school* (pp. 35–53). New York, NY: Routledge.

Simmons, R. G., & Blyth, D. A. (1987). *Moving into adolescence.* New York, NY: Aldine de Gruyter.

Simmons, R. G., Rosenberg, F., & Rosenberg, M. (1973). Disturbance in the self-image at adolescence. *American Sociological Review, 38,* 553–568.

Stupkinsky, R. H., Renaud, R. D., Perry, R. P., Ruthig, J. C., Haynes, T. L., & Clifton, R. A. (2007). Comparing self-esteem and perceived control as predictors of first-year college students' academic achievement. *Social Psychology of Education, 10,* 303–330.

Tobin, R., & Hwang, Y. G. (1997). The dangers of the self-esteem rhetoric in educating children with disabilities. *Education, 118,* 130–132.

Urdan, T., Midgley, C., & Anderman, E. M. (1998). Classroom influences on self-handicapping strategies. *American Educational Research Journal, 35,* 101–122.

Valentine, J. C., DuBois, D. L., & Cooper, H. (2004). The relation between self-beliefs and academic achievement: A meta-analytic review. *Educational Psychologist, 39,* 111–133.

Vuong, M., Brown-Welty, S., & Tracz, S. (2010). The effects of self-efficacy on academic success of first-generation college sophomore students. *Journal of College Student Development, 51,* 50–64.

Weiner, B. (1986). An attributional theory of achievement motivation and emotion. *Psychological Review, 92,* 548–573.

Wigfield, A., & Eccles, J. S. (2002). The development of competence beliefs, expectancies for success, and achievement values from childhood through adolescence. In A. Wigfield & J. S. Eccles (Eds.), *Development of achievement motivation* (pp. 91–120). San Diego, CA: Academic Press.

Wigfield, A., Eccles, J. S., Mac Iver, D., Reuman, D. A., & Midgley, C. (1991). Transitions during early adolescence: Changes in children's domain-specific self-perceptions and general self-esteem across the transition to junior high school. *Developmental Psychology, 27,* 552–565.

Wigfield, A., & Karpathian, M. (1991). Who am I and what can I do? Children's self-concepts and motivation in achievement situations. *Educational Psychologist, 26,* 233–262.

Woolfolk Hoy, A., Hoy, W. K., & Davis, H. A. (2009). Teachers' self-efficacy beliefs. In K. R. Wentzel & A. Wigfield (Eds.), *Handbook of motivation at school* (pp. 627–653). New York, NY: Routledge.

Wylie, R. C. (1974). *The self-concept: Vol. 1. A review of methodological considerations and measuring instruments.* Lincoln: University of Nebraska Press.

Wylie, R. C. (1979). *The self-concept: Vol. 2. Theory and research on selected topics.* Lincoln: University of Nebraska Press.

Zimmerman, B. J., & Bandura, A. (1994). Impact of self-regulatory influences on writing course achievement. *American Educational Research Journal, 31,* 845–862.

CHAPTER 9

Holding High Expectations for Students

Teachers often are encouraged to hold high expectations for their students (e.g., Arnold, 1997). The mantra that "All students can learn," in addition to both political statements and popular movies, promotes the idea that anyone can achieve at high levels if someone "just believes in them." As professionals, however, teachers must consider the empirical evidence and research that underlie such statements. Will holding high expectations for all students lead to superior achievement? If we do hold high expectations, what are the best ways to communicate those expectations to students? Do all students react the same way to high teacher expectations? In this chapter, we examine research that addresses teacher expectations of students and then outline recommendations about how best to hold and communicate appropriate expectations for all students.

DEFINING EXPECTANCIES

The term *expectancy* is used in a variety of ways in education. First, as discussed in Chapter 2, we hold expectations for ourselves as learners. We expect to be more successful at some tasks than at others. For example, an individual might expect greater success at solving algebra problems than at maintaining a strict diet. Our expectancies for success are not general; they are specifically related to tasks and activities that we encounter.

Second, we also have expectations for others. We expect that certain individuals will be successful at certain tasks. Parents know their children well and clearly have different expectations for their performance on different tasks. A parent might have high expectations for a particular child to be successful at swimming, but low expectations for the same child's ability to learn to play the violin. Again, the expectancies that we hold for individuals vary according to tasks.

High expectations for students must be balanced with appropriate academic
support so that students can experience feelings of success at difficult tasks.

Research and Theoretical Perspectives on Expectancies

We have already encountered several motivation theories that include an expectancy
component as a major construct. Some of the earliest research on expectancies is credited
to Tolman (e.g., Tolman, 1932). Indeed, the expectancy construct has a long history both
specifically within the field of educational psychology and more generally across all of
psychology (Zuroff & Rotter, 1985).

Most prominently, expectancy–value theory suggests that an individual's behavior is
shaped by both expectancies for success and perceived values for specific academic tasks
(Eccles, 1983; Wigfield & Eccles, 2000, 2002; Wigfield, Tonks, & Klauda, 2009). Holding positive expectations for personal success is related to enhanced academic achievement (Eccles,
1983; Wigfield & Eccles, 2002). In addition, self-efficacy theory focuses on individuals' perceived abilities to succeed at specific tasks (Bandura, 1986, 1997; Schunk, 1991; Schunk &
Pajares, 2009). An individual who is highly self-efficacious is likely to hold high expectations for personal success. Thus, although self-efficacy theory and expectancy–value theory
are distinct, they overlap a great deal in terms of the expectancy component. What both of
these theories have in common is that they focus on the individual's expectation of success
or failure *for themselves.* A separate line of research has examined the role of our expectations for other people and, particularly, the importance of teachers' expectancies for different students, in terms of those students' ongoing motivation and achievement.

Expectancies in Everyday Life

We all have expectations about people and situations we encounter in our daily lives. These
expectations are based on a range of information, including our personal biases or prior

experiences. Furthermore, once our judgments have been formulated, it may be very difficult to overlook even invalid information and change our expectations. For example, when you are watching a courtroom drama on television and a witness states something that is inappropriate, the lawyer will object, and the judge may tell the jury to disregard the comment. But is it, in fact, possible to disregard the comment? Can you forget something that you clearly heard about a person? Think about recent cases where individuals have been accused of crimes, such as Casey Anthony and former Senator John Edwards. Having heard much of the abundant media coverage of these individuals, will you ever be able to think of them again without recalling the details of their interactions with the legal system?

Stop and Think

Suppose you are given the opportunity to examine your students' previous years' records at your leisure; you are invited to come into the guidance office and peruse your students' files so that you can learn about their academic records, attendance patterns, and disciplinary referrals. Would you accept this offer to look at your students' files? What potential advantages might there be to having information about each student's history? What potential problems can you see?

One of the greatest challenges for teachers is developing the ability to overcome preconceived notions and prior knowledge about students. If a teacher hears from a colleague that a student is a cheater, will the teacher ever be able to think of that student again as honest? If a teacher is told that "Cynthia comes from a bad home," will the teacher ever be able to look at Cynthia's potential in the same way? One would, of course, hope that such prior knowledge about student performance would not affect teachers' behaviors and interactions with students; unfortunately, however, research suggests that such knowledge does affect our interactions with students.

SELF-FULFILLING PROPHECIES

The study of self-fulfilling prophecies dates back to the mid 1900s (e.g., Merton, 1948). A *self-fulfilling prophecy* occurs when teachers' expectations about what students will achieve actually lead to those outcomes. Thus, a teacher who truly believes that a student is gifted may see that the student actually achieves more over time. Similarly, a teacher who expects poor performance from a particular student may eventually induce low achievement. Whereas much of the research on self-fulfilling prophecies has focused on teachers' expectations, others' expectations (e.g., parents) also can lead to self-fulfilling prophecies.

The Pygmalion Study

Rosenthal and Jacobson (1968) conducted one of the most famous studies in psychology on the self-fulfilling prophecy. This study was entitled *"Pygmalion in the Classroom"* after George Bernard Shaw's classic play, in which a professor of phonetics teaches a young working-class woman to present herself as an upper-class lady in London, in the early 20th century.

Using a school in California, Rosenthal and Jacobson administered the Harvard Test of Inflected Acquisition to children in elementary school; teachers were then told that some of the students were identified as children who would "bloom" intellectually during the coming school year. In actuality, the test was an assessment of nonverbal intelligence, and the students who were identified as "bloomers" were chosen randomly.

No other interventions or manipulations were performed with these teachers or students. Follow-up tests indicated that the students who were falsely identified as "bloomers" did, in fact, experience some cognitive benefits. The researchers claimed that this effect was evidence that teachers' raised expectations for those students led to their increased intellectual performance over time. Although the results of this study have been fiercely debated in the literature (e.g., Elashoff & Snow, 1971; Jensen, 1980; Jussim, 2013), most researchers agree that this effect is small but real (Raudenbush, 1984). Research also indicates that Pygmalion-type effects occur in other settings. For example, in one study, nursing home residents were randomly assigned to high- and average-expectancy rehabilitation groups. Although results were mixed, findings did indicate that residents who were in the high-expectancy group experienced more relief from depression and were admitted to hospitals less often than residents in the average-expectancy group (Learman, Avorn, Everitt, & Rosenthal, 1990). In a retrospective article written 25 years after the publication of the original *Pygmalion* study, Rosenthal reviewed evidence supporting the existence of these effects (Rosenthal, 1995).

Research indicates that expectancy effects are stronger for younger (i.e., early elementary school) students than for older students (Kuklinski & Weinstein, 2000, 2001; Rosenthal & Jacobson, 1968). In addition, although teacher expectancy effects on student achievement overall are not very strong, the consensus is that the detrimental effects of negative expectations on student achievement are more powerful than are any beneficial effects of positive expectations on achievement (Brophy & Good, 1974; Cooper & Tom, 1984; Wentzel, 2002).

How Self-Fulfilling Prophecies Work

How might a teacher's expectations of a student influence actual academic performance? An expectation, after all, is a type of cognition: a thought or belief that the teacher holds and that cannot, by itself, bring about any kind of change in the student. The answer is that self-fulfilling prophecies operate over time, through a series of interactions between teachers and students. That is, teacher expectancies do not "work" on their own; rather, they result in differences in the ways in which teachers interact with and instruct students, based on their expectancies. Students, in turn, become aware of the way they are treated by their teachers and benefit both from more challenging and supportive instruction and from their perception that their teacher believes in their ability. Then they respond in kind. Over time, the combination of strengthened self-competence beliefs and good teaching can lead to improved performance. A similar, but opposite cycle of events occurs when teachers form low expectations for individual students.

Lee Jussim and his colleagues have extensively reviewed the literature on teacher expectations and self-fulfilling prophecies. Jussim and his colleagues noted several different models of how self-fulfilling prophecies operate in classrooms, and although those models differ on some points, they all are in agreement about three key issues:

1. Teachers develop erroneous expectations.
2. Those expectations lead teachers to treat high-expectancy students differently than they treat low-expectancy students.
3. Students react to this differential treatment in such a manner as to confirm the originally erroneous expectation (Jussim, Robustelli, & Cain, 2009, p. 361).

Teachers' expectancies are communicated to students in a variety of ways (Cooper, 1983, 1985). One well-known examination of how self-fulfilling prophecies exert their power was developed by Good and Brophy (1978; see also Brophy & Good, 1970, 1974). First, teachers form expectations about individual students. Thus, an English teacher might "expect" Joanna to be an excellent writer and might expect Toby to be a poor writer. Next, the teacher treats the students differently. Thus, the teacher may interact in a more positive manner with Joanna than with Toby. Or the teacher may consider Joanna's errors as learning opportunities, but treat Toby's errors as another sign of his inability as a writer. Or, because of her belief that Toby struggles with writing, the teacher may provide him with less challenging writing assignments or with extra help and resources, even if he has not asked for them. It is important to note that these differences in treatment may not be intentional, or even conscious, on the part of the teacher. That is, it is not necessarily the case that teachers *plan* on treating students differently, but rather that, like all humans, their behavior is partly shaped by their beliefs and biases. Regardless of the teacher's intent, differential treatment communicates to students that the teacher expects different outcomes from different students; thus, Joanna may feel that the teacher expects her to learn from her mistakes, whereas Toby may perceive that the teacher expects him to always "mess up" at writing tasks.

Over time, the differential treatment will affect students' behavior and achievement. Joanna may learn to work hard even when she makes mistakes, whereas Toby may feel helpless and not exert much effort because he may come to believe that his teacher expects him to fail anyway. As these behaviors become reinforced over time, students' behaviors will more closely match the teachers' expectations.

This is, in many ways, a bidirectional process: The teachers' expectations affect the students, and in turn, the students' behavior reinforces the teachers' initial perceptions. Thus, it may be quite difficult for either Joanna or Toby to break this cycle of self-fulfilling prophecies.

Parents' expectations also can affect students. Results of a recent longitudinal study of adolescents and their mothers suggests that self-fulfilling prophecies may have their effects because mothers' beliefs about their children may affect students' future aspirations, which in turn influence academic outcomes (Scherr, Madon, Guyll, Willard, & Spoth, 2011). After controlling for student background characteristics (e.g., socioeconomic status, gender, motivation, and other variables), mothers' beliefs about their adolescent children's future educational attainment (as measured when the students were in the seventh grade) predicted actual educational attainment (e.g., whether or not the students attended college). However, that relation was mediated by adolescents' educational aspirations (i.e., how far they plan to go in school); that is, mothers' beliefs predicted adolescents' aspirations, which in turn predicted their actual attainment. The findings from this study indicate that there are reciprocal interactions between individuals (e.g., parents and their children) that affect beliefs and ultimately behaviors over time. Results of other studies (e.g., Kirk, Lewis-Moss, Nilsen, & Colvin, 2011) also indicate that parental expectations are related to higher educational aspirations in students.

Teacher expectancies exert their power, in part, because they usually are based in truth (Jussim, 1989). That is, teachers' expectancies for student success or failure are good predictors of actual student achievement (Jussim, Eccles, & Madon, 1996). Thus, although self-fulfilling prophecies are real and can both positively and adversely affect student outcomes, it is also important to realize that expectancies do occur naturally, and they often are based, at least in part, on accurate observations made by teachers (e.g., Trouilloud, Sarrazin, Martinek, & Guillet, 2002). The challenge for educators is to be aware of our expectations and to hold open the possibility that students can and will change, so that we continue to provide opportunities for students to prove our low expectations wrong.

MOTIVATION AND EXPECTANCIES

Several theoretical frameworks for achievement motivation have been used to explain expectancy effects in learners. Some of the most prominent theoretical explanations have emerged from expectancy–value theory and from attribution theory.

Expectancy–Value Theory and Expectancies

Expectancy–value theory is most obviously related to teacher expectations. Indeed, the term *expectancy* overlaps both areas of research. Teachers' expectancies for success or failure in their students create a learning environment that most certainly influences student outcomes, including students' own expectancies and values (see Chapter 2).

The types of expectancies teachers hold may have an effect on student outcomes. A key issue is related to teachers' beliefs about the nature of academic ability. Some research suggests that when teachers believe students' poor academic performance reflects an unstable, malleable trait, maladaptive expectancy effects are *less* likely to occur, in comparison to what happens when teachers see lack of ability as a more stable trait in their students (Swann & Snyder, 1980). Indeed, when teachers assume a more developmental perspective and believe that students' abilities will improve in the future, they may hold negative current expectations but still treat their students differently than teachers who believe that low ability will simply never change.

Achievement values are related to teacher expectations in several ways. For example, some researchers have suggested that teachers may hold higher expectancies for students who demonstrably value formal schooling and academic pursuit. Unfortunately, belief in the value of formal schooling may be lower in students from low socioeconomic (SES) backgrounds than in those from middle SES neighborhoods (Eccles & Wigfield, 1985; Mickelson, 1990). In addition, some teachers believe that students of different genders and cultural groups do not value education in general or specific subject areas and, consequently, hold differential expectations for those students' success. Thus, a teacher who believes that her lower SES students do not value education may generalize this belief and treat all her lower SES students differently (i.e., due to the lower expectations) from her higher SES students.

Attributions and Expectancies

Another explanation for the power of teacher expectancies emerges from attribution theory (see Chapter 4). Teachers' initial expectations for students may be influenced by the attributions they make for students' prior successes or failures. Teachers' attributions are affected by prior knowledge about student performance; by demographic factors such as race, socioeconomic status, and gender; and by the teachers' own interactions with students (Peterson & Barger, 1985). For example, a teacher may have heard from another teacher that "Joe is not very good at mathematics." If the new teacher believes Joe's previously poor performance is due to *stable* causes, such as Joe's innate lack of mathematical ability or lack of family support, these attributions may lead to expectations of low performance for Joe. These expectations, then, may lead to a self-fulfilling prophecy (Peterson & Barger, 1985).

As teachers start to treat students differentially, students also make their own attributions. Thus, if Joe feels that his math teacher is treating him in a way that communicates his lack of ability at mathematics, Joe may start to make attributions about his own abilities at math. Joe may make *internal attributions* (e.g., "I'm dumb at math") or *external attributions* (e.g., "That teacher is a jerk"). Unfortunately, many students will internalize the idea that they lack the ability to do well. The student's attributions will then affect the student's subsequent behaviors. If Joe believes that his teacher truly thinks of him as "dumb," then Joe may exert less effort at math or may feel helpless and anxious in the math classroom. In contrast, if Joe believes that the teacher is treating him negatively because the teacher "had a bad week" (that is, makes an *external, unstable* attribution), then this may not adversely affect Joe's self-perceptions as a math student in the long term.

Ultimately, students' behaviors may serve to further confirm or disprove their teachers' attributional beliefs. If Joe still does not exert any effort and continues to get bad grades, then the math teacher's low expectations of performance for Joe will most likely be reinforced. In turn, this may reinforce Joe's beliefs and attributional patterns, thus leading to long-term confirmation of the teacher's beliefs (and low expectations) concerning Joe (Darley & Fazio, 1980).

Self-Efficacy and Expectancies

Self-efficacy refers to individuals' beliefs in their abilities to execute specific behaviors. Reviews by Pajares (1996) and others indicate that self-efficacy is best understood and utilized in terms of specific activities. Thus, a student may feel highly efficacious at doing addition problems but not at all efficacious at doing division problems (see Chapter 8).

Students' self-efficacy beliefs are affected by teachers' expectations. As noted previously, teacher' expectations for student success or failure are interpreted by students and reinforce students' future attitudes and behaviors, as well as teachers' continuing behaviors toward students. Thus, if a teacher holds low expectancies for the performance of a particular student on a particular task, the teacher's interactions with the student and behaviors toward the student may reinforce the student's already low self-efficacy beliefs; in contrast, if a teacher holds high expectations for a student's academic performance on a task, then differential treatment of that student may result in more positive interactions with the student and, thus, enhance the student's self-efficacy.

Consider the following example:

Christina is 8 years old and is learning to add fractions. Christina entered the third grade with low self-efficacy toward all math-related activities. Thus, she does not feel competent as a math student. Her teacher, Mrs. Stein, has been told that Christina is a poor student with weak mathematical skills. Thus, Mrs. Stein holds low expectations for Christina's performance. Christina's poor performance during the first part of the third grade reinforces Mrs. Stein's beliefs about her. Mrs. Stein's tone of voice when talking to Christina suggests that she feels sorry for her. She allows Christina to

Teachers' verbal interactions with students affect student motivation in important ways.

complete fewer problems than her classmates and avoids calling on her to solve problems in class. In addition, Mrs. Stein occasionally rolls her eyes when Christina tries to answer a math question. These types of interactions reinforce Christina's low self-efficacy.

In contrast, differential treatment can also positively affect students' self-efficacy beliefs. If a teacher has high expectations for a student, then the teacher may offer encouraging statements such as "I know you can do this," and provide assistance with difficult projects, for example, by showing the student how to break a large task into manageable steps. High expectations that lead to positive comments and behaviors on the part of the teacher may help students experience genuine success that, in turn, can increase their self-efficacy toward that type of academic task.

Teachers also hold efficacy beliefs about their own abilities as instructors. Teacher efficacy refers to teachers' beliefs about their abilities to positively affect student learning (Ashton & Webb, 1986; Guskey & Passaro, 1994; Klassen, Tze, Betts, & Gordon, 2011; Tschannen-Moran, Woolfolk Hoy, & Hoy, 1998). When teachers believe that they can affect student learning, students are in fact more likely to learn effectively (Ashton & Webb, 1986).

Goal Orientations and Expectancies

The types of expectancies that teachers hold for students may affect the types of goal orientations those students adopt (see Chapter 1). This depends largely on the ways in which teachers communicate their expectancies to their students. Research on students' goal orientations indicates that students who perceive a performance goal structure in classrooms are likely to adopt personal performance goals, and students who perceive a mastery goal structure are likely to adopt mastery goals (Ames, 1992a, 1992b; Urdan, 2010). By definition, a mastery-oriented student is focused on the actual task—that is, on truly mastering the task at hand (Maehr & Anderman, 1993). Eccles and Wigfield (1985) noted that if students with low expectations of success are not motivated to engage fully with academic tasks, teachers might mistake this lack of attention for cognitive and intellectual deficits, rather than as a motivational problem that may be more easily fixable.

> *Suppose that Mr. Tyler holds low expectations for his low-achieving students and high expectations for his high-achieving students. If Mr. Tyler emphasizes grades and test scores in his class, a high achiever might adopt performance goals to demonstrate to Mr. Tyler that she is performing up to his expectations. However, if Mr. Tyler stresses to his students that he defines success in terms of students' effort and persistence, then the student might adopt mastery goals to demonstrate to him that she is meeting his expectations.*
>
> *Now consider the lower achieving students. If Mr. Tyler stresses effort and expects all students to try hard, then a lower achieving student might adopt mastery goals; in contrast, if Mr. Tyler is very focused on grades and communicates to his students that grades are the only way to demonstrate one's competence, then the low achievers are likely to adopt performance goals or, perhaps, even to give up and just not adopt any goals. If students believe that a teacher holds low expectations for them, and the teacher communicates that grades are extremely important in the class, then students may simply give up in such contexts.*

FACTORS THAT AFFECT TEACHER EXPECTATIONS

Teachers' expectations for students' successes and failures are affected by a number of variables. In some cases, teacher expectations may be based on realistic assessments of individual students' performance and needs. In other cases, however, they may be based on invalid assumptions based on students' demographic characteristics or other variables. Countless new teachers who experience academic and behavioral difficulties with their students ask their colleagues for advice; nevertheless, many are asked by their colleagues "Was it a boy or a girl?" "Was it a minority student?" "What part of town does the student come from?" "Was it one of those rich kids?" "Was it an athlete?" Teachers often assume that students' group memberships "cause" students to behave and achieve differently than others. These expectations can lead to self-fulfilling prophecies based on gender, ethnicity, or socioeconomic status. It is important for future teachers to consider these potential assumptions and biases because being aware of such influences may help teachers form more realistic, accurate, and positive expectations for their students.

Gender

Student gender is related to teacher expectations (Chalabaev, Sarrazin, Trouilloud, & Jussim, 2009). For decades, debate has centered on gender differences in subject-area abilities, with many arguing that girls are better at reading and writing and boys are better at mathematics. In reality, gender differences in achievement are highly complex and emanate from a variety of factors (Meece, Glienke, & Askew, 2009; Meece, Parsons, Kaczala, & Goff, 1982). It is important for teachers to remember that, even when differences between the genders are found, they are small differences in average performance by each group. That is, even when differences among groups of students are reported, they tell us nothing about the ability and potential of any individual student. Unfortunately, however, teachers' beliefs about such information certainly affect their interactions with and expectations for students.

Some research has documented teachers' differential treatment of male and female students in classrooms. Brophy and Good (1974) have argued that male students often receive more attention from teachers than female students do. Some other research, however, suggests that female students have more instructional contact with teachers during reading instruction, whereas boys have more contact during math instruction (Leinhardt, Seewald, & Engel, 1979). In addition, male students tend to have more interactions with teachers related to behavioral issues than do female students (Brophy & Good, 1974).

As previously noted, teachers' expectations of male and female students can lead to differential instruction and interaction patterns, which can affect students' self-concepts and behavior. If teachers tend to reprimand boys for their behavior more than they do girls, then the attention paid to boys may reinforce both the boys' behaviors and the teachers' belief that boys are difficult to manage. Over time, boys may internalize the idea that inattention or disruptive behaviors are expected from them, and they may start to see compliant behavior as feminine. Similarly, a teacher who truly believes that girls are not as competent at mathematics as boys may provide different types of feedback to male and female students, thus encouraging differences in attributions and expectations of future success. For example, a boy who performs poorly on a math test may be told that he "didn't try hard enough," whereas a girl with similar performance may be told not to feel bad, because "math is hard."

Race and Social Class

Research suggests that teachers, at times, hold differential expectations for students of different racial and socioeconomic backgrounds (van den Bergh, Denessen, Hornstra, Voeten, & Holland, 2010). Although race and class are related, they are distinct. Both majority and minority students may come from different socioeconomic backgrounds. Family socioeconomic status is a powerful predictor of academic achievement (Takei & Semon Dubas, 1993) and of teachers' expectancies (e.g., Cooper, Baron, & Lowe, 1975). In particular, teachers tend to hold higher expectations of success for mid-SES students than for lower SES students (Baron, Tom, & Cooper, 1985).

Research examining teachers' expectancies and students' ethnicity shows that, in general, teachers hold higher expectations of success for White students than for African American students (Baron et al., 1985). Despite this general trend, it is important to note that these effects are often complex and depend on the variables taken into consideration (Cooper et al., 1975; McKown, Gregory, & Weinstein, 2010; Weinstein, Gregory, & Stambler, 2004). Some of the explanation for teachers' differential expectations may be based in teachers' interpretations of differences in appearance and dress or in behavioral differences that have little to do with intellectual ability. For example, based on Boykin's (1983) identification of movement and verve as important and unique dimensions of African American culture, Neal, McCray, Webb-Johnson, and Bridgest (2003) examined the relations of African American students' movement styles to teacher expectations. These researchers asked middle-school teachers to view videotapes of two students walking; the teachers then completed questionnaires reporting their perceptions of aggression and achievement of the students, as well as their perceptions of whether or not the students needed special education. The results of these question-naires indicated that students who used walking styles that sometimes are preferred by African American males were perceived as lower achievers, as more aggressive, and as more likely to need special education services than students who did not walk in that manner. Neal et al. (2003) described this particular walking style as a "stroll," which is characterized by "swaggered or bent posture, with the head held slightly tilted to the side, one foot dragging, and an exaggerated knee bend (dip)" (p. 50). Given that teach-ers generally prefer students who are compliant and easy to manage, the perception that some students are aggressive or unruly can exacerbate unfavorable expectations of their academic performance.

Lowered expectations for minority students may be particularly common in schools with high percentages of minority students, where teachers may feel as though they have less control and responsibility for student outcomes. For example, high concentrations of African American students in some urban elementary schools are related to lower overall perceptions of teachers' responsibility for student learning (Diamond, Randolph, & Spillane, 2004). Lower expectations for minority students are also, at times, related to lower levels of parental involvement in schools for students of minority children and adolescents (Huss-Keeler, 1997). For example, research indicates that for Latino adolescents, parental involvement is predictive of teacher expectations, which in turn are predictive of students' academic competence and grade point averages (Kuperminc, Darnell, & Alvarez-Jimenez, 2008).

Teachers must be aware of these potential biases so that they can try to overcome them. As noted by Graham (1994), empirical studies have shown that African American students do not display less adaptive forms of motivation than do majority students. Com-mon assumptions that African American, or other minority, students do not value educa-tion or have little confidence in their own abilities are not well supported by the available research. If educators are encouraged to confront their biases early on, and to continue to confront these biases later in their careers, they may be less likely to hold different types of expectations for students of diverse ethnic backgrounds.

HOLDING HIGH EXPECTATIONS FOR LOW-ACHIEVING STUDENTS

As noted at the beginning of this chapter, many statements made about teacher expecta-tions seem to send teachers a "mixed message" in that there is an inherent contradiction in the literature. On one hand are those who claim that teachers' expectations of stu-dents' performance are based on their knowledge of those students' prior achievement. Such a position is consistent with the idea that students at differing achievement levels should receive different types of instruction and challenge, tailored to their needs. On the other hand, however, much of the research discussed in this chapter has focused on teachers potentially underestimating some students and consequently undermining their motivation and learning. Indeed, research indicates that negative expectancies for students are related to poorer academic outcomes; for example, results of one recent study indicated that a negative expectation bias by teachers at the end of primary school is related to poorer educational outcomes five years later (de Boer, Bosker, & van der Werf, 2010).

Currently, much educational rhetoric promotes holding "high expectations" for all students, but it is reasonable to question whether such advice is realistic. Some excellent studies have identified educators who have implemented systems and interventions aimed at holding high and positive expectations for all students. Other research indicates that specific types of instructional techniques are related to high expectations and achievement (Rubie-Davies, 2007). For example, research suggests that in reading instruction for adolescents, the use of authentic literature (as opposed to basal readers; Damber 2009) or forms of theater (Rozansky & Aagasen, 2010) facilitates teachers' ability to hold high expectations and student achievement in reading. To demonstrate the potential efficacy of such programs, we review some of them in the following sections.

Raising Expectations for Low-Achieving High School Students

Rhona Weinstein and her colleagues engaged in a novel experiment, wherein they worked with ninth-grade teachers to raise expectations for low-achieving high-school students. Research of this nature is extremely important, in that it offers rich examples of how teachers examine these issues with their own students. Specifically, in this study a group of teachers, school administrators, and researchers met weekly to examine research and potential changes in practices that would positively affect teacher expectations for low-achieving students.

Changes occurred slowly in the school. One type of change that occurred involved the elimination of tracking, particularly in the domain of English (Weinstein, Madison, & Kuklinski, 1995). The researchers then collected data on students participating in the study and compared it to data on similar students whose teachers were not participating. Comparisons indicated that some improvements did occur for the previously low-achieving students. For example, their grades increased over time, and, at least in the early part of the study, they received fewer disciplinary referrals in school (Weinstein et al., 1991). In other words, the researchers were able to demonstrate some benefits for students when their teachers learned to hold and communicate high expectations for all. Perhaps one of the most important lessons learned from this research, however, is that enhancing expectations for students within a school is a highly complex endeavor and not something that can be achieved easily or quickly (Weinstein et al., 1995). In some ways, it is easier for individual teachers to make changes to their own practice than it is to change the climate in an entire school.

Raising Expectations in Mathematics

You may recall the 1988 film *Stand and Deliver,* which chronicled the experiences of a high-school mathematics teacher named Jaime Escalante. Mr. Escalante worked with low-achieving students in Los Angeles and motivated his students to receive outstanding scores on advanced placement (AP) examinations in calculus. Escalante was inducted into the National Teachers Hall of Fame in 1999 (National Teachers Hall of Fame, 1999). Other teachers at Garfield High School also motivated low achievers to excel in advanced classes.

One of the first groups of Escalante's students who took the AP exam were accused of cheating by the Educational Testing Service; after their scores were invalidated, most of those students took the examination again and still passed the difficult exam. By 1991, 570 students at Garfield High School took AP exams (Jagodzinski, 2001; Santana, 1999).

Jaime Escalante: Mr. Inspiration

Jaime Escalante epitomizes the teacher who holds high expectations for all students. In an interview, Escalante stated the following:

> In my classroom I have a banner with "ganas." It means "desire." And you have to have that desire. Ganas is when the motivation begins. That word is a strong word in my original language. Ganas replaces the word in America "gifted." I cannot accept "gifted." You're going to measure IQ—and I say no. Any student, any [person] to me is gifted. They have something they can do, and I—especially the students—I hold them accountable for what they do. And that's where I make the transformation to motivate them to go for mathematics. You become "gifted" from practicing. Practice assures success. I give you a simple equation, and you do it and do it over and over, and you store that information (Hanson & Graves, 1998).

The story of the students at Garfield High School is important for several reasons. First, it suggests that teachers who truly hold high expectations for their students can indeed motivate them to achieve at high levels. Mr. Escalante's comments illustrate perfectly the belief in students' abilities as changeable. Second, it also emphasizes the power of negative stereotypes: These students' scores may have been invalidated because much of society held low academic expectations for poor minority students. The fact that the Garfield High students did so well academically was interpreted as a problem or anomaly to many people, rather than being seen as evidence that they actually worked diligently and earned their high scores.

Raising Expectations in Low-Income First Graders

Good and Nichols (2001) suggested that first grade is a particularly important and practical time to intervene in classrooms to improve teacher expectations toward low-income children; such interventions may be particularly useful in the domain of reading. Interventions at this early stage in a child's education might help to reduce achievement gaps during the early elementary years. These researchers argued that to successfully raise expectations for this population, several different groups of individuals must be targeted and must work together.

First, *teachers* of low-income students must be better prepared to work with this population. Teachers should be taught basic principles of expectancy research; they should have small classes so that students can receive more individualized attention; they should learn to treat students' social conduct and maturity as distinct from students' academic performance; and they should have opportunities to observe colleagues who work successfully with low-income children.

Second, first-grade *students* should be better prepared for what to expect in first grade. This can be accomplished by having kindergartners spend time during the spring of the kindergarten year in first-grade classrooms. In addition, programs that address the self-regulatory skills of kindergartners should help these students to succeed during first grade.

Third, parents must become educated about how low expectations are communicated to children. Good and Nichols (2001) suggested that parents should visit first-grade classrooms often to get to know the teacher well; parents should be encouraged to ask the teacher quite often to discuss their child's performance; and parents should be invited to observe in the classroom often.

Summary

In this chapter, we have examined teacher expectations. Instructors inevitably form expectations for their students—in some cases positive, in other cases negative. As we have seen, these expectations may lead to self-fulfilling prophecies, where the expectations are reinforced, as are students' behaviors that conform to these expectations. Nevertheless, holding positive expectations for students can lead to numerous beneficial outcomes for students, as well as to better relationships between teachers and students (Pianta, 1999; see Chapter 11).

Some research has identified characteristics of teachers who hold high expectations for their students. In an observational study of teachers with high, average, and low expectancies for their students, Rubie-Davies (2007) found that teachers who held high- and average-level expectations for their students provided frameworks for learning; specifically, they provided detailed instructions and explanations, and they related current lessons to previous lessons. High-expectation teachers also provided their students with more feedback than did low-expectation teachers, and they asked more complex questions than did average- or low-expectancy teachers (Rubie-Davies, 2007).

In summarizing the research, we offer the following recommendations for classroom teachers:

1. *Be aware of your own expectations for students.* All teachers form expectations, and many act on them, albeit often not consciously. All educators must acknowledge that they are not immune to forming expectations and must constantly question their assumptions about students.
2. *Be aware of biases.* Although most of us would not claim to treat students differentially based on demographic characteristics such as gender, race, and socioeconomic status, differential treatment does occur. Again, awareness and an openness to learn more about diverse groups are the most powerful tools to use to combat this tendency.
3. *Remember that students are acutely aware of differential treatment.* Students as young as 6 years old are aware of differential treatment and of the messages that it sends to them. Whereas it is often convenient from an instructional standpoint to organize students into groups (e.g., the "bunnies," the "frogs," and the "tigers"), students are aware of ability differences among these groups. Despite the fact that teachers may go to great lengths to disguise these ability group differences, students typically are aware that the "frogs" do not read as well as the "tigers."
4. *Do not acquire too much information about your students before they arrive in your classrooms.* Many educators believe that knowing a student's academic history will better prepare them to assist the student in learning. This may be true but, as illustrated in this chapter, problems are associated with this prior knowledge. If a teacher knows that a student performed poorly during a previous academic year, it may be difficult for the teacher to ignore this information and to hold high expectations for him or her.
5. *Talk to your colleagues.* Follow the example of Weinstein and her colleagues. Acknowledge that it is possible, albeit difficult, to hold high expectations for all students. Talk with your colleagues about the unique context of your school and how to best hold high expectations for students, given the nature of your particular setting.
6. *Ask school administrators to support professional development in this area.* Experts can be brought in to discuss expectations and

self-fulfilling prophecies with teachers in your school. A modicum of awareness on the part of teachers may have beneficial effects for students, particularly because some of your colleagues may be unaware of how expectancies are subtly communicated to students. Several staff develop-ment programs exist; one of those is TESA (Teacher Expectations and Student Achievement), which is designed to assist teachers in changing the expectancies that are communicated to students (results from studies of the effectiveness of TESA have been mixed; McKown et al., 2010).

Questions to Consider Regarding Expectations of Your Students

1. How aware are you of the types of expectations that you hold for your students?
2. Do you hold different types of expectations for different students?
3. How do the expectations that you hold for your students affect their motivation?
4. Do your expectations reflect gender and ethnic differences in students? Why?
5. Do the types of expectancies that you hold lead to self-fulfilling prophecies?
6. How can you examine and reevaluate your expectations?
7. Do you hold high expectations for all students? Should you hold high expectations for all students?
8. Does your school use certain policies and practices that encourage teachers to have different expectations for different students? If so, how do you feel about that?

LEARNING ACTIVITY 9.1   High Expectations

Imagine that it is the day before the start of a new academic year, and the principal of your school asks you to present a 30-minute workshop on "expectations." What are the most important points that you would try to convey to your colleagues? Would you encourage your colleagues to have the same expectations for all students? How would you address sensitive issues like gender, socioeconomic status, and ethnicity?

LEARNING ACTIVITY 9.2   Self-Fulfilling Prophecies

In this chapter, we reviewed research by Lee Jussim and his colleagues. In summarizing research on self-fulfilling prophecies, these researchers identified three steps that are involved in the development of self-fulfilling prophecies in classrooms:

1. Teachers develop erroneous expectations.
2. Those expectations lead teachers to treat high-expectancy students differently than they treat low-expectancy students.
3. Students react to this differential treatment in such a manner as to confirm the originally erroneous expectation (Jussim et al., 2009, p. 361).

Think about the age group and/or subject areas that you would like to teach. Then, create a scenario in which the three steps just listed could occur, leading to the occurrence of a self-fulfilling prophecy. Finally, think about what you as a teacher could do to intervene at any of these three steps to interrupt this process and prevent the occurrence of potentially damaging self-fulfilling prophecies.

References

Ames, C. (1992a). Achievement goals and the classroom motivational climate. In D. H. Schunk & J. L. Meece (Eds.), *Student perceptions in the classroom* (pp. 327–348). Hillsdale, NJ: Erlbaum.

Ames, C. (1992b). Classrooms: Goals, structures, and student motivation. *Journal of Educational Psychology, 84*(3), 261–271.

Arnold, J. (1997). High expectations for all: Perspective and practice. This we believe and now we must act. *Middle School Journal, 28,* 51–53.

Ashton, P. T., & Webb, R. B. (1986). *Making a difference: Teachers' sense of efficacy and student achievement.* New York, NY: Longman.

Bandura, A. (1986). *Social foundations of thought and action: A social cognitive theory.* Englewood Cliffs, NJ: Prentice-Hall.

Bandura, A. (1997). *Self-efficacy: The exercise of control.* New York, NY: Freeman.

Baron, R. M., Tom, D. Y. H., & Cooper, H. M. (1985). Social class, race, and teacher expectations. In J. B. Dusek (Ed.), *Teacher expectancies* (pp. 251–269). Hillsdale, NJ: Erlbaum.

Boykin, A. W. (1983). The academic performance of Afro-American children. In J. Spence (Ed.), *Achievement and achievement motives* (pp. 324–371). San Francisco, CA: Freeman.

Brophy, J., & Good, T. (1970). Teachers' communication of differential expectations for children's classroom performance: Some behavioral data. *Journal of Educational Psychology, 61,* 365–374.

Brophy, J., & Good, T. (1974). *Teacher-student relationships: Causes and consequences.* New York, NY: Holt, Rinehart and Winston.

Chalabaev, A., Sarrazin, P., Trouilloud, D., & Jussim, L. (2009). Can sex-undifferentiated teacher expectations mask an influence of sex stereotypes? Alternative forms of sex bias in teacher expectations. *Journal of Applied Social Psychology, 39,* 2469–2498.

Cooper, H. M. (1983). Teacher expectation effects. *Applied Social Psychology Annual, 4,* 247–275.

Cooper, H. M. (1985). Models of teacher expectation communication. In J. B. Dusek (Ed.), *Teacher expectancies.* Hillsdale, NJ: Erlbaum.

Cooper, H. M., Baron, R. M., & Lowe, C. A. (1975). The importance of race and social class information on the formation of expectancies about academic performance. *Journal of Educational Psychology, 67,* 312–319.

Cooper, H. M., & Tom, D. Y. H. (1984). Teacher expectation research: A review with implications for classroom instruction. *Elementary School Journal, 85,* 77–89.

Damber, U. (2009). Using inclusion, high demands and high expectations to resist the deficit syndrome: A study of eight grade three classes underachieving in reading. *Literacy, 43,* 43–49.

Darley, J. M., & Fazio, R. H. (1980). Expectancy confirmation processes arising in the social interaction sequence. *American Psychologist, 35,* 867–881.

de Boer, H., Bosker, R. J., & van der Werf, M. P. C. (2010). Sustainability of teacher expectation bias effects on long-term student performance. *Journal of Educational Psychology, 102,* 168–179.

Diamond, J. B., Randolph, A., & Spillane, J. P. (2004). Teachers' expectations and sense of responsibility for student learning: The importance of race, class, and organizational habitus. *Anthropology and Education Quarterly, 35*(1), 75–98.

Eccles, J. S. (1983). Expectancies, values and academic behaviors. In J. T. Spence (Ed.), *Achievement and achievement motivation* (pp. 75–146). San Francisco, CA: Freeman.

Eccles, J. S., & Wigfield, A. (1985). Teacher expectations and student motivation. In J. B. Dusek (Ed.), *Teacher expectations* (pp. 185–226). Hillsdale, NJ: Erlbaum.

Elashoff, J. D., & Snow, R. E. (Eds.). (1971). *Pygmalion reconsidered.* Worthington, OH: Jones.

Good, T. L., & Brophy, J. (1978). *Looking in classrooms.* New York, NY: Harper & Row.

Good, T. L., & Nichols, S. L. (2001). Expectancy effects in the classroom: A special focus on improving the reading performance of minority students in first-grade classrooms. *Educational Psychologist, 36,* 113–126.

Graham, S. (1994). Motivation in African Americans. *Review of Educational Research, 64,* 55–117.

Guskey, T. R., & Passaro, P. D. (1994). Teacher efficacy: A study of construct dimensions. *American Educational Research Journal, 31*(3), 627–643.

Hanson, W., & Graves, B. (1998). *Jaime Escalante: Excellence means "Do it right the first time."*

Retrieved August 5, 2008, from http://www.govtech.com/gt/articles/251178?id=&story_pg=1

Huss-Keeler, R. L. (1997). Teacher perception of ethnic and linguistic minority parental involvement and its relationships to children's language and literacy learning: A case study. *Teaching and Teacher Education, 13,* 171–182.

Jagodzinski, J. (2001). The best teacher in America stands and delivers: The case of Jaime Escalante. *Journal for the Psychoanalysis of Culture and Society, 6*(2), 232–241.

Jensen, A. R. (1980). *Bias in mental testing.* New York, NY: Free Press.

Jussim, L. (1989). Teacher expectations: Self-fulfilling prophecies, perceptual biases, and accuracy. *Journal of Personality and Social Psychology, 57*(3), 469–480.

Jussim, L. (2013). Teachers' expectations. In J. Hattie & E.M. Anderman (Eds.), *International guide to student achievement* (pp. 243–246). New York, NY: Routledge.

Jussim, L., Eccles, J. S., & Madon, S. (1996). Social perception, social stereotypes, and teacher expectations: Accuracy and the quest for the powerful self-fulfilling prophecy. In M. P. Zanna (Ed.), *Advances in experimental social psychology* (Vol. 28, pp. 281–388). San Diego, CA: Academic Press.

Jussim, L., Robustelli, S. L, & Cain, T. R. (2009). Teacher expectations and self-fulfilling prophecies. In K. R. Wentzel & A. Wigfield (Eds.), *Handbook of motivation at school* (pp. 349–380). New York, NY: Routledge.

Kirk, C. M., Lewis-Moss, R. K., Nilsen, C., & Colvin, D. Q. (2011). The role of parent expectations on adolescent educational aspirations. *Educational Studies, 37,* 89–99.

Klassen, R. M., Tze, V. M. C., Betts, S. M., & Gordon, K. A. (2011). Teacher efficacy research 1998–2009: Signs of progress or unfilled promise? *Educational Psychology Review, 23,* 21–43.

Kuklinski, M. R., & Weinstein, R. S. (2000). Classroom and grade level differences in the stability of teacher expectations and perceived differential teacher treatment. *Learning Environments Research, 3*(1), 1–34.

Kuklinski, M. R., & Weinstein, R. S. (2001). Classroom and developmental differences in a path model for teacher expectancy effects. *Child Development, 72,* 1554–1578.

Kuperminc, G. P., Darnell, A. J., & Alvarez-Jimenez, A. (2008). Parent involvement in the academic adjustment of Latino middle and high school youth: Teacher expectations and school belonging as mediators. *Journal of Adolescence, 31,* 469–483.

Learman, L. A., Avorn, J., Everitt, D. E., & Rosenthal, R. (1990). Pygmalion in the nursing home: The effects of caregiver expectations on patient outcomes. *Journal of the American Geriatrics Society, 38*(7), 797–803.

Leinhardt, G., Seewald, A., & Engel, M. (1979). Learning what's taught: Sex differences in instruction. *Journal of Educational Psychology, 71,* 432–439.

Maehr, M. L., & Anderman, E. M. (1993). Reinventing schools for early adolescents: Emphasizing task goals. *Elementary School Journal, 93*(5), 593–610.

McKown, C., Gregory, A., & Weinstein, R. S. (2010). Expectations, stereotypes, and self-fulfilling prophecies in classroom and school life. In J. L. Meece & J. S. Eccles (Eds.), *Handbook of research on schools, schooling, and human development* (pp. 256–274). New York, NY: Routledge.

Meece, J. L., Glienke, B. B., & Askew, K. (2009). Gender and motivation. In K. R. Wentzel & A. Wigfield (Eds.), *Handbook of motivation at school* (pp. 411–431). New York, NY: Routledge.

Meece, J. L., Parsons, J. E., Kaczala, C. M., & Goff, S. B. (1982). Sex differences in math achievement: Toward a model of academic choice. *Psychological Bulletin, 91*(2), 324–348.

Merton, R. K. (1948). The self-fulfilling prophecy. *The Antioch Review, 8,* 193–210.

Mickelson, R. A. (1990). The attitude-achievement paradox among Black adolescents. *Sociology of Education, 63,* 44–61.

National Teachers Hall of Fame. (1999). *Jaime Escalante: National Inductee.* Retrieved August 14, 2008, from http://www.nthf.org/inductee/escalante.htm

Neal, L. I., McCray, A. D., Webb-Johnson, G., & Bridgest, S. T. (2003). The effect of African American movement styles on teachers' perceptions and reactions. *Journal of Special Education, 37,* 49–57.

Pajares, F. (1996). Self-efficacy beliefs in academic settings. *Review of Educational Research, 66*(4), 543–578.

Peterson, P. L., & Barger, S. A. (1985). Attribution theory and teacher expectancy. In J. B. Dusek (Ed.), *Teacher expectancies* (pp. 159–184). Hillsdale, NJ: Erlbaum.

Pianta, R. C. (1999). *Enhancing relationships between children and teachers.* Washington, DC: American Psychological Association.

Raudenbush, S. W. (1984). Magnitude of teacher expectancy effects on pupil IQ as a function of the credibility of expectancy induction: A synthesis of findings from 18 experiments. *Journal of Educational Psychology, 76*(1), 85–97.

Rosenthal, R. (1995). Critiquing Pygmalion: A 25-year perspective. *Current Directions in Psychological Science, 4*(6), 171–172.

Rosenthal, R., & Jacobson, L. (1968). *Pygmalion in the classroom.* New York: Holt, Rinehart and Winston.

Rozansky, C. L., & Aagesen, C. (2010). Low-achieving readers, high expectations: Image theater encourages critical literacy. *Journal of Adolescent and Adult Literacy, 53,* 458–466.

Rubie-Davies, C. M. (2007). Classroom interactions: Exploring the practices of high- and low-expectation teachers. *British Journal of Educational Psychology, 77*(2), 289–306.

Santana, A. (1999). *Jaime Escalante: Mr. Inspiration.* Retrieved July 29, 2008, from http://www.pasadena.edu/about/history/alumni/escalante/escalante.cfm

Scherr, K. C., Madon, S., Guyll, M., Willard, J., & Spoth, R. (2011). Self-verification as a mediator of mothers' self-fulfilling effects on adolescents' educational attainment. *Personality and Social Psychology Bulletin, 37,* 587–600.

Schunk, D. H. (1991). Self-efficacy and academic motivation. *Educational Psychologist, 26,* 207–231.

Schunk, D. H., & Pajares, F. (2009). Self-efficacy theory. In K. R. Wentzel & A. Wigfield (Eds.), *Handbook of motivation at school* (pp. 35–53). New York, NY: Routledge.

Swann, W., & Snyder, M. (1980). On translating beliefs into action: Theories of ability and their application in an instructional setting. *Journal of Personality and Social Psychology, 38,* 879–888.

Takei, Y., & Semon Dubas, J. (1993). Academic achievement among early adolescents: Social and cultural diversity. In R. M. Lerner (Ed.), *Early adolescence: Perspectives on research, policy, and intervention* (pp. 175–190). Hillsdale, NJ: Erlbaum.

Tolman, E. C. (1932). *Purposive behavior in animals and men.* New York: Appleton-Century-Crofts. (Original work published 1949, 1951, Berkeley: University of California Press).

Trouilloud, D. O., Sarrazin, P. G., Martinek, T. J., & Guillet, E. (2002). The influence of teacher expectations on student achievement in physical education classes: Pygmalion revisited. *European Journal of Social Psychology, 32,* 591–607.

Tschannen-Moran, M., Woolfolk Hoy, A., & Hoy, W. K. (1998). Teacher efficacy: Its meaning and measure. *Review of Educational Research, 68*(2), 202–248.

Urdan, T. (2010). The challenges and promise of research on classroom goal structures. In J. L. Meece & J. S. Eccles (Eds.), *Handbook of research on schools, schooling, and human development* (pp. 92–108). New York, NY: Routledge.

van den Bergh, L., Denessen, E., Hornstra, L., Voeten, M., & Holland, R. W. (2010). The implicit prejudiced attitudes of teachers: Relations to teacher expectations and the ethnic achievement gap. *American Educational Research Journal, 47,* 497–527.

Weinstein, R. S., Gregory, A., & Stambler, M. J. (2004). Intractable self-fulfilling prophecies: Fifty years after *Brown v. Board of Education. American Psychologist, 59,* 511–520.

Weinstein, R. S., Madison, S. M., & Kuklinski, M. R. (1995). Raising expectations in schooling: Obstacles and opportunities for change. *American Educational Research Journal, 32*(1), 121–159.

Weinstein, R. S., Soule, C. R., Collins, F., Cone, J., Mehlorn, M., & Stimmonacchi, K. (1991). Expectations and high school change: Teacher-researcher collaboration to prevent school failure. *American Journal of Community Psychology, 19,* 333–363.

Wentzel, K. R. (2002). Are effective teachers like good parents? Teaching styles and student adjustment in early adolescence. *Child Development, 73,* 287–301.

Wigfield, A., & Eccles, J. S. (2000). Expectancy-value theory of achievement motivation. *Contemporary Educational Psychology, 25*(1), 68–81.

Wigfield, A., & Eccles, J. S. (2002). The development of competence beliefs, expectancies for success, and achievement values from childhood through adolescence. In A. Wigfield & J. S. Eccles (Eds.), *Development of achievement motivation: A volume in the educational psychology series* (pp. 91–120). San Diego, CA: Academic Press.

Wigfield, A., Tonks, S., & Klauda, S. L. (2009). Expectancy-value theory. In K. R. Wentzel & A. Wigfield (Eds.), *Handbook of motivation at school* (pp. 55–75). New York, NY: Routledge.

Zuroff, D. C., & Rotter, J. B. (1985). A history of the expectancy construct in psychology. In J. B. Dusek (Ed.), *Teacher expectancies* (pp. 9–36). Hillsdale, NJ: Erlbaum.

CHAPTER 10

Motivational Problems

When the motivational climate of a classroom is not optimal, problems can arise for both students and teachers. Students may engage in a number of maladaptive behavioral, emotional, and cognitive activities when motivation goes awry. Consider the following examples:

> Lori is a seventh grader. She has a test tomorrow in her English class. She spends the entire evening chatting with her friends in an online chat room. She knows she should be studying, but she uses the chat room instead. The next day, Lori fails the test. She justifies this failure to herself and to her friends because she can blame the failure on her time spent in the chat room.
>
> Nadia is a fifth grader. Her teacher always talks about grades and who is doing the best in class. Nadia feels the need to demonstrate her abilities, so she does her work as quickly as she can and, when possible, chooses easy options rather than risking more challenging projects. Nadia doesn't spend time engaging deeply with her school work or thinking about it beyond "getting it done."
>
> Torie is a ninth grader. In her geography class, she often has questions about issues that need clarification or that she doesn't understand. However, she never asks for assistance from the teacher or from her classmates. She is afraid she will look "dumb" to her classmates and to her teacher if she asks too many questions, so she accepts feeling confused, rather than asking for help.

Why do students engage in these behaviors? Most adults and even most of these students would probably admit that they know these behaviors are maladaptive; nevertheless, students continue to engage in these activities both in school and at home.

Student motivation can negatively influence a number of factors. For some students, poor motivation can lead to the avoidance of engaging with academic work; for others, poor motivation can lead to the use of inappropriate academic strategies; for still other students, academic motivation can affect behavior in the classroom.

In this chapter, we explore these motivation-related problems. Specifically, we examine their nature, as well as the motivational factors that often precipitate these difficulties. We first discuss avoidance behaviors, followed by an examination of other motivational problems, including the roles of cognitive strategies and behavior management in student motivation. Finally, we discuss implications for improvement of classroom environments so that students can learn more effectively.

AVOIDANCE BEHAVIORS

What are *avoidance behaviors*? Several different types of avoidance behaviors have been identified. These include the following (Urdan, Midgley, & Anderman, 1998; Urdan, Ryan, Anderman, & Gheen, 2002):

 a. Withdrawing effort
 b. Avoiding or refusing to seek help
 c. Avoiding risk taking
 d. Giving up when faced with challenges
 e. Engaging in self-handicapping strategies

Students engage in *avoidance behaviors* when they "move away from, or avoid, some perceived threat in the learning context" (Urdan et al., 2002, p. 56). The examples of Lori, Nadia, and Torie represent avoidance behaviors. Students who engage in avoidance behaviors try to avoid having to deal with difficult learning situations. Thus, Lori chooses to spend her evening in the chat room because she doubts her ability to perform well on her English test. By not studying, she avoids the implication that she lacks ability in English. Nadia avoids academic challenges because she is afraid of risking a lower grade. Torie avoids asking questions in her geography class so that she will not appear to be unintelligent to her friends or to her teacher.

Avoidance behaviors are generally maladaptive. Few teachers would want their students to engage in these behaviors. Nevertheless, research indicates that the types of instructional practices that teachers use in their classrooms can create an environment that encourages some students to engage in avoidance behaviors. This is very important because decisions that you make as a teacher regarding how you will deliver instruction to your students can influence the likelihood of your students using some of these problematic avoidance strategies.

Although they appear maladaptive, avoidance behaviors actually do serve a useful purpose for some students, at least in the short term. Martin Covington (1992) has argued that students engage in these types of behaviors to protect their sense of self-worth. Specifically, when students engage in avoidance behaviors, they are able to deflect negative thoughts, perceptions, and comments from themselves and, thus, protect their own positive self-beliefs (Covington, 1992). Students engage in avoidance behaviors to maintain positive perceptions of themselves as students. That is, if a student does not feel academically competent in a certain subject area, the student may adopt avoidance behaviors so that the student won't feel badly about himself or herself. Thus, if Lori spends the evening chatting with her friends, she may be able to protect her self-worth, even if she fails the test, because she can "blame" the failure on the behavior (i.e., chatting), rather than on lack of ability. In other words, Lori can still feel good about herself, despite her failure. Of course, the long-term outcomes of Lori's behavior will be increasingly negative, as her lack of effort leads to more and more failure experiences.

FIGURE 10-1 Review of Four Personal Goal Orientations		
	Approach	**Avoid**
Mastery	Goal is to master the task, to develop ability.	Goal is to avoid misunderstanding the task.
Performance	Goal is to demonstrate ability on the task, particularly in relation to others.	Goal is to avoid appearing incompetent or "dumb" at the task.

AVOIDANCE BEHAVIORS AND GOAL ORIENTATIONS

Most of the research on avoidance behaviors emanates from goal orientation theory (Ames, 1992a, 1992b; Dweck & Leggett, 1988; Harackiewicz, Barron, Pintrich, Elliot, & Thrash, 2002; Pintrich, 2000). Recall that goal orientation theorists argue that students pursue mastery and performance goals and that these goals can either emphasize approach or avoidance components (see Figure 10-1). In addition, goal orientation theorists argue that teachers' instructional practices can foster the perception of an emphasis on either mastery or performance goals in their classes; these perceptions are referred to as a *classroom mastery goal structure* or a *classroom performance goal structure*. When students perceive that a classroom has a mastery goal structure, they believe that the teacher focuses on effort, task mastery, and *developing* ability. In contrast, when students perceive that a classroom has a performance goal structure, they believe that the teacher focuses on competition, relative ability, and the *demonstration* of ability (Kaplan, Middleton, Urdan, & Midgley, 2002; Midgley, 2002).

Why would goal orientations or goal structures lead to avoidance behaviors? Turner and her colleagues (Turner et al., 2002) noted that when classrooms are perceived as being focused on *mastery,* students are unlikely to feel threatened and, thus, may not need to use avoidance strategies. In contrast, when a classroom is perceived as being focused on *performance* (and when performance is what is rewarded by the teacher), then students may come to believe that certain strategies (e.g., asking for assistance from the teacher) will draw attention to their lack of ability. Such students might not choose to use strategies such as help-seeking that could truly assist them to become more effective learners. As we will review later in this chapter, much evidence suggests that performance goals and the perception of a performance goal structure are related to greater engagement in avoidance behaviors than are mastery goals and perceptions of a mastery goal structure (Butler & Neuman, 1995; Turner et al., 2002; Urdan et al., 2002).

TYPES OF AVOIDANCE BEHAVIORS

Several types of behaviors represent avoidance strategies. As we will see, the emergence and maintenance of these behaviors are related to the types of goals that students pursue and that students perceive as being emphasized in their classrooms.

Self-Handicapping

Self-handicapping is a process through which students deliberately try to externalize their failures to preserve their self-esteem or self-worth (Berglas & Jones, 1978; Covington, 1992;

FIGURE 10-2 Examples of Academic Self-Handicapping Strategies

Strategy	If performance is low, this can be justified because students can say that they didn't do well because . . .
"Fooling around" the night before a test or a quiz	. . . they fooled around.
Getting involved in too many activities	. . . of all their other commitments.
Finding reasons not to study (not feeling well, having to help parents with chores, having to babysit for a sibling)	. . . they didn't have time to prepare.
Letting friends keep a student from paying attention in class or from doing homework	. . . their friends were distracting them.
Purposely not trying hard in class	. . . they just didn't try hard enough.
Putting off doing classwork until the last minute	. . . they delayed doing their work for too long.

Source: Midgley et al. (2000).

Urdan et al., 2002). Students engage in self-handicapping strategies to avoid looking dumb or incompetent in school (Covington, 1992). Urdan and his colleagues (2002) noted that although self-handicapping is similar to the process of attribution, there is an important difference: Self-handicapping is a deliberate, *proactive* strategy that students use to influence others' beliefs about their abilities; in contrast, an attribution is the true belief that the student has about the reasons for his or her successes or failures. Attributions are made after a student experiences success or failure. Self-handicapping is generally a problematic avoidance strategy and has been linked to anxiety and negative affect (Thompson & Richardson, 2001). Midgley and her colleagues (2000) have identified several examples of self-handicapping behaviors. These are summarized in Figure 10-2.

In the example that opened this chapter, Lori deliberately spends the night before her exam chatting with her friends. This is a self-handicapping strategy because she purposefully chooses to engage in an activity (chatting) that will allow her to subsequently justify her failure on the exam to that activity. In contrast, after the failure, if Lori really believes that her failure was due to a lack of ability, that subsequent belief would be an *attribution*.

REASONS STUDENTS ENGAGE IN SELF-HANDICAPPING BEHAVIORS Students engage in self-handicapping behaviors when they do not expect to succeed at an academic task. In particular, students who maintain low self-perceptions of ability, or who truly are low in measured ability, are likely to engage in self-handicapping behaviors.

But why would students deliberately set themselves up for failure? If a student knows that she should study, why would she deliberately do something else, like chat with her friends or go to the movies? Researchers have been interested in the causes of self-handicapping for the past two decades. In recent years, however, they have begun to examine specifically the relations of motivational variables to self-handicapping.

Studies of the relations between motivation variables and self-handicapping generally indicate that self-handicapping is related to perceptions of a performance goal structure in the classroom (Midgley & Urdan, 2001; Urdan et al., 1998). That is, when students believe that success in a class is defined by demonstrating one's ability, getting good grades, and outperforming others, the emergence of self-handicapping behaviors may be more likely. In addition, other research indicates that self-handicapping is associated both with personal extrinsic goals (Midgley & Urdan, 1995) and with personal performance-avoid goals (Midgley & Urdan, 2001). Thus, students who are focused either on getting good grades or on avoiding looking "dumb" or incompetent may be more likely to adopt self-handicapping strategies than other students.

Several studies have also examined the relations of mastery goals and mastery goal structures to self-handicapping. Turner and her colleagues (2002) found that perceptions of a mastery goal structure were predictive of lower levels of self-handicapping in a large sample of upper-elementary-school students. In addition, Midgley and Urdan (2001) found that both personal mastery goals and perceptions of a mastery goal structure were related to lower levels of self-handicapping in a sample of eighth graders. When students believe their teachers value real understanding and progress, and when they adopt those goals for themselves, they are less likely to engage in self-handicapping behaviors that work against real learning.

Avoidance of Help-Seeking

Many motivation researchers are interested in students' tendencies to seek help when they are experiencing difficulties with their work. When students actively seek help, they learn material more effectively (Newman & Schwager, 1992). However, when students experience motivational problems, or when they perceive that the classroom climate does not support their motivation, students may avoid seeking help from the teacher or from others.

Whether or not a student will seek help has much to do with the type of learning environment in the classroom, as well as with the student's personal characteristics and goals. Certainly, shy students may be less likely to seek help than their more socially oriented peers, particularly when asking help from someone of the opposite sex (DePaulo, Dull, Greenberg, & Swaim, 1989). Nevertheless, some students deliberately avoid seeking help, although they know they would benefit from assistance. This behavior is often rooted in motivational issues.

WHY STUDENTS AVOID SEEKING HELP Why would students not ask for help when they know that assistance is needed to succeed? Generally, research indicates that perceptions of a mastery goal structure in the classroom are related to *less* avoidance of help-seeking. That is, students who perceive that the classroom supports effort, improvement, and task mastery may feel more comfortable asking for assistance with difficult academic tasks. With regard to personal goals, it appears that students who endorse mastery goals at an individual level are also less likely to avoid seeking help, whereas students who endorse performance goals are more likely to avoid seeking help.

Several researchers have examined the relations of perceived classroom goal structures to help-seeking. Ryan and her colleagues (Ryan, Gheen, & Midgley, 1998) found that when students perceive a mastery goal structure, they are less likely to report that they avoid seeking help in the classroom. In a different sample, Turner and her colleagues (2002) also found that perceptions of a mastery goal structure are related to less avoidance of help-seeking. Butler and Neuman (1995) found that students are more likely to seek help when they are learning in an environment that stresses task mastery; when students learn in a performance-oriented environment, they explain their avoidance of help-seeking as a means of covering up their inability to do the work.

Other studies have examined the relations of personal mastery and performance goals to the avoidance of help-seeking. Ryan and Pintrich (1997), Ryan, Hicks, and Midgley (1997), and Middleton and Midgley (1997) have all reported that the avoidance of help-seeking is more likely with personal performance goals and less likely with personal mastery goals. Important evidence also shows that students will be more likely to seek help from teachers for bullying and violence in school settings when the students have positive relationships with their teachers and perceive the presence of a supportive climate in the school (Eliot, Cornell, Gregory, & Fan, 2010; Yablon, 2010).

Stop and Think

Have you ever engaged in any avoidant behaviors? Why? Were these strategies helpful to you? Did they ultimately cause any problems for you?

Summary of Avoidance Behaviors and Motivation

The use of avoidance behaviors such as self-handicapping and the avoidance of help-seeking is quite predictable. Students will be more likely to use these strategies when they are highly focused on grades and performance; they will be less likely to engage in them when they are focused on mastery, effort, and improvement. Fortunately, students' personal goals and classroom goal structures are malleable; therefore, it may be possible for educators to create motivational learning environments where such avoidance behaviors are unlikely to occur.

OTHER MOTIVATIONAL PROBLEMS   Whereas avoidance behaviors are quite common, other issues can also arise due to motivational problems in classrooms. When teachers create environments that are not conducive to students' needs, motivational problems can be quite serious. In most of these cases, problems in the classroom result in maladaptive cognitions and behaviors in students. Fortunately, changing these facets of the classroom environment often can improve student outcomes considerably. We describe some of these important issues in the next sections.

MOTIVATION AND STRATEGY USE

Cognitive strategies refer to the ways that students think while solving problems. The type of motivational climate that is supported in a classroom actually can affect students' abilities to solve problems effectively. Depending on the type of motivational climate that you as the teacher foster in your classroom, students may elect to utilize either effective or ineffective cognitive strategies. Thus, it is extremely important for teachers to acknowledge the potential relation between student motivation and cognitive strategy usage. You, as the classroom teacher, will influence how students think about their academic work through the choices that you make daily related to student motivation.

Although cognitive strategies can be examined in a variety of ways, motivation researchers often describe two types of strategies: *deep cognitive strategies* and *surface cognitive strategies.*

Deep Cognitive Strategies

Deep strategies most closely resemble what the popular literature refers to as "critical thinking." When students utilize deep cognitive-processing strategies, they engage in strategies that allow them to truly examine and ponder the academic task at hand. Deep strategies are desirable because they allow students to really learn, understand, and apply material for the long term.

Some Deep Cognitive Strategies

- Relating new information to prior knowledge
- Monitoring one's understanding of new material
- Organizing or outlining work
- Asking oneself questions or generating new examples related to new information

---

Research clearly indicates that the use of deep-level cognitive processing strategies is related to the endorsement of mastery goals. Specifically, when students are focused on mastering a task, they are more likely to engage in effective learning strategies (Ames & Archer, 1988; Nolen, 1988; Pintrich & de Groot, 1990; Wolters, Yu, & Pintrich, 1996). In contrast, research regarding performance approach goals is mixed, with some studies finding positive relations between deep strategy use and performance-approach goals (Wolters et al., 1996) and other studies yielding no relation between performance approach goals and effective strategy use (Kaplan & Midgley, 1997).

Surface Cognitive Strategies

In contrast to deep strategies, surface strategies are quick and easy strategies that will allow the student to complete tasks and memorize the material being studied with as little effort as possible. Surface strategies are usually undesirable because they do not necessarily lead to long-term or robust retention of material.

Some Surface Strategies

- Rote memorization of lists
- Reading texts as quickly as possible without thinking about content in depth
- Writing down the first answer that comes to mind
- Rehearsal (repeating information over and over again)

Research indicates that the use of surface-level strategies is related inversely to mastery goals; that is, when students endorse mastery goals, they are less likely to use these strategies (E. M. Anderman & Young, 1994; Garcia, Pintrich, & Educational Resources Information Center [U.S.], 1991; Pintrich, Marx, & Boyle, 1993).

Students' motivational problems can be misinterpreted as behavioral problems.

Stop and Think

When do you use deep cognitive strategies? When do you use surface cognitive strategies? Do you associate your own use of these two different types of strategies with the instructional practices used by your teachers?

MOTIVATION AND BEHAVIOR MANAGEMENT

It is important to consider motivational processes such as self-regulation when examining the causes of behavior management problems in classrooms (McCaslin et al., 2006). Teachers and students maintain diverse beliefs about classroom-based behavioral problems and behavior management (Woolfolk Hoy & Weinstein, 2006). Nevertheless, most students, parents, and teachers would agree that when students are not motivated to learn or are not *engaged* with academic tasks, behavioral problems may arise; in contrast, when students are interested in their work, they are less likely to be tempted to engage in alternative, off-task activities.

Stop and Think

Try to recall a time when you misbehaved in school. Do you remember the class where this occurred? How motivated were you in that particular class?

Consider the following two students, both of whom are fourth graders:

Nancy is working on a science project. She doesn't understand the purpose of the project, and she thinks the project is boring. It is difficult for her to pay attention to her work. When another student tries to distract her, she is happy to start talking with the other student.

Lynnette is writing a short story. She loves writing, and she is completely engrossed in this project. She feels that her project is important, and she is proud of her work. When another student tries to distract her, she tells the student to leave her alone because she wants to finish her story.

The difference between these two situations is that Lynnette is engaged with her work, whereas Nancy is not. Students are *engaged* when they are psychologically and emotionally involved with their academic tasks (Fredericks, Blumenfeld, & Paris, 2004; Skinner & Belmont, 1993; Turner et al., 1998). Julianne Turner and Debra Meyer are two researchers who have studied *involvement*, which is similar to engagement. They found that teachers can create contexts that encourage involvement. Specifically, they found that high-involvement mathematics classrooms tend to have the following characteristics (Turner et al., 1998):

1. *Students are pushed to understand the material.* When students do not demonstrate an understanding of the work, teachers assist the students until they are sure that each student has reached an appropriate level of understanding.
2. *Errors are viewed constructively.* Students' mistakes are viewed as opportunities for learning. Teachers in high-involvement classrooms don't criticize students for making mistakes, but use the opportunity to find out where the students' cognitive processing went awry.
3. *Teachers are enthusiastic about the material they are teaching.* When teachers communicate that they value the material they are teaching, this enthusiasm is often contagious; students sense their teachers' enthusiasm and often internalize these positive attitudes.

When teachers create classroom contexts that support engagement and involvement, students are less likely to misbehave. If a student is engrossed in an academic task, he or she may be less likely to become distracted by peers. In addition, if most students in the class are engaged with their work, there will be fewer distractions overall.

In addition, it is important for teachers to have supportive relationships with their students; students are likely to show respect for teachers whom they perceive as caring. However, a caring teacher is more than just a teacher who is "nice" to students because that type of caring is an insufficient way to get students to learn effectively and behave (L. H. Anderman, Patrick, Hruda, & Linnenbrink, 2002); rather, effective caring involves true demonstrations by the teacher that he or she cares about the students as learners (Davis, 2003; Pianta, 1999; Wentzel, 1997).

Anderman, Andrezejewski, and Allen (2011) observed high-school teachers who had been identified by their students as providing environments that were supportive of student motivation and engagement. All the identified teachers maintained effective classroom management while simultaneously building positive relationships with their students. For example, in an 11th-grade chemistry class, one teacher always began class with what he called "News of Interest," during which he allotted time for students to share information from their daily lives. Students spoke about such things as upcoming school-based activities, but also personal and community news. In addition, all the observed teachers provided students with a degree of autonomy, for example, selecting their own groups for laboratory activities, choosing where to sit in the classroom, and leaving for the restrooms without seeking permission. Whereas many teachers might see these strategies as potential triggers for problematic behaviors, when teachers use these strategies along with other effective motivation strategies, students will not necessarily take advantage of these freedoms. Second, in the effective classrooms, teachers used discretion when they encountered off-task behaviors. For example, the authors described one example in which a female student put her head down on the desk during class; the teacher approached the student quietly and corrected her without drawing undue attention to the situation.

Developmental Differences and Behavior Management

When students are motivated, they are less likely to engage in inappropriate behaviors. Nevertheless, it is important to realize that students of different ages will experience different behavioral issues, and these issues relate to academic motivation in different ways.

During the elementary-school years, student misbehavior often is not as serious as it may be during the middle-school and high-school years. It is easier for teachers to redirect students back to the task at hand during the elementary years, compared to during secondary education. For example, a second-grade student who is off task and talking to a neighbor will probably be more responsive to a teacher redirecting the student's attention toward the task than will a ninth grader.

During the secondary years, problematic behaviors may also be more serious. For example, the occurrence of bullying in a high-school classroom may have serious ramifications for students both inside and outside the classroom. Thus, whereas a teacher may be able to redirect a student's attention momentarily in the classroom, the larger problem of being bullied may affect motivation and learning outside the classroom.

It is particularly important for elementary-school teachers to examine ways of redirecting misbehavior. As developmental researchers have shown, motivational beliefs develop, change, and solidify over time (Wigfield & Eccles, 2002); consequently, if student misbehavior consistently leads to less engagement and poorer motivation during the elementary-school years, this pattern may become ingrained and more difficult to eliminate as students become adolescents.

Cultural Values and Behavior Management

One area that has received relatively little attention in the research literature is the effects of students' cultural values on their classroom behavior. It is inappropriate to assume that students of all ethnic groups maintain similar cultural values; indeed, students from different backgrounds maintain diverse values and beliefs.

Tyler, Haines, and Anderman (2006) reviewed the literature on cultural values of different ethnic groups in the United States. These authors cautioned that it is important when examining this literature to recall that there is much diversity *within* each ethnic group (e.g., Native Americans actually consist of more than 500 distinct tribal nations). Nevertheless, some values appear to be somewhat consistent across such subgroups. If classroom environments do not espouse similar values, students may feel less of a connection to the classroom and, potentially, may seem to violate the rules of the classroom more often.

For example, African American students often prefer classrooms that emphasize *communalism* (e.g., acknowledging the importance of interpersonal interactions and mutual interdependence), *movement*, and *verve* (e.g., sensory stimulation). Nevertheless, as noted by Boykin and his colleagues, most American classrooms do not espouse these values, and this mismatch between African American students' values and classroom norms may result in behavioral problems for some students (Boykin, Tyler, & Miller, 2005). Interestingly, experimental research indicates that low-income African American children learn extremely well when classroom contexts do incorporate these culturally relevant themes (Boykin, 1983; Boykin, Lilja, & Tyler, 2004).

SIDEBAR: Suggestions for Motivating Culturally Diverse Students

1. *Learn about your students' cultures.* Don't be afraid to admit that you do not know about certain cultural preferences. Immerse yourself in books, videos, and Web sites to learn about aspects of the students' cultures that you can incorporate into your teaching.

2. *Talk to your students about their cultures.* You can learn much from your students. Talk to them about their preferences, their customs, and their families. By incorporating some of this information into your teaching, you may engage some students who have not previously felt engaged in your class.

3. *Talk to parents.* You can learn so much from your students' parents. Don't be afraid to ask them about their family and community traditions and values, and be willing to incorporate newly learned information into your curricula.

4. *Acknowledge and accept the fact that students use different forms of discourse.* For example, many African Americans interact with a form of communication known as *call-response,* in which listeners provide encouragement and commentary while someone else is speaking (Gay, 2000). Whereas this type of communication may be seen as interrupting others and interpreted as a form of misbehavior by some teachers, a culturally sensitive teacher is aware that thwarting this type of communication may harm a minority student's motivation.

5. *Try to learn about your students' lives outside school.* Taking an interest in what your students do in their daily lives before and after school may help you to better understand students' in-class behavior. Indeed, knowing something about a student's family life may allow you as the teacher to understand that misbehavior in the classroom is situated for many students within larger social and familial issues. For example, some research suggests that ethnic minority girls who live in single-parent households with their mothers may be at greater risk for involvement in behavioral infractions than similar girls in two-parent households (Mokrue, Chen, & Elias, 2012). If you as the teacher are aware of the family situations of some of your students, it may help you to better understand the complexities underlying any misbehavior.

6. *Consult with other professionals.* Almost all public schools have either school psychologists or school social workers available for consultation. These individuals are well prepared to help you as the classroom teacher deal with complex behavioral issues. You should not feel that you are alone in strategizing about ways to handle complex behavioral problems; many professionals with expertise in this area are available to assist you. School psychologists in particular can help teachers to assess whether a different set of instructional strategies might be more effective for a student who is engaged in problematic behaviors.

It is, therefore, extremely important for teachers to be sensitive to the cultural values of their students. This is important even if only one student in the classroom has cultural values that differ from the majority. The use of culturally relevant pedagogy will lead to both motivational and behavioral benefits for students from all ethnic backgrounds (Gay, 2000).

MOTIVATION AND ANXIETY

Test anxiety as it relates to assessment is presented in a previous chapter (see Chapter 4). As was noted, many students experience anxiety during testing situations, and this anxiety can affect their performance on tests adversely (Zeidner, 1998). Nevertheless, it is also possible for students to experience motivation-related anxiety under other (nontesting) conditions.

For example, some students may experience anxiety when they have a performance-avoidant goal orientation. Consider the following example:

> *Lindsay always gets very nervous and anxious in her French class. She does not like the way her voice sounds when her teacher calls on her and makes her speak in French. She wants to avoid being embarrassed, and she does not want to appear incompetent as a French speaker. Thus, she tries as hard as she can to avoid being called on to speak in class. She often is successful, but she experiences much anxiety every day as a result of her avoidance goal.*

In this example, Lindsay's motivational orientation toward avoidance may be causing her to experience anxiety during her French class. Thus, it is possible for students to experience anxiety as a result of their motivational beliefs.

In addition, teachers' instructional practices can also induce feelings of anxiety in some students. For example, some students may experience anxiety in physical education classes, particularly if they are not very good at sports (Ridgers, Fazey, & Fairclough, 2007). Consider the following example:

> *Ethan is in the eighth grade. He has never been very good at sports and has often had unpleasant experiences during physical education (PE). His PE teacher organizes many team-based competitive activities during class. Specifically, the teacher often picks two "captains" and then allows the captains to alternate choosing members for their respective teams. Ethan is almost always one of the last students who is chosen for a team, causing him to experience much anxiety prior to and during his physical education class.*

In this example, Ethan's anxiety can potentially be avoided by changing the strategy for choosing teams. The PE teacher could use a number of alternative methods for choosing teams; for example, the teacher could have students count off by two's (one, two, one, two, etc.), and then make the "ones" into a team and the "twos" into a team. He could also plan lessons that balance team-based activities with others that are completed individually and noncompetitively. These changes could go a long way to alleviating Ethan's anxiety.

As educators, we sometimes do not realize that the instructional practices we use can cause anxiety (and sometimes debilitating anxiety) for our students. It is important for us to consider the possibility that we may be causing unnecessary stress in our students sometimes. Informal conversations with students often provide us with important information about such issues. In addition, informal, anonymous surveys or feedback sheets can be used occasionally to solicit feedback from students.

MOTIVATION AND LEARNED HELPLESSNESS

When students experience learned helplessness, they perceive little relation between their behaviors and outcomes. Dweck (1986) described children who experience a "helpless" pattern of achievement behavior as avoiding challenge and not persisting when encountering difficulty. Such feelings of helplessness can lead to negative affect, depression, and feelings of hopelessness and anxiety (Dweck, 1986; Seligman, 1975).

Consider the following example:

> Ghita does her math homework every night. However, whenever she takes a math test, she fails. She feels that there is no relation between her persistence at doing math homework and her continued failure on math exams. Ghita believes that she is "dumb" when it comes to math and that there isn't much that she can do to change that. Thus, when she encounters a difficult math task, she just "gives up" rather than trying to apply the strategies she has learned. Ghita feels frustrated and quite depressed about her experiences in math.

In this example, Ghita has developed learned helplessness. She does not feel that there is a relation between her behavior (doing math homework) and the outcome (failing math tests). Ghita experiences highly negative affect after these continued failures.

It is difficult to help students who experience learned helplessness; however, it is possible to alter this pattern of negative thinking. Specifically, teachers need to work to change students' attributions after failures.

Earlier in the book we discussed students' fixed and entity beliefs about intelligence. Recently, Dweck has referred to these as "mind-sets" (Dweck, 2006). Specifically, individuals who hold a *fixed mind-set* believe that their abilities are set at specific levels and cannot change, whereas individuals who hold a *growth mind-set* believe that their talents and abilities can be developed and improved.

Students who experience learned helplessness quite likely also have a fixed mind-set. In the preceding example, Ghita probably attributes her failures on math examinations to a lack of mathematical ability. Ghita does her homework nightly but still fails. Ghita probably believes that her ability in mathematics is fixed and that she simply is not capable of successfully completing math problems.

One possible solution would be for a teacher to examine Ghita's study skills. For example, Ghita may be doing the homework assignments but not spending any time studying or practicing solving math problems under simulated test conditions. She may be using surface learning strategies, such as trying to memorize superficial steps to solving problems, rather than focusing on understanding the mathematical properties in question. If Ghita is shown new study strategies and allowed to practice them, her math test performance may improve. When Ghita learns to attribute her poor performance to inappropriate strategies, rather than an innate lack of ability, her new beliefs will break the learned helplessness cycle. Changing attributional beliefs may be quite difficult for teachers or parents alone; this might be a particularly good situation in which to consult with a school psychologist.

MOTIVATION AND APATHY

As noted by Brophy (2004), perhaps the most difficult motivational problem for teachers is the apathetic student: one who simply does not care about anything at school and does not want to learn. Student apathy can occur in just about any subject area, although teachers of some subject areas may encounter more apathy than others. For example, history teachers often note that students are apathetic toward learning about historical events that seem to

The apathetic student is one of the greatest challenges for teachers.

have little relevance to students' lives (Kaiser, 2010). Such students may engage in minimal amounts of work to stay out of trouble, but they generally don't care at all about academics. Consider the following example:

> Logan is a 10th-grade student. He does not like coming to school. He isn't particularly interested in any of his classes, and he does the minimal amount of academic work. He does not spend much time studying at home, and he does not have a good relationship with any of his teachers.

Students such as Logan represent true motivational challenges for educators. How do you "motivate" a student who appears to be totally unmotivated?

Brophy (2004) suggested that educators can enhance motivation even in students with serious motivational deficits, such as Logan. For example, a student like Logan might benefit from the use of incentives or rewards. Although rewards may undermine intrinsic motivation in some students (Deci, Koestner, & Ryan, 2001), they may foster at least some engagement in students who have no intrinsic motivation to lose. Another suggestion is to try to develop a close personal relationship with the student. Alienated students probably do not feel a sense of belonging in their schools (Juvonen, 2006); therefore, the development of a positive relationship with a teacher may help improve feelings of belonging. Brophy also suggested that educators working with apathetic students need to build on the students' preexisting interests. For example, if an English teacher discovers that an apathetic student loves to read comics, then the teacher might assign a special project to that student, wherein the student can develop her own "comic strip," representing a novel that is being read in class. Finally, Brophy noted that some apathetic students may not have an appropriate repertoire of strategies to be successful in school. Teachers can work with these students to teach them some self-regulatory strategies (e.g., how to study for a math test); then, if these students begin to experience more academic success as a result of these newly learned strategies, their motivation may be enhanced.

AVOIDING MOTIVATION-RELATED BEHAVIORAL PROBLEMS

From the perspective of motivation, teachers can use certain strategies, such as the following, to deter the occurrence of behavioral problems in the classroom:

1. *Promote mastery goals whenever possible.* To avoid motivational problems, teachers should do their best to promote the mastery of material. When students truly believe that the goals of instruction support task mastery, effort, and improvement, they are likely to become more engaged with tasks and, consequently, should be off task less and misbehave less. They are also less likely to engage in maladaptive behaviors, such as self-handicapping and avoiding help-seeking.

2. *Avoid promoting grades and competition.* Whereas testing and grading will always exist, they don't have to be the focus of instruction. When the focus of instruction is on testing and grades, students often will take academic shortcuts or may engage in problematic avoidant behaviors, such as self-handicapping.

3. *Create an environment in which students can readily and easily seek assistance.* If students become frustrated with a task and feel that they can't easily acquire assistance, they may stop concentrating on the task and become distracted and engage in problematic behaviors. Students may choose to avoid seeking help for a variety of reasons. Teachers should actively encourage students to seek assistance from both the teacher and peers. In addition, teachers should provide ways for students to be able to seek help privately (e.g., after class, by going up to the teacher's desk and asking quietly for help).

4. *Encourage the use of deep cognitive-processing strategies.* When students solve problems as quickly and easily as they can, they often lose interest in the problem and may get off task and misbehave, and they often are not rewarded for engaging in complex thinking strategies. Teachers can set up reward structures in their classrooms that encourage students to engage in complex thinking and to take academic risks. For example, a teacher might offer to award part of a grade on an assignment for creativity in problem solving (i.e., students are rewarded for developing a novel method for solving a problem).

5. *Use culturally relevant pedagogy.* Students from different ethnic and cultural backgrounds may prefer to learn in different ways; when the values espoused in the classroom do not meet the expectations of individual students, behavioral problems may be more likely to occur. Educators must acknowledge and understand that students who come from different cultural backgrounds may use different communication

styles in the classroom. Whereas it may not be possible to meet all the needs of all students every day, it is possible to gear instruction toward students' varied cultural backgrounds over several days so that all students feel they are appreciated and valued.

6. *Understand the complex and important relation between motivation and behavior management.* Teachers must think carefully about how, when, and why students misbehave. At times, students misbehave simply because they are bored or not engaged with the academic task. Teachers should plan lessons that will keep students engaged and on task. This may be particularly challenging with apathetic students, but even students who display little interest in academics can become more motivated.

7. *Consider the developmental levels of your students.* As discussed throughout this book, some motivational strategies will be more effective with younger students, and some will be more effective with older students. Teachers should consider the developmental appropriateness, not only of their curriculum content, but also of their approaches to supporting and maintaining their students' engagement.

8. *Promote a positive climate in your classroom.* Too often as educators we focus on negative aspects of classrooms and learning (e.g., stopping bad behaviors), rather than focusing on the promotion of positive behaviors and emotions in the classroom. Teachers need to be cognizant of this tendency and work to promote students' experience of positive emotions on a regular basis (Conoley & Conoley, 2009).

Prevention of Avoidance Behaviors

Kimberly Baron is a curriculum coordinator for high-school foreign languages and fine arts in a large urban school district. She has taught foreign language classes for many years. She has developed a number of instructional practices that deter her students from engaging in avoidance behaviors. Kim has found that engagement in avoidance behaviors by students is particularly common in foreign language classes because many students experience high levels of anxiety associated with learning a new language. In particular, they often are nervous about speaking the new language, particularly in front of their peers. Kim starts her first-year foreign language classes each year by having her students read the book *The Cow That Went Oink* (Most, 1990). This book is a story about the process of learning a language; the contents of the book demonstrate to the students that making mistakes is a natural part of learning a foreign language. Through the use of this book, Kim illustrates to her students that they all will make mistakes as they learn a new language; she emphasizes that in her opinion, something is only considered a "mistake" if the student refuses to attempt to correct it. When students use the new language incorrectly, Kim treats that as a learning opportunity. She does not allow her students to say, "I don't know. . ."; if they do, she responds to them with statements such as "I'll come right back to you; use your notes and other resources [e.g., your books, your speaking partner] to try to come up with the answer." These strategies encourage Kim's students to seek help, to not give up, and to be willing to take risks.

Summary

In this chapter, we have examined some issues associated with maladaptive forms of academic motivation. As discussed, students occasionally use maladaptive strategies (e.g., self-handicapping), particularly when they encounter difficult academic work. It is important for teachers to understand the reasons why students might use these problematic strategies. Teachers can identify these problems in their students and can intervene quickly to redirect students toward the use of more positive motivational strategies.

Questions to Consider Regarding Motivational Problems

1. How can a teacher get a student to understand that the student is engaging in self-handicapping strategies?
2. How can a teacher encourage adaptive help-seeking in the classroom? How can teachers make students feel inconspicuous when requesting help?
3. What are some issues related to culture and ethnicity that must be considered when assisting students with motivational problems?
4. How might you assist a student who exhibits "learned helplessness" behaviors?

LEARNING ACTIVITY 10.1   Behavior Management and Motivation

Consider the following scenario:

Ottavia is a fifth-grade student in your class. You noticed recently that every day during group reading time, she is off task and acting silly. Although the other four students in her reading group try to stay on task and work on their reading, Ottavia is often off task, either doing something else, daydreaming, or distracting others.

Considering what you have learned about the relations between the types of instructional practices that teachers use and student motivation, what are some things that you could do, using motivation theory and research, to get Ottavia to become more engaged? What are some specific instructional practices that you could implement, either with Ottavia or with the entire group, to encourage Ottavia to stay on task and engaged?

References

Ames, C. (1992a). Achievement goals and the classroom motivational climate. In D. H. Schunk & J. L. Meece (Eds.), *Student perceptions in the classroom* (pp. 327–348). Hillsdale, NJ: Erlbaum.

Ames, C. (1992b). Classrooms: Goals, structures, and student motivation. *Journal of Educational Psychology, 84*(3), 261–271.

Ames, C., & Archer, J. (1988). Achievement goals in the classroom: Students' learning strategies and motivation processes. *Journal of Educational Psychology, 80*(3), 260–267.

Anderman, E. M., & Young, A. J. (1994). Motivation and strategy use in science: Individual differences and classroom effects. *Journal of Research in Science Teaching, 31*(8), 811–831.

Anderman, L. H., Andrzejewski, C. E., & Allen, J. (2011). How do teachers support students' motivation and learning in their classrooms? *Teachers College Record, 113*, 969–1003.

Anderman, L. H., Patrick, H., Hruda, L. Z., & Linnenbrink, E. A. (2002). Observing classroom goal structures to clarify and expand goal theory. In C. Midgley (Ed.), *Goals, goal structures, and patterns of adaptive learning* (pp. 243–278). Mahwah, NJ: Erlbaum.

Berglas, S., & Jones, E. E. (1978). Drug choice as a self-handicapping strategy in response to noncontingent success. *Journal of Personality and Social Psychology, 36*, 405–417.

Boykin, A. W. (1983). The academic performance of Afro-American children. In J. Spence (Ed.), *Achievement and achievement motives* (pp. 324–371). San Francisco, CA: Freeman.

Boykin, A. W., Lilja, A. J., & Tyler, K. M. (2004). The influence of communal versus individual learning context on the academic performance of African American elementary school students. *Learning Environments Journal, 7*, 227–244.

Boykin, A. W., Tyler, K. M., & Miller, O. A. (2005). In search of cultural themes and their expression in the dynamics of classroom life. *Urban Education, 40*(5), 521–549.

Brophy, J. (2004). *Motivating students to learn* (2nd ed.). Mahwah, NJ: Erlbaum.

Butler, R., & Neuman, O. (1995). Effects of task and ego achievement goals on help-seeking behaviors and attitudes. *Journal of Educational Psychology, 87*, 261–271.

Conoley, C. W., & Conoley, J. C. (2009). Positive psychology for educators. In R. Gilman, E. S. Huebner, & M. J. Furlong (Eds.), *Handbook of positive psychology in schools* (pp. 463–476). New York, NY: Routledge.

Covington, M. V. (1992). *Making the grade: A self-worth perspective on motivation and school reform.* New York, NY: Cambridge University Press.

Davis, H. A. (2003). Conceptualizing the role and influence of student–teacher relationships on children's social and cognitive development. *Educational Psychologist, 38*, 207–234.

Deci, E. L., Koestner, R., & Ryan, R. M. (2001). Extrinsic rewards and intrinsic motivation in education: Reconsidered once again. *Review of Educational Research, 71*(1), 1–27.

DePaulo, B. M., Dull, W. R., Greenberg, J. M., & Swaim, G. W. (1989). Are shy people reluctant to ask for help? *Journal of Personality and Social Psychology, 56*(5), 834–844.

Dweck, C. S. (1986). Motivational processes affecting learning. *American Psychologist, 41*, 1040–1048.

Dweck, C. S. (2006). *Mindset: The new psychology of success.* New York, NY: Random House.

Dweck, C. S., & Leggett, E. L. (1988). A social-cognitive approach to motivation and personality. *Psychological Review, 95*(2), 256–273.

Eliot, M., Cornell, D., Gregory, A., & Fan, X. (2010). Supportive school climate and student willingness to seek help for bullying and threats of violence. *Journal of School Psychology, 48*, 533–553.

Fredericks, J., Blumenfeld, P. C., & Paris, A. (2004). School engagement: Potential of the concept, state of the evidence. *Review of Educational Research, 74*, 59–109.

Garcia, T., Pintrich, P. R., & Educational Resources Information Center (U.S.). (1991). *The effects of autonomy on motivation, use of learning strategies, and performance in the college classroom* [microform]. Washington, DC: U.S. Dept. of Education Office of Educational Research and Improvement Educational Resources Information Center.

Gay, G. (2000). *Culturally responsive teaching: Theory, research, and practice.* New York, NY: Teachers College Press.

Harackiewicz, J. M., Barron, K. E., Pintrich, P. R., Elliot, A. J., & Thrash, T. M. (2002). Revision of achievement goal theory: Necessary and illuminating. *Journal of Educational Psychology, 94*(3), 638–645.

Juvonen, J. (2006). Sense of belonging, social bonds, and school functioning. In P. A. Alexander & P. H. Winne (Eds.), *Handbook of educational psychology* (2nd ed., pp. 655–674). Mahwah, NJ: Erlbaum.

Kaiser, C. (2010). Redrawing the boundaries: A constructivist approach to combating student apathy in the secondary history classroom. *The History Teacher, 43*, 223–232.

Kaplan, A., Middleton, M. J., Urdan, T., & Midgley, C. (2002). Achievement goals and goal structures. In C. Midgley (Ed.), *Goals, goal structures, and patterns of adaptive learning* (pp. 21–53). Mahwah, NJ: Erlbaum.

Kaplan, A., & Midgley, C. (1997). The effect of achievement goals: Does level of perceived academic-competence make a difference? *Contemporary Educational Psychology, 22*(4), 415–435.

McCaslin, M., Bozack, A. R., Napoleon, L., Thomas, A., Vasquez, V., Wayman, V., & Zhang, J. (2006). Self-regulated learning and classroom management: Theory, research, and considerations for classroom practice. In C. M. Evertson & C. S. Weinstein (Eds.), *Handbook of classroom management: Research, practice, and contemporary issues* (pp. 223–252). Mahwah, NJ: Erlbaum.

Middleton, M. J., & Midgley, C. (1997). Avoiding the demonstration of lack of ability: An underexplored aspect of goal theory. *Journal of Educational Psychology, 89,* 710–718.

Midgley, C. (Ed.). (2002). *Goals, goal structures, and patterns of adaptive learning.* Mahwah, NJ: Erlbaum.

Midgley, C., Maehr, M. L., Hruda, L. Z., Anderman, E. M., Anderman, L. H., Freeman, K. E., . . . Urdan, T. (2000). *Manual for the patterns of adaptive learning scales.* Ann Arbor: University of Michigan.

Midgley, C., & Urdan, T. (1995). Predictors of middle school students' use of self-handicapping strategies. *Journal of Early Adolescence, 15*(4), 389–411.

Midgley, C., & Urdan, T. (2001). Academic self-handicapping and achievement goals: A further examination. *Contemporary Educational Psychology, 26*(1), 61–75.

Mokrue, K., Chen, Y. Y., & Elias, M. (2012). The interaction between family structure and child gender on behavior problems in urban ethnic minority children. *International Journal of Behavioral Development, 36,* 130–136.

Most, B. (1990). *The cow that went oink.* Orlando, FL: Harcourt.

Newman, R. S., & Schwager, M. T. (1992). Student perceptions and academic help-seeking. In D. H. Schunk & J. L. Meece (Eds.), *Student perceptions in the classroom* (pp. 123–146). Hillsdale, NJ: Erlbaum.

Nolen, S. B. (1988). Reasons for studying: Motivational orientations and study strategies. *Cognition and Instruction, 5,* 269–287.

Pianta, R. C. (1999). *Enhancing relationships between children and teachers.* Washington, DC: American Psychological Association.

Pintrich, P. R. (2000). An achievement goal theory perspective on issues in motivation terminology, theory, and research. *Contemporary Educational Psychology, 25*(1), 92–104.

Pintrich, P. R., & de Groot, E. V. (1990). Motivational and self-regulated learning components of classroom academic performance. *Journal of Educational Psychology, 82*(1), 33–40.

Pintrich, P. R., Marx, R. W., & Boyle, R. A. (1993). Beyond cold conceptual change: The role of motivational beliefs and classroom contextual factors in the process of conceptual change. *Review of Educational Research, 63*(2), 167–199.

Ridgers, N. D., Fazey, D. M. A., & Fairclough, S. J. (2007). Perceptions of athletic competence and fear of negative evaluation during physical education. *British Journal of Educational Psychology, 77*(2), 339–349.

Ryan, A. M., Gheen, M. H., & Midgley, C. (1998). Why do some students avoid asking for help? An examination of the interplay among students' academic efficacy, teachers' social-emotional role, and the classroom goal structure. *Journal of Educational Psychology, 90*(3), 528–535.

Ryan, A. M., Hicks, L. H., & Midgley, C. (1997). Social goals, academic goals, and avoiding seeking help in the classroom. *Journal of Early Adolescence, 17,* 152–171.

Ryan, A. M., & Pintrich, P. R. (1997). Should I ask for help? The role of motivation and attitude in adolescents' help-seeking in math class. *Journal of Educational Psychology, 89,* 329–341.

Seligman, M. E. P. (1975). *Helplessness: On depression, development, and death.* San Francisco, CA: Freeman.

Skinner, E. A., & Belmont, M. J. (1993). Motivation in the classroom: Reciprocal effects of teacher behavior and student engagement across the school year. *Journal of Educational Psychology, 85,* 571–581.

Thompason, T., & Richardson, A. (2001). Self-handicapping status, self-handicaps and reduced practice effort following success and failure feedback. *British Journal of Educational Psychology, 71,* 151–170.

Turner, J. C., Meyer, D. K., Cox, K. E., Logan, C., DiCintio, M., & Thomas, C. T. (1998). Creating contexts for involvement in mathematics. *Journal of Educational Psychology, 90*(4), 730–745.

Turner, J. C., Midgley, C., Meyer, D. K., Gheen, M. H., Anderman, E. M., Kang, Y., & Patrick, H. (2002). The classroom environment and students' reports of avoidance strategies in mathematics: A multimethod study. *Journal of Educational Psychology, 94*(1), 88–106.

Tyler, K., Haines, R. T., & Anderman, E. M. (2006). Identifying the connection between culturally relevant motivation and academic performance among ethnic minority youth. In D. McInerney, M. Dowson, & S. Van Etten (Eds.), *Research on sociocultural influences on motivation and learning: Vol. 6. Effective schools* (pp. 61–103). Greenwich, CT: Information Age Press.

Urdan, T., Midgley, C., & Anderman, E. M. (1998). Classroom influences on self-handicapping strategies. *American Educational Research Journal, 35*, 101–122.

Urdan, T., Ryan, A. M., Anderman, E. M., & Gheen, M. (2002). Goals, goal structures, and avoidance behaviors. In C. Midgley (Ed.), *Goals, goal structures, and patterns of adaptive learning* (pp. 55–83). Mahwah, NJ: Erlbaum.

Wentzel, K. R. (1997). Student motivation in middle school: The role of perceived pedagogical caring. *Journal of Educational Psychology, 89*, 411–419.

Wigfield, A., & Eccles, J. S. (2002). The development of competence beliefs, expectancies for success, and achievement values from childhood through adolescence. In A. Wigfield & J. S. Eccles (Eds.), *Development of achievement motivation: A volume in the educational psychology series* (pp. 91–120). San Diego, CA: Academic Press.

Wolters, C. A., Yu, S. L., & Pintrich, P. R. (1996). The relation between goal orientation and students' motivational beliefs and self-regulated learning. *Learning and Individual Differences, 8,* 211–238.

Woolfolk Hoy, A., & Weinstein, C. S. (2006). Student and teacher perspectives on classroom management. In C. M. Evertson & C. S. Weinstein (Eds.), *Handbook of classroom management: Research, practice, and contemporary issues* (pp. 181–219). Mahwah, NJ: Erlbaum.

Yablon, Y. B. (2010). Student-teacher relationships and students' willingness to seek help for school violence. *Journal of Social and Personal Relationships, 27*, 1110–1123.

Zeidner, M. (1998). *Test anxiety: The state of the art.* New York, NY: Plenum.

Motivational Classrooms for All Learners

Students experience different types of relationships in school. In particular, they have relationships with peers and with teachers. Thus, as researchers have noted for some time, the classroom is a highly social environment (L. H. Anderman, 1999; Juvonen & Weiner, 1993; Juvonen & Wentzel, 1996; Roeser, Urdan, & Stephens, 2009; Ryan & Patrick, 2001; Urdan & Maehr, 1995). These relationships affect students' academic performance, their motivation, and their behaviors both in and out of school. In this chapter, we consider the effects of interpersonal relationships on various outcomes. In addition, we discuss strategies that teachers can use to facilitate the development of positive relationships between and among students and faculty.

THE CLASSROOM SOCIAL ENVIRONMENT

Students' interactions with other individuals affect a number of psychological and educational outcomes (Harter, 1996). The social environment of the classroom is particularly complex. Indeed, the social organization of classrooms can be thought of in many different ways. Students interact with many different individuals during any school day, and all these interactions can affect students' academic motivation. The social environment of the classroom can also be examined in numerous ways.

Social interactions in the classroom encompass the following (Patrick & Ryan, 2005; Ryan & Patrick, 2001):

- Students' perceptions about how they are expected to interact with their teachers
- Students' perceptions about how they are expected to interact with their peers

Teachers' instructional practices and interactions with students have important effects on the classroom social environment.

- Students' perceptions of being accepted and belonging in a specific class and the school as a whole
- The ways in which teachers promote mutual respect toward all members of the classroom community
- The ways in which teachers encourage students to interact during academic tasks
- The ways in which teachers promote a sense of community in the classroom
- The ways in which teachers provide academic and social support for students

In addition, it is particularly important to recall that in middle schools and high schools, students often spend all or part of their day moving between classrooms; thus, students' perceptions of the learning environment of the school as a whole are related strongly to their experiences within individual classrooms each day. Finally, given the increased use of technology in classrooms, it is important to acknowledge that social interactions can occur via the Internet and other forms of electronic communication; thus students' perceptions about how they are supposed to interact with others via technology is a new but important consideration as well.

Classroom climate is the term often used to characterize the overall character of a classroom (Moos & Moos, 1978). The climate of a classroom is affected by a variety of factors, including the relationships among students and teachers, the type of discourse used by students and teachers, the behavioral policies incorporated, the leadership styles of teachers, and even the nonverbal interactions between and among teachers and students (Brophy, 2006; Davis, 2003). Positive and supportive classroom climates are related to enhanced student engagement and academic achievement (Reyes, Brackett, Rivers, White, & Salovey, 2012). In summarizing guidelines for "good teaching," Brophy lists having a "supportive classroom climate" at the top of his list (p. 775).

RELATIONSHIPS WITH TEACHERS

Consider the following examples of students' relationships with their teachers:

> *Paulo is a seventh grader. He generally does not like school. He misbehaves, and he does not get good grades. Paulo finds himself in the assistant principal's office at least once or twice per week, and he often faces in-school suspension. However, Paulo has a great relationship with his science teacher, Mr. Tyler. He visits with Mr. Tyler between classes at least once per day. In addition, he often comes in to talk with Mr. Tyler before school. Mr. Tyler always makes time for Paulo and is glad to talk with and spend time with him.*
>
> *Kathie is a 12th grader. She is an excellent writer and aspires to be a journalist. Kathie has a wonderful relationship with her English teacher, Mrs. Erlbaum. Mrs. Erlbaum recognizes Kathie's talents, encourages her, and talks with her about her career goals. Kathie feels that Mrs. Erlbaum inspires her to do her best work.*
>
> *Joe is a fourth grader. He has a very adversarial relationship with his teacher, Mrs. Albertson. He believes that she does not like him. No matter what he does, he feels that she seems frustrated with him, makes faces at him, and is always angry with him. Joe feels that he can't do anything to please her. He often does not want to go to school because he does not want to spend time with Mrs. Albertson.*

In each of these situations, the relationships that the students have with their teachers clearly affect their behavior and their learning. A positive relationship with a teacher can inspire and motivate a student, whereas a bad relationship with a teacher can truly hinder a student's progress.

Stop and Think

Think about your own educational experiences and about the teachers that you had for your own classes. What were your relationships with your teachers like? Does any teacher stand out as having had an especially good relationship with you? What about one that had a bad relationship with you?

As noted by several researchers, the relationships that students have with their teachers are important for all students, but they may be particularly important for students who are at risk for academic failure and for dropping out of school (Berand, 1992; Pianta, 1999; Wentzel, 1997, 1998). When students have become disengaged and are only minimally interested in their academic work, a positive relationship with a teacher may be the one reason that some students continue to come to school daily.

Developmental Differences

Students' relationships with their teachers take on different meanings at different times in students' academic lives. At some points, teachers are perceived as supportive, caring extensions of the family, whereas, at other times, they are perceived as adversarial "enemies of the state."

The ways teachers communicate with young children affect motivation and learning.

ELEMENTARY-SCHOOL TEACHERS Children's experiences with elementary-school teachers often represent their first experiences with adults outside the home. Thus, children may be extremely nervous about spending much of their day with other adults. Nevertheless, a supportive and caring elementary-school teacher can make a tremendous difference in a child's transition from the home into school.

Students' early experiences in school are very important and can have a tremendously powerful effect on their future school experiences. A study examining a large sample of first graders who had been identified as "at risk" found that children who experienced classrooms that provided both strong emotional and instructional support achieved at higher levels and had better relationships with their teachers than did children in less supportive classrooms (Hamre & Pianta, 2005).

Some research with elementary-age children indicates that the nature of teachers' interactions with their students affects academic motivation. Turner and her colleagues have examined this phenomenon in depth. In one of their studies, Turner and colleagues (1998) examined the nature of discourse between teachers and students in seven elementary classrooms. They examined the relations between *scaffolding* and student motivation. When teachers *scaffold* student learning, they consistently engage their students as co-creators of learning; more specifically, the teacher guides student learning when it is necessary and encourages each student to take ownership of the learning process (Palincsar, 1986; Rogoff, 1990). The work of Turner and her colleagues indicated that students reported greater levels of involvement in mathematics in classrooms where teachers scaffolded mathematics instruction through whole-class discussions. In addition, they found that high levels of student involvement were associated with classrooms in which teachers (a) pressed students to understand the material, (b) treated errors made by students as opportunities for learning, and (c) talked openly about and demonstrated their own interest in mathematics.

ffolding Motivation and Instruction

rner et al., 2002) examined motivational scaffolding in mathematics
veyed to students through the language (discourse) that teachers use
dents on a daily basis. Turner et al. described motivational scaffolding
The following are examples of each:

l Discourse: The teacher helps students to understand material, prompt-
what they have learned.

tional Discourse: The teacher asks students to provide correct answers
t to do, without providing explanations for why the students need to do

nal Discourse: The teacher uses language that focuses on learning and
ting positive emotions and collaboration.
- *Nonscaffolded Instructional Discourse:* The teacher talks about students' errors, promoting negative affect and social comparisons among students.

Adapted from Turner et al. (2002) and Perry, Turner, & Meyer (2006).

MIDDLE-SCHOOL TEACHERS During the middle-school years, students are more likely to experience academic, motivational, and behavioral problems than previously (E. M. Anderman & Mueller, 2010; Carnegie Council on Adolescent Development, 1989). During early adolescence, students receive support from a variety of sources, including teachers, peers, and families (Wentzel, 1998). The nature of teachers' interactions with students, however, changes during this period, and students' relationships with teachers can be both positive and negative during the early adolescent years. In particular, however, research indicates that students perceive teachers as more evaluative and focused on grades and performance during middle school than during elementary school (E. M. Anderman & Midgley, 1997; Harter, 1996; Midgley, Anderman, & Hicks, 1995).

Furthermore, middle-school students' relationships with teachers generally are characterized as less warm than during elementary school. For example, research suggests that middle-school teachers are less trusting of students than are elementary-school teachers and that middle-school teachers believe more in having to control and apply disciplinary techniques to children than do elementary-school teachers (Midgley, Feldlaufer, & Eccles, 1988).

Nevertheless, negative relationships with middle-school teachers are not inescapable. Research conducted by Wentzel and her colleagues indicates that early adolescents' perceived support from teachers is related to adaptive outcomes in middle-school students, such as their interest in class and the pursuit of prosocial classroom goals (i.e., following classroom rules and norms; Weiner, 1985). In summarizing some of the research in this area, Wentzel and Battle (2001) noted that middle-school students describe caring and supportive teachers in much the same way that authoritative parents are described:

> Specifically, they describe caring teachers as those who demonstrate democrat-
> ic and egalitarian communication styles designed to elicit student participation
> and input, who develop expectations for student behavior and performance in
> light of individual differences and abilities, who model a "caring" attitude and

interest in their instruction and interpersonal dealings with students, and who provide constructive rather than harsh and critical feedback. (p. 101)

Thus, when students in the middle grades perceive their teachers as treating all students fairly and as caring and aware of individual differences (rather than as being harsh and excessively critical), students are likely to develop important, respectful, and meaningful relationships with their teachers.

A study of middle-school students by Ryan and Patrick (2001) found that students report higher levels of academic self-efficacy and self-regulation when they perceive their teachers as promoting mutual respect in the classroom. In addition, when students perceive their middle-school teachers as being supportive, the students are less likely to engage in disruptive behaviors and are more likely to exhibit the characteristics of self-regulated learners (Ryan & Patrick, 2001).

Consider the following example of the way that a practicing middle-school teacher builds positive relationships with his students:

Ryan Alexis is a middle-school band teacher. He is well known in his school district for being an outstanding teacher and for his ability to motivate his students. As evidence of the positive influence that he has on students, many of his students voluntarily enroll in extra band opportunities both during the school day and even after school. Mr. Alexis attributes much of the motivation in his band students to the fact that he works hard to develop strong personal relationships with them. Mr. Alexis says that "getting to know them one on one," and "getting to know them as people" are his primary goals. Mr. Alexis uses deliberate and specific strategies to develop these relationships with his students. For example, he often will ask his students on a Monday morning about how they spent their weekends; he circulates the room while students are preparing their instruments at the beginning of class and while they are cleaning up at the end of class, and just chats with them—he asks students about their brothers and sisters, about their parents, and even about what they had for breakfast. He also lets students know about things that he is doing in his own life (e.g., where he is going to go on a vacation), so that they can better relate to him. In addition, he asks his band students to send him postcards when they travel, and he hangs those in the band room. Interestingly, Mr. Alexis noted that during his first year of teaching, he had just focused on teaching the music content; after that first year, once he started to work on developing personal relationships with his middle-school students, he noticed that his students became much more highly motivated. Mr. Alexis truly believes that students will want to try harder in class if teachers take the time to show that we care about them as individuals.

The strategies used by Mr. Alexis can be incorporated into other teachers' daily practices. For example, teachers in other subject areas can engage in informal conversations with students in between classes, before school, or after school. Teachers also can express interest in their students' personal lives by asking students to describe events and personally relevant issues in some of their assignments. For example, a language arts teacher could ask students to focus a writing assignment on a topic of personal interest; a social studies teacher could ask students to evaluate two political candidates and describe which one aligns more closely with the student's life experiences. (Recall the chemistry teacher described in Chapter 10, who began class with time for "News of Interest" every day.)

HIGH-SCHOOL TEACHERS   The high-school years often are experienced as troublesome for some adolescents. Some of these problems result from poor relationships and inter-actions with teachers. High schools often are larger in size than middle schools, and teachers in larger schools often are characterized as being less warm and more control-ling than are teachers in smaller schools, such as middle schools and elementary schools (Eccles et al., 1993).

In addition, high schools often are quite bureaucratic (Dornbusch & Kaufman, 2001). This bureaucratic nature of the high-school environment may make it both more difficult for adolescents to develop personal relationships with teachers and, simultaneously, all the more important for adolescents to have these positive relationships. Indeed, a caring "friend" among the faculty might truly be what a student needs to help her find her way through the bureaucracies of modern high schools. Many adolescents do manage to develop meaningful relationships with teachers during the high-school years. In addition, some research indicates that student athletes, in particular, may benefit from their rela-tionships with their coaches (Reinboth & Ntoumanis, 2004).

Teachers can take particular advantage of the fact that high-school students are con-sidering various options for the future (e.g., going to college; joining the military; getting a job), and use those as starting points for conversations. Many students would be delighted to know that one of their teachers wanted to talk about future plans. You may not feel confident in your ability to advise students on these issues, but just expressing interest can mean a great deal to many adolescents.

The Importance of Relationships with Teachers

Why should we care about the relationships that teachers have with students? These relationships are important for many reasons. First, students spend much time with their teachers; in fact, some may spend more time with their teachers than with their parents, particularly if the parents spend a great deal of time at work. Because much research suggests that all individuals need to have caring, strong, positive relationships to maintain psychological and physiological well-being (e.g., Baumeister & Leary, 1995), it makes sense that students' relationships with their teachers are important. In addition, because students often acquire knowledge through observational learning of their teach-ers as models, students will be more likely to develop efficacy for a particular skill that is being modeled by the teacher if the student has a good relationship with the teacher (Schunk, 1989).

Second, teachers are the primary conduits of information to students. When students and teachers maintain good relationships, less time may be spent on unpleasant interac-tions (e.g., discipline), which should afford more time for students and teachers to interact over learning tasks. Students who have good relationships with their teachers may simply learn more and more effectively than students with less positive relationships. As noted by Wentzel (2009), when students have good relationships with their teachers, students feel better about themselves overall and experience greater emotional well-being, which in turn may facilitate children's engagement with classroom experiences, thus enhancing their learning.

Third, students' relationships with their teachers may help to alleviate psychological stress (Patrick, 1997; Wentzel & Battle, 2001). Although research in this area is nascent, Wentzel and her colleagues suggest that positive relationships between teachers and students

Teachers can develop positive relationships with their students by interacting with them outside formal instruction.

may help build feelings of competence in students; these feelings of competence, in turn, may lead to enhanced learning and psychological health.

Fourth, positive relationships with teachers may prevent some students from dropping out of school. A student who is trying to decide whether or not to quit school might be convinced to stay if that student had a positive, caring relationship with one or several teachers. This may be particularly true for minority students. For example, a recent study of Chicano/Latino school dropouts indicated that many students reported that they dropped out of school because of low expectations from their teachers and perceptions of differential treatment by school authorities (Davison Aviles, Guerrero, Barajas Howarth, & Thomas, 1999).

Fifth, the types of relationships that teachers have with their students may have an impact on long-term outcomes. For example, some evidence indicates that young children who have better relationships with their teachers may be less likely to be retained when they are identified as not being ready to move on to the next grade (Pianta & Steinberg, 1992). In addition, a study by Brengden and her colleagues found that both boys and girls who are verbally abused by teachers during childhood are more likely to exhibit behavior problems, and girls are less likely to have obtained a high-school diploma, when followed-up at the age of 23 (Brengden, Wanner, Vitaro, Bukowski, & Tremblay, 2007).

Finally, management of student behavior often is easier when teachers have good relationships with their students. Imagine trying to gain control of a rowdy room full of seventh graders; now imagine trying to do this if you have very poor, unsupportive relationships with your students. Although management of behavior is complex for even the most experienced teachers, research suggests teachers who are exceptionally effective at managing classroom behavior spend time during the year building relationships with their students (Holt, Hargrove, & Harris, 2011).

What It Means to Be a "Caring" Teacher

Educators often hear much rhetoric about the need to care for their students. Nevertheless, there are different types of "caring." Consider the following examples:

> *Mr. West cares about his students. He asks them how they are feeling every day, and he talks to them about their personal issues and concerns.*
>
> *Ms. Casto cares about her students. She pays attention to their individual abilities and difficulties as learners, and she points out to her students individually how they can improve their skills.*
>
> *Mr. Lockwood cares about his students. He makes a point of telling each student at least once per week that he or she is an important member of the classroom.*

These three types of caring all represent different ways that teachers can demonstrate their concern for students' well-being. Mr. West is the type of teacher who cares about students' personal lives; he provides an environment in which his students can express feelings and can share information with a trusted adult. Ms. Casto expresses a different type of caring in which she nurtures students as individual learners. And Mr. Lockwood expresses care for his students by acknowledging each of them as important members of his classroom community.

Stop and Think

Are some expressions of care and concern more important than others for students' learning and motivation? What are the different effects of these caring attitudes on student outcomes?

RESEARCH ON TEACHER CARING   A growing body of research indicates that when teachers express caring attitudes toward their students, beneficial outcomes accrue (Noddings, 1988, 2005). Certainly, teachers have different ways to express their concerns for their students, but an important point is that any ways that teachers can express genuine care and concern for their students will result in positive benefits for the students.

Several researchers have examined the relations between students' perceptions of having caring teachers and important educational outcomes. Wentzel (1997) found that when middle-school students perceive their teachers as caring, the students are more likely to pursue prosocial goals (e.g., sharing what they have learned with other classmates), to pursue social-responsibility goals (e.g., trying to do what the teacher asks), and to report exerting effort toward their school work.

Wentzel (1996) has also examined the ways that students describe caring teachers. In one study, she asked students to list three characteristics of such teachers. Results indicated that being perceived as a "caring" teacher was associated with democratic interaction styles, high expectations for student achievement, and positive encouragement and feedback (Wentzel, 1996, 1997).

EXPRESSING CARE TO ALL STUDENTS   Whereas it is important to try to express caring to all students, it may also be difficult for teachers to do so. Teachers get to know their students quite well, and their interactions with students are affected by prior knowledge about students' behaviors, abilities as learners, and background characteristics.

We know that, at times, teachers do express preferences for some students in their classrooms over other students. For example, there is evidence that the grades that students receive in classrooms sometimes are related to how much teachers like individual students (e.g., Hadley, 1954). In addition, we also know that teachers are often perceived as treating some students differently than others (Jussim, Robustelli, & Cain, 2009; Kuklinski & Weinstein, 2000). Thus, teachers may be perceived as treating "smart" students differently from students with lower ability levels.

RELATIONSHIPS WITH PEERS

Relationships with peers are extremely important and have crucial influences on development during childhood and adolescence (Berndt, 1992; Berndt & Keefe, 1996; Ladd, Herald-Brown, & Kochel, 2009; Parker & Asher, 1993; Rubin, Bukowski, & Parker, 1998a; Wentzel, Baker, & Russell, 2009). Children's and adolescents' relationships with their peers are related to many educational variables, including successful transitions between elementary- and middle-grades schools (Aikens, Bierman, & Parker, 2005), risk factors later in life (e.g., participation in criminal activity, dropping out of school; (Hartup, 1993; Parker & Asher, 1987), academic motivation (Berndt & Keefe, 1996; Ladd et al., 2009), academic achievement (Epstein, 1983; Wentzel & Caldwell, 1997), and dropping out of school (Hymel, Comfort, Schonert-Reichl, & McDougall, 1996). In addition, students often value social aspects of their lives more than they value academic issues, particularly during the adolescent years (Wentzel, 1996); consequently, relationships with peers are particularly important sources of behavioral influence during this period.

Types of Peer Groups

It is important to distinguish among various combinations of peer groups. A variety of different terms are used in the literature because studies of peer influences emanate from diverse fields, including educational psychology, developmental psychology, social psychology, and even sociology and anthropology. Consider the following example:

> *Marla is 15 years old. She has three very close friends, with whom she spends most of her time; these four close friends share many interests, beliefs, and preferences. This group of friends spends much of their free time together, particularly on the weekends and during school vacations. Marla and her friends consider themselves to be among the most popular girls in the school. However, while in school, this small group of friends also tends to interact with a larger group of popular students.*

This description should seem quite familiar. Whereas many students have a small group of very close and reciprocal friendships, they also usually belong to a larger community of peers who share similar interests and/or social reputations. This represents the important distinction between cliques and crowds. A *clique* is a small, intimate group of friends, whereas a *crowd* is a larger group of individuals who usually share some common interests or characteristics (Brown, 1990; Rubin, Bukowski, & Parker, 1998b; Ryan, 2000). Thus, Marla's small group of four close friends is a *clique,* whereas

Adolescents tend to socialize with peers who have similar academic abilities.

the larger group of students with whom they interact at school is a *crowd.* Most children and adolescents also report having one or two *best friends,* in addition to being members of cliques and crowds (Hartup, 1993). It is important to note that not all students belong to cliques (Ennett & Bauman, 1996). Whereas some students become members of such friendship groups, other students are socially isolated or move from one group to another.

Crowds are larger groups that often are representative of social structures in the school. Typical groups have names such as jocks, nerds, druggies, cheerleaders, and popular kids. Crowds are particularly common in middle schools and high schools, and membership is generally based on a student's reputation among peers. It is possible (although rather uncommon) for a student to belong to more than one crowd at the same time; for example, a student could be considered to be both a jock and a druggie (Brown, 2004).

Effects of Peer Relationships on Academic Outcomes

Students' relationships with their peers affect both motivation and achievement. Whereas there are some similarities in these patterns, there are also important distinctions.

EFFECTS OF PEER RELATIONSHIPS ON ACADEMIC ACHIEVEMENT The friends with whom children and adolescents associate influence how, what, and why students learn in school.

Stop and Think

Think about your closest friends from your own childhood and adolescence. Did they get grades similar to yours? Did they influence your study habits?

In general, students who have friends who do well in school also tend to do well in school, whereas students who socialize with lower achieving peers also tend to perform poorly in school (Epstein, 1983). This has many explanations. One is related to ability grouping (see Chapter 5). When students are grouped by ability for instruction, they will obviously spend more time in school with the other students in those same classes. Thus, students in high-ability classes are likely to become friendly with other high-ability students, whereas students in low-ability classes are likely to develop friendships with other low-ability peers. Because students often do not move easily between ability tracks or groups, these peer groups may remain stable for long periods of time, thus enhancing the development of friendships with similar peers.

EFFECTS OF PEER RELATIONSHIPS ON MOTIVATION   The company that children and adolescents keep is also related to their achievement motivation. Indeed, students often tend to spend time with peers who share similar attitudes and dispositions toward academic work. For example, some research indicates that children's and adolescents' friends in the classroom display similar levels of academic engagement with classroom tasks (Kindermann, 1993; Kindermann, McCollam, & Gibson, 1996). In addition, students who perceive that their peers are supportive of academics are more likely to value academics themselves (Vitoroulis, Schneider, Vasquez, Soteras de Toro, & Gonzales, 2012). Kindermann examined naturally occurring peer groups in elementary-school classrooms and studied these groups during one academic year. Results indicated that, at the beginning of the school year, children spent time with students who held similar motivational beliefs. Although the peers reorganized somewhat during the year, the motivational characteristics of the groups were preserved.

Much of the research on the relations between peer relationships and academic motivation originated in goal orientation theory. Several researchers have demonstrated that students develop goals that are specifically related to their friendships at school (L. H. Anderman, 1999; L. H. Anderman & E. M. Anderman, 1999; Patrick, Hicks, & Ryan, 1997; Ryan, Hicks, & Midgley, 1997; Ryan, Kiefer, & Hopkins, 2004; Wentzel, 1996). More specifically, these researchers have conceptualized three types of social goals that students are motivated to pursue:

> *Relationship goal:* The goal is to have close, personal, reciprocal relationships with one or several friends.
>
> *Status goal:* The goal is to be a member of a popular peer group.
>
> *Responsibility goal:* The goal is to follow the classroom rules and be a "good citizen."

The types of social goals that students have in school are related to their academic motivation. For example, research indicates that during early adolescence, the pursuit of responsibility goals is related to being mastery oriented toward academic tasks, whereas the pursuit of relationship goals and status goals is related to being performance oriented (L. H. Anderman & E. M. Anderman, 1999). Students who are focused on peer relationships and popularity may be more likely to compare themselves with their peers in generating their own self-perceptions of competence and ability. In contrast, students who endorse responsibility goals may focus more on task mastery because they are interested in pleasing the teacher; if the teacher's goal is for students to master a particular academic task, then pursuit of the teacher's goal may lead to the simultaneous pursuit of the student's goal.*

---

*Other researchers (e.g., Dowson & McInerney, 2001) have described other types of social goals.

SCHOOL BELONGING

Beyond direct interpersonal relationships with teachers and peers, students also differ in the degree of affiliation and acceptance they experience in relation to their schools in general (L. H. Anderman & Freeman, 2004; Goodenow, 1993). Consider the following two hypothetical students:

> *Josh is a sixth grader; he enjoys coming to school every day. He feels like school is a "home away from home." He is particularly fond of his school because he has good friends and because he feels that his teachers and fellow students care about him. For example, when he was absent one day last week, several of his friends and teachers asked him what was wrong and if he was feeling better when he returned the next day.*
>
> *Carey is a ninth grader. She does not enjoy coming to school. She feels like she is just a "number" rather than a "name" in her school. She feels as if nobody would notice if she didn't attend school for several weeks. She does not feel as if teachers or many other students really care about her as an individual.*

Josh feels a strong sense of belonging in his school, whereas Carey does not. These student perceptions are very important because feeling a sense of identification or belonging within one's own school is related to a host of important educational and psychological outcomes (L. H. Anderman & Freeman, 2004; Finn, 1989; Juvonen, 2006; Osterman, 2000), including motivation (Goodenow & Grady, 1993), achievement (E. M. Anderman, 2002; L. H. Anderman, 2003; Kuperminc, Darnell, & Alvarez-Jimenez, 2008), less engagement in risky behaviors (Resnick et al., 1997), lower levels of misconduct at school (Demanet & Van Houtte, 2012), and positive affect (L. H. Anderman, 1999).

Carol Goodenow was one of the first researchers to examine the concept of *school belonging*. She developed measures to examine and measure students' subjective sense of belonging in school and in their classes. It is worth examining such measures because they provide a more thorough understanding of the makeup of psychological constructs. Goodenow's measure consists of items such as the following:

> *"I feel like a real part of this school."*
>
> *"People here notice when I'm good at something."*
>
> *"Most teachers at this school are interested in me."*
>
> *"Other students in this school take my opinion seriously."* (Goodenow & Grady, 1993)

Studies examining the reasons why students drop out of school often indicate that not feeling a sense of belonging is a reason for dropping out of school (Berktold, Geis, & Kaufman, 1998; Hymel et al., 1996).

Although belonging is related to academic outcomes (Finn, 1989), some research also suggests that perceptions of school belonging are related to other psychological outcomes. For example, some research suggests that students who reported high levels of school belonging were less likely to report feelings of depression, social rejection, and behavioral problems (E. M. Anderman, 2002).

Common planning time for teachers helps "small learning communities" to be effective.

School Belonging and Motivation

Is academic motivation related to perceptions of school belonging? It is plausible that when many students in a school are academically motivated, those who feel a sense of belonging in that school will be more likely to adopt similar motivational beliefs. Some recent research has specifically examined the relations between perceptions of school belonging and academic motivation.

Research generally indicates that students who perceive a sense of belonging display adaptive patterns of motivation. These studies have been conducted from a variety of theoretical perspectives. For example, Goodenow and her colleagues examined the relations of school belonging with students' expectancies and values. Results of one study indicated that middle-school students' sense of belonging was related positively to both expectancies for success and to achievement values (Goodenow, 1993). These relations have been demonstrated across a variety of ethnic groups, including African American and Hispanic American students (Goodenow & Grady, 1993). Other studies (L. H. Anderman, 2003) also indicate the existence of positive relations between students' expectancies for success and perceptions of school belonging.

Other researchers have examined school belonging using a goal orientation theory perspective. L. H. Anderman and E. M. Anderman (1999) examined relations between perceptions of school belonging and changes in mastery and performance goals. Even after controlling for a host of other variables, students' sense of belonging was related to increases in mastery goals and decreases in performance goals over time. L. H. Anderman (2003) found that school belonging was related strongly and positively to perceptions of a classroom mastery goal orientation over time. Similarly, Walker (2012) found that perceptions of both classroom mastery and performance goal structures were related to perceptions of school belonging in a sample of high school students.

Small Learning Communities

One movement that has become popular in recent years is the creation of *small learning communities* within larger schools, which have been conceptualized and operationalized in a number of different ways. When teachers in a large school create a small learning community, they create an environment in which students can feel a sense of belonging.

Many strategies can be used to create small learning communities. Some examples include the following:

- Creating smaller "schools within schools," wherein smaller cohorts of students travel together throughout all or part of the day and share teachers
- Creating common preparation times for teachers, so that the instructional needs of individual students can be discussed across a group of teachers
- Separating some students (e.g., ninth graders) into a separate wing of the school; this may be particularly helpful for students making a transition into a new school
- Establishing an advisor/advisee system, in which all students are assigned an advisor who regularly meets with the student to make sure that his or her needs are being met

The use of small learning communities within larger schools may be particularly helpful for students with special needs (Dukes & Lamar-Dukes, 2006). For example, a student with a learning disability in the area of reading may be more effectively educated if the student's teachers across a variety of subjects (e.g., English, mathematics, science, and social studies) can work together with a special educator to provide the most inclusive and effective academic tasks for that particular student. Small learning communities may also be particularly effective for ethnic minority students (Conchas & Noguera, 2004).

Nevertheless, merely restructuring a school does not guarantee success. Indeed, some efforts to develop small learning communities within larger schools have resulted in improvements in the working and teaching environments for instructional staff but few long-term effects on actual student learning (Supovitz, 2002). It is important for a school that is developing small learning communities to have all instructional and support staff working collaboratively to make this innovation as effective as possible (Oxley, 2001).

EFFECTIVE SMALL LEARNING COMMUNITIES   Schools can follow available guidelines when attempting to create small learning communities. Whereas each school ultimately must consider its own needs and goals, some common characteristics are associated with effective small learning communities. A report issued by the Northwest Regional Educational Laboratory (Cotton, 2001) suggests that the elements that are related to successful small learning communities include the following:

- *Autonomy:* Effective small learning communities make their own decisions and bring about change from within, rather than having external consultants come in and "tell" the school what to do.
- *Separateness:* In effective small learning communities, students often are physically and psychologically separated into different corridors or wings within the school. Thus, a physical separateness helps the small learning community to establish its own identity within the larger school.
- *Distinctiveness:* The small learning community must stand out from the rest of the school in a specific way. This could be its location, its goals, or a theme that guides the work of the small learning community.

- *Motivation:* The participants in successful small learning communities want to be part of such communities. Successful small learning communities include teachers and students who want to be part of such an organization, rather than having been forced or coerced to participate.
- *Identity:* Successful small learning communities have easily identifiable themes, visions, and goals for the community.
- *Focus on student learning:* Successful small learning communities keep enhanced student learning outcomes as the primary goal and focus. Whereas numerous benefits are derived from small learning communities, successful reforms maintain learning as the primary goal of all students and personnel involved.
- *Personalization:* Effective small learning communities allow teachers and students to truly get to know each other on a personal level. This is one of the ways in which a sense of belonging is integral to successful small learning communities.
- *Elimination of ability grouping/tracking:* If school personnel wish to create an environment in which all students feel accepted, it may be helpful to eliminate ability grouping. As soon as ability tracks are present, a focus on differential ability is inevitable because some students are "better" learners than others. As noted previously, it is difficult to eliminate ability grouping; nevertheless, educators must realize that the message mixed ability grouping sends to students and parents is that some students inevitably learn better than others do.
- *Teacher continuity:* In many successful small learning communities, students stay with the same teachers for multiple academic years. This may be difficult for teachers, as they must prepare instructional materials for new classes as students move into higher grades; nevertheless, this continuity is an important component of successful small learning communities.
- *Parent and community involvement:* Successful small learning communities include parent and community members in the communities' activities. This may include involvement in decision making, as well as with actual instructional activities.
- *Support for teaching:* In successful small learning communities, teachers are supported by their colleagues. For example, teachers who are members of the same teaching team work together collaboratively to create positive learning environments. In addition, schools must provide appropriate professional development so that these teachers can be successful in working with smaller populations of students. It may be particularly helpful for teachers to be able to network and communicate with colleagues at other schools where small learning communities are also being implemented.
- *Multiple forms of assessment:* School administrators who run successful small learning communities think about assessment quite creatively. Assessment needs to occur at both the student level and the unit level (i.e., evaluating the overall effectiveness of the small learning community). Although most schools will continue to use standardized assessments, the type of learning that occurs in small learning communities may be truly different from learning that occurs in more traditional settings. Therefore, a variety of assessments should be used. For example, if students participate in more collaborative learning, then assessments that reflect the artifacts that students produce as groups should be considered. In addition, the effectiveness of the small learning community should be assessed via school personnel; these assessments should reflect the goals of each individual small learning community.

RECOMMENDATIONS FOR PROMOTING POSITIVE LEARNING ENVIRONMENTS

The creation of positive learning environments that enhance student motivation is important and complex. Students need to feel motivated, cared for, valued, and respected; any one of these individually is an important and yet difficult-to-achieve outcome. Having all these elements together simultaneously is quite challenging.

TARGET

A well-known acronym in the motivation literature is *TARGET*. This term was originated by Joyce Epstein and subsequently has been adapted and used by a number of researchers, most notably Ames (1990) and Maehr and Midgley (e.g., Maehr & Midgley, 1996). The TARGET acronym represents six dimensions of instructional practice, each of which teachers must consider to develop a truly motivational environment in their classrooms.

Specifically, educators should consider these six dimensions daily to design motivationally engaging academic lessons: (1) the nature of academic *tasks*, (2) the amount of *autonomy* (choice and control) that students have during the lesson, (3) the ways in which students are *recognized* for their achievements, (4) the ways that students are *grouped* for instruction, (5) how student work is *evaluated,* and (6) the way *time* is used. Table 11-1 provides specific examples of ways that teachers can think about and implement each of these six dimensions.

TABLE 11-1   TARGET Dimensions

TARGET Dimension	Explanation	Example
Task	Teachers should consider the motivational consequences of academic tasks.	A teacher chooses to teach principles of physics using skateboards because students in the class love skateboarding.
Autonomy	Teachers should provide students with opportunities to feel a sense of control or choice.	An English teacher allows his students to write essays about any short story that the class read during the past month, rather than about one preselected story.
Recognition	Students should be recognized for effort and improvement, as well as for their achievements.	A teacher writes an encouraging note to a student who recently has been displaying a great deal of effort.
Grouping	Grouping should be flexible and based on students' interests, not merely on ability.	A teacher creates reading groups based on students' interests and reorganizes these groups monthly.
Evaluation	Varied forms of evaluation should be used, so that all students can demonstrate their learning.	A social studies teacher uses a variety of different forms of assessment: sit-down exams, take-home exams, projects, essays, and oral presentations.
Time	Time should be used creatively, effectively, and efficiently.	A teacher who has a double (blocked) instructional period only twice per week plans special lessons that will take more time for those 2 days.

The TARGET acronym is supported by much research (Ames, 1990; E. M. Anderman & Maehr, 1994; E. M. Anderman, Maehr, & Midgley, 1999; Maehr & Midgley, 1996; Patrick, Anderman, Ryan, Edelin, & Midgley, 2001). Classroom teachers can use this acronym when planning instruction. In particular, this acronym can be used as a checklist. It would only take most teachers a few minutes daily to think about the day's lessons and examine which of the dimensions of TARGET are addressed. As demonstrated by Ames, when teachers consider these six dimensions and incorporate them into instruction, student motivation can be greatly enhanced.

Summary

General Recommendations for Promoting Positive Motivational Environments

We recommend that teachers interested in creating positive learning environments consider their goals and the support that they have from their colleagues. It can be quite frustrating when one teacher's efforts to create positive environments are undermined by another teacher's contradictory practices (Maehr & Midgley, 1996).

If the faculty in a given school decides to focus on changing the school environment, we recommend that all teachers commit to this endeavor. In addition, each teacher should be encouraged to think about each of the following issues every day; specifically, all teachers should reflect on a daily basis how they are accomplishing each of the following during class time:

- *Caring.* Teachers must consider specifically how they are communicating to their classes that they care about each student as an individual learner. It may not be possible to communicate directly with each student on an individual basis each day, but a teacher should be able to note by the end of the week how he or she has specifically communicated a message of individual caring to each student.
- *Promoting a sense of belonging.* Research indicates that belonging is enhanced when students perceive that their teachers promote a sense of mutual respect and emphasize openness to multiple opinions and points of view (L. H. Anderman, 2003; L. H. Anderman & Freeman, 2004). Teachers and students would benefit if teachers remind themselves regularly about what they plan to do in class to promote this sense of belonging. For example, a teacher might decide to remind students on a daily basis that everyone in the class has a valuable opinion and that students in the class must respect each others' comments and thoughts about the lesson.
- *Optimal motivation for individual students.* Teachers must consider individual students' motivational profiles. As the year progresses, teachers will realize that different types of motivational frameworks are effective with different students (Perry, Turner, & Meyer, 2006). For example, some students may respond better to extrinsic incentives, whereas others may respond well to engagement with intrinsically interesting activities. A teacher may not be able to structure a class to always meet each student's motivational profile but should be able to adapt instruction so that all students' needs are met over the course of a semester. Teachers can have conversations with their students about motivation to ascertain the best way to motivate a particular student (McCaslin & Good, 1996).

Teachers' relationships with their students are very important.

- *Peer climate.* Teachers should also consider the type of environment that peers in the classroom are promoting. Whereas teachers can't control all aspects of peer interaction in school, they can demand a certain level of dignity and mutual respect within their own classrooms. When students see that teachers across their classes consistently foster respectful environments, they are likely to feel a greater sense of belonging to the school as a whole and, consequently, be more comfortable asking questions and taking on challenging tasks. In contrast, if students perceive that teachers allow teasing or bullying to occur (Smith & Brain, 2000), classroom and school environments will more likely be perceived as being unsupportive.

LEARNING ACTIVITY 11.1   Using TARGET

For this activity, develop a lesson (you pick the grade level and subject area). Briefly describe as many aspects of the lesson as you can. Then, using the TARGET acronym, identify one action you can take in each of the six dimensions of TARGET to foster positive motivational outcomes for your students.

LEARNING ACTIVITY 11.2   School Belonging

The principal in your school has asked a small group of teachers to develop five strategies that the school can implement next year to enhance a sense of belonging among the students. Working in a small group, identify and explain the five strategies that you would suggest, Keep in mind that schools often do not have large budgets for projects of this nature, so think about initiatives that can be implemented at little to no additional cost to the school.

References

Aikens, J. W., Bierman, K. L., & Parker, J. G. (2005). Navigating the transition to junior high school: The influence of pre-transition friendship and self-system characteristics. *Social Development, 14*(1), 42–60.

Ames, C. (1990, April). *The relationship of achievement goals to student motivation in classroom settings.* Paper presented at the American Educational Research Association, Boston, MA.

Anderman, E. M. (2002). School effects on psychological outcomes during adolescence. *Journal of Educational Psychology, 94*, 795–809.

Anderman, E. M., & Maehr, M. L. (1994). Motivation and schooling in the middle grades. *Review of Educational Research, 64*(2), 287–309.

Anderman, E. M., Maehr, M. L., & Midgley, C. (1999). Declining motivation after the transition to middle school: Schools can make a difference. *Journal of Research and Development in Education, 32*, 131–147.

Anderman, E. M., & Midgley, C. (1997). Changes in achievement goal orientations, perceived academic competence, and grades across the transition to middle-level schools. *Contemporary Educational Psychology, 22*(3), 269–298.

Anderman, E. M., & Mueller, C. (2010). Middle school transitions and adolescent development. In J. Meece & J. S. Eccles (Eds.), *Handbook of research on schools, schooling, and human development* (pp. 198–215). New York, NY: Routledge.

Anderman, L. H. (1999). Classroom goal orientation, school belonging and social goals as predictors of students' positive and negative affect following the transition to middle school. *Journal of Research and Development in Education, 32*(2), 89–103.

Anderman, L. H. (2003). Academic and social perceptions as predictors of change in middle school students' sense of school belonging. *Journal of Experimental Education, 72*, 5–22.

Anderman, L. H., & Anderman, E. M. (1999). Social predictors of changes in students' achievement goal orientations. *Contemporary Educational Psychology, 25*, 21–37.

Anderman, L. H., & Freeman, T. M. (2004). Students' sense of belonging in school. In P. R. Pintrich &

M. L. Maehr (Eds.), *Advances in motivation and achievement: Vol. 13. Motivating students, improving schools: The legacy of Carol Midgley* (pp. 27–63). Amsterdam, The Netherlands: JAI Press.

Baumeister, R. F., & Leary, M. R. (1995). The need to belong: Desire for interpersonal attachments as a fundamental human motivation. *Psychological Bulletin, 117*, 497–529.

Berand, B. (1992). Westing resiliency in kids: Protective factors in the family, school, and community. *Prevention Forum, 12*, 3.

Berktold, J., Geis, S., & Kaufman, P. (1998). *Subsequent educational attainment of high school dropouts* (No. NCES 98085). Washington DC: National Center for Education Statistics.

Berndt, T. J. (1992). Friends' influence on students' adjustment to school. *Educational Psychologist, 34*, 15–29.

Berndt, T. J., & Keefe, K. (1996). Friends' influence on school adjustment: A motivational analysis. In J. Juvonen & K. R. Wentzel (Eds.), *Social motivation: Understanding children's school adjustment* (pp. 248–278). New York, NY: Cambridge University Press.

Brengden, M., Wanner, B., Vitaro, F., Bukowski, W., & Tremblay, R. E. (2007). Verbal abuse by the teacher during childhood and academic, behavioral, and emotional adjustment in young adulthood. *Journal of Educational Psychology, 99*, 26–38.

Brophy, J. (2006). Observational research on generic aspects of classroom teaching. In P. A. Alexander & P. H. Winne (Eds.), *Handbook of educational psychology* (2nd ed., pp. 755–780). Mahwah, NJ: Erlbaum.

Brown, B. B. (1990). Peer groups and peer culture. In S. S. Feldman & G. R. Elliott (Eds.), *At the threshold: The developing adolescent* (pp. 171–196). Cambridge, MA: Harvard University Press.

Brown, B. B. (2004). Adolescents' relationships with peers. In R. Lerner & L. Steinberg (Eds.), *Handbook of adolescent psychology* (pp. 363–394). New York, NY: Wiley.

Carnegie Council on Adolescent Development. (1989). *Turning points: Preparing American youth for the 21st century.* New York, NY: Carnegie Corporation.

Conchas, G. Q., & Noguera, P. A. (2004). Understanding the exceptions: How small schools support the achievement of academically successful black boys. In N. Way & J. Y. Chu (Eds.), *Adolescent boys: Exploring diverse cultures of boyhood* (pp. 317–337). New York, NY: New York University Press.

Cotton, K. (2001). *New small learning communities: Findings from recent literature*. Portland, OR: Northwest Regional Educational Laboratory.

Davis, H. A. (2003). Conceptualizing the role and influence of student–teacher relationships on children's social and cognitive development. *Educational Psychologist, 38*, 207–234.

Davison Aviles, R. M., Guerrero, M. P., Barajas Howarth, H., & Thomas, G. (1999). Perceptions of Chicano/Latino students who have dropped out of school. *Journal of Counseling and Development, 77*(4), 465–473.

Demanet, J., & Van Houtte, M. (2012). School belonging and school misconduct: The differing role of teacher and peer attachment. *Journal of Youth and Adolescence, 41*, 499–514.

Dornbusch, S. M., & Kaufman, J. G. (2001). The social structure of the American high school. In T. Urdan & F. Pajares (Eds.), *Adolescence and education: General issues in the education of adolescents* (pp. 61–93). Greenwich, CT: Information Age Publishing.

Dowson, M. & McInerney, D. M. (2001). Psychological parameters of students' social and work-avoidance goals: A qualitative investigation. *Journal of Educational Psychology, 93*, 35–42.

Dukes, C., & Lamar-Dukes, P. (2006). Special education: An integral part of small schools in high schools. *High School Journal, 89*(3), 1–9.

Eccles, J. S., Midgley, C., Wigfield, A., Miller-Buchanan, C. M., Reuman, D., Flanagan, C., & Mac Iver, D. (1993). Development during adolescence: The impact of stage-environment fit on young adolescents' experiences in schools and in families. *American Psychologist, 48*(2), 90–101.

Ennett, S., & Bauman, K. (1996). Adolescent social networks: School, demographic, and longitudinal considerations. *Journal of Adolescent Research, 11*, 194–215.

Epstein, J. L. (1983). The influence of friends on achievement and affective outcomes. In J. L. Epstein & N. Karweit (Eds.), *Friends in school: Patterns of selection and influence in secondary schools* (pp. 177–200). New York, NY: Academic Press.

Finn, J. D. (1989). Withdrawing from school. *Review of Educational Research, 59*, 117–142.

Goodenow, C. (1993). Classroom belonging among early adolescent students: Relationships to motivation and achievement. *Journal of Early Adolescence, 13*(1), 21–43.

Goodenow, C., & Grady, K. E. (1993). The relationship of school belonging and friends' values to academic motivation among urban adolescent students. *Journal of Experimental Education, 62*(1), 60–71.

Hadley, S. (1954). A school mark: Fact or fancy? *Educational Administration and Supervision, 40*, 305–312.

Hamre, B. K., & Pianta, R. C. (2005). Can instructional and emotional support in the first-grade classroom make a difference for children at risk of school failure? *Child Development, 76*(5), 949–967.

Harter, S. (1996). Teacher and classmate influences on scholastic motivation, self-esteem, and level of voice in adolescents. In J. Juvonen & K. R. Wentzel (Eds.), *Social motivation: Understanding children's school adjustment* (pp. 11–42). Cambridge, England: Cambridge University Press.

Hartup, W. W. (1993). Adolescents and their friends. *New Directions for Child Development, 60*, 3–22.

Holt, C., Hargrove, P., & Harris, S. (2011). An investigation into the life experiences and beliefs of teachers exhibiting highly effective classroom management skills. *Teacher Education and Practice, 24*, 96–113.

Hymel, S., Comfort, C., Schonert-Reichl, K., & McDougall, P. (1996). Academic failure and school dropout: The influence of peers. In J. Juvonen & K. R. Wentzel (Eds.), *Social motivation: Understanding children's school adjustment* (pp. 313–345). Cambridge, England: Cambridge University Press.

Jussim, L., Robustelli, S. L., & Cain, T. R. (2009). Teacher expectations and self-fulfilling prophecies. In K. R. Wentzel & A. Wigfield (Eds.), *Handbook of motivation at school* (pp. 349–380). New York, NY: Routledge.

Juvonen, J. (2006). Sense of belonging, social bonds, and school functioning. In P. A. Alexander & P. H. Winne (Eds.), *Handbook of educational psychology* (2nd ed., pp. 655–674). Mahwah, NJ: Erlbaum.

Juvonen, J., & Weiner, B. (1993). An attributional analysis of students' interactions: The social consequences of perceived responsibility. *Educational Psychology Review, 5*, 325–345.

Juvonen, J., & Wentzel, K. R. (1996). *Social motivation: Understanding children's school adjustment.* Cambridge, England: Cambridge University Press.

Kindermann, T. A. (1993). Natural peer groups as contexts for individual development: The case of children's motivation in school. *Developmental Psychology, 29*, 970–977.

Kindermann, T. A., McCollam, T. L., & Gibson, E. (1996). Peer network and students' classroom engagement during childhood and adolescence. In J. Juvonen & K. R. Wentzel (Eds.), *Social motivation: Understanding children's school adjustment.* Cambridge, England: Cambridge University Press.

Kuklinski, M. R., & Weinstein, R. S. (2000). Classroom and grade level differences in the stability of teacher expectations and perceived differential teacher treatment. *Learning Environments Research, 3*(1), 1–34.

Kuperminc, G. P., Darnell, A. J., & Alvarez-Jimenez, A. (2008). Parent involvement in the academic adjustment of Latino middle and high school youth: Teacher expectations and school belonging as mediators. *Journal of Adolescence, 31*, 469–483.

Ladd, G. W., Herald-Brown, S. L., & Kochel, K. P. (2009). Peers and motivation. In K. R. Wentzel & A. Wigfield (Eds.), *Handbook of motivation at school* (pp. 323–348). New York, NY: Routledge.

Maehr, M. L., & Midgley, C. (1996). *Transforming school cultures.* Boulder, CO: Westview Press.

McCaslin, M., & Good, T. (1996). *Listening in classrooms.* New York, NY: Harper Collins.

Midgley, C., Anderman, E. M., & Hicks, L. H. (1995). Differences between elementary and middle school teachers and students: A goal theory approach. *Journal of Early Adolescence, 15*(1), 90–113.

Midgley, C., Feldlaufer, H., & Eccles, J. S. (1988). The transition to junior high school: Beliefs of pre- and posttransition teachers. *Journal of Youth and Adolescence, 17*(6), 543–562.

Moos, R. H., & Moos, B. S. (1978). Classroom social climate and student absences and grades. *Journal of Educational Psychology, 70*, 263–269.

Noddings, N. (1988). An ethic of caring and its implications for instructional arrangements. *American Journal of Education, 96*, 215–230.

Noddings, N. (2005). *The challenge to care in schools: Alternative approaches to education* (2nd ed.). New York, NY: Teachers College Press.

Osterman, K. F. (2000). Students' need for belonging in the school community. *Review of Educational Research, 70*(3), 323–367.

Oxley, D. (2001). Organizing schools into small learning communities. *NASSP Bulletin, 85*(625), 5–16.

Palincsar, A. S. (1986). The role of dialogue in providing scaffolded instruction. *Educational Psychologist, 21*, 73–98.

Parker, J. G., & Asher, S. R. (1987). Peer relations and later personal adjustment: Are low-accepted children at risk? *Psychological Bulletin, 102*(3), 357–389.

Parker, J. G., & Asher, S. R. (1993). Friendship and friendship quality in middle childhood: Links with peer group acceptance and feelings of loneliness and social dissatisfaction. *Developmental Psychology, 29*(4), 611–621.

Patrick, H. (1997). Social self-regulation: Exploring the relations between children's social relationships, academic self-regulation, and school performance. *Educational Psychologist, 32*, 209–220.

Patrick, H., Anderman, L. H., Ryan, A. M., Edelin, K., & Midgley, C. (2001). Teachers' communication of goal orientations in four fifth-grade classrooms. *Elementary School Journal, 102*, 35–58.

Patrick, H., Hicks, L., & Ryan, A. M. (1997). Relations of perceived social efficacy and social goal pursuit to self-efficacy for academic work. *Journal of Early Adolescence, 17*, 109–128.

Patrick, H., & Ryan, A. (2005). Identifying adaptive classrooms: Dimensions of the classroom social environment. In K. A. Moore & L. H. Lippman (Eds.), *What do children need to flourish? Conceptualizing and measuring indicators of positive development* (pp. 271–287). New York, NY: Springer.

Perry, N. E., Turner, J. C., & Meyer, D. K. (2006). Classrooms as context for motivating learning. In P. A. Alexander & P. H. Winne (Eds.), *Handbook of educational psychology* (2nd ed., pp. 327–348). Mahwah, NJ: Erlbaum.

Pianta, R. C. (1999). *Enhancing relationships between children and teachers.* Washington, DC: American Psychological Association.

Pianta, R. C., & Steinberg, M. (1992). Teacher-child relationships and the process of adjusting to school. *New Directions for Child Development, 57,* 61–80.

Reinboth, M., & Ntoumanis, N. (2004). Dimensions of coaching behavior, need satisfaction, and the psychological and physical welfare of young athletes. *Motivation and Emotion, 28(3),* 297–313.

Resnick, M. D., Bearman, P. S., Blum, R. W., Bauman, K. E., Harris, K. M., Jones, J., . . . Udry, J. R. (1997). Protecting adolescents from harm: Findings from the National Longitudinal Study on Adolescent Health. *Journal of the American Medical Association, 278,* 823–832.

Reyes, M. R., Brackett, M. A., Rivers, S. E., White, M., & Salovey, P. (2012). Classroom emotional climate, student engagement, and academic achievement. *Journal of Educational Psychology, 104,* 700–712.

Roeser, R. W., Urdan, T. C., & Stephens, J. M. (2009). School as a context of student motivation and achievement. In K. R. Wentzel & A. Wigfield (Eds.), *Handbook of motivation at school* (pp. 381–410). New York, NY: Routledge.

Rogoff, B. (1990). *Apprenticeship in thinking: Cognitive development in social context.* New York, NY: Oxford University Press.

Rubin, K. H., Bukowski, W., & Parker, J. G. (1998a). Peer interactions, relationships, and groups. In W. Damon & N. Eisenberg (Eds.), *Handbook of child psychology: Vol. 3. Social, emotional, and personality development* (5th ed., pp. 619–700). Hoboken, NJ: Wiley.

Rubin, K. H., Bukowski, W., & Parker, J. G. (1998b). Peer interactions, relationships, and groups. In W. Damon (Ed.), *Handbook of child psychology: Vol. 3. Social, emotional, and personality development* (pp. 619–700). New York, NY: Wiley.

Ryan, A. (2000). Peer groups as a context for the socialization of adolescents' motivation, engagement, and achievement in school. *Educational Psychologist, 35,* 101–111.

Ryan, A. M., Hicks, L. H., & Midgley, C. (1997). Social goals, academic goals, and avoiding seeking help in the classroom. *Journal of Early Adolescence, 17(2),* 152–171.

Ryan, A. M., Kiefer, S. M., & Hopkins, N. B. (2004). Young adolescents' social motivation: An achievement goal perspective. In P. R. Pintrich & M. L. Maehr (Eds.), *Motivating students,*

improving schools: The legacy of Carol Midgley (pp. 301–330). Amsterdam, The Netherlands: Elsevier/JAI.

Ryan, A. M., & Patrick, H. (2001). The classroom social environment and changes in adolescents' motivation and engagement during middle school. *American Educational Research Journal, 38(2),* 437–460.

Schunk, D. H. (1989). Self-efficacy and achievement behaviors. *Educational Psychology Review, 1,* 173–208.

Smith, P. K., & Brain, P. (2000). Bullying in schools: Lessons from two decades of research. *Aggressive Behavior, 26,* 1–9.

Supovitz, J. A. (2002). Developing communities of instructional practice. *Teachers College Record, 104(8),* 1591–1626.

Turner, J. C., Meyer, D. K., Cox, K. E., Logan, C., DiCintio, M., & Thomas, C. T. (1998). Creating contexts for involvement in mathematics. *Journal of Educational Psychology, 90(4),* 730–745.

Turner, J. C., Midgley, C., Meyer, D. K., Gheen, M., Anderman, E. M., Kang, Y., & Patrick, H. (2002). The classroom environment and students' reports of avoidance strategies in mathematics: A multimethod study. *Journal of Educational Psychology, 94,* 88–106.

Urdan, T., & Maehr, M. L. (1995). Beyond a two-goal theory of motivation and achievement: A case for social goals. *Review of Educational Research, 65(3),* 213–243.

Vitoroulis, I., Schneider, B. H., Vasquez, C. C., Soteras de Toro, M., & Gonzales, Y. S. (2012). Perceived parental and peer support in relation to Canadian, Cuban, and Spanish adolescents' valuing of academics and intrinsic academic motivation. *Journal of Cross Cultural Psychology, 43,* 704–722.

Walker, C. O. (2012). Student perceptions of classroom achievement goals as predictors of belonging and content instrumentality. *Social Psychology of Education, 15,* 97–107.

Weiner, B. (1985). An attribution theory of achievement motivation and emotion. *Psychological Review, 92,* 548–573.

Wentzel, K. R. (1996). Social goals and social relationships as motivators of school adjustment. In J. Juvonen & K. R. Wentzel (Eds.), *Social motivation: Understanding children's school adjustment* (pp. 226–247). Cambridge, England: Cambridge University Press.

Wentzel, K. R. (1997). Student motivation in middle school: The role of perceived pedagogical caring. *Journal of Educational Psychology, 89*, 411–417.

Wentzel, K. R. (1998). Social relationships and motivation in middle school: The role of parents, teachers, and peers. *Journal of Educational Psychology, 90*(2), 202–209.

Wentzel, K. R. (2009). Students' relationships with teachers as motivational contexts. In K. R. Wentzel & A. Wigfield (Eds.), *Handbook of motivation at school* (pp. 301–322). New York: NY: Routledge.

Wentzel, K. R., Baker, S., & Russell, S. (2009). Peer relationships and positive adjustment at school. In R. Gilman, E. S. Huebner, & M. J. Furlong (Eds.), *Handbook of positive psychology in schools* (pp. 229–243). New York, NY: Routledge.

Wentzel, K. R., & Battle, A. A. (2001). Social relationships and school adjustment. In T. Urdan & F. Pajares (Eds.), *Adolescence and education: General issues in the education of adolescents* (pp. 93–118). Greenwich, CT: Information Age Publishing.

Wentzel, K. R., & Caldwell, K. (1997). Friendships, peer acceptance, and group membership: Relations to academic achievement in middle school. *Child Development, 68*, 1198–1209.

Index